BRITISH POLITICS AND THE ENVIRONMENT IN THE LONG NINETEENTH CENTURY

BRITISH POLITICS AND THE ENVIRONMENT IN THE LONG NINETEENTH CENTURY

Edited by
Peter Hough

Volume I
Discovering Nature and Romanticizing Nature

LONDON AND NEW YORK

First published 2024
by Routledge
4 Park Square, Milton Park, Abingdon, Oxon OX14 4RN

and by Routledge
605 Third Avenue, New York, NY 10158

Routledge is an imprint of the Taylor & Francis Group, an informa business

© 2024 selection and editorial matter, Peter Hough; individual owners retain
copyright in their own material.

The right of Peter Hough to be identified as the author of the editorial
material, and of the authors for their individual chapters, has been asserted in
accordance with sections 77 and 78 of the Copyright, Designs and Patents
Act 1988.

All rights reserved. No part of this book may be reprinted or reproduced or
utilised in any form or by any electronic, mechanical, or other means, now
known or hereafter invented, including photocopying and recording, or in any
information storage or retrieval system, without permission in writing from
the publishers.

Trademark notice: Product or corporate names may be trademarks or
registered trademarks, and are used only for identification and explanation
without intent to infringe.

British Library Cataloguing-in-Publication Data
A catalogue record for this book is available from the British Library

ISBN: 978-1-032-04782-9 (set)
ISBN: 978-1-032-04784-3 (Volume I) hbk
ISBN: 978-1-003-19465-1 (Volume I) ebk

DOI: 10.4324/9781003194651

Typeset in Times New Roman
by Apex CoVantage, LLC

CONTENTS

VOLUME I   DISCOVERING NATURE AND ROMANTICIZING NATURE

Acknowledgements	xi
Note on Copy-Texts	xii
General Introduction	xiii

PART 1
Discovering Nature: Science and the Environment in Nineteenth-Century Britain   1

Chronology of Science and the Environment in the Nineteenth Century   3

Volume I Part 1 Introduction   5

1.1
Biodiversity Decline   13

1. *The Natural History and Antiquities of Selborne*   17
   GILBERT WHITE

2. *Letter to Joseph Banks*   23
   WILLIAM ROXBURGH

3. *Tracts Relative To The Island Of St. Helena: Written During A Residence Of Five Years*   27
   ALEXANDER BEATSON

4. *Residence in Cape Town, and Rambles in the Vicinity*   37
   WILLIAM JOHN BURCHELL

v

CONTENTS

5. *Principles of Geology*   43
CHARLES LYELL

6. *Origin of the Species*   49
CHARLES DARWIN

7. *The natural history of man: comprising inquiries into the modifying influence of physical and moral agencies on the different tribes of the human family*   59
JAMES COWLES PRICHARD

8. *Abstract of Mr. J. Wolley's researches in Iceland respecting the gare-fowl or great auk*   65
ALFRED NEWTON

9. *Presidential Address (British Ecological Society)*   71
ARTHUR TANSLEY

1.2
Resource Depletion   **75**

10. *An Essay on the Principle of Population*   79
THOMAS MALTHUS

11. *On the Checks to Population*   87
WILLIAM FORSTER LLOYD

12. *Economic Value of Population*   97
WILLIAM FARR

13. *The Coal Question; An Inquiry concerning the Progress of the Nation, and the Probable Exhaustion of our Coal-mines*   105
WILLIAM JEVONS

14. *On the fluctuations in the herring fisheries*   115
JOHN CLEGHORN

15. *Inaugural Address. Fisheries Exhibition, London*   121
THOMAS HUXLEY

CONTENTS

16. *On Forest Schools*   129
    JOHN CROUMBIE BROWN

17. *Forestry in Some of its Economic Aspects*   135
    WILLIAM SOMERVILLE

1.3
Pollution   **141**

18. *On the Use of the Arsenic in Agriculture – Poisoning by*
    Arsenic, and Symptoms of Cholera – The Possible Effect
    of the Game Laws   145
    HENRY W. FULLER

19. *On the Mode of Communication of Cholera*   151
    JOHN SNOW

20. *Air and rain: the beginnings of a chemical climatology*   157
    ROBERT ANGUS SMITH

21. *Observations on the Filth of the Thames*   163
    MICHAEL FARADAY

22. *'Pollution of Glamorganshire Rivers'*   167
    CARDIFF RURAL SANITARY AUTHORITY

23. *On Radiation Through the Earth's Atmosphere*   173
    JOHN TYNDALL

24. *Smoke abatement: a lecture delivered in the lecture room*
    of the International Health Exhibition   181
    ERNEST HART

25. *The Destruction of Daylight. A Study in the*
    Smoke Problem   191
    JOHN GRAHAM

References   195

vii

CONTENTS

PART 2
**Romanticizing Nature: Environmental Conservation
as a Nationalistic Artistic and Political Movement in
Nineteenth-Century Britain**   **199**

Chronology of Environmental Conservation as a Nationalistic
    and Artistic Movement in the Nineteenth Century   201

Volume I Part 2 Introduction   203

2.1
Aesthetes and Conservation   **211**

26. 'The Raven'   215
    SAMUEL TAYLOR COLERIDGE

27. *The Excursion*   219
    WILLIAM WORDSWORTH

28. 'In Memoriam A.H.H.'   227
    ALFRED TENNYSON

29. *A Protest Against the Extension of Railways in
    the Lake District*   237
    JOHN RUSKIN

30. *Silas Marner*   245
    GEORGE ELIOT

31. *Under an Elm-Tree; or, Thoughts in the Country-Side*   253
    WILLIAM MORRIS

32. 'Remembrances'   259
    JOHN CLARE

33. *Our Common Land*   265
    OCTAVIA HILL

34. *Black Beauty*   273
    ANNA SEWELL

viii

CONTENTS

35. *The Waters of Edera*   279
LOUISE DE LA RAMÉE (AKA OUIDA)

36. *My Days and Dreams*   285
EDWARD CARPENTER

37. *My First Summer in the Sierra*   293
JOHN MUIR

2.2
Conserving Nature and the Aristocracy   **297**

38. *Emma*   301
JANE AUSTEN

39. *Rural Rides*   307
WILLIAM COBBETT

40. *Sybil*   315
BENJAMIN DISRAELI

41. *Signs of the Times*   321
THOMAS CARLYLE

42. 'The Dorsetshire Labourer'   329
THOMAS HARDY

43. *London Zoological Society*   337
THOMAS STAMFORD RAFFLES

44. *The Game Animals of Africa (dedicated to Herbrand Russell)*   343
RICHARD LYDEKKER

45. *Nature Reserves: Formation of a New Society*   349
CHARLES ROTHSCHILD

2.3
Conservation and Fear of the Future   **353**

46. *The Doom of the Great City. Being the Narrative of a Survivor*   357
WILLIAM DELISLE HAY

CONTENTS

47. *The Plunder of the Earth*   363
ALFRED RUSSEL WALLACE

48. *The National Standard of Physical Health*   371
REGINALD BRABAZON (LORD MEATH)

49. *The Heart of the Empire*   383
CHARLES MASTERMAN AND PHILIP WHITWELL WILSON, EDS.

50. *A Modern Utopia*   391
H.G. WELLS

References   397

Index   400

ACKNOWLEDGEMENTS

I was approached to put together this series by Rachel Douglas, Editor of Routledge's Historical Resources Programme, and I thank her for putting her faith in me to deliver this. My family, as always, have been a great source of support and encouragement in my work. In particular, I am indebted to my mum, Sandra Hough, and father-in-law, Norman Say, for lending me several useful books that greatly aided my research. I am thankful also to Dave Humphreys, who acted as a reviewer of the overall content of the series. His enthusiasm for the concept and choice of texts was a great source of encouragement.

NOTE ON COPY-TEXTS

The following extracts have been transcribed as per the original source; however, exceptions occur where the quality of the original texts was poor and therefore would not reproduce well. Breaks between excerpts (which may cover sentences, paragraphs or chapters) are indicated thus:

. . .

In order to fit texts comfortably to the pages of this edition, certain liberties have been taken with the format of the originals.

GENERAL INTRODUCTION

BRITAIN'S INDUSTRIAL TAKE-OFF

Britain in the nineteenth century, in many ways, is where environmentalism started. It is here that the world's first Industrial Revolution took place, radically changing the relationship between humanity and the natural world. Polluting mines and factories proliferated, urbanization both shrunk and commodified the countryside and the existence of many natural resources and animals became threatened as never before. Since the Industrial Revolution, most of these environmental changes have come to be subject to legal limitations but the overall fundamental shift in the human relationship with nature has largely persisted. None of these environmental changes were new or unique to Britain and Ireland in that age but their significance greatly intensified and fundamentally changed the world. The systematic enclosure of common lands, such as woodlands and village greens, largely began in the seventeenth century. Smoke pollution from coal had been a concern in England since at least the early fourteenth century. British deforestation can also be dated back to the Middle Ages. Going back even a millennium further, aurochs (an ancestor of cattle) were hunted and farmed to extinction in the British Isles in the Bronze Age. Similar forms of environmental change had also been occurring in many other parts of the world for many centuries. However, it was in the industrializing UK and its Empire in the nineteenth century that these sorts of changes greatly accelerated and fundamentally altered the balance between the human and non-human worlds.

This radical change has come increasingly to be recognized as a new geological era, the 'Anthropocene'. Crutzen and Stoermer are widely credited with introducing the term *Anthropocene* in 2000, suggesting that it should succeed the Holocene as the contemporary geological epoch. Holocene had been introduced by the pioneering British geologist of the nineteenth century Charles Lyell, profiled in Volume I Part 1 of this series, to denote the post-glacial epoch dating back to around 10,000 BCE. Crutzen and Stoermer reasoned that the rate of population growth, urbanization, loss of natural wetlands, resource depletion and climate change of the contemporary age constituted a paradigm shift.

Considering these and many other major and still growing impacts of human activities on earth and atmosphere, and at all, including global, scales, it seems to us more than appropriate to emphasize the central role of mankind in geology and ecology by proposing to use the term "anthropocene" for the current geological epoch.

(Crutzen & Stoermer 2000: 17)

Crutzen and Stoermer furthermore suggested that the starting point of this new geological age was the industrial revolution in Britain and, more particularly, James Watt's refinement of the steam engine in 1784 (Crutzen & Stoermer 2000). Watt had worked on steam engines for some time before this, building on the research of Thomas Newcomen, but from this time on this power source could readily be deployed in ways that revolutionized Britain's factories, mills and modes of transport. The eponymizing of the great scientist in the unit of power (Watt) makes the significance of this invention plain.

With the onset of industrialization change in the British landscape moved from evolution to revolution. The population of Manchester grew from 27,000 in 1773 to 75,000 in 1801 as the cotton industry mechanized and expanded (Markham 1994: 12). Between 1801 and 1911 Middlesbrough swelled from a 25 strong hamlet on the mouth of the Tees to a major town of 104,767, on the back of steel production and becoming a key conduit for imports and exports through the North Sea (McCord & Rowe 1977). This urbanization was occurring elsewhere in Western Europe but at nowhere near the same rate. The proportion of Great Britain's population that was urban grew from 20% in 1800 to 62% in 1890. In contrast, in the same time period, urban France grew from 9% to 26%, Germany from 6% to 28% and the Scandinavian countries from 5 to 13% (de Vries 1984: 45–46). On the back of its industrialization British society and its environment similarly underwent radical change linked to this urbanization.

Britain's global prominence, reach and rich natural resource base in the nineteenth century allowed her to take advantage of the technical advances of the age born of the Enlightenment. The textile industry led the way in the industrial revolution and Britain's economic take-off. Late eighteenth-century innovations, such as Hargreaves' 'Spinning Jenny' which multiplied the number of cotton threads that could be spun into textiles, and Arkwrights 'Water Frame', which speeded up and improved the spinning process through water power, made Britain the world leader in the 'rag trade'. These, along with other innovations and then the application of steam power, propelled the cotton trade to new heights. Imports of pure cotton, principally from the Empire and the US, soared and exports of textiles produced from this in new factories grew at an even greater rate: rising 1,500% between 1820 and 1840 (Stearns 2013: 30).

Coal mining also intensified, essentially replacing wood as the country's key fuel source. This was fortunate since the latter had long been depleted in the British Isles, whilst there were huge reserves of the former. Britain's energy policy hence shifted from having to import timber to becoming self-sufficient in coal and able to make earnings on exporting what it did not need. The resultant economic take-off fuelled further mechanization and technological innovation, intensifying industrialization and growth. Coal production more than quadrupled between 1830 and 1870 and came to exceed the rest of the world put together (Stearns 2013: 37). As with textiles, this greatly boosted British export earnings but also serviced a huge growth in domestic demand. British homes and businesses consumed five times as much coal as the rest of Europe put together (O'Brien 2022: 135). The high costs of technological innovation could be absorbed by a booming economy, unlike in other countries coming to acquire this scientific know-how to potentially follow suit, such as across the channel in France. Hence the first phase of the Industrial Revolution was largely a British affair. Conscious of this sudden advantage, the British government also looked to keep it that way for as long as possible, enacting laws proscribing the export of new industrial technologies and also the men who invented them. Later in the nineteenth century, Britain came to embrace free trade but in the early stages of the Industrial Revolution she sought to guard her comparative advantage in a protectionist manner.

THE BIRTH OF ECOLOGY

Although a strong case can be made to suggest that environmentalism was born in Britain, the academic appreciation of this first emerged elsewhere. The science of understanding matters of environmental change emerged in the nineteenth century and was given the name *ecology* by the Prussian biologist Haeckel (Haeckel 1866). The science of ecology brought recognition of natural systemic phenomena linking disparate life forms such as food chains, the carbon cycle and evolution and an understanding of humanity's place within this environment. Published shortly before this first usage of the term ecology, US diplomat's George Perkins Marsh's *Man and Nature* in 1864 is widely regarded as the first ecological book in that it used empirical data to prove the effects of human activity on woodlands and waterways. Drawing on research Marsh carried out while serving as US ambassador to Italy in Rome, *Man and Nature* begins with an overview of how much of the forested and fertile Roman Empire had become unproductive arid wasteland through overproduction. Hence Marsh was discussing desertification over half a century before the term came to be employed. The book was also ahead of its time in foreseeing the links between deforestation and flooding because of the role played by riverside trees. Whilst *Man and Nature* is more of a scientific than polemical work, in examining the effects of major engineering projects – like the Suez and Panama Canals – on nature and questioning their legitimacy there is no doubt that Marsh sowed the seed of political ecology. 'We can never know how wide a circle of disturbance we produce in the harmonies of nature when we throw the smallest pebble into the ocean of organic life' (Marsh 1864: 549).

The British were slower to embrace this new science of ecology than Germany or the US. In practice, the Germans acted sooner against deforestation and the decline of birds and fish than the British. The US embraced conservation ahead of their former rulers, albeit led by a British émigré, John Muir. A number of explanations can be offered for the study of ecology not originating in the place where the changes it was comprehending were most apparent. For a start, certain geographical characteristics distinguished the British from other industrializing states and their empires. The UK itself was a relatively small country with a benign climate and a notable absence of natural hazards or obvious 'warnings' of environmental change. In the modern age at least, there was no British equivalent to the highly visible demise of the bison from the American plains.

Furthermore, in spite of the scale of urbanization, the British rural landscape was actually less radically altered than that of comparable countries, such as Germany and the US. Although it was a different story in Ireland and the Highlands of Scotland, much of British agriculture modernized but did so mostly through rationalization and the incorporation of innovative methods within the existing farming framework. British government investment focused on the modernization of industry not agriculture and the new huge, highly mechanized 'factory farms' that transformed the rural landscapes of the US and Prussia were far less apparent in England, Wales and the Scottish lowlands. In addition, resistance to encroachment on the commons and rural wildernesses was relatively successful in Britain compared to Germany and other states (Winter 1999: 15). The scale of the British empire also allowed her to absorb and be less conscious about resource depletion. Timber shortages did not trouble the British as much as the Germans since local deforestation had been going on for centuries without any apparent cause for concern. In addition, the fact that they had led the world in industrialization bred a sense of British exceptionalism and blinkeredness. British exceptionalism fed cornucopianism and a belief that they could invent themselves out of problems born of change (as with the much economic thought in the US from the 1980s). Even though British science had proven that overfishing was a problem and that diseases like cholera were transmitted through water British diplomats often treated these 'inconvenient truths' as non-tariff barriers in negotiating with other governments for international health regulations and marine conservation regimes.

Geopolitical factors also offer some insight as to why Marsh's pioneering ecological message was less influential in Britain than it was in most states. The US and Britain were rivals in the nineteenth-century world and anti-American sentiment possibly coloured British judgement. As we see in several examples in this series, there was far more British intellectual cooperation with the Germans than the Americans and, in this sense, the nineteenth century was markedly different than the twentieth. London and Washington had gone to war over Canada in 1815 and clashed diplomatically over the hunting of fur seals in the Arctic. Indeed, the Russians sold Alaska to the US in 1867 partly in order to stir up that transatlantic rivalry. In this context the views of an American diplomat were not as influential as we might today imagine. Marsh's innovative thinking was widely panned in the British press and academic journals. Physician to the royal family Sir Henry Holland in the Edinburgh Review dismissed Man and Nature as 'rather florid and

xvi

ambitious' (Holland 1864 quoted in Winter 1999: 30). Marsh's arguments allied to British exceptionalism meant that he was dismissed in many quarters as partial and ignorant of human ingenuity. Furthermore, since his ecological message was more one of the practical sustainability of resources (not, then, a major British concern) than a romantic reverence for nature that characterized early British environmentalists, it did not necessarily chime even with emergent environmental thought in Britain (Winter 1999: 28–39).

Historical and political factors can also be offered to help explain the Germans and US Americans being more receptive to ecological thinking. Germany and US as relatively new countries had less of an old elite establishment to stifle new thinking and change. It is hard to imagine Muir having risen to have the ear of the government had he remained in Scotland and not emigrated. Whereas British scientists and romantic writers advocating for nature were often challenging the establishment, the likes of Goethe and Humboldt were the embodiment of Germanness not radical outsiders. Germany and US were also born with far more devolved political systems forged to bring together diverse states. Federalism lends itself more to rural bottom-up challenges than centralized states with long-established concentrations of power. This continues to be the case in Germany today if we consider the prominence of the Green Party relative to the UK (although not, of course, in the US). The conscious 'creation' of the US and Germany also meant that there was more emphasis on identity in their brands of nationalism and nature came to form an important part of this. The pioneer spirit of the American settlers and the reverence for traditional forest forest-dwelling Germanic tribes gave nature a notable prominence in their process of nation-building. In contrast, British national identity was constructed in more abstract terms, celebrating being a world leader and pioneer of industrialization and free trade; essentially the opposite of identifying with nature. Urbanization and industry were often promoted and embraced as patriotic. Nicknames like 'The Big Smoke' for London or 'The Black Country' for the Birmingham conurbation allude to polluted landscapes but were terms of affection and, indeed, remain so. Similarly, the grand monickers of Ironopolis for Middlesbrough and Cottonopolis for Manchester, celebrating their industry and growth, belied the squalor of those rapidly growing towns.

Britain, of course, also had more to lose than other countries in addressing the perennial problem of balancing profits and pollution. Smoke might seem an obvious social menace but the blackening skies above Britain's bustling cities were not always viewed with foreboding. Chimney fumes could be seen to symbolize progress and a modernization of the economy and domestic living. Even if it could be acknowledged that urban smogs were proliferating and rivers were beginning to stink and ceasing to contain fish a 'where there's muck there's brass' mentality could often tolerate such inconveniences. As we see in Part 1 of this volume, the public showed little initial appetite for smoke-reducing domestic fire technologies when they came onto the market. Indeed, a romanticization of the open hearth still lingers today. An aversion to 'do-gooders' and the 'nanny state' has, perhaps, always been a prominent British trait. In 1854, *The Times* reported approvingly on the sacking of public health pioneer Edwin Chadwick, who they referred to as a 'medical tyrant', asserting that the British public would: 'prefer to take our chance of cholera and the rest than be bullied into health' (*Times* 1854: 8).

However, the pollute-or-profit dichotomy is, of course, too simplistic. Many aspects of industrialization can be in the public's interest. The emergence of the sustainable development paradigm as the consensual position at the global level from the 1980s, built on the need to balance economic growth and environmental conservation, illustrates this. As Indian prime minister Indira Gandhi famously stated at the 1972 UN Convention on the Human Environment in Stockholm: 'poverty is the worst pollution'. Great scientific and social advances occurred alongside each other in industrializing Britain. At one level the rise of the factory system and the enclosure and commodification of common rural lands were indicative of greedy, exploitative capitalism at its worst. However, at another, they did fuel an economic boom and served to modernize the country with many societal payoffs (such as street lighting and public transport). The first Enclosures Act of 1709 was very much framed in terms of the need to increase production in the face of the evidence of population growth that would later motivate Thomas Malthus to warn that the food supply was soon to be overtaken by demand. On the back of the burgeoning factories of the cities and mechanization and rationalization of the agricultural sector British gross domestic product per capita doubled in the century between 1760 and 1860, having fluctuated between periods of slow growth and decline in the centuries preceding the industrial revolution (Crafts 1985).

Nevertheless, it gradually became obvious and unignorable that there was a cost to this growth in both public and environmental terms. Economists and scientists needed to grapple with the emerging facts that supplies of timber, fish and even coal were finite; animals could be hunted to extinction; and that the air and waters could be ruined by smoke and waste deposits. Huntsmen, also, would need to face up to the realities of biodiversity decline, if only for the sake of their 'sport'. Artists and writers railed against the aesthetic costs of urban sprawl and the despoilment of the countryside by railway lines, dams and deeper deforestation. Politicians of all persuasions needed to reconcile themselves with or resist the profound social changes resulting from industrialization. Political conservatives rallied to the cause of resisting change as the last vestiges of the old feudal order of lord and peasant were being swept away. Socialists emerged to defend a new working class from the negativities of factory work and urban living. Liberals broadly welcomed the changes as a route to a modernized and reformed Britain but also came to recognize that pollution and negative aspects of urban living challenged their laissez faire instincts and necessitated a state role in new kinds of reform. The UK's prominence in the world grew on the back of industrialization but it also gradually became apparent that there were costs to this extended global role also. Questions of national sustainability quickly became questions of imperial sustainability as resources in the colonies also came under strain. Furthermore, the costs of military supremacy – both economic and environmental – spiralled as warfare industrialized. Almost all aspects of public and private life

xviii

in the British Isles came to be rapidly redefined in the changing landscape of the nineteenth century.

Pollution and biodiversity decline, to a large degree, define contemporary environmentalism and political ecology: a political movement generally held to have been around for only sixty or so years. In the 1960s, the emergence of acid rain, large-scale marine oil pollution and the possible extinction of whales, birds and other animals as major international concerns put environmentalism on the international political map. From the 1980s climate change amplified a range of environmental concerns and the central arguments that frame political ecology today. However, these political dilemmas did not suddenly manifest themselves from the 1960s. These challenges had previously become very much apparent during the industrialization and proto-globalization of the nineteenth century. Contrary to much popular appreciation, acid rain, climate change and biodiversity-decline were both apparent and appreciated in the nineteenth-century world. Although the notion of an Anthropocene is a recent one, Kelly opines that an 'anthropocentric consciousness' started to emerge in the early nineteenth century as scientific enquiry across a number of countries began to provide evidence of human activities permanently changing the environment (Kelly 2018: 9). Similarly, Grove and Damodaran argue that the 1860s represented the "first environmental decade" and, alongside Marsh, cite the particular importance of British scientists of the age towards this, including Darwin, Roxburgh, Beatson and Croumbie Brown who are all profiled in Volume I Part 1 (Grove & Damodaran 2006). For Wall, the final two decades of the nineteenth century in the UK were the formative years of ecological political thought. He cites the radical proto eco-socialism of William Morris and Edward Carpenter and emergence of vegetarian and animal rights movements in support of the assertion that political ecology was born up to eighty years before what is generally suggested. Wall notes that it can be demonstrated that these late Victorian thinkers meet twenty-seven of the twenty-nine distinguishing features of political ecology famously highlighted by probably the contemporary age's leading British exponent of this ideology, Jonathon Porritt (Wall 1994: 1–10; Porritt 1984).

THIS SERIES

Part 1 of Volume I of this series examines how the scientific advances that both propelled and were then catalysed by the Industrial Revolution also spawned the scientific discipline of ecology. Three key dimensions of scientific enquiry with important ecological relevance are examined: biodiversity, resource depletion and pollution.

The towering scientific figure of the age, Charles Darwin, spearheaded the appreciation of the interconnectedness of nature with his evolutionary theory and so essentially defined biodiversity. Darwinism built on insights into the evolutionary nature of geology from Charles Lyell and botany by William Roxburgh, Alexander Beatson and William John Burchell. Before them all, Gilbert White's insights on how birds relate to other species and the world in general essentially gave birth to naturalism. Darwinism subsequently moulded new thinking on environmental determinism, most notably through the thinking of James Cowles Prichard on human evolution and Alfred Newton on ornithology and the extinction of species. Moving into the twentieth century the profound interdependence of life-forms, forming the basis of more radical forms of ecology, was given expression in the notion of an ecosystem by Arthur Tansley.

Concerns about resource depletion came to not only inform but also divide opinion amongst scientists and economists in industrializing Britain. At the outset of the Industrial Revolution, economist Thomas Malthus pioneered concerns about overpopulation, the notion that demand would come to exceed demand supply on a global scale. William Forster Lloyd reinforced this message with the tragedy-of-the commons parable which warned of land erosion if open spaces were left unregulated. However other economists, such as William Farr, disagreed with these pessimistic assessments, putting more faith in human ingenuity and technological innovation to meet increased demand. In relation to particular resources the naturalist John Cleghorn coined the expression and rationalized 'overfishing', John Croumbie Brown advanced an appreciation of deforestation and economist William Jevons reasoned that even the rich British coal seams would not last forever. However, as with the overarching population question there were significant dissenters to this message of resource loss, with the most-renowned scientist of the age Thomas Huxley declaring that 'the most important sea fisheries, such as the cod fishery, the herring fishery, and the mackerel fishery, are inexhaustible' (Huxley 1883). Gradually, however, the consensus shifted away from such optimistic assessments, as more pessimistic evidence emerged and controls began to be imposed on fishing and forestry management schemes introduced.

In a similar fashion to how scientific evidence of biodiversity and resource depletion would eventually overcome wishful thinking, in time pollution gradually came to be acknowledged as more than some 'muck' accompanying the 'brass'. British scientists of the nineteenth century were prominent in the emergence of evidence of the harmful effects of pollutants which, a century later, would form the basis for the take-off of political ecology. Medic John Snow famously proved that the deadly cholera epidemics that swept the country and the world that century were transmitted via water and legendary scientist Michael Farraday helped popularize the necessity of curbing river pollution for health reasons. Around the same time, the less-celebrated Henry W. Fuller pioneered an appreciation of hazardous pesticide use and the fact that deadly pollutants could pass through the food chain by poisoning a cat! Smoke pollution came to be accepted as more than an ugly side effect of industrialization through the research and campaigning of men like Ernest Hart and John Graham. Although not at the time recognized as the threat it is today, the fact that the Earth's climate could change as a consequence of pollution was also proven through the scientific work of Irishman John Tyndall.

Part 2 of Volume I profiles how the rapidly changing landscape and society of the UK fed into the emergent nationalism of the country and its constituent nations.

The subjective and fluid ideology of nationalism is often forged from what a group of people fear they may be at risk of losing. For the British in the nineteenth century, seemingly secure in Europe and leading the world, this manifested itself internally in fears for the loss of traditional rural life and associated values seen to define the country. Many aesthetes railed against the brutality, ugliness and ungodliness of industrialization. A new movement of romantic poets led by Samuel Taylor Coleridge and William Wordsworth lamented the loss of nature through modernization and glorified the past. Leading artists and aesthetes, such as William Morris and John Ruskin, expressed their frustrations not only through their art but in direct political action, seeking to preserve the countryside against industrial and urban encroachment.

The changing social order of Britain became the key focus of much literature of the age lamenting the loss of the old order of landed gentry. Jane Austen and Thomas Hardy remain amongst the country's most revered novelists today for, in different ways, providing social comment on the demise of feudal England. The leading conservative politician of the age, Benjamin Disraeli, turned to novels to highlight a similar message of the dangers inherent in allowing the country's aristocracy to be usurped by a new urban middle class of industrialists. The polemical writings of leading and influential political commentators William Cobbett and Thomas Carlyle portrayed British nationalism as the resistance to threats posed by urban-focused liberalism. Whilst this defence of the old feudal order was a manifestation of social rather than environmental conservatism, many of the age's aristocrats themselves did come to play important roles in the preservation of nature. Thomas Stamford Raffles and the Duke of Bedford became key pioneers of global animal conservation whilst Charles Rothschild trailblazed the systematic conservation of the British countryside.

As the evidence of the moral and environmental pollution of Britain's cities became apparent in the late nineteenth century an eclectic range of politicians and novelists came to express their nationalistic fears of the future of the country in these terms. The national security implications of the physical degeneration of young men due to urban living were highlighted by Lord Meath, citing early defeats in the Second Boer War as evidence. Other politicians, such as Charles Masterman and Philip Whitwell Wilson, focused more on the moral degeneration of urban dwellers and the threats posed by this to national and imperial power. In literature, doomsday science fiction became popular on the back of public fears, with novels such as William Deslisle Hay's *The Doom of the Great City* imagining London coming to be destroyed by an escalation of the 'peasouper' fogs which had come to regularly blight the capital.

In Volume II Part 1, the political implications of industrialization in the environmental context are examined. The early phase of the Industrial Revolution came close to having commensurate societal effects. Rural Britain rebelled against job losses resulting from the switch of emphasis on the national economy to the cities. In urbanizing Britain, the mechanization of work and greater uncertainties of industrial employment also bred resentment and protest. Political commentators from abroad, such as French liberal Alexis De Tocqueville and Prussian radical socialist

Friedrich Engels, observed at close hand the desperate living and working conditions of workers in Britain's new industrial landscape. Prominent domestic literary figures, such as Charles Dickens, added their voices to the blackening air of discontent sweeping the country. The Liberals took advantage of this social unrest and came to dominate British politics in the middle of the century with a programme of sweeping reform. Liberal governments not only embraced their traditional cause of free trade but also came to recognize a socially protectionist role for the state in line with the utilitarianist philosophy of Jeremy Bentham: acting so as to maximize societal happiness. The politics of public health was hence initiated by the Benthamite civil servant Edwin Chadwick with boards of health created to bring sanitation and pollution controls to Britain's expanding cities. Despite some initial resistance by industry bosses and something of a backlash against this new role for the state by the conservatives, political measures curbing urban pollution subsequently evolved.

The logic of utilitarianism allied to the urban moral degeneration arguments also saw cruelty to animals become part of the reformist agenda of nineteenth-century British politics. More radical animal rights sentiments were apparent in the age, such as those of John Oswald and Lewis Gompertz, but it was the notion of the corrupting effects on the abusers that largely defined the advance of the political campaign and the gradual emergence of prohibitive legislation. Animal abuse by the rural and urban poor was hence addressed before hunting by the gentry and vivisection came into focus. Nevertheless, these more elitist forms of animal usage did gradually come into purview and the politically ecological notion that rights extended beyond humans began to emerge.

The commons of village greens and woodlands similarly came to be an important political battleground in the nineteenth century, although in this case this was the continuation of a longer struggle against the enclosures (private sales) of such land going back a couple of centuries. Liberal reformist politicians, including George Shaw Lefevre and Robert Hunter, rallied to this cause in England and essentially created the conservationist measures, such as public rights of way, that frame discussions on urban expansion today. In Scotland campaigners like Alexander MacKenzie and James Bryce pioneered even further reaching reforms giving land rights back to Highland crofters evicted in the Clearances and wider public access to the mountains of this region.

Volume II Part 2 explores the imperial and foreign policy causes and consequences of environmental change in the UK. Once the finite nature of resources started to become apparent the sustainability of not only the country but also the empire came into focus. Even millions starving to death away from Britain, in famines in Ireland and India, were not enough to erode a commitment to market forces. However, when the core of the empire started to be directly affected by resource depletion thinking began to change. As we see, deforestation and biodiversity decline in the colonies came to be recognized as important political issues largely due to their effects on timber imports and big game hunting opportunities.

The amoral necessity that tends to inform imperial and foreign affairs more than domestic policy manifested itself in the intensification of the long-standing phenomenon of military ecocide: the deliberate destruction of natural resources in warfare. In the titanic power struggle against France early in the nineteenth century and in resisting colonial insurgency in Ceylon, India, New Zealand, Malay, South Africa and Nigeria we see the regular recourse to 'scorched earth' tactics by the British. Such military methods can be dated back to ancient times but the industrialization of warfare and a recognition of the centrality of resources to the war effort brought the burning of enemy crops and disruption of their water supplies to prominence many centuries after such practices had started to be declared beyond the pale.

The late nineteenth century then saw the UK, reluctantly at first, become a party in the first emergence of global environmental policy, on the basis of concerns about both resource sustainability and military ecocide. Maritime resources on the high seas (beyond sovereign reach) started to be regulated as fishing and hunting clearly came to exhaust supplies. The desire not to be deprived of big game for hunting also came to internationalize as part of the 'Scramble for Africa' which saw the European imperial powers begin to cooperate and harmonize their standards in order not suffer a comparative disadvantage. At the close of the century, as part of the Hague Convention, some prohibitions on military ecocide then came to be codified and the UK recognized that they could not afford to be behind the normative curve on this emergent area of international law.

By the twentieth century industrialization, environmental change and ecology were very much international concerns but the origins of these epoch-defining changes can be located in nineteenth-century Britain.

Manchester in 1840 www.historic-uk.com/HistoryUK/HistoryofBritain/Cotton-Industry/

REFERENCES

Crafts, N. (1985) *British Economic Growth During the Industrial Revolution*. New York: Oxford University Press.

Crutzen, P. & Stoermer, E. (2000) 'The Anthropocene'. *IGBP Global Change Newsletter* 41: 17–18.

Grove, R. & Damodaran, V. (2006) 'Imperialism, Intellectual Networks, and Environmental Change Origins and Evolution of Global Environmental History, 1676–2000: Part I', *Economic and Political Weekly*, 41(41) (Oct. 14–20): 4345–4354.

Haeckel, E. (1866) *Generelle Morphologie der Organismen*, Berlin: Verlag von Georg Reimer.

Holland, H. (1864) 'Review of Man and Nature', *Edinburgh Review* 120: 464: 500.

Kelly, J. (2018) 'Anthropocenes A Fractured Picture' in *Rivers of the Anthropocene*.

Lyell, C. (1832) *Principles of geology, being an attempt to explain the former changes of the Earth's surface, by reference to causes now in operation*. Volume 2, London: John Murray.

Markham, A. (1994) *A Brief History of Pollution*, London: Routledge.

Marsh, G. (1864) *Man and Nature* (reprint 1965) Cambridge USA: Harvard University Press.

McCord, N., & Rowe, D. (1977) Industrialisation and Urban Growth in North-East England. *International Review of Social History*, 22(1), 30–64.

O'Brien, P. (2022) Was the British industrial revolution a conjuncture in global economic history? *Journal of Global History*, 17(1), 128–150.

Porritt, J. (1984) *Seeing Green: Politics of Ecology Explained*, Oxford: Oxford University Press.

Stearns, P. (2013) *The Industrial Revolution in World History (4th ed)*, Boulder CA: Westview.

The Times (1854) August 1st.

Vries, J., de. (1984) *European Urbanization 1500–1800*. Cambridge, MA: Harvard University Press.

Wall, D. (1994) *Green History. A Reader in Environmental Literature, Philosophy and Politics*, London: Routledge.

Winter, J. (1999) *Secure from Rash Assault: Sustaining the Victorian Environment*, Berkeley: University of California Press.

Part 1

DISCOVERING NATURE
Science and the Environment in Nineteenth-Century Britain

CHRONOLOGY OF SCIENCE AND THE ENVIRONMENT IN THE NINETEENTH CENTURY

1789   Gilbert White publishes *The Natural History and Antiquities of Selbourne*

1792   Gas lights invented by William Murdoch

1798   Thomas Malthus publishes *An Essay on the Principle of Population*

1814   First steam train invented by George Stephenson

1826   Zoological Society of London established

1830   First commercial rail service opens between Liverpool and Manchester

1830–32 First British Cholera epidemic

1831   Charles Darwin's *Beagle* voyage to South America

1832   Charles Lyell publishes *Principles of Geology*

1836   Marsh Test for detecting arsenic pollution created.

1847–49 Second Cholera epidemic

1851   Arsenic Act

1854   John Snow's closure of Broad Street water pump in London proves aquatic transmission of cholera during third epidemic (which killed at least 23,000).

1854   Bessemer Steel converter invented

1855   'Overfishing' coined as a term by John Cleghorn

1858   The 'Great Stink' pollution of the Thames.

1859   Charles Darwin's *Origin of the Species* published.

1863   John Tyndall's *On Radiation Through the Earth's Atmosphere* published

1864   X Club set up by Thomas Huxley

1866   William Jevons's *The Coal Question* . . . published

1873   Major London smog

1881   Smoke Abatement Exhibition in London

1884   Marine Biological Association established

1889   First Forestry Lectureship established at Edinburgh University.

1892   Major London smog

1903   International Council for the Exploration of the Seas established

DOI: 10.4324/9781003194651-2

VOLUME I PART 1 INTRODUCTION

Environmental science – or ecology – was born in the nineteenth century. Although it was apparent, and, to some extent, appreciated before then, the human impact on nature in terms of pollution, resource depletion and species decline only came to be properly understood in light of the unprecedentedly rapid scientific and technological development of that age. Underpinning this was the fact that resource extraction was greatly accelerated by technological advances. Largely on the back of coke-fuelled blast furnace technology, pig iron production in Britain grew from 17,000 to 1.5 million tons between 1740 and 1840 and then doubled again in the following decade (Nature 1933: 335). This also made Britain the overwhelming world leader in this industry before other states, such as the US and Germany, began to follow suit in the late nineteenth century. In the 1860s, however, Britain then became the leading player of the 'steel age' after the scientist Henry Bessemer had invented a new revolutionary process for cheaply mass-producing this alloy and key building material utilizing the plentiful pig iron.

The Industrial Revolution, hence, was based on the huge growth of building materials (such as steel), new sources of energy (such as steam power and the internal combustion engine), new machinery (such as the Spinning Jenny that revolutionized cotton manufacturing) and new methods of transport and communications (such as trains and radio). British good fortune, in terms of its natural resource base and global reach born of imperialism, made it a world leader in all these areas. Political actions also ensured that the First Industrial Revolution from the 1760s to 1830s was largely confined to Britain since legal restrictions were imposed on the export of new technologies and the industrialists themselves. A series of acts from the eighteenth century banned the export of new tools and machines used in cotton and silk manufacturing and printing (Jeremy 1973: 26–27). Inevitably, Britain could not keep a lid on this forever, and the genie eventually got out of the bottle and across the Channel, but this protectionism did help keep her advantage for a number of years.

Britain, as the world's wealthiest, most technologically advanced and most powerful state of the nineteenth century, was central to the emergence of environmentalism in two very different ways. First, Britain's technological development, scientific research and imperial reach were very important in the recognition and addressing

DOI: 10.4324/9781003194651-3

5

VOLUME I PART 1 INTRODUCTION

of emerging problems, such as acid rain, smog, overpopulation, deforestation and the spread of contagious diseases. Second, however, British leadership in industrialization, trade and imperial expansion also made it a key creator of many of these newly appreciated concerns. Nineteenth-century Britain was central to the conceptualization of environmental problems but also a key architect of them.

BIODIVERSITY DECLINE

Extinctions were well documented prior to the scientific revolutions of the nineteenth century, as with the infamous demise of the dodo due to hunting on the French colony of Mauritius in the seventeenth century. The advent of natural history as a discipline, led by English pastor Gilbert White, allowed for a greater understanding of the numbers and movements of fauna more dispersed and mobile than the dodo to put such developments into context. Darwin's evolutionary theory then provided evidence on the profound interconnectedness of fauna and flora, including humanity, that fully laid the foundations for the science of ecology. It was German biologist Ernst Haeckel who coined the term *ecology* and is probably the best claimant to the title of founder of this new discipline (Haeckel 1866). The science of ecology brought recognition of natural systemic phenomena linking disparate life forms such as food chains, the carbon cycle and an understanding of humanity's place within this environment. Haeckel, though, was a close associate of Darwin and – as many of the examples in this Part of the volume testify – Anglo-German scientific cooperation in this era was more extensive than might popularly be imagined. Prior to their twentieth-century collisions, Britain and the uniting Germany shared extensive royal and cultural links and this spilled over into the realms of scientific work. John Tyndall and Roberts Angus Smith, profiled in this Part of the volume for their pioneering work on climate change and acid rain, did their PhDs in German universities. There was stronger funding for scientific research and a larger take-up of science degrees in Germany (MacLoed 1971: 228). Cooperation with Germany hence became important for the advancement of British and global science. Consequently, the British were not necessarily the scientific leaders their economic and technological status might suggest. The journal *Nature* even lamented that Germany and other states such as the US were now far ahead and that science had "all but died in England" (MacLoed 1971: 205; Nature 1871: 302). The 'X club' of scientists established by Thomas Huxley in 1864, which met informally although regularly for nearly thirty years seeking to modernize and professionalize British science, reflected this concern. Huxley's compatriots in the group, who were all inspired in different ways by Darwinism, included John Tyndall and John Lubbock – featured elsewhere in this series – and George Busk, Edward Frankland, Thomas Hirst, Joseph Hooker, William Spencer and William Spottiswood. The X Club were also largely from outside of the British establishment. None of these leading lights of British science were Oxbridge-educated, and three of them had acquired their doctorates in Germany (MacLoed 1971: 200–201).

6

As discussed in the series introduction, conservation formed a key part of the German national identity coming to find political expression in their unification process and this was less hindered by economic interests than in Britain. German science was part of the establishment and the science of ecology less of an 'inconvenient truth' to business elites than in Britain. There also a stronger state role in education in Germany, particularly in the Prussian universities and new technical colleges. British universities were, in the main, resistant to shifting the emphasis from the classics and the arts to sciences as Huxley and the X Club were imploring. In contrast, Von Humboldt, Prussia's leading scientific mind, was placed in charge of the country's whole educational system in 1809 and moulded what would become the much-envied German model (Roderick & Stephens 1982).

Collaboration with Germany and other European states hence came to be a feature of British scientific enquiry in the late nineteenth century, although this was already internationally focused. Cross-European intellectual cooperation had grown in the eighteenth and early nineteenth centuries in spite of political divisions. Britain's prominent imperial presence also contributed to this international outlook. Whilst the environmentally damaging taming of perceived savagery, both human and non-human, characterized many imperial conquests there was also an observable trend for a maturing of colonial systems so that they became more sustainable in both an economic and political sense. A Malthusian appreciation of the finite nature of resources, particularly in terms of the relationship between timber and naval power, was one dimension of this. In addition, the emerging science of botany came to be linked to both the exploration of new lands and the management of existing colonies (Grove 1995). In the late eighteenth century, British explorer James Cook's legendary voyages charting Australia and the South Pacific included Joseph Banks and Johann Reinhold Forster, the leading British and Prussian botanists of their day. Cook himself was a cartographer and astronomer and this merging of science and exploration in cross-national ventures became a feature of European imperialism. In particular, a professional appreciation of the flora and fauna of colonies and the world in general became a component of imperial rule.

As also foretold in Cook's voyages, the transnational nature of emerging *epistemic communities* (transnational networks of experts) of botanists came to manifest itself in a significant degree of cross-imperial learning. The development of botanical gardens on Mauritius by the French from the eighteenth century, aiming to conserve species, was imitated by British governors and botanists in the East India Corporation and, particularly, in a major experiment on the remote Atlantic island of St Helena (Grove 1995: 332–242). St Helena was chosen consciously as a conduit between India and the West Indies to facilitate imperial exchanges of crops and in order to learn about conservation, climate and reforestation. In particular, William John Burchell, a botanist at St Helena and then in India, researched links between deforestation and soil erosion and flooding. At around the same time, the governor, Alexander Beatson (an open admirer of the eighteenth-century

French governor of Mauritius Pierre Poivre), demonstrated a very early appreciation of climate change in noting the increased prominence of droughts across the world (Grove 1995: 358). Beatson was as much a scientist as a colonial administrator and his work *Tracts* is known to have influenced Charles Darwin, whose *Origin of the Species* cites evidence from St Helena on the impact of encroachment by human and other life forms on ecosystems.

Although born of it, some of the age's botanists in Britain and Europe even came to be somewhat critical of imperialism. Prior to Darwin the greatest naturalist of his age, the Prussian Alexander Von Humboldt – an associate of Banks and Forster – even linked South American deforestation to European colonizers.

> By felling the trees which cover the tops and sides of the mountains, men in all climates seem to bring upon future generations two calamities at once; want of fuel and a scarcity of water.
>
> (Von Humboldt 1819: 143)

Whilst it was more common to blame the premodern ignorance of indigenous peoples for resource depletion in the European colonies and neo-European colonies (such as the US, Australia and New Zealand), some cross-cultural learning also took place as the ingrained sustainability of many local cultures became appreciated. Oneness with nature characterized many of the cultures of Europe's imperial subjects, such as Hindus, Buddhists and Native American peoples, and this came to be appreciated and appropriated. Hence, we can see some instances of the traditional knowledge of colonials being valued. The French and British in Canada, for instance, learned the arts of sustainable beaver fur trapping from working with indigenous peoples (Beinart & Hughes 2007: 41). Most British colonial encounters were built on assumptions of British superiority to indigenous primitivism but there were exceptions to this exceptionalism. As we see, the botanist Burchell was keen to draw on local knowledge in his research in India, St Helena and South Africa. Although some protégés of Darwin used evolutionary theory as a framework for developing racist theories of white supremacism, others, such as James Cowles Prichard, showed how ecological science actually dispelled the notion of Caucasian or even human exceptionalism. Although, as we will see in the next part of the volume, environmentalism came to be embraced by aesthetes and aristocrats for reasons of social as much as natural conservation, ecology ultimately was still a child of science.

RESOURCE DEPLETION

When environmental politics fully took off in the 1960s concerns about resource depletion due to unsustainable population growth at the global level were a key catalyst. Overpopulation, both at the local and global levels, appeared to risk eating up the world's food and fuel with catastrophic consequences. Paul Ehrlich's *Population Bomb*, predicting mass starvation across a swathe of the world, became a best seller, and birth control was put firmly on the agenda at the United Nations (Ehrlich 1968). At the micro level, the growing problems of desertification and deforestation came to be more squarely linked with the fact that they were occurring in the parts of the world that had not developed and 'achieved' replacement level fertility (a birth rate falling to roughly equal the death rate and so slow population growth). Garret Hardin's *Tragedy of the Commons* called for action to relinquish 'the freedom to breed' to avert 'common' resources – such as fish outside territorial waters – being depleted to everyone's cost (Hardin 1968). Both Ehrlich and Hardin, however, were actually reviving old arguments first developed by British economists in the nineteenth century.

The first well-known expression of concern that this phenomenon could lead to the world becoming overpopulated came at the end of the eighteenth century with the publication of *An Essay on the Principle of Population* by the British economist Thomas Malthus. Malthus reasoned that the Earth's 'carrying capacity' of resources – particularly food – would soon be exceeded, for '[T]he power of population is indefinitely greater than the power in the earth to produce subsistence for man' (Malthus 1798: 23–24). A Malthusian doomsday never came but not because his line of argument was flawed. The world's population and resource consumption grew at a rate greater than ever in history in the proceeding century, but so did its carrying capacity as a result of the Industrial Revolution, which served to improve crop yields and resource extraction. The Neo-Malthusians of the 1960s and 1970s came to be challenged and derided for over-pessimism as the 'Green Revolution' led to increases in food production in the global South in the 1980s, but this, too, was a rerun of a nineteenth-century dialectic. As evidenced in the selected extracts of this volume part, the likes of William Farr and Thomas Huxley saw human ingenuity and technological advance as a means of increasing the food and fuel supply to meet expanding demand.

In another revival of nineteenth-century economic thinking, in 1968 the 'Neo-Malthusian' US ecologist Garrett Hardin popularized a cautionary parable first aired over a century earlier by the British economist William Forster Lloyd on the finite quality of shared resources. Lloyd described how open access to the traditional English village green was leading to their ruin because of an abuse of the privilege by villagers in overgrazing their cattle on this land (Hardin 1968). This practice had gone on for centuries and worked well but an unsustainable increase in the number of cattle being grazed was eroding the land and ruining the common resource for all. The most literal version of the tragedy of the commons manifested itself in the legal and political battles over enclosures onto England's common lands, discussed in Volume I Part 2 and Volume II Part 1. This was mostly framed as an aesthetic concern but the erosion of key resources through overuse was an issue economists and scientists turned their attention to in the nineteenth century, as they came to again from the 1960s.

British industrialization and economic growth were largely fuelled by coal, which essentially superseded timber as the core energy source and so obscured the longer-term demise of that resource. However, it did start to dawn on some

VOLUME I PART I INTRODUCTION

thinkers that the 'coal age' could not last forever. As far back as the late eighteenth century, John Williams warned that

> [w]hen our coal mines are exhausted, the prosperity and glory of this flourishing and fortunate island are at an end. Our cities and great towns must then become ruinous heaps for want of fuel, and our mines and manufactories must fail from the same cause, and then consequently our commerce must vanish. In short, the commerce, wealth, importance, glory, and happiness of Great Britain will decay and gradually dwindle to nothing, in proportion as our coal and other mines fail; and the future inhabitants of this island must live, like its first inhabitants, by fishing and hunting.
>
> (Williams 1789: 172–173)

This was an early manifestation of what today is known as the 'resource curse theory', the dangers of 'putting all of your eggs in one basket', most typically applied to countries dependent on oil exports. The industrial revolution seemed to alleviate such fears by allowing both coal extraction and usage to become more efficient. However, economist William Jevons reframed the question of British dependence on coal by reasoning that greater efficiency was not enough since this also served to make coal more attractive and so drive up demand. In doing so, Jevons essentially pre-empted the notion of sustainable development by over a century. Scientists and economists also came to question the sustainability of fishing and forestry but came up against the perennial barrier of short-term economic interests. British economic interests could blind authorities to scientific reason, as we have seen in recent times with climate change and the sometimes denialist stances of governments in countries like the US and Australia. Here again, the internationalism of science became important. The Germans were a step ahead of the British on the sustainability of forestry and fishing, but gradually, this came to be recognized and German expertise was then utilized in pioneering forestry management schemes in the British Empire. On the sustainability of marine foods, it was German scientists who took up the mantle of overfishing from an obscure Scots thinker John Cleghorn before the British finally came to see reason and abandon the wishful notion, supported by eminent scientists such as Huxley, that the seas' harvests were limitless.

POLLUTION

As with resource depletion, the heightened public health threats posed by pollution became starkly apparent in industrializing Europe and North America in the nineteenth century. Over a century before the phenomenon formed the vanguard of the environmentalist social movement in Europe, acid rain was identified by British chemist Robert Angus Smith in 1859 and subsequently campaigned about by foresters and scientists in Germany (where Angus Smith had previously lived and studied) in the 1860s (Reed 2014; Dominick 1992). Similarly, the science of climate change was established that decade by the pioneering work of Irish scientist John Tyndall on the effect of the presence of 'greenhouse gasses' in the Earth's atmosphere. Again, this UK-based research actually emanated from a transnational epistemic community. Perhaps most notably Swedish chemist Svante Arrhenius, later a Nobel Prize winner, published a paper which can lay claim to have established the link between fossil fuel emissions and global warming (Arrhenius 1896). Human-induced climate change was not portrayed as a threat to life by Arrhenius or Tyndall, but the fact that the link between industrialization and environmental change was identified over 120 years ago is instructive if we consider how appropriate action on the dire human consequences of this today is hampered by industrialists and politicians wilfully ignoring this for supposed national interests.

As the countries at the forefront of the industrial revolution – and the scientific advances and social changes associated with this – Britain, Germany and Sweden pioneered environmental policy in Europe. In Britain, the Alkali Act was enacted in 1863 due to recognition that the new booming Leblanc soda production process (invented in France) was filling the atmosphere with hydrochloric acid, and in recognition of his role in identifying this, Angus Smith was appointed head of the Alkali Inspectorate set up to implement new industrial restrictions (Reed 2014). In a similar illustration of the catalytic effect of scientific discoveries on environmental policy still evident today, the Public Health Acts of 1848, 1872 and 1875 and the River Pollution Prevention Act of 1876 followed the establishment of the link between water pollution and cholera in Britain by Dr John Snow. Five major public inquiries fed into the 1876 act to establish solid grounds for imposing costs on British industry to develop clean technology (Pontin 2014: 766). It was a similar story elsewhere in an industrializing and modernizing Europe. In Germany, the Technische Anleitung Luft in 1895 was a clean air act passed by the Reich which, in keeping with the new state's devolved political system, permitted stricter than federal restrictions on industry to be imposed by Lander (Hanf & Jansen 1998: 278–9). Sweden introduced its first Public Health Act in 1874, establishing public health boards in all major towns to monitor water and air quality, and Finland followed suit five years later. Across Europe, the fact that the Industrial Revolution required taming in spite of its huge contribution to economic growth was well-established by the end of the nineteenth century.

The urban accumulation of smoke from burning coal was a far more obvious and long-standing problem than the complex atmospheric consequences of acid or greenhouse gas emissions. As the medic and campaigner Ernest Hart outlines in his lecture profiled here, London smog was being debated in parliament as far back as the early fourteenth century. However, by the nineteenth century, the frequency of such events allied to the hard evidence of their medial consequences prompted action to be taken even if this was to come at some economic cost. The 1755 Great Fog is sometimes considered to have been the dawn of a new era of regular bouts of smoke pollution in the capital and a 'fog season' even came to be talked about (Luckin 2003: 34). By the 1873 Great Fog, advances in statistical collation and analysis provided solid evidence of jumps in the mortality rate, particularly amongst the very old and young, in relation to these events (*Ibid*: 45). Measures limiting and technologies minimizing smoke pollution came to be enacted towards the end of the century as public alarm grew at this most visible manifestation of industrialization. It was a similar story with river pollution, which also became impossible to ignore.

These pioneering anti-pollution measures are somewhat neglected in much analysis of environmental policy because they were not eco-centric. They were motivated by the saving of human lives rather than curbing pollution to save birds, as was the case in the 1960s when US biologist Rachel Carson kick-started political ecology by highlighting the effects of synthetic chemicals such as DDT. However, these public health interventions were environmental in so far that they were protecting the air and water in ways that were contrary to economic interests for the sake of human health. The primary motivation for contemporary policy on climate change, ozone depletion or pollution in general is essentially the same. Whilst there is a significant wider environmental cost to these problems it is still the threat to human life that frames these issues as matters of urgency. This use of scientific reason to meet the human interest was in line with the utilitarianism of Bentham and the liberals, particularly prevalent in Britain in this age (Pontin 2014). Again, vested economic interests had to be overcome to make the case that these were just side effects to the overall progress produced by industrialization and urbanization. Essentially, the same balancing act continues to be carried out today.

1.1

BIODIVERSITY DECLINE

Editorial Headnote

1720 (Selborne, Hampshire)–1793

Often styled as 'England's first ecologist', the Reverend Gilbert White was a clergyman and writer on nature (a combination that came to be termed 'parson naturalist'). White was Oxford-educated and then followed the family tradition of entering the church. He was ordained as a deacon in 1749 and served the cloth whilst maintaining a private passion for gardening and nature. He also remained a fellow of Oxford University for life after attaining this position but lived almost exclusively at his beloved home in the picturesque village of Selborne on the South Downs.

This, White's most noted work, is often held to be the first major publication on natural history and is estimated to be the fourth-most published book in the English language (Guardian 2018). The book contains detailed and lengthy observations on many animal species – and how they are interconnected – collated from his specialized journal designed by his friend Daines Barrington, one of the principal correspondents in this book. As is evidenced in the selected passage, White's observations offered new insights into the migratory patterns of birds, which he communicated to fellow enthusiasts. In line with the selected extract, much of the book's content consists of letters from White to fellow naturalists. Thomas Pennant, to whom he is writing in the selected extract, was also a prominent naturalist who published books on zoology. This spirit of collaborative research remains an essential feature of environmental enquiry today, given the complexity of the data being collated and analysed. White's colourful and fluent writing style, which was informed by his religious faith and love of nature, contributes greatly to the popularity of the work, but the book's enduring legacy lies in his ability to marry this to a rigorous scientific methodology. White died just four years after this groundbreaking book was published by his brother Benjamin (Gilbertwhiteshouse 2022).

Nearly a century after his death, the Selborne Society was founded in honour of Gilbert White, by George and Theresa Musgrave, in 1885 to pursue the 'Preservation of Birds, Plants and Pleasant Places'. This became a hugely influential organization containing such luminaries as the poet Alfred Tennyson and the campaigners Robert Hunter and Octavia Hill, all featured elsewhere in this book series. White's legacy is still very much apparent in Britain today. The Gilbert White Museum in Selborne stands at the former home of this ecological pioneer, where he made his name and carried out much of his valuable research. Furthermore, the museum's environs on Selborne Common are preserved by the National Trust, a hugely significant pressure group, created by the Selborne Society.

pp. 54–59

1

THE NATURAL HISTORY AND ANTIQUITIES OF SELBORNE

Gilbert White

Source: Gilbert White, *The Natural History and Antiquities of Selborne* (1789)

Letter IX
To Thomas Pennant, Esquire
SELBORNE, Aug. 17, 1768.

DEAR SIR,

I HAVE now, past dispute, made out three distinct species of the willow-wrens *(motacillae trochili)* which *constantly* and *invariably* use distinct notes. But, at the same time, I am obliged to confess that I know nothing of your willow-lark. In my letter of *April* the 18th, I had told you peremptorily that I knew your willow-lark, but had not seen it then: but, when I came to procure it, it proved, in all respects, a very *motacilla trochilus;* only that it is a size larger than the two other, and the yellow-green of the whole upper part of the body is more vivid, and the belly of a clearer white. I have specimens of the three sorts now lying before me; and can discern that there are three gradations of sizes, and that the least has black legs, and the other two flesh-coloured ones. The yellowest bird is considerably the largest, and has it's quill-feathers and secondary feathers tipped with white, which the others have not. This last haunts only the tops of trees in high beechen woods, and makes a sibilous grasshopper-like noise, now and then, at short intervals, shivering a little with its wings when it sings; and is, I make no doubt now, the *regulus non cristatus* of *Ray;* which he says

"*cantat voce stridulâ locustae.*"

Yet this great ornithologist never suspected that there were three species.

Letter XX
To Thomas Pennant, Esquire
Selborne, October 8, 1768.

DEAR SIR,

It is, I find, in zoology as it is in botany: all nature is so full, that that district produces the greatest variety which is the most examined. Several birds, which are

DOI: 10.4324/9781003194651-5

17

said to belong to the north only, are, it seems, often in the south. I have discovered this summer three species of birds with us, which writers mention as only to be seen in the northern counties. The first that was brought me (on the 14th of May) was the sandpiper, tringa hypoleucus: it was a cock bird, and haunted the banks of some ponds near the village; and, as it had a companion, doubtless intended to have bred near that water. Besides, the owner has told me since, that, on recollection, he has seen some of the same birds round his ponds in former summers.

The next bird that I procured (on the 21st of May) was a male red-backed butcher bird, lanius collurio. My neighbour, who shot it, says that it might easily have escaped his notice, had not the outcries and chattering of the white-throats and other small birds drawn his attention to the bush where it was: its craw was filled with the legs and wings of beetles.

The next rare birds (which were procured for me last week) were some ring-ousels, turdi torquati.

This week twelve months a gentleman from London, being with us, was amusing himself with a gun, and found, he told us, on an old yew hedge where there were berries, some birds like blackbirds, with rings of white round their necks: a neighbouring farmer also at the same time observed the same; but, as no specimens were procured little notice was taken. I mentioned this circumstance to you in my letter of November the 4th, 1767 (you, however, paid but small regard to what I said, as I had not seen these birds myself); but last week, the aforesaid farmer, seeing a large flock, twenty or thirty of these birds, shot two cocks and two hens: and says, on recollection, that he remembers to have observed these birds again last spring, about Lady-day, as it were, on their return to the north. Now perhaps these ousels are not the ousels of the north of England, but belong to the more northern parts of Europe; and may retire before the excessive rigour of the frosts in those parts; and return to breed in the spring, when the cold abates. If this be the case, here is discovered a new bird of winter passage, concerning whose migrations the writers are silent: but if these birds should prove the ousels of the north of England, then here is a migration disclosed within our own kingdom never before remarked. It does not yet appear whether they retire beyond the bounds of our island to the south; but it is most probable that they usually do, or else one cannot suppose that they would have continued so long unnoticed in the southern counties. The ousel is larger than a blackbird, and feeds on haws; but last autumn (when there were no haws) it fed on yew-berries: in the spring it feeds on ivy-berries, which ripen only at that season, in March and April.

I must not omit to tell you (as you have been so lately on the study of reptiles) that my people, every now and then of late, draw up with a bucket of water from my well, which is 63 feet deep, a large black warty lizard with a fin-tail and yellow belly. How they first came down at that depth, and how they were ever to have got out thence without help, is more than I am able to say.

My thanks are due to you for your trouble and care in the examination of a buck's head. As far as your discoveries reach at present, they seem much to corroborate my suspicions; and I hope Mr . . . . may find reason to give his decision in my favour; and then, I think, we may advance this extraordinary provision of nature as a new instance of the wisdom of God in the creation.

As yet I have not quite done with my history of the oedicnemus, or stone curlew; for I shall desire a gentleman in Sussex (near whose house these birds congregate in vast flocks in the autumn) to observe nicely when they leave him (if they do leave him), and when they return again in the spring; I was with this gentleman lately, and saw several single birds.

Window at Gilbert White's House
https://images.app.goo.gl/j3PLQtUPbru9SxRC8

Editorial Headnote

1751 (Ayrshire)–1815

William Roxburgh was a Scots surgeon and botanist often styled as the 'father of Indian botany'. He published many acclaimed works collating and describing botanical species accompanied by his own illustrations. In particular, Flora Indica, published in 1820 five years after his death, is generally held to be the first detailed catalogue of the flora of the Indian subcontinent (Roxburgh 1820).

Roxburgh studied medicine at Edinburgh University and then joined the East India Company as a surgeon's mate in 1772. He rose through the ranks and gradually assumed more of a role as a naturalist for the company. In 1793, he was appointed superintendent of the Calcutta Botanic Garden, taking over from its founder Robert Kyd on his death. The garden is still a prominent research institute and tourist attraction today. Botanical research of this age was very much carried out in the imperial context. As evident in this letter, some of Roxburgh's work involved posting seeds for trial cultivation around different parts of the Empire, including St Helena in the South Atlantic.

Although not founded as an official botanical gardens until 1840, as the letter testifies, Kew Gardens had been in operation as a repository of flora specimens from around the world since 1759. Joseph Banks (1743–1820), to whom Roxburgh is writing, was the pivotal figure behind the development of Kew Gardens and a legendary figure in botany, having made his name accompanying Captain James Cook on his famous voyage to Australia and the South Pacific on board the Endeavour from 1768–1771. The fact that the Endeavour's landing place in Australia came to be named Botany Bay is a testament to Banks and his discipline's significance.

Roxburgh had a busy private life, fathering twelve children by three wives. However, he was plagued by poor health, as is evident in the letter, and eventually returned to Scotland as a consequence of this in 1813. He stopped off at St Helena on the return journey from India, where he collated a list of that island's plants which later came to be cited in Beatson's Tracts, featured in the next extract of this volume. Roxburgh died in Edinburgh just two years after returning back home. A memorial in the Calcutta Botanical Gardens commemorates this pioneering botanist and several plant species are named in his honour, including Roxburghia (Jstor 2022).

2

LETTER TO JOSEPH BANKS

William Roxburgh

Source: William Roxburgh, *Letter to Joseph Banks* (1795)

Calcutta 25th April 1795

Dear Sir

I have it not in my power to refer to your kind letter by the Royal Admiral, as I am now from home on account of bad health, to which I have been more or less afflicted with ever since I left the Coast, but more so far these last two or three months, however I am again a little better, and just able to write you by this conveyance, should my health be restored I shall remain here, if it is not, I mean to request permission to go the length of the Cape of Good Hope to try what effect the change may have.

With this you have a list of the plants going on the Royal Admiral under the care of Mr Good for the Royal Gardens at Kew, it is unfortunate that I should be confined at this time, otherwise the collection would have been much more extensive, our new nursery man Mr Smith, brought out, in high preservation, as good collection of plants however we still want a great many of those I pointed out to the Directions last year, particularly a large supply of Myrtus [Pincuta?]

Agrastis [indecipherable] of Konig is too valuable a grass to permit one to let it remain longer neglected, I have therefore sent three large packages of the [seed?] by Peter Good, the person who has charge of the plants for the Royal Gardens, one is for you, one for those Gardens & the third for St Helena.

Copies of the first seventeen numbers of my descriptions go by this conveyance to the Directors, No. 18 is that of Nerium tinitorium, they have it in duplicate, I wish they may supply you with my last corrected copy, which was sent to them from Madras in 1792 or 93. In looking over the originals which my writer was copying these seventeen I blush at the numerous errors & had I not the greatest confidence in your kindness & attention, I would request the whole to be suppressed

I must observe that the plant named in the list [Lovicteasia?] trifoliata is a very elegant small tree, & that I have not yet seen the pericarp, its flowers agree perfectly with the character of L: my [avieda?] articullata is no doubt your

DOI: 10.4324/9781003194651-6

23

Liphananthus, of which you gave Mr Smith a sketch, it is no doubt a didynamous
plant & comes near Clerodenrum [Clerodendrum]

> I have the honour to be with much respect
> Dear Sir
> your most obedt
> Humble Servt
> W Roxburgh
> Sir J. Banks Bart

Editorial Headnote

1758 (Fife)–1830

Alexander Beatson was a senior army officer who also carried out important research and published, widely and influentially, on the subject of botany. Beatson saw service in India in the Fourth Anglo–Mysore War of the late 1790s and published an account of his experiences on his return to England in 1800. He then took up the position of Governor of the remote South Atlantic island colony of St Helena (which was administered by the East India Corporation) between 1808 and 1813.

As he describes in the extract, during his tenure as governor of St Helena Beatson had to put down a mutiny in 1811 when a number of soldiers protested against measures he had introduced to restrict the availability of alcoholic spirits. As an isolated and desolate stop-off between Britain and her Asian colonies St Helena had acquired a reputation as an ill-disciplined and inhospitable outpost. However, as well as improving law and order on the island, Beatson was able to use his position to advance scientific understanding by carrying out what were highly effective and influential agricultural experiments on growing potatoes and other forms of vegetation. As documented in the below extract, cultivation on St Helena greatly improved during Beatson's tenure, vindicating his view that it was possible to overcome the island's apparent arable limitations by giving greater consideration to its soil and climate. Of wider and longer-lasting ecological importance were Beatson's observations on the particular prevalence of droughts on St Helena and how this linked to the onset of famines. This research contributed to the understanding of climate science and particularly the El Nino effect – an episodic upsurge in air pressure over a period of about four years (Grove 1995: 344–346).

Perhaps most notably, this work, Tracts, came to be widely cited by Charles Darwin in the groundbreaking Origin of the Species a few decades later. Darwin drew on Beatson's evidence from St Helena, to compare with his research on the Galapagos, to understand the impact of encroachment by human and other life-forms on what we now know as ecosystems. Such islands represented effective testing grounds for scientific research. Environmental change and degradation were more readily observable on isolated islands than the urbanizing European landscape. The contribution of William Roxburgh, profiled previously, to Beatson's research is also acknowledged in this extract.

Beatson combined agricultural research with his military career for the rest of his life.

pp. vii–xii

3

TRACTS RELATIVE TO THE ISLAND OF ST. HELENA: WRITTEN DURING A RESIDENCE OF FIVE YEARS

Alexander Beatson

Source: Alexander Beatson, *Tracts Relative To The Island Of St. Helena: Written During A Residence Of Five Years* (1816)

PREFACE

It had long been very generally supposed that St. Helena was a rocky and unproductive island; mostly devoid of soil; scantily supplied with water; subject to severe and unusual droughts; abounding with rats, and wholly incapable of extensive cultivation, or improvement.

Whether these notions have originated with early writers, or in hearsay information of passing visitors, or in wilful misrepresentation to answer particular ends, it is unnecessary in this place to enquire. It will be sufficient to observe, that they were very prevalent, both in England and at St. Helena, at the period of my appointment to the Government; and that soon after my arrival, having reason to believe they were neither supported by facts nor appearances, I considered it my duty fully to investigate the whole; so as to ascertain whether or not those obstacles to improvement really did exist.

The means that were pursued will be found interspersed throughout the first part of this Work. The results have been most satisfactory; for they have not only exposed the fallacy of all such notions, but have most clearly demonstrated that many parts of St. Helena, so far from being desolate and barren, are pre-eminently fertile; that the island, in general, is capable of the highest improvements, both in the cultivation of corn, and all sorts of vegetables; and in raising valuable plantations of fruit and timber trees.

Being aware that investigations of this nature could only be interesting to a few, and that there are certain points on which information will naturally be expected in a work treating of St. Helena, I have therefore endeavoured to adapt it to a more general class of readers. Accordingly, I have prefixed an Introductory Chapter, which comprises Geological Facts, tending to illustrate the primary formation of the island; Observations on its Mineral and Vegetable Productions; Soil and

DOI: 10.4324/9781003194651-7

Climate, and Seasons; capabilities of Improvement, and on its singular Strength and Security as a Military Station.

These additional subjects, together with a detailed account of the Mutiny in 1811 (the only historical event deserving notice since the year 1808), and a List of Indigenous and Exotic Plants growing at St. Helena, and some other matters contained in the Appendix, will put the reader in full possession of every material fact that has come to my knowledge, or that has occurred, during my residence of five years. The whole is illustrated by Six Views of the most interesting parts, and by a Geological Plan and Elevation. I therefore indulge a hope, that this attempt to convey to the public more just ideas of this extraordinary island, may prove acceptable.

The List of Plants, or a Flora of the island, was communicated by my deceased friend Doctor Roxburgh, a few days before his death. It is therefore the last work of that indefatigable botanist; whose meritorious exertions in improving botanical science, and in applying it to useful economical purposes, are well known to the public.

The Views are engraved by that excellent artist Mr. W. Daniell, from the drawings of my friend Samuel Davis, Esq. They are most faithful representations, and are peculiarly valuable, as illustrations of the geological and military observations.

The Plan and Elevation of the Island are compiled from the Survey, and the measurement of heights, taken by Major Rennell; and from some other documents.

In a book entitled "Tracts," I did not deem it necessary to touch upon the history of St. Helena: I wished also to preserve uniformity, by confining this work wholly to subjects that have never yet appeared before the public; and to prevent enlarging it beyond the bounds I had prescribed. To those who are desirous of information upon the localities of the island, from the period of its discovery to the year 1807, I beg to recommend to their perusal Mr. Brooke's History of St. Helena, published in 1808; which is drawn from the most authentic sources, and is replete with accurate information.

In attempting to introduce improvements upon an island where the arts of agriculture were little understood; where lands were cultivated by manual labour, without the aid of animals; and where prejudices in favour of old customs were strong, it was obvious there could be no hope of amendment without the evidence of successful examples.

It was therefore necessary to have recourse to experiments. Ploughs, and other implements were introduced; the shooting population was increased by the introduction of about three hundred Chinese; and an improved system of husbandry was carried on, under the direction of an experienced Norfolk farmer. But it was a long time before the generality of the islanders would even look at these improvements. They regarded them as "mere foolishness;" said "they might do very well in England; but that in a mountainous country the plough could never answer; that their forefathers had done very well with the hoe, and they saw no use or necessity for these new things."

At length, however, when they did perceive the facility with which extensive fields were broken up; the rapidity with which they were prepared by the plough, and the excellent crops of potatoes and corn that were raised, they acknowledged the superiority of English farming; and many of the most respectable soon afterwards followed the example.

Besides giving examples in the use of the plough, and in the new culture of potatoes, and of corn, it was deemed proper to explain the principles, and to point out the advantages of the new husbandry. With this view, I prepared short agricultural essays, (detailing the progress and results of the experiments) which were printed, for general Information, in the St. Helena Monthly Register. Thirty of those essays have been selected for the First Part of this Work. They are placed in the order in which they were written. The Table of Contents points out the sections wherein the several subjects are at first discussed, or afterwards resumed; so that no inconvenience can arise from this arrangement: on tile contrary, it was the only mode of shewing the progressive steps that were taken to convey useful information to the landholders; and to excite amongst them a Spirit of emulation in cultivation and planting.

The complete success which has attended my efforts to improve the husbandry of St. Helena; and, above all, to substitute the plough for the spade and hoe, are circumstances not undeserving the attention of those who have valuable estates in the West India islands. According to Mr. Bryan Edwards's statement, founded upon his own experience, it appears, that by using the plough, in the operation of holing a sugar plantation, the labour of slaves is only about one-twentieth part of that which is required when the same work is performed by the hoe. In breaking up lands, and preparing them for corn and potatoe crops at St. Helena, it might easily be proved, that the reduction of manual labour, by the use of the plough, has been in a much greater proportion.

If, then, the plough were employed wherever the nature of the lands will admit, in all those countries where the hoe is in general use, and consequently where the demand for manual labour is excessive, it seems reasonable to infer, that such a change would be productive of infinite advantage. The necessity for manual labour would thereby be reduced, and the bodily fatigue of the unfortunate slaves would be lessened; which would, in all probability, lead to a greater increase of the present stock. By such means, all those inconveniences, whether real or imaginary, that are apprehended from the abolition of the Slave Trade, might, in the course of a few years, be effectually removed.

Since the abolition of slavery at St. Helena, which took place in the year 1792, there has been an augmentation in the black population, which consists of three classes: the slaves of individuals; the Company's slaves; and free blacks. It was intended to have shown the actual augmentation during a period of nineteen years, that is, since 1793: but, upon examining the lists in my possession, it was found that, until the year 1803, the Company's slaves and free blacks were excluded. On this account I have been obliged to confine the comparison to the period between the years 1803 and 1812; by which there appears to have been an increase of 148 from a stock of 1539 men, women, and children.

. . .

Pp: 36–43

SECTION VII

On Potatoes – two Crops in the Year – extensive Culture recommended – solid Nourishment of, compared with Flour – Culture of Corn recommended as a green or dry Fodder for Cattle – former heavy Losses in Cattle ascribed to improvident management – Notices of dry Seasons, and Losses in Cattle, from the year 1724 to 1792. – Seasons of Drought produced by the Operation of some general Cause – severe Drought at St. Helena in 1791–2 pervaded the Peninsula of India; and felt at Montserrat in the West Indies.

"LEEK to the Welsh, to Dutchmen BUTTER'S dear,
Of Irish swains POTATOE is the cheer." GAY

DOCTOR ADAM SMITH, in his *Wealth of Nations*, observes, that, "the chairmen, porters, and coal-heavers in London, and those unfortunate women who live by prostitution, the strongest men, and the most beautiful women perhaps in the British dominions, are said to be, the greater part of them, from the lowest rank of people in Ireland, who are generally fed with *Potatoes.* No food can afford a more decisive proof of its nourishing quality, or of its being peculiarly suitable, to the health of the human constitution."

If this able writer had visited St. Helena, or had been aware of the practice of raising *two crops* a year from the same land, or of producing 36,000 pounds of *Potatoes* annually from an acre, without manure, which Colonel Broughton has found to be the average of his crops at Long Wood, which is by no means the richest land here, it would have afforded him even a much greater contrast, and a more forcible comparison than he has drawn between the produce of an acre of *Potatoes* and an acre of *Wheat* in England. The former he rates at only twelve thousand pounds weight; the latter at two thousand, and allowing "half the weight of *Potatoes*, to go to water, (a very large allowance)," he infers that "one acre of *Potatoes* producing 6000 weight of solid nourishment, is equal to three times the quantity produced from an acre of *Wheat*."

It is evident therefore, that the same train of argument applied to this island, would make the annual produce of one acre of *Potatoes,* in solid nourishment, equal to *nine* acres of *Wheat* in England.

From the peculiar advantages which St. Helena enjoys in the extraordinary produce, as well as in the excellent quality of this invaluable root, it is evident that the extensive culture *of Potatoes,* is deserving the utmost attention, not merely as a food for man but for cattle and livestock of all kinds. The imports of flour, rice and paddy, and of salted meat, might thus be diminished, the island might easily be made to abound with every necessary of life, which is assuredly the best mode of depressing the present exorbitant prices; and the diminution of those wants which are obtained from other countries, would no doubt, have the effect of retaining, amongst the cultivators of the soil, a very great proportion of the sums that are annually paid for foreign supplies.

The annual consumption of flour is about 1600 barrels, which would cost in England, including the barrels, according to the invoice per Walmer Castle in 1807, £8674. If freight and charges he added at £5. per ton, and rating six barrels to a ton, this would be 266 tons, or £1330, making the total cost of 1600 barrels of flour, when landed here, £10,004.

Now from what has been said, and following Doctor Adam Smith's deductions, I will proceed to shew that an equal quantity of the "solid nourishment" contained in 1600 barrels of flour might be obtained in *Potatoes,* from thirty-three acres of this island, and admitting the rent, and the labour in cultivating the *two* crops annually, at even 30 pounds per acre, which is a very large sum, and particularly when the plough management is introduced, that for nine hundred and ninety pounds sterling there might be raised of wholesome nourishing food, a substitute or equivalent, for what costs when brought to this island, more than ten thousand pounds sterling! Sixteen hundred casks of flour, at 370 pounds each, contain 592,000 pounds, and thirty-three acres of *Potatoes* at 36,000 pounds per annum, would be 1,188,000, the half of which being 594,000 pounds, is "the solid nourishment," according to Doctor Adam Smith: which is even *more* than that contained in the above number of casks of flour.

Mr. Parmentier found, from a number of experiments, that good bread might be made from equal quantities of flour and potatoes. No doubt, two thirds of flour to one third of potatoes would be better: and some of this sort made here by a neighbour who well understands the comforts and good things of this life, was superior to any bread I ever tasted on this island. I would recommend a trial to the St. Helena bakers; they would find by this mixture that the bread has a fresher taste, and that it has the property of keeping better than that which is made of the flour imported from England: besides, by making flour go farther, they could afford to dispose of bread at a cheaper rate than that made wholly from flour.

I trust that these remarks will stimulate our landholders to their own interests, and that we shall soon have at least an hundred acres of potatoes added to the present cultivation. By this I do not mean to exclude the use of flour, but I am fully persuaded, that the advantage and convenience arising even from this addition in feeding man and livestock, would soon lead to a more extensive culture. In a year or two the inhabitants would thus become far less dependent on foreign imports; and the potatoe culture upon an enlarged scale, would also enable the landholders to give a portion to their cattle, at those times when they are much reduced by the impoverished state of the pastures; by this the lives of many might be saved during an unfavourable season. But the more effectually to guard against the fatal consequences that may justly be apprehended from a dry season, under the present management of cattle, I cannot too strongly recommend the expediency of alternate crops of potatoes and corn: the latter might be raised as at the Cape of

Good Hope, either as a dry or green fodder; and of which there might always be a certain supply particularly when the rains have only partially failed: this was most clearly proved in February and November, 1810, as will appear from what is stated in page 28 of the printed Laws and Ordinances, and in pages 51 and 76 of the Goat papers.

Further advantages would result from the alternate crops of potatoes and corn, since they would preserve the lands in good heart; and if some attention were paid to manuring, it would prevent them being exhausted, and becoming unprofitable, which they often have been by continually repeating the potatoe crops. It is, moreover, the opinion of eminent agriculturists that such a rotation would; in a great measure, secure potatoes against the ravages of the caterpillar.

What eminent advantages does the whole of this easy system of management hold out! I am firmly resolved to pursue it; for I have often seriously reflected on the great losses that have been sustained here by the planters. I have endeavoured to discover the causes, which I cannot but ascribe, almost entirely, to improvident management. No care whatever is taken to guard against evils similar to what have frequently visited this remote spot on the globe. In 1738 the planters lost 555 head of cattle, and the Company 132. The total number that perished at that time, from the extreme dryness of the weather, was 687. This is a dreadful warning. What a blow would such a season give to the landholders of the present day! For there is absolutely not the smallest precaution taken to avert it. I cannot behold this picture without apprehension; for the value of the number of cattle that died in 1738, (and a far greater number in 1791 and 1792) at the present market price, may be fairly rated at 6 to 8000 pounds, sterling.

To excite a serious attention in the minds of the landholders, who have almost the whole of their property in cattle, and more strongly to impress them with the dreadful consequences of trusting wholly to pasture lands, and in the hope also they will pay some attention to the facts and hints I now set before them, I shall conclude these remarks with a brief statement of every notice I can find on record, that relates to the visitations of unfavourable seasons, and to the calamities which have been experienced by preceding generations.

Notices regarding bad Seasons and Losses in Cattle, extracted from the Consultations, and from Letters from the Court of Directors.

In the year 1724, February 12. – Bad seasons for 4 or 5 years past: in dread of a famine.

1738, June 13. – Losses sustained in cattle, by the late dryness in the weather.

			Cattle.
Loss to the inhabitants	–	–	555
Ditto Company	–	–	132
		Total	687

RELATIVE TO THE ISLAND OF ST. HELENA

1739, May 4th. – Rainy seasons had failed for the last 4 or 5 years.

1747, March 9th. – Rains failed last season.

April 11. – Unusual drought for several months past.

May 26. – On account of the grass lands being burnt up by the continuation of dry weather, cattle were fed, during six weeks with plantain trees.

1748, May 10th. – Yams so scarce, that only 32 soldiers can be supplied weekly.

1752, August 3. – A failure of rain for some time past.

February 22. – Heavy rains fell on the 20th instant.

1759, December 7th. – For want of rain, the island and cattle in bad condition. The Court of Directors recommend promoting the increase of stock of all kinds.

1772, January 8. – Long continuance of dry weather occasioned great diminution in the number of cattle.

1774, December 23. – The island restored to a flourishing state.

1779, May 17. – The island in a distressed situation from the present drought – and from the loss and poverty of cattle.

July 19. – Great mortality among the cattle.

1780, April 17. – The Company's flock of sheep in bad condition "from the long drought and present failure of our summer rains."

June 5. – The island in a distressed state.

1781, March 1. – Torrents damaged Sandy Bay fortifications.

June 2. – The island had sustained severe drought for three years.

1791, April 13. – Colonel Brooke informs Doctor Anderson at Madras, that while the grass is burnt up, his Guinea grass, at High Knoll, looked "green and beautiful."

May 30. – Thirty-two of the Company's cattle (including calves) died during six months. The Company's stock on July 11, was 340 cattle.

October 21. – The season continued alarmingly dry – the crops of potatoes failed – the yam grounds grown very unprofitable – and numbers of the cattle have died.

| 1792, April 9. – | Company's cattle, December 31 | – | – | 369 |
| | Dead | – | – | 91 |

Here it appears that one fourth of the Company's stock died.

1792, August 17. – The planters petition to Government, representing that they "have, by the late drought, lost one half of their stock of cattle."

Philosophers of all ages have built a hope of being able to discover by repeated observations, some rules concerning the variations of seasons, and changes in the weather, convinced that such discoveries would be of the highest utility, especially in agriculture; because by foreseeing, even in part, the circumstances of the seasons, we should have it in our power to prevent, at least in some degree, the losses arising from them. But from the imperfection of our present knowledge of this subject, it is impossible to account for the uncertainty in the fall of rain. Most countries whether mountainous or flat are subject to it and it would seem from experience and comparisons, that the variations which have taken place, have sometimes been effected by the operation of some general cause. The severe drought felt here in 1791 and 1792 was far more calamitous in India. Doctor Anderson states, in a letter to Colonel Kyd, dated the 9th of August, 1792, that owing to a failure of rain, during the above two years, one half of the inhabitants in the northern circars had perished by famine; "and the remainder were so feeble and weak, that on the report of rice coming from the Malabar coast, 5000 poor people left Rajamundry, and very few of them reached the sea-side, although the distance is only 50 miles." The Doctor further observes "that betwixt the latitudes 16° and 18° on the coast of Coromandel, there was so little rain during the years 1764, 1765, and 1766, that the country was desolated by famine." It appears by Mr. Bryan Edwards's History of the West Indies, that the season of 1791–2 were unusually dry at the island of Montserrat.

It will be observed, by the extracts I have given, that no notice is taken of dry seasons at those periods; and that the greatest continuance of seasons *uncomplained of*, was betwixt the years 1724 and 1738. This interval was fourteen years. Now as there has been no serious drought since 1792, it should be kept in mind that the present interval of favourable seasons, being nineteen years, already exceeds any other on record. We know not how soon another visitation may take place. Let us then be wise and prudent, from dear bought experience, and use every means in our power to be prepared for it.

15th August, 1811.

Editorial Headnote

1781 (London)–1863

William John Burchell was the archetypal Victorian polymath. Amongst other things, he was a notable botanist, explorer, artist, linguist and cartographer. His plant specimens are still held at Kew Gardens and some of his insect collection remains on display at the Oxford University Museum. His father was a botanist, and Willliam followed in his footsteps and, after a private education at Raleigh House Academy in Mitcham, served an apprenticeship in botany at Kew before embarking on a career in this subject (Cleverley 1987: 3).

In his twenties, Burchell appeared to change his vocational ambitions and travelled to St Helena intending to initiate a merchant career. Shortly after arriving, however, he became disillusioned with commerce and abandoned that to become a teacher and botanist on the island. This remote South Atlantic outcrop has hence played a surprisingly prominent role in the advance of botanical science, given the previously described work Beatson and Roxburgh also carried out there. Beyond botanical significance were Burchell's observations in diaries he kept whilst on St Helena which provided important insights on the links between deforestation and flooding and soil erosion (Grove 1995: 349).

From St Helena, Burchell sailed to South Africa in 1810 and conducted research on a four-year expedition on the invitation of Jan Jansens, the governor of the Dutch Cape Colony. He collected a huge number of specimens and wrote the work profiled here chronicling his findings. The internationalism of scientific endeavour is very apparent in the extract with Burchell taking to learning Dutch and working freely with other nationalities in the course of carrying out his research. In particular, Burchell stands out for being uncharacteristically respectful of indigenous knowledge in his thinking, as is apparent in this extract with his appeal to take heed of the insights of all ethnic groups and even slaves. The Hottentots, to whom he refers, were the native peoples of the region.

Burchell later made a similar voyage to Brazil in 1825 and carried out extensive botanical research there also. However, on returning to England in 1830 he gradually became a more reclusive figure. He suffered from depression and ended his own life back home in Fulham. He eventually came to be buried in a local church graveyard, in spite of his suicide, after a campaign for this usual restriction for internment to be lifted by his sister (Clevereley 1987: 36). A number of animal species have been named in his honour, including Burchell's zebra, native to Southern Africa (Stewart & Warner 2012).

pp. 11–15

4

RESIDENCE IN CAPE TOWN, AND RAMBLES IN THE VICINITY

William John Burchell

Source: William John Burchell, *Residence in Cape Town, and Rambles in the Vicinty* (1822)

CHAPTER 2

I HAD brought with me letters of introduction to the Governor, to the Colonial Secretary, and to several English families; and had, above four years and a half before, been so fortunate as to become personally known to General Jansens the last Dutch governor, and to several officers of his suite, among whom was Dr. Lichtenstein, the present professor of natural history in the university at Berlin. On being informed of my intention of visiting the colony, they voluntarily offered letters and friendly recommendations to many Dutch and German families residing there.

Among these, the Reverend Frederick Hesse, the Lutheran minister, was more particularly mentioned to me; and a correspondence having from that time continued to subsist between us, I now decided on repairing to his house; having first secured a lodging at the "English Hotel." The reception which I met with, was such as to prepossess me with a favourable opinion of the place and of its inhabitants. He would not allow that I should take up my abode elsewhere than at his house during my stay in Cape Town; and the friendly kindness of his manners at last persuaded me to accept his hospitality. The lateness of the evening did but just permit me to present another letter of introduction, and to pay a visit to an old acquaintance: but as I walked along the streets, the remaining twilight was still sufficient both to excite and to satisfy much of my curiosity; and I was particularly struck with the elegant style of architecture, regularity, and cleanness of the town.

Thus passed my first African day. Gratified by every thing I had met with, when I retired to rest, a train of pleasing reflections and anticipations long kept me from sleep.

27th

The next morning I presented my letters to the Governor the Earl of Caledon, who expressed with much politeness his inclination and readiness to forward my views.

DOI: 10.4324/9781003194651-8

A letter of introduction to the Deputy Colonial Secretary, Major (now Colonel) Bird, was the means of my obtaining afterwards much polite attention from that gentleman. He was then filling the office of the Colonial Secretary Mr. Alexander, to whom I was already personally known, but who was absent on a mission to England. To the friendship of Mr. Alexander, and a voluntary offer of several letters of introduction, I feel a pleasure in ascribing some of the advantages which I enjoyed.

28th

This, and the greater part of the two following days, were occupied in delivering my letters to such gentlemen as were living in Cape Town; in introductions to others; in receiving the friendly visits of several who now renewed a former acquaintance; in getting my baggage ashore; and in executing several little commissions with which I had been charged.

I had at this time decided on nothing more than the general outlines of the plan for my future travels, agreeable to an intention of exploring the less frequented or unknown parts of Africa, for the purpose of becoming acquainted with its inhabitants, and of increasing my own knowledge by the addition of whatever facts I might have the opportunity of observing. Being accountable to no one for the result of my visit to this country, I felt the more at ease to decide on any arrangement best suited to my views; and determined on delaying my intended journey, until I should have collected some information respecting the country, and acquired some experience and knowledge of its customs and peculiarities.

Besides which, a knowledge and proper pronunciation of the Dutch language, according to the Cape dialect, and even according to the corrupt dialect of the Hottentots, was not among the least important preparations for a journey of research in this part of Africa. For I am convinced that many incorrect and absurd things, which have been written about this Colony, would never have been said, had the writers been sufficiently acquainted with the language to converse with every class of its inhabitants. To be qualified for judging of the character of these inhabitants, it is not enough to live mingled with the better part of society; the Boors must be heard, the Hottentots must be heard, and the slaves must be heard. It is an observation which Hollanders have often made, that on their first arrival they could not readily comprehend the meaning of a Hottentot when he spoke in Dutch; while it was evident to them that the Hottentot had still more difficulty in understanding that language in its pure and grammatical state. The English language may be said to be quite unknown to the natives beyond the colonial boundary, and even within that line it is very little understood, excepting in Cape Town.

I resolved, therefore, to consider Cape Town as my place of abode for a few months, expecting that a part of this time would be well employed in making collections in Natural History; thus saving myself the labour of bringing from a distance that which might here more easily be procured close at hand. Much of this time would be required for purchasing and collecting together a multitude of things necessary for such a journey, and for finding a number of Hottentots both qualified and willing to accompany me; for it was soon evident that such must be my only companions.

29th

As soon as my baggage was all safely landed, and I had got over the first bustle of introductions and visits, my curiosity to see the environs of the town could not longer be restrained; and Mr. Hesse proposed that we should this afternoon take a walk round the *Lion Mountain.*

As we passed along the western skirts of the town, I continued to admire the cleanness and good appearance of the houses, and the magnificence of the surrounding mountains. Owing to its great height and undivided form, *Table Mountain* does not at first appear to be so distant from the town as it really is; but as we approach, it seems to recede gradually, disclosing to the observer its enormous mass, and apparently, at every step, towering higher and higher above his head.

As soon as we had passed the houses, my attention, in spite of myself, was entirely engrossed by the rich and wonderful variety of plants that grew in every spot. In the bushes, weeds, and herbage by the road-side, at every step I recognised some well-known flower which I had seen nursed with great care in the green-houses of England.

A little farther on, we came to some plants of the great American Aloe (*Agave Americana*), in flower. This noble plant is frequently used for forming hedges; and when they stand close together, their thorny leaves present an impregnable barrier to cattle, and even to men. Their leaves, six feet long, and flower-stems of thirty feet in height, present a truly gigantic specimen of the plants commonly termed "flowers." Of these and the surrounding scenery I afterwards made a drawing.

Editorial Headnote

1797 (Forfarshire)–1875

Charles Lyell was a Scottish geologist and a major figure in the full emergence of that discipline in the nineteenth century.

Lyell was born in a stately home in Scotland, but his family moved to the New Forest when he was a young child. He studied law at Oxford and then initiated a legal career whilst always maintaining a private passion for geology and natural history. Poor eyesight allied with acknowledging his true love saw Lyell abandon the legal profession and fully embrace geology, lecturing in the subject at Cambridge and travelling extensively in the course of researching many publications in this area. These travels also afforded him ample opportunities to indulge in his favourite pastime of mountain climbing, an appropriate and natural spin-off for a geologist.

Lyell is often styled as the 'father of geology' such were his contributions to the discipline. Notably, he developed the theory of 'uniformitarianism', first articulated by James Hutton in the eighteenth century, which argued that all the Earth's physical features were formed gradually over time through natural forces acting on them, such as with erosion. This contrasted with the orthodoxy of the time, 'catastrophism', which held that physical features were formed by sudden major changes, such as huge earthquakes and floods. This paradigm was more readily relatable for many Christians since biblical events such as the Noah's Ark story could be accommodated within it. In the latter half of the nineteenth century, however, most geologists were won over by Lyell's reasoning and uniformitarianism became the orthodoxy (Wool 2001).

In the selected extract, Lyell examines how humanity has come to have an impact on nature, in addition to phenomena such as climate and gravity. In doing so he pre-empts the contemporary idea of the Anthropocene: a geological age moulded by humans. This is made explicit in the highly ecological observation that there is 'reasonable doubt, whether, upon the whole, we fertilize or impoverish the lands which we occupy'. The biodiversity consequences of deforestation, desertification and human alterations to the landscape are all questioned in this regard.

The holistic, gradual and continual logic of geological uniformitarianism in particular appealed to Charles Darwin in developing his theory of evolution regarding flora and fauna, and Lyell is widely cited in the Origin of the Species (discussed next in this volume). The two also became close friends.

Lyell was knighted 1848 and is buried in Westminster Abbey. Amongst many commemorations of his life, the highest mountain in Yosemite National Park and craters on the Moon and Mars are named after him.

pp. 146–150

5

PRINCIPLES OF GEOLOGY

Charles Lyell

Source: Charles Lyell, *Principles of Geology* (1832)

Every new condition in the state of the organic or inorganic creation, a new animal or plant, an additional snow-clad mountain, any permanent change, however slight in comparison to the whole, gives rise to a new order of things, and may make a material change in regard to some one or more species. Yet a swarm of locusts, or a frost of extreme intensity, may pass away without any great apparent derangement; no species may be lost, and all may soon recover their former relative numbers, because the same scourges may have visited the region, again and again, at some former periods. Every plant that was incapable of resisting such a degree of cold, every animal which was exposed to be entirely cut off by famine, in consequence of the consumption of vegetation by the locusts, may have perished already, so that the subsequent recurrence of similar catastrophes is attended only by a temporary change.

We are best acquainted with the mutations brought about by the progress of human population, and the growth of plants and animals favoured by man. To these, therefore, we should, in the first instance, turn our attention. If we conclude, from the concurrent testimony of history and of the evidence yielded by geological data, that man is, comparatively speaking, of very modern origin, we must at once perceive how great a revolution in the state of the animate world the increase of the human race, considered merely as consumers of a certain quantity of organic matter, must necessarily cause.

It may, perhaps, be said, that man has, in some degree, compensated for the appropriation to himself of so much food, by artificially improving the natural productiveness of soils, by irrigation, manure, and a judicious intermixture of mineral ingredients conveyed from different localities. But it admits of reasonable doubt, whether, upon the whole, we fertilize or impoverish the lands which we occupy. This assertion may seem startling to many, because they are so much in the habit of regarding the sterility or productiveness of land in relation to the wants of man, and not as regards the organic world generally. It is difficult, at first, to conceive, if a morass is converted into arable land, and made to yield a crop of grain, even of moderate abundance, that we have not improved the capabilities of the habitable surface – that we have not empowered it to support a larger quantity

DOI: 10.4324/9781003194651-9

of organic life. In such cases, a tract, before of no utility to man, may be reclaimed and become of high agricultural importance, but it may yield, at the same time, a scantier vegetation. If a lake be drained and turned into a meadow, the space will provide sustenance to man and many terrestrial animals serviceable to him, but not perhaps so much food as it previously yielded to the aquatic races.

If the pestiferous Pontine Marshes were drained and covered with corn like the plains of the Po, they might, perhaps, feed a smaller number of animals than they do now; for these morasses are filled with of herds of buffaloes and swine, and they swarm with birds, reptiles, and insects.

The felling of dense and lofty forests which covered, even within the records of history, a considerable space on the globe, now tenanted by civilized man, must usually have lessened the amount of vegetable food throughout the space where these woods grew. We must also take into our account the area covered by towns, and a still larger surface occupied by roads.

If we force the soil to bear extraordinary crops one year, we are, perhaps, compelled to let it lie fallow the next. But nothing so much counterbalances the fertilizing effects of human art as the extensive cultivation of foreign herbs and shrubs, which, although they are often more nutritious to man, seldom thrive with the same rank luxuriance as the native plants of a district. Man is, in truth, continually striving to diminish the natural diversity of the stations of animals and plants in every country, and to reduce them all to a small number fitted for species of economical use. He may succeed perfectly in attaining his object, even though the vegetation be comparatively meagre, and the total amount of animal life be greatly lessened.

Spix and Martius have given a lively description of the incredible number of insects which lay waste the crops in Brazil, besides swarms of monkeys, flocks of parrots and other birds, as well as the paca, agouti, and wild swine. They describe the torment which the planter and the naturalist suffer from the musquitoes, and the devastation of the ants and blattae; they speak of the dangers to which they were exposed from the jaguar, the poisonous serpents, lizards, scorpions, centipedes, and spiders. But with the increasing population and cultivation of the country, observe these naturalists, these evils will gradually diminish; when the inhabitants have cut down the woods, drained the marshes, made roads in all directions, and founded villages and towns, man will by degrees triumph over the rank vegetation and the noxious animals, and all the elements will second and amply recompense his activity.

The number of human beings now peopling the earth is supposed to amount to eight hundred millions, so that we may easily understand how great a number of beasts of prey, birds, and animals of every class, this prodigious population must have displaced, independently of the still more important consequences which have followed from the derangement brought about by man in the relative numerical strength of particular species.

Let us make some inquiries into the extent of the influence which the progress of society has exerted, during the last seven or eight centuries, in altering the distribution of our indigenous British animals. Dr. Fleming has prosecuted this inquiry with his usual zeal and ability, and in a memoir on the subject has enumerated the best-authenticated examples of the decrease or extirpation of certain species during a period when our population has made the most rapid advances. We shall offer a brief outline of his results.

The stag, as well as the fallow deer and the roe, were formerly so abundant that, according to Lesley, from five hundred to a thousand were sometimes slain at a hunting-match; but the native races would already have been extinguished, had they not been carefully preserved in certain forests. The otter, the marten, and the polecat, were also in sufficient numbers to be pursued for the sake of their fur; but they have now been reduced within very narrow bounds. The wild cat and fox have also been sacrificed throughout the greater part of the country, for the security of the poultry-yard or the fold. Badgers have been expelled from nearly every district which at former periods they inhabited.

Besides these, which have been driven out from some haunts, and everywhere reduced in number, there are some which have been wholly extirpated; such as the ancient breed of indigenous horses, the wild boar, and the wild oxen, of which last, however, a few remains are still preserved in the parks of some of our nobility. The beaver, which was eagerly sought after for its fur, had become scarce at the close of the ninth century, and, by the twelfth century, was only to be met with, according to Giraldus de Barri, in one river in Wales, and another in Scotland. The wolf, once so much dreaded by our ancestors, is said to have maintained its ground in Ireland so late as the beginning of the eighteenth century (1710), though it had been extirpated in Scotland thirty years before, and in England at a much earlier period. The bear, which in Wales was regarded as a beast of the chase equal to the hare or the boar, only perished as a native of Scotland in the year 1057.

Many native birds of prey have also been the subjects of unremitting persecution. The eagles, larger hawks, and ravens, have disappeared from the more cultivated districts. The haunts of the mallard, the snipe, the redshank, and the bittern, have been drained equally with the summer dwellings of the lapwing and the curlew. But these species still linger in some portion of the British isles; whereas the large capercailzies, or wood grouse, formerly natives of the pine-forests of Ireland and Scotland, have been destroyed within the last fifty years. The egret and the crane, which appear to have been formerly very common in Scotland, are now only occasional visitants.

The bustard (Otis tarda), observes Graves in his British Ornithology, 14 was formerly seen in the downs and heaths of various parts of our island, in flocks of forty or fifty birds; whereas it is now a circumstance of rare occurrence to meet with a single individual." Bewick also remarks, "that they were formerly more common in this island than at present; they are now found only in the open counties of the south and east, in the plains of Wiltshire, Dorsetshire, and some parts of Yorkshire." In the few years that have elapsed since Bewick wrote, this bird has entirely disappeared from Wiltshire and Dorsetshire.

DISCOVERING NATURE

These changes, we may observe, are derived from very imperfect memorials, and relate only to the larger and more conspicuous animals inhabiting a small spot on the globe; but they cannot fail to exalt our conception of the enormous revolutions which, in the course of several thousand years, the whole human species must have effected.

Editorial Headnote

1809 (Shrewsbury)–1882

Charles Darwin was and remains a towering figure of science for his groundbreaking theory of evolution in life forms that came to be known as Darwinism (a term coined by his protégé Thomas Huxley, profiled later in this volume part).

Darwin is generally held to have been an unexceptional scholar as a child but became captivated by natural history as a young man. He initially studied medicine at Edinburgh, but his father, sensing his lack of commitment, switched him to Cambridge, where he studied the wider sciences and fully discovered his passion for nature. In 1831, he enrolled as a naturalist on the HMS Beagle surveying wildlife on the west coast of South America in a five-year voyage. On his return, Darwin worked on his thoughts for some twenty years before finally writing Origin of the Species in which he sets out his paradigm-shifting but also controversial theories.

According to Darwin's revolutionary theory, all species are connected and evolve through the process of 'natural selection'. Characteristics that help an organism survive, compete and reproduce are passed down through generations and so they evolve. Humans – and all other organisms – have evolved in this way to become distinct from other species they are nevertheless related to. As he outlines in the extract, Darwin was influenced by his friend Charles Lyell's pioneering work on geology in appreciating the notion of gradual progressive change in nature.

Evolutionary theory was controversial for challenging the creationism of Christian thought and the 'Godliness' of nature which underpinned most leading naturalists of the day. As Darwin states in this extract, however, he did not consider that the scientific paradigm shift his theory required necessarily contradicted a belief in God. Beyond arousing some religious ire, the application of evolutionary theory to humanity itself in 'social Darwinism' also came to be highly contentious. Herbert Spencer, referred to by Darwin in this passage, coined the phrase 'survival of the fittest' as a basis for opposing welfare and defending societal elitism. It should be noted, though, that Darwin himself was never an advocate for political applications (or misapplications) of his scientific thought, such as in the advocacy of eugenics or racial superiority.

The theory of evolution was not Darwin's only enduring scientific legacy. In his remarkable career, he also offered many other influential insights on matters of natural science, including on atolls, the relationship between earthworms and soil and phototropism (how plant growth is affected by light). Darwin was plagued by poor health throughout his life but lived until his seventies. He is buried at Westminster Abbey (Encyclopedia Britannica).

pp. 459–490

6

ORIGIN OF THE SPECIES

Charles Darwin

Source: Charles Darwin, *Origin of the Species* (1859)

"RECAPITULATION AND CONCLUSION"

I have now recapitulated the facts and considerations which have thoroughly convinced me that species have been modified, during a long course of descent. This has been effected chiefly through the natural selection of numerous successive, slight, favourable variations; aided in an important manner by the inherited effects of the use and disuse of parts; and in an unimportant manner, that is in relation to adaptive structures, whether past or present, by the direct action of external conditions, and by variations which seem to us in our ignorance to arise spontaneously. It appears that I formerly underrated the frequency and value of these latter forms of variation, as leading to permanent modifications of structure independently of natural selection. But as my conclusions have lately been much misrepresented, and it has been stated that I attribute the modification of species exclusively to natural selection, I may be permitted to remark that in the first edition of this work, and subsequently, I placed in a most conspicuous position – namely, at the close of the Introduction – the following words: "I am convinced that natural selection has been the main but not the exclusive means of modification." This has been of no avail. Great is the power of steady misrepresentation; but the history of science shows that fortunately this power does not long endure.

It can hardly be supposed that a false theory would explain, in so satisfactory a manner as does the theory of natural selection, the several large classes of facts above specified. It has recently been objected that this is an unsafe method of arguing; but it is a method used in judging of the common events of life, and has often been used by the greatest natural philosophers. The undulatory theory of light has thus been arrived at; and the belief in the revolution of the earth on its own axis was until lately supported by hardly any direct evidence. It is no valid objection that science as yet throws no light on the far higher problem of the essence or origin of life. Who can explain what is the essence of the attraction of gravity? No one now objects to following out the results consequent on this unknown element of attraction; notwithstanding that Leibnitz formerly accused Newton of introducing "occult qualities and miracles into philosophy."

DOI: 10.4324/9781003194651-10

I see no good reason why the views given in this volume should shock the religious feelings of any one. It is satisfactory, as showing how transient such impressions are, to remember that the greatest discovery ever made by man, namely, the law of the attraction of gravity, was also attacked by Leibnitz, "as subversive of natural, and inferentially of revealed, religion." A celebrated author and divine has written to me that "he has gradually learnt to see that it is just as noble a conception of the Deity to believe that He created a few original forms capable of self-development into other and needful forms, as to believe that He required a fresh act of creation to supply the voids caused by the action of His laws."

Why, it may be asked, until recently did nearly all the most eminent living naturalists and geologists disbelieve in the mutability of species? It cannot be asserted that organic beings in a state of nature are subject to no variation; it cannot be proved that the amount of variation in the course of long ages is a limited quality; no clear distinction has been, or can be, drawn between species and well-marked varieties. It cannot be maintained that species when intercrossed are invariably sterile, and varieties invariably fertile; or that sterility is a special endowment and sign of creation. The belief that species were immutable productions was almost unavoidable as long as the history of the world was thought to be of short duration; and now that we have acquired some idea of the lapse of time, we are too apt to assume, without proof, that the geological record is so perfect that it would have afforded us plain evidence of the mutation of species, if they had undergone mutation.

But the chief cause of our natural unwillingness to admit that one species has given birth to clear and distinct species, is that we are always slow in admitting great changes of which we do not see the steps. The difficulty is the same as that felt by so many geologists, when Lyell first insisted that long lines of inland cliffs had been formed, and great valleys excavated, by the agencies which we see still at work. The mind cannot possibly grasp the full meaning of the term of even a million years; it cannot add up and perceive the full effects of many slight variations, accumulated during an almost infinite number of generations.

Although I am fully convinced of the truth of the views given in this volume under the form of an abstract, I by no means expect to convince experienced naturalists whose minds are stocked with a multitude of facts all viewed, during a long course of years, from a point of view directly opposite to mine. It is so easy to hide our ignorance under such expressions as the "plan of creation" or "unity of design," &c., and to think that we give an explanation when we only restate a fact. Any one whose disposition leads him to attach more weight to unexplained difficulties than to the explanation of a certain number of facts will certainly reject the theory. A few naturalists, endowed with much flexibility of mind, and who have already begun to doubt the immutability of species, may be influenced by this volume; but I look with confidence to the future, – to young and rising naturalists, who will be able to view both sides of the question with impartiality. Whoever is led to believe that species are mutable will do good service by conscientiously expressing his conviction; for thus only can the load of prejudice by which this subject is overwhelmed be removed.

Several eminent naturalists have of late published their belief that a multitude of reputed species in each genus are not real species; but that other species are real, that is, have been independently created. This seems to me a strange conclusion to arrive at. They admit that a multitude of forms, which till lately they themselves thought were special creations, and which are still thus looked at by the majority of naturalists, and which consequently have all the external characteristic features of true species, – they admit that these have been produced by variation, but they refuse to extend the same view to other and slightly different forms. Nevertheless they do not pretend that they can define, or even conjecture, which are the created forms of life, and which are those produced by secondary laws. They admit variation as a *vera causa* in one case, they arbitrarily reject it in another, without assigning any distinction in the two cases. The day will come when this will be given as a curious illustration of the blindness of preconceived opinion. These authors seem no more startled at a miraculous act of creation than at an ordinary birth. But do they really believe that at innumerable periods in the earth's history certain elemental atoms have been commanded suddenly to flash into living tissues? Do they believe that at each supposed act of creation one individual or many were produced? Were all the infinitely numerous kinds of animals and plants created as eggs or seed, or as full grown? and in the case of mammals, were they created bearing the false marks of nourishment from the mother's womb? Undoubtedly some of these same questions cannot be answered by those who believe in the appearance or creation of only a few forms of life, or of some one form alone. It has been maintained by several authors that it is as easy to believe in the creation of a million beings as of one; but Maupertuis' philosophical axiom "of least action" leads the mind more willingly to admit the smaller number; and certainly we ought not to believe that innumerable beings within each great class have been created with plain, but deceptive, marks of descent from a single parent.

As a record of a former state of things, I have retained in the foregoing paragraphs, and elsewhere, several sentences which imply that naturalists believe in the separate creation of each species; and I have been much censured for having thus expressed myself. But undoubtedly this was the general belief when the first edition of the present work appeared. I formerly spoke to very many naturalists on the subject of evolution, and never once met with any sympathetic agreement. It is probable that some did then believe in evolution, but they were either silent, or expressed themselves so ambiguously that it was not easy to understand their meaning. Now things are wholly changed, and almost every naturalist admits the great principle of evolution. There are, however, some who still think that species have suddenly given birth, through quite unexplained means, to new and totally different forms: but, as I have attempted to show, weighty evidence can be opposed to the admission of great and abrupt modifications. Under a scientific point of view, and as leading to further investigation, but little advantage is gained by believing that new forms are suddenly developed in an inexplicable manner from old and widely different forms, over the old belief in the creation of species from the dust of the earth.

It may be asked how far I extend the doctrine of the modification of species. The question is difficult to answer, because the more distinct the forms are which we consider, by so much the arguments in favour of community of descent become fewer in number and less in force. But some arguments of the greatest weight extend very far. All the members of whole classes are connected together by a chain of affinities, and all can be classed on the same principle, in groups subordinate to groups. Fossil remains sometimes tend to fill up very wide intervals between existing orders.

Organs in a rudimentary condition plainly show that an early progenitor had the organ in a fully developed condition; and this in some cases implies an enormous amount of modification in the descendants. Throughout whole classes various structures are formed on the same pattern, and at a very early age the embryos closely resemble each other. Therefore I cannot doubt that the theory of descent with modification embraces all the members of the same great class or kingdom. I believe that animals are descended from at most only four or five progenitors, and plants from an equal or lesser number.

Analogy would lead me one step farther, namely, to the belief that all animals and plants are descended from some one prototype. But analogy may be a deceitful guide. Nevertheless all living things have much in common, in their chemical composition, their cellular structure, their laws of growth, and their liability to injurious influences. We see this even in so trifling a fact as that the same poison often similarly affects plants and animals; or that the poison secreted by the gallfly produces monstrous growths on the wild rose or oak-tree. With all organic beings excepting perhaps some of the very lowest, sexual production seems to be essentially similar. With all, as far as is at present known the germinal vesicle is the same; so that all organisms start from a common origin. If we look even to the two main divisions – namely, to the animal and vegetable kingdoms – certain low forms are so far intermediate in character that naturalists have disputed to which kingdom they should be referred. As Professor Asa Gray has remarked, "The spores and other reproductive bodies of many of the lower algae may claim to have first a characteristically animal, and then an unequivocally vegetable existence." Therefore, on the principle of natural selection with divergence of character, it does not seem incredible that, from such low and intermediate form, both animals and plants may have been developed; and, if we admit this, we must likewise admit that all the organic beings which have ever lived on this earth may be descended from some one primordial form. But this inference is chiefly grounded on analogy and it is immaterial whether or not it be accepted. No doubt it is possible, as Mr. G. H. Lewes has urged, that at the first commencement of life many different forms were evolved; but if so we may conclude that only a very few have left modified descendants. For, as I have recently remarked in regard to the members of each great kingdom, such as the Vertebrata, Articulata, &c., we have distinct evidence in their embryological homologous and rudimentary structures that within each kingdom all the members are descended from a single progenitor.

When the views advanced by me in this volume, and by Mr. Wallace, or when analogous views on the origin of species are generally admitted, we can dimly foresee that there will be a considerable revolution in natural history. Systematists will be able to pursue their labours as at present; but they will not be incessantly haunted by the shadowy doubt whether this or that form be a true species. This, I feel sure and I speak after experience, will be no slight relief. The endless disputes whether or not some fifty species of British brambles are good species will cease. Systematists will have only to decide (not that this will be easy) whether any form be sufficiently constant and distinct from other forms, to be capable of definition; and if definable, whether the differences be sufficiently important to deserve a specific name. This latter point will become a far more essential consideration than it is at present; for differences, however slight, between any two forms if not blended by intermediate gradations, are looked at by most naturalists as sufficient to raise both forms to the rank of species.

Hereafter we shall be compelled to acknowledge that the only distinction between species and well-marked varieties is, that the latter are known, or believed, to be connected at the present day by intermediate gradations, whereas species were formerly thus connected. Hence, without rejecting the consideration of the present existence of intermediate gradations between any two forms we shall be led to weigh more carefully and to value higher the actual amount of difference between them. It is quite possible that forms now generally acknowledged to be merely varieties may hereafter be thought worthy of specific names; and in this case scientific and common language will come into accordance. In short, we shall have to treat species in the same manner as those naturalists treat genera, who admit that genera are merely artificial combinations made for convenience. This may not be a cheering prospect; but we shall at least be free from the vain search for the undiscovered and undiscoverable essence of the term species.

The other and more general departments of natural history will rise greatly in interest. The terms used by naturalists, of affinity, relationship, community of type, paternity, morphology, adaptive characters, rudimentary and aborted organs, &c., will cease to be metaphorical, and will have a plain signification. When we no longer look at an organic being as a savage looks at a ship, as something wholly beyond his comprehension; when we regard every production of nature as one which has had a long history; when we contemplate every complex structure and instinct as the summing up of many contrivances, each useful to the possessor, in the same way as any great mechanical invention is the summing up of the labour, the experience, the reason, and even the blunders of numerous workmen; when we thus view each organic being, how far more interesting – I speak from experience – does the study of natural history become!

A grand and almost untrodden field of inquiry will be opened, on the causes and laws of variation, on correlation, on the effects of use and disuse, on the direct action of external conditions, and so forth. The study of domestic productions will rise immensely in value. A new variety raised by man will be a more important and interesting subject for study than one more species added to the infinitude of already recorded species. Our classifications will come to be, as far as they can be so made, genealogies; and will then truly give what may be called the plan of creation. The rules for classifying will no doubt become simpler when we have a definite object in view. We possess no pedigrees or armorial bearings; and we have to discover and trace the many diverging lines of descent in our natural genealogies, by characters of any kind which have long been inherited. Rudimentary organs will speak infallibly with respect to the nature of long-lost structures. Species and groups of species which are called aberrant, and which may fancifully be called living fossils, will aid us in forming a picture of the ancient forms of life. Embryology will often reveal to us the structure, in some degree obscured, of the prototype of each great class.

When we feel assured that all the individuals of the same species, and all the closely allied species of most genera, have within a not very remote period descended from one parent, and have migrated from some one birth-place; and when we better know the many means of migration, then, by the light which geology now throws, and will continue to throw, on former changes of climate and of the level of the land, we shall surely be enabled to trace in an admirable manner the former migrations of the inhabitants of the whole world. Even at present, by comparing the differences between the inhabitants of the sea on the opposite sides of a continent, and the nature of the various inhabitants on that continent, in relation to their apparent means of immigration, some light can be thrown on ancient geography.

The noble science of Geology loses glory from the extreme imperfection of the record. The crust of the earth with its imbedded remains must not be looked at as a well-filled museum, but as a poor collection made at hazard and at rare intervals. The accumulation of each great fossiliferous formation will be recognised as having depended on an unusual concurrence of favourable circumstances, and the blank intervals between the successive stages as having been of vast duration. But we shall be able to gauge with some security the duration of these intervals by a comparison of the preceding and succeeding organic forms. We must be cautious in attempting to correlate as strictly contemporaneous two formations, which do not include many identical species, by the general succession of the forms of life. As species are produced and exterminated by slowly acting and still existing causes, and not by miraculous acts of creation; and as the most important of all causes of organic change is one which is almost independent of altered and perhaps suddenly altered physical conditions, namely, the mutual relation of organism to organism, – the improvement of one organism entailing the improvement or the extermination of others; it follows, that the amount of organic change in the fossils of consecutive formations probably serves as a fair measure of the relative though not actual lapse of time. A number of species, however, keeping in a body might remain for a long period unchanged, whilst within the same period several of these species by migrating into new countries and coming into competition with foreign associates, might become modified; so that we must not overrate the accuracy of organic change as a measure of time.

In the future I see open fields for far more important researches. Psychology will be securely based on the foundation already well laid by Mr. Herbert Spencer, that of the necessary acquirement of each mental power and capacity by gradation. Much light will be thrown on the origin of man and his history.

Authors of the highest eminence seem to be fully satisfied with the view that each species has been independently created. To my mind it accords better with what we know of the laws impressed on matter by the Creator, that the production and extinction of the past and present inhabitants of the world should have been due to secondary causes, like those determining the birth and death of the individual. When I view all beings not as special creations, but as the lineal descendants of some few beings which lived long before the first bed of the Cambrian system was deposited, they seem to me to become ennobled. Judging from the past, we may safely infer that not one living species will transmit its unaltered likeness to a distant futurity. And of the species now living very few will transmit progeny of any kind to a far distant futurity; for the manner in which all organic beings are grouped, shows that the greater number of species in each genus, and all the species in many genera, have left no descendants, but have become utterly extinct. We can so far take a prophetic glance into futurity as to foretell that it will be the common and widely-spread species, belonging to the larger and dominant groups within each class, which will ultimately prevail and procreate new and dominant species. As all the living forms of life are the lineal descendants of those which lived long before the Cambrian epoch, we may feel certain that the ordinary succession by generation has never once been broken, and that no cataclysm has desolated the whole world. Hence we may look with some confidence to secure future of great length. And as natural selection works solely by and for the good of each being, all corporeal and mental endowments will tend to progress towards perfection.

It is interesting to contemplate a tangled bank, clothed with many plants of many kinds, with birds singing on the bushes, with various insects flitting about, and with worms crawling through the damp earth, and to reflect that these elaborately constructed forms, so different from each other, and dependent upon each other in so complex a manner, have all been produced by laws acting around us. These laws, taken in the largest sense, being Growth with Reproduction; Inheritance which is almost implied by reproduction; Variability from the indirect and direct action of the conditions of life and from use and disuse: a Ratio of Increase so high as to lead to a Struggle for Life, and as a consequence to Natural Selection, entailing Divergence of Character and the Extinction of less-improved forms. Thus, from the war of nature, from famine and death, the most exalted object which we are capable of conceiving, namely, the production of the higher animals, directly follows. There is grandeur in this view of life, with its several powers, having been originally breathed by the Creator into a few forms or into one; and that, whilst this planet has gone cycling on according to the fixed law of gravity, from so simple a beginning endless forms most beautiful and most wonderful have been, and are being evolved.

Editorial Headnote

1786 (Herefordshire)–1848

James Cowles Prichard was a physician and anthropologist who made a major contribution to the appreciation that all humans are part of a single species.

As a child, Prichard was educated at home and raised as a Quaker. He remained devoutly Christian throughout his life but converted to Anglicanism. In 1802, he took up a medical apprenticeship before going to study medicine at Edinburgh University. At university, he honed a secondary interest in anthropology, and his dissertation came to form the basis of The Natural History of Man. After completing his medical doctorate, Prichard took up a physician position in Bristol. His research included several important contributions to the understanding of psychopathy and insanity, including coining the expression 'senile dementia'. As a result of this, in 1845, he was appointed as the wonderfully titled Commissioner of Lunacy (a body set up that year to oversee asylums) in London.

Prichard's best-known work, however, was in the emerging discipline of ethnology, the study of the human race. He was a prominent member of the Ethnological Society, including serving as its president (1847–8). His thesis that humanity is part of a single species, rather than made up of separate races, was in line with Darwinian evolutionary theory in applying the idea of 'natural selection' to how we have evolved. This view is made evident in the following extract, by his citing the examples of the divergent physical appearances of Eskimos and Namibians. In stating that man 'modifies the agencies of the elements upon himself; but do not these, agencies also modify him', Prichard is also advancing the idea of environmental determinism. Physical differences between people around the world are a consequence of adaptation to climatic and other environmental factors rather than their origins in separate species of humanity. This set him apart from critics such as the US physician Charles Caldwell, who advanced a popularly accepted pluralist theory of human origins – or polygenism – positing that humanity was made up of four races: Caucasian, Mongolian, American Indian and African (Caldwell 1851). Caldwell was a slave owner and used polygenism – and the discredited science of phrenology (linking skull shape to intellect) – as a justification for this and the asserted racial superiority of Caucasians. Caldwell's, rather than Prichard's, position persuaded most anthropologists and people in general in the mid-nineteenth century, but this changed, and the latter view is now almost universally accepted. Prichard hence made a huge contribution to challenging racial prejudice, as well as advancing the important environmental principle that humanity is part of and conditioned by the natural world (Driver 1988).

pp. 1–5

7

THE NATURAL HISTORY OF MAN: COMPRISING INQUIRIES INTO THE MODIFYING INFLUENCE OF PHYSICAL AND MORAL AGENCIES ON THE DIFFERENT TRIBES OF THE HUMAN FAMILY

James Cowles Prichard

Source: James Cowles Prichard, *The natural history of man: comprising inquiries into the modifying influence of physical and moral agencies on the different tribes of the human family* (1855)

SECTION 1

Introductory Observations

The organised world presents no contrasts and resemblances more remarkable than those which we discover on comparing mankind with the inferior tribes. That creatures should exist so nearly approaching to each other in all the particulars of them physical structure, and yet differing so immeasurably in their endowments and capabilities, would be a fact hard to believe, if it were not manifest to our observation. The differences are every where striking: the resemblances are less obvious in the fulness of their extent, and they are never contemplated without wonder by those who, in the study of anatomy and physiology, are first made aware how near is man in his physical constitution to the brutes. In all the principles of his internal structure, in the composition and functions of his parts, man is but an animal. The lord of the earth, who contemplates the eternal order of the universe, and assumes to communion with its invisible Maker, is a being composed of the same materials, and framed on the same principles, as the creatures which he has tamed to be the servile instruments of his will, or slays for his daily food. The points of resemblance are innumerable, they extend to the most recondite arrangements of that mechanism which maintains instrumentally the physical life of the body, which brings forward its early development, and admits, after a given period, its decay, and by means of which is prepared a succession of similar

DOI: 10.4324/9781003194651-11

beings destined to perpetuate the race. If it be inquired in what the still more remarkable difference consists, it is by no means easy to reply. By some it will he said that man, while similar in the organisation of his body to the lower tribes, is distinguished from them by the possession of an immaterial soul, a principle capable of conscious feeling, of intellect and thought. To many persons it will appear paradoxical to ascribe the endowment of a soul to the inferior tribes in the creation; yet it is difficult to discover a valid argument that limits the possession of an immaterial principle to man. The phenomena of feeling, of desire and aversion, of love and hatred, of fear and revenge, and the perception of external relations manifested in the life of brutes, imply, not only through the analogy which they display to the human faculties, but likewise from all that we can learn or conjecture of their particular nature, the superadded existence of a principle distinct from the mere mechanism of material bodies. That such a principle must exist in all beings capable of sensation, or of anything analogous to human passions and feelings, will hardly he denied by those who perceive the force of arguments which metaphysically demonstrate the immaterial nature of the mind. There may be no rational grounds for the ancient dogma that the souls of the lower animals were imperishable like the soul of man: this is, however, a problem which we are not called upon to discuss; and we may venture to conjecture that there may he immaterial essences of divers kinds, and endowed with various attributes and capabilities. But the real nature of these unseen principles eludes our research: they are only known to us by their external manifestations. These manifestations are the various powers and capabilities, or rather the habitudes of action, which, characterise the different orders of beings, diversified according to their several destinations. Among the most remarkable of these phenomena are the results of that impulse peculiar to man, which urges him to attempt and to persevere through long successive ages in the effort to obtain a conquest over the physical agencies of the elements, and to render subservient to his uses and wants the properties of surrounding bodies. While the lower tribes live every where resistless slaves to the agencies of material nature, the mere sport of their destiny, or of the lot which external conditions impose upon them, without making an effort to modify the circumstances which limit their capability of existence, man, on the contrary, gains victories over the elements, and turns the most powerful and even the most formidable of their agencies to the promotion of his own pleasure and advantage. Hence it comes to pass that man is a cosmopolite; that while, among the wild inhabitants of the forest, each tribe can exist only on a comparatively small tract of the earth's surface, man, together with those creatures which he has chosen for his immemorial companions, and has led with him in all his wanderings, is capable of living under every clime, from the shores of the Icy Sea, where the frozen soil never softens under his feet, to the burning sands of equatorial plains, where even reptiles perish from heat and drought. But here an inquiry is suggested which opens to our view a wide and interesting field of investigation. It is, whether man has not received from his Maker, besides his mental sagacity and effective contrivance, yet another principle of accommodation, by which he becomes fitted to possess and occupy the whole earth. He modifies the agencies of the elements upon himself; but do not these, agencies also modify him? Have they not rendered him in his very organisation different in different regions, and under various modes of existence imposed by physical and moral conditions? How different a being is the Esquimaux, who, in his burrow amid northern ices, gorges himself with the blubber of whales, from the lean and hungry Namibian, who pursues the lion under a vertical sun! And how different, whether compared with the skin-clad and oily fisher of the icebergs, or with the naked hunter of the Sahara, are the luxurious inmates of Eastern harems, or the energetic and intellectual inhabitants of the cities of Europe! That so great differences in external conditions, by the double influence of their physical and moral agency, should have effected during a long series of ages remarkable changes in the tribes of human beings subjected to their operation, – changes which have rendered these several tribes fitted in a peculiar manner for their respective abodes, – is by no means an improbable conjecture; and it becomes something more than a conjecture, when we extend our view to the diversified breeds of those animals which men have domesticated, and have transferred with themselves from one climate to another. Considered in this point of view, it acquires, perhaps, the character of a legitimate theory, supported by adequate evidence and by an extensive series of analogous facts. But we must not omit to observe that to this opinion there is an alternative, and one which many persons prefer to maintain, namely, that the collective body of mankind is made up of different races, which have differed from each other in their physical and moral nature from the beginning of their existence. To determine which of these two opinions is the best entitled to assent, or at least to set before my readers a clear and distinct notion of the evidence that can he brought to hear upon the question, will he my principal object in the following work.

I cannot enter upon the inquiry above stated, and proceed to discuss it as a mere question of natural history, without briefly adverting, in the first place, to some considerations with which it is connected, and particularly without offering a few remarks on the relation which it hears to the history of mankind contained in the Sacred Scriptures.

Editorial Headnote

1829 (Geneva)–1907

Alfred Newton was a professor of comparative anatomy at Cambridge University but is most renowned as a zoologist and a major pioneering figure in ornithology. In particular, he published several important works on birds, was the founder of the British Ornithologists Union and campaigned successfully for the legal protection of sea birds. His book A Dictionary of Birds (1893) is particularly well recognized for its contribution to the rapidly emerging discipline of ornithology.

Newton came from a rich family, with wealth built on the slave trade in the Caribbean, and his father, William, was an MP. Throughout his life he remained deeply religious and socially and politically conservative. Nevertheless, this did not deter him from embracing new scientific thinking. In particular, in spite of his Christian faith, he was greatly influenced by Darwin and applied his theory of evolution to his studies of ornithology.

Utilizing a research grant, Newton travelled with his friend Jon Wolley – whom he had met as a student at Cambridge – to Scandinavia in 1855 hoping to find that the great auk had not been rendered extinct by hunting, as had come to be reported. Sadly, however, he learned that this was indeed the case from meeting Icelandic bird hunters in the course of his research. The world's last pair of great auks (also known as gare-fowls as Newton refers to them) had been killed and their eggs also smashed. In reaching this dis-spiriting conclusion, Newton was able to document the precise occasion of a notorious extinction. It has subsequently been suggested that the last great auks in the British Isles were similarly killed in 1840 on the remote (now uninhabited) Hebridean island of St Kilda by 'superstitious natives' (Rackham 1986: 38). Wolley died in 1859, and Newton collated his friend's research and correspondence with him, as in this extract from an article published in the journal Ibis (of which Newton was editor).

Newton later served as the colonial secretary of Mauritius, the location of an earlier and even more infamous bird driven to extinction: the dodo, where he continued his studies. On his death in 1907, an obituary in Nature wrote:

> While zoological, and more especially ornithological, science has been deprived of one of its most illustrious students and exponents by the death of Alfred Newton, Cambridge has sustained an even more severe blow scientifically and socially. For not only has she lost in the late occupant of the chair zoology a distinguished professor and working zoologist, and a great benefactor to her zoological museum, but likewise a social figure, whose place can never be exactly filled.
>
> (Nature 1907: 179)

pp. 390–394

8

ABSTRACT OF MR. J. WOLLEY'S RESEARCHES IN ICELAND RESPECTING THE GARE-FOWL OR GREAT AUK

Alfred Newton

Source: Alfred Newton, *Abstract of Mr. J. Wolley's researches in Iceland respecting the gare-fowl or great auk* (1861)

The last gare-fowls known to have occurred in Iceland were two in number, caught and killed in 1844 by a party, of which our excellent host at Kyrkjuvogr, Vilhjalmur Hakonarsson, was the leader. They were bought, singularly enough, by Herr Christian Hansen, son of that Hansen I have before alluded to as having been (though, in the first instance, against his will) so dread a scourge to the race. From him they passed to Herr Möller, then the apothecary at Reykjavik, who, previously to having them skinned, prevailed upon M. Vivien (a French artist) to paint a picture of one of the dead birds, which picture now hangs in the house of his successor, Herr Randrup, the present apothecary in the capital of Iceland. As many persons may regard these birds as the latest survivors of their species, I may perhaps be excused for relating at some length the particulars of their capture, the more so as this will serve to explain the manner followed on former occasions.

The party consisted of fourteen men: two of these are dead, but with all the remaining twelve we conversed. They were commanded, as I have just said, by Vilbjalmui, and started in an eight-oared boat from Kyrkjuvogr, one evening between the 2nd and 5th of June, 1844.

The next morning early they arrived off Eldey. In form the island is a precipitous stack, perpendicular nearly all round. The most lofty part has been variously estimated to be from fifty to seventy fathoms in height; but on the opposite side a shelf (generally known as the "Underland") slopes up from the sea to a considerable elevation, until it is terminated abruptly by the steep cliff of the higher portion. At the foot of this inclined plane is the only landing-place; and further up, out of the beach of the waves, is the spot where the gare-fowls had their home. In this expedition but three men ascended: Jon Brandsson, a son of the former leader, who had several times before visited the rock, with Sigurdr Islefsson and

DOI: 10.4324/9781003194651-12

Ketil Ketilsson. A fourth, who was called upon to assist, refused, so dangerous did the landing seem. As the men I have named clambered up, they saw two gare-fowls sitting among the numberless other rock-birds (Uria troile and Alca iorda), and at once gave chase. The gare-fowls showed not the slightest disposition to repel the invaders, but immediately ran along under the high cliff, their heads erect, their little wings somewhat extended. They uttered no cry of alarm, and moved, with their short steps, about as quickly as a man could walk. Jon with outstretched arms drove one into a corner, where he soon had it fast. Sigurdr and Ketil pursued the second, and the former seized it close to the edge of the rock, here risen to a precipice some fathoms high, the water being directly below it. Ketil then returned to the sloping shelf whence the birds had started, and saw an egg lying on the lava slab, which he knew to be a gare-fowl's. He took it up, but finding it was broken, put it down again. Whether there was not also another egg is uncertain. All this took place in much less time than it takes to tell it. They hurried down again, for the wind was rising. The birds were strangled and cast into the boat, and the two younger men followed. Old Jon, however, hesitated about getting in, until his foreman threatened to lay hold of him with the boat-hook; at last a rope was thrown to him, and he was pulled in through the surf. It was "such Satan's weather," they said, but once clear of the breakers they were all right, and reached home in safety. Next day Vilhjalniur started with the birds for Reykjavik to take them to Herr Carl F. Siemsen, at whose instance this particular expedition had been undertaken; but on the way he met Hansen, to whom he sold them for eighty Rigsbank-dollars (about £9). According to Professor Steenstrup the bodies are now preserved in spirit in the Museum of the University of Copenhagen, but respecting the ultimate fate of the skins I am not quite sure.

Several other expeditions besides those to which I have here adverted no doubt took place between the years 1830 and 1844, but I cannot at present give either the dates or the results. Herr Siemsen informed Mr. Wolley that twenty-one birds and nine eggs had passed through his hands; but this account contains other details, which are certainly inaccurate. If all the stories we received can be credited, the whole number would reach eighty-seven. I should imagine sixty to be about the real number. Of these a large portion went to the Royal Museum at Copenhagen, as is stated by the late Etatsraad Keinhardt; a good many more passed into the hands of Herr Brandt, whose son informed Mr. Wolley that, in or since the year 1835, his father had had nine eggs, and I suppose birds to match. Two eggs were also purchased by a certain Snorri Ssemonasson then living at Keflavik, but what became of them I do not know. I have also learnt, on undoubted authority, that the late Herr Mechlenburg has had in all eight birds and three eggs. From this naturalist, in April, 1844, Mr. John Hancock, by the intervention of Mr. John Sewell, of Newcastle, received a bird and an egg, which are now in his collection, with the information that they were taken together with another bird and another egg, a year or two previously, on an island "at the north-east side of Iceland." A wrong locality was probably furnished on purpose to mislead Herr Mechlenburg; but the fact of his never having had more than three eggs, of which two came into his possession in, or shortly before, the year 1844, entirely disposes of Dr. Kjaerbolling's assertion to which I have before alluded. Thus it is pretty evident that most of the specimens of the great auk and its eggs which now exist in collections were obtained from Eldey between the years 1830 and 1844.

From what has been already stated, it will be seen how great Mr. Wolley's industry in collecting information was; yet I must add a few more words. In former days, the gare-fowls were, in summer time, so constantly observed in the sea by the fishermen, that their appearance was thought but little of. The people from Kyrkjuvogr and Sudrues used to begin to see them when they arrived off Hafnaberg, and from thence to lleykjancs rost. We were told by many people that they swam with their heads much lifted up, but their necks drawn in; they never tried to flap along the water, but dived as soon as alarmed. On the rocks they sat more upright than either guillemots or razorbills, and their station was further removed from the sea. They were easily frightened by noise, but not by what they saw. They sometimes uttered a few low croalis. They have never been known to defend their eggs, but would bite fiercely if they had the chance when caught. They walk or run with little, short steps, and go straight like a man. One has been known to drop down some two fathoms off the rock into the water. Finally, I may add that the colour of the inside of their mouths is said to have been yellow, as in the allied species.

In 1846 Eldey was visited by Vilhjalmur and a party, and no gare-fowls could be found. In 1858 Mr. Wolley and I remained at Kyrkjuvogr, with two short intervals, from May 21st to July 14th. Our chief object was to reach not only Eldey, but the still more distant Geirfugladrangr, on which probably no man has set foot since the Swedish Count, in 1821, with so much difficulty reached it. Boats and men were engaged, and stores for the trip laid in; but not a single opportunity occurred when a landing would have been practicable. I may say that it was with heavy hearts that we witnessed the season wearing away without giving us the wished-for chance. The following summer was equally tempestuous, and no voyage could be attempted. Last year (1860), on the 13th of June, Vilhjalmur successfully lauded on Eldey, but he found no trace of a greak auk, and the weather prevented his proceeding to the outer island. Later in the year a report reached Copenhagen, which was subsequently published in the newspaper 'Flyveposten' (No. 273), to the effect that two eggs of this bird had been taken on one of the skerries and sold in England for fabulous prices. Through the kind interest of several friends, 1 think I am in a position to assert that the statement is utterly false. The last accounts I have received from Iceland, under date of June 20th, in the present year (1861), make no mention of any expedition this summer. I am not very sanguine of a successful result, but I trust yet to be the means of ascertaining whether, at the sinking of the true Geirfuglasker, some of the colony, deprived of their wonted haunt, may not have shifted their quarters to the Geirfugladrangr, as others, we presume, did to Eldey, and to this end I have taken, and shall continue to take, the necessary steps.

Editorial Headnote

1871 (London)–1955

Arthur Tansley was an influential botanist perhaps best known for coining the term ecosystem in the 1930s but who was also a significant pioneer of the science of ecology long before that. Tansley was born into a wealthy middle-class London family and privately educated. He then studied at University College London and Cambridge and subsequently embarked on an academic career in Botany at those same universities. He worked with Herbert Spencer on his work The Principles of Biology and was a good friend of the author H.G. Wells, profiled later in this Part 2 of this volume.

Tansley co-founded the British Vegetation Committee in 1904, and in 1913, this body transformed into the British Ecological Society, with Tansley as its first president. The society launched the Journal of Ecology, extracted in the following, the world's first academic ecological periodical. The early history of the science of ecology is described by Tansley in the speech. In particular, he acknowledges his debt to Eugenius Warming, a Danish botanist and key founder of the discipline.

Tansley fought in and was injured in the Great War. It was at this time that he developed a secondary research interest in Freud and psychoanalysis. He later came to be analysed by him and published in this area as well as coming to link psychological and psychoanalytical insights into the study of nature as the ideas of universal interconnectedness that would underpin the concept of the ecosystem evolved. Tansley later came to define an ecosystem accordingly:

> But the more fundamental conception is, as it seems to me, the whole system (in the sense of physics), including not only the organism-complex, but also the whole complex of physical factors forming what we call the environment of the biome – the habitat factors in the widest sense. Though the organisms may claim our primary interest, when we are trying to think fundamentally we cannot separate them from their special environment, with which they form one physical system. It is the systems so formed which, from the point of view of the ecologist, are the basic units of nature on the face of the earth. Our natural human prejudices force us to consider the organisms (in the sense of the biologist) as the most important parts of these systems, but certainly the inorganic "factors" are also parts – there could be no systems without them, and there is constant interchange of the most various kinds within each system, not only between the organisms but between the organic and the inorganic. These ecosystems, as we may call them, are of the most

DISCOVERING NATURE

various kinds and sizes. They form one category of the multitudinous physical systems of the universe, which range from the universe as a whole down to the atom.

(Tansley 1935: 299)

Politically, Tansley was a socialist, and there is an egalitarian logic apparent in his ecosystem concept based on a universal and non-hierarchical notion of interconnectedness and self-regulation. Indeed, Tansley's thinking formed the basis for some radical strains of political ecology that came to emerge several decades later. Deep Green Ecology, pioneered in 1973 by Norwegian thinker Arne Naess, is built on the principle of 'biospherical egalitarianism', assigning equal value to all life-forms (or, at least, sentient beings). The animal liberation movement and radical non-governmental organizations like Earth First have been influenced by this philosophy which views the 'shallow green' mere consideration of eco-centric values as insufficient and calls for liberal notions of human rights to be extended to the non-human world. Australian philosopher Peter Singer (1979: 123), for example, has controversially and provocatively suggested that, since it has no perception of its own existence; 'the life of a newborn [baby] is of less value than the life of a pig, dog or a chimpanzee'.

Science and politics combined in Tansley's famous criticism of the South African botanist/statesman Jan Smuts and his popularization of holism as an alternative ecological concept of interconnectedness and self-regulation. Amongst other things, Tansley objected to holism because Smuts – a pioneer of apartheid – applied the biological logic of interconnectedness to justify racial segregation (on the grounds that African whites and blacks were separate self-regulating systems; Anker 2002).

Tansley was knighted in 1950, five years before his death.

pp. 194–196

9

PRESIDENTIAL ADDRESS (BRITISH ECOLOGICAL SOCIETY)

Arthur Tansley

Source: Arthur Tansley, *Presidential Address (British Ecological Society;* 1914)

My task to-day is a very honourable one, and brings with it no inconsiderable sense of responsibility. For however much I may wish to refrain from exalting the office of President of this very young Society, whose future it is difficult to foresee with any approach to certainty, it is impossible to forget altogether that this is the first presidential address to the first ecological society-so far as my knowledge goes-the world has seen.

First let me congratulate the Society on a successful opening year. Our numbers are markedly higher than it was estimated at the outset they would be, and it is most satisfactory to note that practically every one who has joined the Society has joined as a full member, which was certainly unexpected. That result is due no doubt to the feeling that the Journal-to which full members alone are entitled – is the chief, though it is by no means the only, advantage the Society has to offer to its members. And the fact that so many people have joined the Society, in place of simply subscribing to the Journal as members of the public, shows further, I think, that we have not estimated too highly the privileges of attending the meetings and excursions, and the other advantages of membership.

THE JOURNAL

I congratulate the Society on possessing, in Dr Cavers, an able editor of the Journal, whose notices of ecological papers are models of lucidity and thoroughness. Dr Cavers's work in this respect is of first importance to the Society, for on the excellence of the Journal the prestige of the Society will largely depend, and on its circulation outside the membership we must largely rely for our funds. I spent the whole of last summer in the United States, and wherever I met plant-ecologists, who are far more numerous among professional botanists in that country than is the case in the British Isles, I was greeted with the heartiest and most welcome congratulations, not only on the foundation of this Society, but especially on the excellent start made by our Journal. More than 50 copies of the Journal

DOI: 10.4324/9781003194651-13

are already subscribed for in the United States – a number which I am confident, from what I heard, will be largely increased in the near future. I am very glad to be able to announce that American ecologists are co-operating with us to help the Jouinal take the place in the periodical literature of botany which we believe it should occupy. We have succeeded in securing for it articles by several of the leading workers in that country. Such cordial support at the outset from a country in which ecology is valued more highly than anywhere in the world is a very great asset to a young Society like ours, with all its reputation to make. It behooves us on our part to do our very best to keep the Journal up to the high standard that will rightly be expected of it.

THE POSITION OF ECOLOGY IN BRITAIN

Ecology is in some respects in a difficult position in this country today. Many of us believe with Clements that it is "The central and vital part of botany." Probably all of us members of this Society believe that it has a very great future. There can be no doubt that it makes a vivid and widespread appeal to the younger generation of botanists, and to very many who are not professional botanists, it gives a new point of view and quite a new interest to botany. But for all that it has not yet attained the general recognition among botanists which we feel it ought to have. It occupies a very small, in many cases almost a negligible, place in our University curricula. In some quarters, it is more or less covertly sneered at. Now it is absolutely of no use to get angry about these things. The only wise course is to discover the causes, to do our best to remedy those which are within our control, and to wait patiently for the others to disappear, as they assuredly will do in course of time if our belief in the subject is well founded. Let me deal with the last class first, and get them out of the way, for it is pleasanter, as well as much more profitable, to discuss matters we may hope to control than to dilate on the weakness of our fellows. The most important is the natural conservatism of the adherents of the older and well-established branches of a subject, which tends to carry with it dislike and distrust of anything new. And when to this is added some tincture of jealousy of the attraction of a newer area of development for the younger workers, the feeling I have alluded to is seen to be natural enough, however much we may deplore it.

SCOPE AND FUNCTIONS OF ECOLOGY

In the case of a new subject which attains very striking results in a short time, such for instance as genetics, the position is, so to speak, taken by assault, and whatever distrust and jealousy there may be, it very soon ceases to be articulate. But in the case of ecology it is different. We can point to no great body of well-established and remarkable results obtained within a short time, and striking the imagination by their novelty and obvious importance. We claim for ecology that it is before all things a way of regarding the plant world, that it is par excellence the study of plants for their own sakes as living beings in their natural surroundings,

PRESIDENTIAL ADDRESS (BRITISH ECOLOGICAL SOCIETY)

of their vital relations to these surroundings and to one another, of their social life as well as their individual life, and that is why we put it in the forefront of botanical science.

Ecology is most emphatically not merely the study of plant communities as such. That is a common error, based of course on the fact that while the general ecological point of view has been more or less familiar for many years, though with certain notable exceptions its pursuit has not in the past been particularly zealous nor particularly scientific, it was Warming's book which in 1896 first presented any part of it in a definite and systematic form capable of making an immediate impression, and Warming's book dealt mainly with plant communities. But the scope of the subject is clearly much wider. Ecology is not in fact primarily a specialised branch of botany at all, but a way of regarding plant life. As such and firmly based on plant-physiology, it should yield in the first place the most fitting method of dealing with plant life in an elementary course, for under its unifying viewpoint the most fundamnental facts about plants as we know them at present can be most naturally arranged and presented to the greatest educational advantage. As a subject of research the field of ecology is so vast and varied, and as yet so largely undeveloped, that we cannot be surprised at having to meet the charge of vagueness and diffuseness from those who lack the imagination or the will to understand its immense potentialities. The vast and as yet largely undeveloped content of ecology is in fact at once its present weakness and, as it seems to me, its immense potential strength. We are like miners standing over a goldfield of unquestionable richness, but as yet tested only here and there. We scarcely know where to begin, and how to locate the richest bodies of ore. We are also novices in the best methods of mining, or, in other words, our technique is still in a rudimentary condition. Much of the mining is going to be both difficult and laborious, and many of us are inadequately trained. Small wonder then that our demeanour is often hesitating and uncertain, and that we are subject to the scepticism, if not to the jeers, of those who have other mines to work, and are not likely to be specially anxious that ours should be too remunerative an undertaking. And this initial attitude of hesitation and uncertainty brings with it another result – a tendency to shirk the serious problems of the subject on the part of the weaker workers in the field, a tendency well expressed by Clements in 1905, though his words are happily somewhat less true now than they were nine years ago, "development has begun on the surface and has scarcely penetrated beneath it." In its extreme expression this tendency takes the form of lists of species, often incorrectly determined, representing badly defined and incorrectly apprehended vegetation units, which often indeed have no real existence, and illustrated by inferior photographs; or perhaps of loose descriptions of supposed adaptations to habitat conditions. These are forms of activity which we can only deplore and do our utmost to discourage. There can be little surprise if they bring down upon some of the published work the charge of triviality which is often made, and quite justly made, so far as such work is concerned. The mental characteristics which this kind of thing betrays are not, however, by any means unapparent in a good deal of the published work in other branches of botany.

1.2

RESOURCE DEPLETION

Editorial Headnote

1766 (Dorking)–1834

Thomas Malthus was an economist and is still well known today for his influential theory on the links between population growth and resources, which has come to be known as Malthusianism.

Malthus was from a wealthy family and was educated at home by his father, an academic and close friend of philosophers David Hume and Jean-Jacques Rousseau. After this, he went on to study at Cambridge and took orders to become a curate of the Church of England.

On the Principle of Population was effectively an extended pamphlet and its brevity succeeded in giving his arguments a quick and widespread impact. Malthus then followed up this short work of 1798 with a much more extensive second edition in 1803 utilizing more supporting data. In doing so he expanded on his central thesis that 'the power of population is indefinitely greater than the power in the earth to produce subsistence for man'. The reasoning was that, since food production increased at a linear rate whilst human reproduction occurred at an exponential rate, the Earth would soon come to exceed its carrying capacity. Hence, Malthus advocated taking steps to check population growth, such as promoting sexual abstinence and having marriages later in life (he disapproved of contraception on religious grounds).

His avowed empiricism made Malthus a pessimist, viewing famines, poverty and diseases as inevitable and not altogether undesirable given the over-arching threat of global overpopulation. He was sceptical of notions that human ingenuity and reason could alter the well-supported fact that global demand was soon to exceed supply. The references to the pioneer of anarchism, William Godwin, in the text allude to Malthus's contention that he was placing reason over wishful thinking. In particular, Godwin's individualism was at odds with Malthus's belief that people needed saving from themselves.

Although socially conservative, Malthus was an economic liberal who was close friends with and influenced by David Ricardo, the most prominent proponent of market forces of his day. As is evident in this volume part and Volume II, his conviction that famines were inevitable and that seeking to counter them with aid was both futile and counter-productive (for distorting market forces) came to influence British policy domestically and in the colonies.

Malthus is also known to have been an influence on Charles Darwin as the great scientist admitted in his autobiography:

> I happened to read for amusement Malthus on Population, and being well prepared to appreciate the struggle for existence which everywhere goes on from long-continued observation of the habits of animals and plants,

it at once struck me that under these circumstances favourable variations would tend to be preserved, and unfavourable ones to be destroyed. The results of this would be the formation of a new species. Here, then I had at last got a theory by which to work.

(Darwin 1969: 119–20)

Malthus took up a position as professor of history and political economy at the East India Company College at Haileybury, Hertfordshire, in 1805 and remained there for the rest of his working life (Encyclopedia Britannica).

10

AN ESSAY ON THE PRINCIPLE OF POPULATION

Thomas Malthus

Source: Thomas Malthus, *An Essay on the Principle of Population* (1798)

CHAPTER 1

Question stated – Little prospect of a determination of it, from the enmity of the opposing parties – The principal argument against the perfectibility of man and of society has never been fairly answered – Nature of the difficulty arising from population – Outline of the principal argument of the Essay

THE GREAT AND UNLOOKED FOR DISCOVERIES that have taken place of late years in natural philosophy, the increasing diffusion of general knowledge from the extension of the art of printing, the ardent and unshackled spirit of inquiry that prevails throughout the lettered and even unlettered world, the new and extraordinary lights that have been thrown on political subjects which dazzle and astonish the understanding, and particularly that tremendous phenomenon in the political horizon, the French Revolution, which, like a blazing comet, seems destined either to inspire with fresh life and vigour, or to scorch up and destroy the shrinking inhabitants of the earth, have all concurred to lead many able men into the opinion that we were touching on a period big with the most important changes, changes that would in some measure be decisive of the future fate of mankind.

It has been said that the great question is now at issue, whether man shall henceforth start forwards with accelerated velocity towards illimitable, and hitherto unconceived improvement, or be condemned to a perpetual oscillation between happiness and misery, and after every effort remain still at an immeasurable distance from the wished-for goal.

Yet, anxiously as every friend of mankind must look forwards to the termination of this painful suspense, and eagerly as the inquiring mind would hail every ray of light that might assist its view into futurity, it is much to be lamented that the writers on each side of this momentous question still keep far aloof from each

DOI: 10.4324/9781003194651-15

DISCOVERING NATURE

other. Their mutual arguments do not meet with a candid examination. The question is not brought to rest on fewer points, and even in theory scarcely seems to be approaching to a decision.

The advocate for the present order of things is apt to treat the sect of speculative philosophers either as a set of artful and designing knaves who preach up ardent benevolence and draw captivating pictures of a happier state of society only the better to enable them to destroy the present establishments and to forward their own deep-laid schemes of ambition, or as wild and mad-headed enthusiasts whose silly speculations and absurd paradoxes are not worthy the attention of any reasonable man.

The advocate for the perfectibility of man, and of society, retorts on the defender of establishments a more than equal contempt. He brands him as the slave of the most miserable and narrow prejudices; or as the defender of the abuses of civil society only because he profits by them. He paints him either as a character who prostitutes his understanding to his interest, or as one whose powers of mind are not of a size to grasp any thing great and noble, who cannot see above five yards before him, and who must therefore be utterly unable to take in the views of the enlightened benefactor of mankind.

In this unamicable contest the cause of truth cannot but suffer. The really good arguments on each side of the question are not allowed to have their proper weight. Each pursues his own theory, little solicitous to correct or improve it by an attention to what is advanced by his opponents.

The friend of the present order of things condemns all political speculations in the gross. He will not even condescend to examine the grounds from which the perfectibility of society is inferred. Much less will he give himself the trouble in a fair and candid manner to attempt an exposition of their fallacy.

The speculative philosopher equally offends against the cause of truth. With eyes fixed on a happier state of society, the blessings of which he paints in the most captivating colours, he allows himself to indulge in the most bitter invectives against every present establishment, without applying his talents to consider the best and safest means of removing abuses and without seeming to be aware of the tremendous obstacles that threaten, even in theory, to oppose the progress of man towards perfection.

It is an acknowledged truth in philosophy that a just theory will always be confirmed by experiment. Yet so much friction, and so many minute circumstances occur in practice, which it is next to impossible for the most enlarged and penetrating mind to foresee, that on few subjects can any theory be pronounced just, till all the arguments against it have been maturely weighed and clearly and consistently refuted.

I have read some of the speculations on the perfectibility of man and of society with great pleasure. I have been warmed and delighted with the enchanting picture which they hold forth. I ardently wish for such happy improvements. But I see great, and, to my understanding, unconquerable difficulties in the way to them. These difficulties it is my present purpose to state, declaring, at the same time, that so far from exulting in them, as a cause of triumph over the friends of innovation, nothing would give me greater pleasure than to see them completely removed.

The most important argument that I shall adduce is certainly not new. The principles on which it depends have been explained in part by Hume, and more at large by Dr Adam Smith. It has been advanced and applied to the present subject, though not with its proper weight, or in the most forcible point of view, by Mr Wallace, and it may probably have been stated by many writers that I have never met with. I should certainly therefore not think of advancing it again, though I mean to place it in a point of view in some degree different from any that I have hitherto seen, if it had ever been fairly and satisfactorily answered.

The cause of this neglect on the part of the advocates for the perfectibility of mankind is not easily accounted for. I cannot doubt the talents of such men as Godwin and Condorcet. I am unwilling to doubt their candour. To my understanding, and probably to that of most others, the difficulty appears insurmountable. Yet these men of acknowledged ability and penetration scarcely deign to notice it, and hold on their course in such speculations with unabated ardour and undiminished confidence. I have certainly no right to say that they purposely shut their eyes to such arguments. I ought rather to doubt the validity of them, when neglected by such men, however forcibly their truth may strike my own mind. Yet in this respect it must be acknowledged that we are all of us too prone to err. If I saw a glass of wine repeatedly presented to a man, and he took no notice of it, I should be apt to think that he was blind or uncivil. A juster philosophy might teach me rather to think that my eyes deceived me and that the offer was not really what I conceived it to be.

In entering upon the argument I must premise that I put out of the question, at present, all mere conjectures, that is, all suppositions, the probable realization of which cannot be inferred upon any just philosophical grounds. A writer may tell me that he thinks man will ultimately become an ostrich. I cannot properly contradict him. But before he can expect to bring any reasonable person over to his opinion, he ought to shew that the necks of mankind have been gradually elongating, that the lips have grown harder and more prominent, that the legs and feet are daily altering their shape, and that the hair is beginning to change into stubs of feathers. And till the probability of so wonderful a conversion can be shewn, it is surely lost time and lost eloquence to expatiate on the happiness of man in such a state; to describe his powers, both of running and flying, to paint him in a condition where all narrow luxuries would be contemned, where he would be employed only in collecting the necessaries of life, and where, consequently, each man's share of labour would be light, and his portion of leisure ample.

I think I may fairly make two postulata.

First, That food is necessary to the existence of man.

Secondly, That the passion between the sexes is necessary and will remain nearly in its present state.

These two laws, ever since we have had any knowledge of mankind, appear to have been fixed laws of our nature, and, as we have not hitherto seen any alteration in them, we have no right to conclude that they will ever cease to be what they now are, without an immediate act of power in that Being who first arranged the system of the universe, and for the advantage of his creatures, still executes, according to fixed laws, all its various operations.

I do not know that any writer has supposed that on this earth man will ultimately be able to live without food. But Mr Godwin has conjectured that the passion between the sexes may in time be extinguished. As, however, he calls this part of his work a deviation into the land of conjecture, I will not dwell longer upon it at present than to say that the best arguments for the perfectibility of man are drawn from a contemplation of the great progress that he has already made from the savage state and the difficulty of saying where he is to stop. But towards the extinction of the passion between the sexes, no progress whatever has hitherto been made. It appears to exist in as much force at present as it did two thousand or four thousand years ago. There are individual exceptions now as there always have been. But, as these exceptions do not appear to increase in number, it would surely be a very unphilosophical mode of arguing to infer, merely from the existence of an exception, that the exception would, in time, become the rule, and the rule the exception.

Assuming then my postulata as granted, I say, that the power of population is indefinitely greater than the power in the earth to produce subsistence for man. Population, when unchecked, increases in a geometrical ratio. Subsistence increases only in an arithmetical ratio. A slight acquaintance with numbers will shew the immensity of the first power in comparison of the second. By that law of our nature which makes food necessary to the life of man, the effects of these two unequal powers must be kept equal.

This implies a strong and constantly operating check on population from the difficulty of subsistence. This difficulty must fall somewhere and must necessarily be severely felt by a large portion of mankind.

Through the animal and vegetable kingdoms, nature has scattered the seeds of life abroad with the most profuse and liberal hand. She has been comparatively sparing in the room and the nourishment necessary to rear them. The germs of existence contained in this spot of earth, with ample food, and ample room to expand in, would fill millions of worlds in the course of a few thousand years. Necessity, that imperious all pervading law of nature, restrains them within the prescribed bounds. The race of plants and the race of animals shrink under this great restrictive law. And the race of man cannot, by any efforts of reason, escape from it. Among plants and animals its effects are waste of seed, sickness, and premature death. Among mankind, misery and vice. The former, misery, is an absolutely necessary consequence of it. Vice is a highly probable consequence, and we therefore see it abundantly prevail, but it ought not, perhaps, to be called an absolutely necessary consequence. The ordeal of virtue is to resist all temptation to evil.

This natural inequality of the two powers of population and of production in the earth, and that great law of our nature which must constantly keep their effects equal, form the great difficulty that to me appears insurmountable in the way to the perfectibility of society. All other arguments are of slight and subordinate consideration in comparison of this. I see no way by which man can escape from the weight of this law which pervades all animated nature. No fancied equality, no agrarian regulations in their utmost extent, could remove the pressure of it even for a single century. And it appears, therefore, to be decisive against the possible existence of a society, all the members of which should live in ease, happiness, and comparative leisure; and feel no anxiety about providing the means of subsistence for themselves and families.

Consequently, if the premises are just, the argument is conclusive against the perfectibility of the mass of mankind.

I have thus sketched the general outline of the argument, but I will examine it more particularly, and I think it will be found that experience, the true source and foundation of all knowledge, invariably confirms its truth.

. . .

pp. 7–8 (Chapter 2)

Let us now take any spot of earth, this Island for instance, and see in what ratio the subsistence it affords can be supposed to increase. We will begin with it under its present state of cultivation.

If I allow that by the best possible policy, by breaking up more land and by great encouragements to agriculture, the produce of this Island may be doubled in the first twenty-five years, I think it will be allowing as much as any person can well demand.

In the next twenty-five years, it is impossible to suppose that the produce could be quadrupled. It would be contrary to all our knowledge of the qualities of land. The very utmost that we can conceive, is, that the increase in the second twenty-five years might equal the present produce. Let us then take this for our rule, though certainly far beyond the truth, and allow that, by great exertion, the whole produce of the Island might be increased every twenty-five years, by a quantity of subsistence equal to what it at present produces. The most enthusiastic speculator cannot suppose a greater increase than this. In a few centuries it would make every acre of land in the Island like a garden. Yet this ratio of increase is evidently arithmetical. It may be fairly said, therefore, that the means of subsistence increase in an arithmetical ratio. Let us now bring the effects of these two ratios together.

The population of the Island is computed to be about seven millions, and we will suppose the present produce equal to the support of such a number. In the first twenty-five years the population would be fourteen millions, and the food being also doubled, the means of subsistence would be equal to this increase. In the next twenty-five years the population would be twenty-eight millions, and the means of subsistence only equal to the support of twenty-one millions. In the next period, the population would be fifty-six millions, and the means of subsistence just sufficient for half that number. And at the conclusion of the first century the population would be one hundred and twelve millions and the means of subsistence only equal to the support of thirty-five millions, which would leave a population of seventy-seven millions totally unprovided for.

A great emigration necessarily implies unhappiness of some kind or other in the country that is deserted. For few persons will leave their families, connections, friends, and native land, to seek a settlement in untried foreign climes, without some strong subsisting causes of uneasiness where they are, or the hope of some great advantages in the place to which they are going.

But to make the argument more general and less interrupted by the partial views of emigration, let us take the whole earth, instead of one spot, and suppose that the restraints to population were universally removed. If the subsistence for man that the earth affords was to be increased every twenty-five years by a quantity equal to what the whole world at present produces, this would allow the power of production in the earth to be absolutely unlimited, and its ratio of increase much greater than we can conceive that any possible exertions of mankind could make it.

Taking the population of the world at any number, a thousand millions, for instance, the human species would increase in the ratio of – 1, 2, 4, 8, 16, 32, 64, 128, 256, 512, etc. and subsistence as – 1, 2, 3, 4, 5, 6, 7, 8, 9, 10, etc. In two centuries and a quarter, the population would be to the means of subsistence as 512 to 10: in three centuries as 4096 to 13, and in two thousand years the difference would be almost incalculable, though the produce in that time would have increased to an immense extent.

No limits whatever are placed to the productions of the earth; they may increase for ever and be greater than any assignable quantity. Yet still the power of population being a power of a superior order, the increase of the human species can only be kept commensurate to the increase of the means of subsistence by the constant operation of the strong law of necessity acting as a check upon the greater power.

Editorial Headnote

1794 (Buckinghamshire)–1852

William Forster Lloyd was a mathematician and economist best remembered for developing the economic paradox known as The Tragedy of the Commons, later widely applied in political ecology.

Lloyd was from a privileged background – the son of a wealthy rector – and was educated at Westminster School and Oxford University. He then embarked on an academic career and had his first work published in 1830 on the contentious issue of corn pricing.

As the extract illustrates, Lloyd was an economic liberal and protégé of Malthus, albeit with some less socially conservative views on marriage and reproduction. Later in the extract, Lloyd makes his best-known modification to Malthusianism by explaining how seemingly infinite shared resources were, in fact, finite. He describes how the traditional English village green, conventionally open to all villagers, had become an endangered resource because of an abuse of the privilege by villagers in overgrazing their cattle. As the practice had gone on for centuries, it had been assumed that it always could, but it had emerged that an increase in the number of cattle above an optimum level was eroding the land and ruining the common resource for all. Hence, in spite of his economic liberal sensibilities, Lloyd was acknowledging limits to relying on Adam Smith's metaphorical Invisible Hand of market forces in the distribution of resources (Clarke 2004).

Neither Lloyd nor his paradox were particularly well known in his time but became popularized over a century later when in 1968 the 'Neo-Malthusian' US ecologist Garrett Hardin adapted the tragedy of the commons to global commons (outside sovereign jurisdiction) such as clean air, fresh water and high-seas fish stocks, endangered by states continuing to exploit or pollute them oblivious to the fact that the cumulative effect of this would eventually be their depletion for all (Hardin 1968). This greatly contributed to the emergence of political ecology because it posed revolutionary questions about core political values such as economic growth, technological development and sovereignty. 'Ruin is the destination toward which all men rush, each pursuing his own best interest in a society that believes in the freedom of the commons' (Hardin 1968: 1244). Hardin's solution to the problem, like Lloyd's, was population control, and this subsequently became a major international political concern in the late 1960s and early 1970s.

pp. 473–477

11

ON THE CHECKS TO POPULATION

William Forster Lloyd

Source: William Forster Lloyd, *On the Checks to Population* (1833).

LECTURE I

I proposed to consider, in this and in the following Lecture, the checks to population. We have seen that the increase of food cannot keep pace with the theoretical rate of increase of population. Since, therefore, food is essential to the existence of man, it is obvious, that, with reference to the increase of numbers actually possible, the theoretical power of multiplication can be of little moment, and that, whatever be its extent, the actual excess of the births above the deaths must be determined according to the inferior-progression of the supply of food. In considering therefore the condition of any country in respect to its population, we have two rates of increase to which to direct our attention; viz. first, the theoretical rate, or in other words, as I explained in a former Lecture, that amount of the annual excess of the births above the deaths, which would be possible, and might he expected to have a real existence, were the supply of food abundant, and were no part of the people cramped in their circumstances: and secondly, the actual rate of increase, or the annual excess of the births above the deaths really occurring.

It is necessary, I say, to attend to these two rates of increase, because the difference between them is the measure of the amount of existences repressed, and it is in the mode by which the repression is effected, that the happiness or misery of every people is essentially involved. The superabundant tendency to increase must of necessity be repressed by some one mode of repression or another. So far is absolutely unavoidable. But there are material differences in the possible modes of repression, and it is of importance to ascertain the circumstances, which favour them respectively, and tend to give the predominance to any one of them in particular. The modes of repression are the same as what have been called the checks to population. It is obvious that the theoretical rate of increase, that is, the theoretical excess of the births above the deaths, may be reduced to the dimensions of the increase actually possible, in two ways, namely, either by a diminution in the births, or an increase in the deaths. Mr. Malthus therefore distinguishes the checks into two principal classes, the preventive, which restrain the number of the actual births, and prevent its being as great as the theoretical number: and

DOI: 10.4324/9781003194651-16

the positive, which swell the number of the deaths, and increase them beyond the proportion due to the natural law of mortality in the human species. There is reason to believe, as I intimated in a previous Lecture, that the poverty and hard living, which in many cases operate to the destruction of life, have in other cases the effect of diminishing fecundity. So far as they produce this latter effect they are preventive checks. Promiscuous intercourse, beyond a certain degree, prevents the birth of children, and therefore belongs to the same class. But the most important branch of the preventive check consists in, what is termed by Mr. Malthus, moral restraint. For an explanation of its nature, I will read his own description of it "The preventive check," he observes, "as far as it is voluntary, is peculiar to man, and arises from that distinctive superiority of his reasoning faculties, which enables him to calculate distant consequences. The checks to the indefinite increase of plants and irrational animals are all either positive, or, if preventive, involuntary. But man cannot look around him, and see the distress which frequently presses on those who have large families; he cannot contemplate his present possessions or earnings, which he now nearly consumes himself, and calculate the amount of each share, when, with very little addition, they must be divided, perhaps, among seven or eight, without feeling a doubt whether, if he follow the bent of his inclinations, he may be able to support the offspring which he may probably bring into the world. In a state of equality, if such can exist, this would be the simple question. In the present state of society other considerations occur. Will he not lower his rank in life, and be obliged to give up in a great measure his former habits? Does any mode of employment present itself by which he may reasonably hope to maintain a family? Will he not at any rate subject himself to greater difficulties, and more severe labour than in his single state? Will he not be unable to transmit to his children the same advantages of education and improvement that he had himself possessed? Does he even feel secure that, should he have a large family, his utmost exertions can save them from rags and squalid poverty, and their consequent degradation in the community? And may he not be reduced to the grating necessity of forfeiting his independence, and of being obliged to the sparing hand of charity for support? "These considerations are calculated to prevent, and certainly do prevent, a great number of persons in all civilized nations from pursuing the dictate of nature in an early attachment to one woman." This is Mr. Malthus' account of the operation of that branch of the preventive check termed moral restraint. I now proceed to what he says about the positive checks. "The positive checks to population are extremely various, and include every cause, whether arising from vice or misery, which in any degree contributes to shorten the natural duration of human life. Under this head, therefore, may he enumerated all unwholesome occupations, severe labour and exposure to the seasons, extreme poverty, had nursing of children, great towns, excesses of all kinds, the whole train of common diseases and epidemics, wars, plague, and famine." Now, if we examine the particulars mentioned by Mr. Malthus, we shall see, that, though they embrace all the checks arising, either directly or indirectly, from a want of food, yet they are not limited to these alone. They go much further, and include checks which must exist in every stage of society, as well while an immense expanse of fertile land remains unappropriated, as when every acre of land in the country has been cultivated like a garden. In every stage of society the period of infancy is helpless, and the prospect of a family must always carry with it the prospect of some division of a limited command of wealth, or otherwise of greater difficulties and more severe labour than in a single state. Wealth is never to be had for nothing, and to have to maintain those who contribute no addition to it, must of course imply either a deduction from the existing stock, or a compensation derived either from increased labour or extraneous sources.

An American, we will suppose, settles in the woods, marries and has a family. He clears his ground, builds his house, plants an orchard, incloses his fields. As time rolls on, he acquires experience, obtains a knowledge of the localities, finds out the most advantageous channels of trade, his orchard becomes productive, the cultivation of his land becomes more easy, he improves his habitation, every year adds to his comforts, and eventually he surrounds himself with many of the conveniences and luxuries of refined life. In a word, his daily enjoyments depend much more on accumulation, than on the daily labour of himself or of his family. His children are brought up participating in all these advantages. Thus comfortably situated at home, have they no cause for hesitation, or for an interval of preparation, before they venture upon marriage? Surely they have, and so long as man is a reasoning animal, and not only food but all the conveniences and luxuries of life are not to be had for nothing, motives for prudential restraint must present themselves, more or less imperiously, in every condition of society.

Again, as to the positive checks. The whole train of common diseases and epidemics, war and plague, are contained in the list. But these, as a whole, are not, either mediately or immediately, the effects of a deficiency of food. The cholera, for example, has appeared in America, to say the least of it, in a form as severe as in England; and though in England it has been most destructive in the abodes of poverty, yet neither has it altogether spared the rich. The like may be said of wars, and other evils which we bring upon ourselves. They are not universally the result of a scarcity of the means of subsistence. Many would, perhaps, be startled on being told, that they have anything to do with it. Yet I think that, on consideration, they would agree with an observation of Mr. Malthus, that the causes of war, in their remote ramifications, are not unconnected with it. The late war, for example, was owing, in a very considerable degree, to the apprehension entertained by the aristocracy of the contagion of the French revolution. But they would have had less ground for apprehension, had the bulk of the people been easy in their condition. Few will deny that an easy command of subsistence is almost a panacea for discontent among the lower classes. Suppose that the cases, in which prudential restraint arises from the fear of a want of sustenance, were clearly distinguishable, by some manifest token, from those in which it depends on other motives. Suppose also poverty, by which I here mean misery produced by want, to have diseases of its own, wars of its own, and other modes of destruction of its own, all marked by some specific difference, and never to use any tools, or instruments of death, not peculiarly appropriated to its own department. Then the view of the subject would be comparatively simple, and we might draw a hard line of distinction between the different checks, separating them into two classes, and placing on one side of the line all those motives, and all those diseases and other causes, which diminish fecundity or destroy life, and which arise from a scarcity of the means of subsistence; and on the other, all causes productive of the same effect, but originating in moral and physical circumstances totally independent of this scarcity. Now, though in the natural course of events, causes appertaining to both of these classes are commonly intermixed in their operation, and cannot be disentangled, and though, perhaps, scarcely a single case of diminished fecundity or of death, in which poverty is concerned, be the result of poverty alone, yet these circumstances constitute no objection to our distinguishing in imagination the quantities of the effects due to each description of causes. A line, or the equivalent of a line, parting the quantities of the effects, must exist in nature, though not visible to the eye of the philosopher, and we are at liberty to reason respecting the quantities placed on each side of this line in the same manner as if its position were actually ascertained.

We shall thus have a third rate of increase, viz. a theoretical rate, which might be expected to have a real existence, were not only food always abundant, but also all wars, all diseases, and other causes in any way tending to diminish fecundity, or to extinguish human life before the completion of the natural term of longevity, to be utterly removed. The three rates will then stand as follows: First, we shall have a theoretical rate, derived from the supposition of the absence, not only of a scarcity of food, but also of all other causes whatever, which tend to diminish fecundity, or prematurely to weaken or destroy the human frame. Let us assume this to be such as would double population in ten years. Secondly, we shall have another theoretical rate, derived from the supposition of the absence only of a scarcity of food, and not of the other causes of retardation unconnected with this scarcity. This is not, like the other, merely an imaginary case, but one of which examples may be found; and according to this rate it has appeared in a former Lecture that population would probably, in this country, double itself at the least in thirty-five years. Thirdly, there is the actual rate which occurs in every country under its existing circumstances, and which, at the present time, and in this country, is that of a duplication in forty-nine or fifty years. With respect to these different rates of increase we may remark, that the first is the most stable of all, and that though its exact quantity is difficult to be ascertained, yet, whatever it is, it is nearly invariable, and, if it can be rightly assumed to give a rate of duplication in ten years at any particular time and place, the same assumption will be equally applicable to all times and places. The second is much less stable, and oscillates between limits widely distant, according to the varieties of different countries in respect of climate, and in the same country at different times, according as it is cleared, drained, and improved, and according to the advance of its inhabitants in the knowledge of medicine, and in their command of the conveniences of life. Though however not accurately geometrical, it yet preserves those main features of a geometrical progression, which are essential with regard to practical considerations, viz. that the increase of one period furnishes the power of a greater increase in the next, and this without any limit.

. . .

Pp. 481–483

In the actual business of life, we commonly find some labourers out of employment, and more at one time than at another. So long however as the whole stock of food is sufficient for the possible maintenance of all, want of employment does not arise from an absence of demand for labour in general. It depends on more partial causes. The inability of the labourers to change at pleasure the quality and direction of their capacity to labour, and to adjust it to the varying tastes and demands of those who have the food of the country at their disposal, will prevent some from obtaining employment, whenever such variations may occur. Another impediment consists in the difficulty of arranging contracts-a difficulty, which is periodically increased or mitigated by oscillations in the currency. A third arises out of the greater trustiness and greater ability to labour of some than others, while all insist on an equal recompense. Abstracting however from all these disturbing causes, with which I am not now concerned, we may safely lay down the general proposition, that the channel of employment can always receive as many labourers as can live; from which it follows, that employment will be coextensive with the ability to labour, and may be considered simply as an appointed mean, for obtaining a ticket entitling the bearer to a proportional share of the general stock of subsistence. In the case before us, therefore, where the children are able to labour from the moment of birth, they can immediately earn their ticket which is to give them a share; not a definite share, (containing a precise weight in pounds or ounces,) but a share determined by the proportion of the whole number of tickets to the food which is to be divided. Suppose an unmarried man to be able to command by his labour, of the general stock of food, one part out of ten million parts. If he marries, and has children requiring as much more, he and his children will command two out of ten million and one parts. All the privation therefore, which his family entails on him, consists in the difference between one out of ten million, and one out of ten million and one parts. This difference in a single case is of course imperceptible. All the other members of the society are, however, subjected to the like privation, and the ten million differences thence arising constitute in fact the new share acquired by his family. In this case, therefore, as well as under a community of goods, there is a want of appropriation to each person of the consequences of his own conduct. All suffer through the act of one, and no encouragement to moral restraint is offered to individuals. I have here proceeded on the tacit assumption of the stock of food being a given quantity. That assumption renders the case a little easier, but it is evident that it is not essential to the conclusion. The whole food of a country divided by the sum of its population, constitutes the share of each person. Here, the food is the numerator, and the population the denominator of a fraction. In order that this fraction shall diminish, it is not necessary that the numerator shall continue stationary while the denominator increases: it is sufficient that it shall not increase as fast; and this is the case with food, which, we know, cannot increase as rapidly as an unchecked population. I have also stated that the channel of employment can receive as many labourers as can possibly be maintained. It is to be remarked, however, that neither is the truth of this proposition essential to the conclusion. It is sufficient that all persons, young and old, shall have an equal chance of obtaining employment, even though there be not employment adequate for all. If there be no established order of succession among the labourers; no claim, that is, to a priority of admission, and no permanency in the possession of a place once obtained in the field of employment; then, though a man may know that it can contain no more, yet he will have no reason for expecting that his children cannot find their way into it. He will know that by their entrance some will be cast out, but he will consider this as a chance, to which all, whether married or unmarried, are equally liable. Being himself exposed to it, in innumerable instances, from the increase of population resulting from the marriages of others, he will not anticipate any sensible increase of danger to himself, from the competition of his own children. Amongst so many, he would reckon it hard, were he the person, on whom, in a particular instance, the lot should fall. In short, upon the supposition of all being able to obtain employment, the inference is, that the consequences of the act of one will be equally divided between all: on the supposition of the field of employment admitting only a certain number, these consequences fall undivided upon some one unlucky person. But before the drawing of the lottery, since the chances of all are equal, we must in idea consider them as divisible. The motives therefore are the same upon both suppositions, and in both cases the encouragement to moral restraint is equally wanting.

It will serve to illustrate the subject, if we compare the relation subsisting between the cases of two countries, in one of which the constitution of society is such as to throw the burden of a family entirely on the parents, and in the other such that the children maintain themselves at a very early age, with that subsisting between the parallel cases of inclosed grounds and commons; the parallel consisting in what regards the degree of density, in which the countries are peopled, and the commons are stocked, respectively. Why are the cattle on a common so puny and stunted? Why is the common itself so bare-worn, and cropped so differently from the adjoining inclosures? No inequality, in respect of natural or acquired fertility, will account for the phenomenon. The difference depends on the difference of the way in which an increase of stock in the two cases affects the circumstances of the author of the increase. If a person puts more cattle into his own field, the amount of the subsistence which they consume is all deducted from that which was at the command, of his original stock; and if, before, there was no more than a sufficiency of pasture, he reaps no benefit from the additional cattle, what is gained in one way being lost in another. But if he puts more cattle on a common, the food which they consume forms a deduction which is shared between all the cattle, as well that of others as his own, in proportion to their number, and only a small part of it is taken from his own cattle. In an inclosed pasture, there is a point of saturation, if I may so call it, (by which, I mean a barrier depending on considerations of interest,) beyond which no prudent man will add to his stock. In a common, also, there is in like manner a point of saturation. But the position of the point in the two cases is obviously different. Were a number of adjoining pastures, already fully stocked, to be at once thrown open, and converted into one vast common, the position of the point of saturation would immediately be changed. The stock would be increased, and would be made to press much more forcibly against the means of subsistence. Now, the field for the employment of labour is in fact a common, the pasture of which is free to all, to the born and to the unborn, to the present tenants of the earth and to all who are waiting for admission. In the common for cattle, the young animal begins an independent participation in the produce, by the possession of a set of teeth and the ability to graze. In the common for man, the child begins a similar participation, by the possession of a pair of hands competent to labour. The tickets for admission being so readily procurable, it cannot happen otherwise, than that the commons, in both cases, must be constantly stocked to the extreme point of saturation. It appears then, that, neither in the actual condition of the labouring classes, nor under a system of equality with a community of labour and of goods, when the increase in the resources of the society is so slow as to require prudence in reference to marriage, is the obligation of such prudence sufficiently divided and appropriated. In neither case, if individuals are prudent, do they alone reap the benefit, nor, if they are imprudent, do they alone feel the evil consequences. The helplessness of the first few years of life operates indeed, to a certain degree, as a weight in favour of individual prudence. But this is not enough. It ought to be an adequate weight. Nobody would maintain, that, were the helplessness to continue only for nine or ten days, or for nine or ten weeks, or for nine or ten months, it would offer a sufficient incentive to abstinence. Why then should there be any peculiar virtue in nine or ten years? If the pressure of a family during that period is disregarded, the public is not saved from the subsequent inconvenience. It does not follow, that, because the children are able to maintain themselves, as it is called, or, in other words, to purchase by their labour their daily bread, nobody else is the worse for their being brought into the world. Were this a just inference, it would be equally just could they work for their living from the moment of birth, as under the abstract hypothesis. I shall return to this subject in the next Lecture.

Editorial Headnote

1807 (Shropshire)–1883

William Farr was a physician and statistician, and it is in the coming together of these disciplines – epidemiology – that his legacy is greatest.

Farr was born into a poor rural Shropshire family – in Kenley near Much Wenlock – and adopted as a young boy by a local squire, Joseph Pryce. He was apprenticed in apothecary and qualified in this profession in 1832. Pryce left him an inheritance on his death, permitting him to fund medical studies in France, Switzerland and University College London. In 1839, however, he switched to a career with the General Registrar Office (GRO) – whose principal task was compiling the data for the recently established national census. Three years into his career with the GRO, he became statistical superintendent – a role he maintained for the rest of his working life. Farr's chief legacy was enhancing understanding of morbidity, advancing both the study of epidemiology and the cause of social reform.

Farr was widely published, particularly in The Lancet, and made huge contributions to the emergent discipline of epidemiology and particularly in understanding the spread of the deadly diseases cholera and smallpox. He initially supported the orthodox miasma theory of the spread of disease but came to recognize that John Snow was right in suggesting that cholera was transmitted through water rather than the air. His work laid the foundations for the International Classification of Diseases, still a mainstay of epidemiology today. Farr's research also led him to argue that hunger was underrepresented as a cause of death and so distorting statistical records (Driver 1988).

In counter to the prevailing orthodoxy in demography, highlighted in the previous sections, Farr was essentially anti-Malthusian and argued that the supply and demand projections in that paradigm were far too rigid. He reasoned that food production could be increased through human ingenuity and that reproduction rates can naturally reduce through social change. In particular, Farr helped develop the notion of 'human capital' – that people can be a resource and are not just a cost. Hence, in this extract, he puts a positive price on people and estimates that the UK population is worth about £5.25 million. This logic long pre-empted Cornucopian arguments that emerged in economics in the 1980s, most notably by Julian Simon (Simon 1981), to rebuff the advocacy of radical birth control measures by neo-Malthusians such as Paul Ehrlich. This Malthus–Farr dialectic essentially still frames debates on overpopulation today.

pp. 59–64

12

ECONOMIC VALUE OF POPULATION

William Farr

Source: William Farr, *Economic Value of Population* (1877)

Various attempts have been made to estimate the amount and the increase of the capital of the United Kingdom. The most recent attempt of the kind has been made by the chief of the statistical department of the Board of Trade. The value of the most important part of the capital of the United Kingdom and the increase have yet to be determined; I mean the economic value of the population itself. To this I propose to call attention briefly. As lands, houses, railways, and the other categories in the income tax schedules are of value, because they yield annual returns; so, for the same reason, and on the same principle, the income of the population derived from pay of every kind for professional or other services and wages can be capitalized; not precisely, it is true, unless the income of every person living were returned at least as nearly as the incomes subject to income tax; but sufficiently near to the true value to show that the value of the population itself is the most important factor in the wealth of the country.

It will be sufficient to state here that the capitalization of personal incomes always proceeds upon the determination of the present value at any age of the future annual earnings at that and all future ages; hence the value of future wages rises from the date of birth, when it is a notable quantity; is highest in the labouring classes at the age of 25; and declines as age advances, until in extreme age, when no wages are earned, it disappears. The living by the Life Table are most numerous in childhood, and gradually fall off till they are all extinct; and so in the population enumerated at the Census the numbers decline from the first year to the ultimate year of age. While the rates of wages rise rapidly from birth to the age of manhood, and afterwards decline, the numbers living constantly decline. Taking a series of observations on the wages of agricultural labourers' some years ago at different ages; determining their value by a Life Table at five per cent. rate of interest for each age; and multiplying the numbers living by these values, it is found that the mean gross value at all ages is 349*l*. But the mean value of the subsistence of the labourer as child and man, determined by the same method, is about 199*l*.; and deducting this sum from 349*l*. there remain 150*l*. as the mean net value of the male population, estimated by this standard of the agricultural

DOI: 10.4324/9781003194651-17

DISCOVERING NATURE

labourer. To extend the value to the whole population, including females, the standard might be lowered from 150*l.* to 110*l.* a head.

Then multiplying the population of the United Kingdom by 110 we have as the aggregate value £3,640 million; this including only as much of the income as approximates in annual amount to the wages of agricultural labourers. Only a small part of it is subject to assessment under the income tax schedules. The gross assessment under the income tax affords the means of estimating the value of incomes exceeding 100*l.* a year under Schedules D. and E.; excluding companies, mines, and works, these profits and salaries amount to £214 million a year, to which about £92 million a year may be added for incomes above 30*l.* and below 100*l.* a year; thus making the aggregate of such incomes £306 million a year; which when the assessments of B. (farmers') are added becomes £373 million a year. Deduct the half of this revenue as due to external capital, and as required for the necessary sustenance of farmers, tradesmen, and professional men and there remain £186½ million a year as pure profit; which cannot be capitalized as a perpetuity inasmuch as the interest is limited by the lives of the producers, but taking life contingencies into account may be capitalized at ten years' purchase. This makes the value of these incomes £1,865 million. Allowing £255 million for the part of the incomes of about a million people paying the income tax previously valued in the £3,640 million, and for other deductions, £1,610 million remain, which, added to the £3,640 million already obtained, make £5,250 million.

Thus by capitalizing the earnings, fees, salaries, wages of the professional, mercantile, trading, and working classes, £5,250 million are obtained as an approximation to the value which is inherent in the people, and may be fairly added to the capital in land, houses, cattle or stock, and other investments. The amount would be increased by taking into account the rise of wages, and the income omitted in the returns of Schedule D. With an industrial Census an accurate estimate can be made of this most important part of the capital of the country. The minimum value of the population of the United Kingdom, men, women, and children, is 159*l.* a head; that is the value inherent in them as a productive, money-earning race. The incomes chiefly under schedules D., E., and B., raise the mean value from 110*l.* to 150*l.* (see above).

Again, it must be borne in mind that the value under Schedule A. is dependent upon the population; where there is little population land itself is of little value. The increase of the value of house property is directly due to the increased numbers and earnings of the inhabitants. The railways yield no profit where there is no population. The profits of quarries, mines, ironworks (Schedule D.), and other concerns are mainly due to the skill and industry of the masters and men who work them. Upon the other hand the products of human industry are multiplied a hundredfold by the tools, machinery, steam power, and all the appliances which capital commands and represents. Should the population of a country decay, the value of its capital might sink to the vanishing point.

What I wish further to point out is that during the 392 years this office has existed there have been added to the population of the United Kingdom 7,619,759 people who, valued as land is valued by the annual yield of net profit, constitute an addition of £1,212 million to the wealth of the nation.

The value of labour – that is of working men – varies, and is greatest where there is the greatest facility for profitable use, and where it is in greatest demand. Thus a large stream of the population of England flows to the Metropolis; and England is to the United Kingdom what the Metropolis is to England. So the populations of Ireland and Scotland flow into England, where they find more profitable employment, and are of more value than they are at home.

For the same and other reasons large armies of the population of the United Kingdom passed into the colonies and the United States; during the thirty-nine and a half years (1837–76) the excess of births over deaths was nearly 16 millions, of which nearly 8 millions augmented the ranks of the population at home, and more than 8 millions settled in other lands; chiefly in the midst of the old English stock of the United States and in the Colonies extending from Canada in America, to Africa and to Australasia.

Of the 8,013,267 people who must have left the country, only about 6,580,000 are accounted for by the Emigration Commissioners, whose returns were imperfect in two ways; they neither included the whole of the emigrants nor recognised emigrants returning recently in large numbers.

The emigrants are chiefly adults married and unmarried; the men greatly exceeding the women in number. A few infants accompany their parents. Valuing the emigrants as the agricultural labourers have been valued at home – taking age and service into account – the value of emigrants in 1876 was 175*l.* per head.

If we may venture to apply this standard to the whole period it will follow that the money value of the 8,000,000 people that left England, Scotland, and Ireland in the years 1837–76 was £1400 million, or on an average about 35,000,000*l.* a year. In round numbers taking into account their aptitude to earn wages in future years at the home rates the annual industrial army that went out was worth at starting 35,000,000*l.* Many of the emigrants are skilled artizans, and considerable numbers are returned as farmers, gentlemen, professional men, and merchants; some of whom no doubt carried away a certain amount of capital which is not here brought into account.

The policy of the people of this country has thus been a policy of progress; instead of resting as they were in 1837, they have added since that year on an average of 192,873 souls annually to the population at home, and sent 202,868 sons and daughters to seek their fortune abroad in other fields of labour. The women, instead of to 644,214 children, who would just replace the population removed by deaths, have given birth to 1,039,987 annually, at a certain loss of their own lives with intermingled sorrows and joys such as befall mothers in rearing children: while the men instead of expending the whole of their gains on themselves have devoted a large share to their wives and families; besides that, as we have seen, the external wealth of the country has increased, as the nation has, without conquering territory or levying heavy contributions on its European neighbours.

99

The value of men varies with their earnings, which differ considerably in the colonies from the earnings of agricultural labourers at home; and on the whole before the civil war the emigrants to the United States got higher wages, and at the same time gave a higher value to the territory.

It may be contended that emigration is a loss to the mother country. It seems so. It is like the export of precious goods for which there is no return. But experience proves that simultaneously with this emigration there has been a prodigious increase of the capital of the country, especially in recent years. Wages have risen, and the value of the labourer has risen in proportion. In Norfolk, where wages are intermediate between the rates in the north and south, the rise has apparently been about 20 per cent.; so a fifth may be added to the estimated value of the workman. When the man leaves the village where he was born and bred, he leaves the market open to his fellows; he removes to a field where his work is in demand, and carries his fortune with him. It is the same when he emigrates to the colonies. His parents in rearing him have expended their gains in the way most agreeable to themselves. They have on an average five children, instead of two or three, or none. Taking a wider view, the emigrants create articles of primary use with which in exchange they supply the mother country; they have sent to England in the 39 years wheat, cotton, wool, gold to the value of hundreds of millions. What is of still more vital importance, they grow into new nations; they multiply discoveries; by confederation they will be to the Anglo-Saxon race outposts of strength across the Atlantic, in the Pacific, in South Africa, and in Australasia on the flank of India. And, moreover, to all it is an advantage to speak a wide spread language, and thus to be in social, literary, and scientific communion with millions of the same race. The increasing numbers enable them, advanced as they are in the arts, in the sciences, and in civil government, to do more for the good of kindred races; and to endow them with advantages which could not be attained in other ways for centuries. They govern India.

The economic value of the population depends very much on their command over the powers of nature; which they acquire by education. Put barbarians in possession of the land, the mines, the manufactures, the machines, the ships, the triumphant position of these islands on the sea between two continents, and what would be the result? Another Asia Minor, Egypt, or Syria? The better educated the English people become, the more skilful they will become, and the more valuable in an economic sense they will be. The clever artisan is worth more than the rude labourer. Now the art of reading and writing their own language is by no means proof of complete education, or of any technical training, but it is a proof that men in possession of it are preparing to enter on the heritage of thought, and knowledge, and sentiment, which men of all ages have bequeathed to mankind, and which is enshrined in the writers of an admirable language.

In 1837 not more than 58 in 100 men and women possessed this art; but there has been progress, and I have year by year assiduously noted the increase of their numbers in the 39 years, so that I am now able to report, that instead of 58, eighty-one in a hundred write their names in the marriage registers.

It is evident that there are other elements on which the economic value of the working population depends; and foremost among them stand health and long life. The longer men live, and the stronger they are, the more work they can do. Epidemic diseases in rendering life, render wages, insecure. These diseases are most fatal in cities whither the population – to secure all the advantages of the division of labour – have been congregating every year in increased numbers: villages have become populous or have grown into towns; so the population has been growing denser. And that by a definite law, other things being equal, tends to increase weakness, sickness, and mortality. There have been counteracting agencies in operation in the thirty-nine years. Asiatic cholera was epidemic in England in 1831–2; influenza followed at intervals in 1833, 1837, and 1847; and laid thousands of the population low; in 1848–9 the cholera epidemic in England and Wales alone was fatal to fifty-three thousand people; its ravages in every corner of the kingdom were described; the conditions of its diffusion and fatality were brought to light, and the further investigations of the slighter epidemics of 1854 and 1866 prove that this plague is under the control of science. Other epidemics have since been fatal especially to children, and fever has struck at prince and peers as well as peasants; but upon the whole the great zymotic diseases have been quelled. Plague in its various forms has been kept at bay by a series of defences based upon minute precautions. In some epidemics I found it necessary to publish daily particulars respecting deaths in the Metropolis. By pursuing such inquiries, year after year, not only many of the causes that induce sickness and destroy life have been discovered, but observations of the same kind have shown that their removal has been followed by health and longer, more vigorous life. The economic value of the population of several towns has been increased by sanitary measures. The truths established, the facts ascertained, the remedies discovered in the thirty-nine years past await their full administrative applications in the years to follow; and the savings of time wasted in sickness, as well as of precious lives prematurely lost in youth and manhood, will enhance the value of the population to an incalculable extent. The famines so fatal in Ireland are not likely to recur; part of the population has emigrated to England or to America, and the intelligent landowners of Ireland, through the extension of the Poor Law, now insure their countrymen against death by starvation. The same beneficient law has in the thirty-nine years been extended to the Highlands of Scotland. Every improvement in health recorded makes it clearer and clearer that the gloom of sickness and premature death flies away before sanitary measures; and when the qualified health officers whom the Universities are offering to examine, are in suitable positions under enlightened local authorities all over the country they will no doubt prove as efficient in preventing as their medical brethren are in treating sickness. The result on human happiness cannot be calculated; but a future Industrial Census will show in a very definite shape its effect in raising the economic value of the population. The mean lifetime by the English Life Table is 40.86 years; by the Healthy Life Table it is 49.0 years, which is attainable in every well organized State. It is fair to assume that if a fifth part be added to the mean lifetime, at least a fifth part will be added to the worth of a living and labouring population. Upon this estimate £1,050 million will be added to the economic value of the population of the kingdom. Its value will increase with its numbers, and so will the value of its emigrating thousands.

Editorial Headnote

1835 (Liverpool)–1882

William Stanley Jevons was an influential economist renowned for pioneering what can now be seen as a politically ecological perspective from within that discipline in questioning the conventional wisdom on supply and demand in relation to the sustainability of resources.

Jevons was educated chiefly in the sciences at University College London (UCL) but then entered academia as a philosopher/economist. He suffered from depression and resigned his position as a professor at UCL in 1880. He died only two years later in a drowning accident swimming in the sea at Hastings (Stanford 2015).

Perhaps the most lasting legacy of this economist's work is that his name continues to be eponymized in the term Jevons paradox, applied to questions of the sustainability of resources. The Jevons paradox refers to the point that having sustainable resources is more complicated than improving production efficiency in order to raise supply and so meet growing demands. This is because improving efficiency in extracting and utilizing resources through technological innovation will also be likely to make the product more attractive and increase demand. This, then, is an important counter to cornucopian arguments – such as those advanced by Farr in the previous section – that technological innovation can be relied upon to increase the supply of resources and circumvent Malthusian depletion due to population growth.

In The Coal Question, Jevons argues that increased efficiency in coal use in Britain was not enough to safeguard her leadership in this industry, even though she led the world both in terms of resources and their efficient extraction and use. Increased efficiency also reduces the costs of using a resource and so gives an economic incentive for industry and the public to demand more of it. Jevons hence was pessimistic about the prospects of Britain becoming sustainable in coal and advocated developing alternative energy sources such as hydroelectric and solar power (although, of course, not petrol or gas since these had yet to be developed as energy sources). This seems particularly prescient in the context of today's climate crisis a century and a half after this was written. Jevons also reasons that, given the folly of vainly pursuing world resource leadership, the current British economic comparative advantage should be utilized for the public good in terms of social reforms such as ending child labour and improving education.

Jevons's logic could be said to have been vindicated in the following century. The UK passed peak coal production in 1913 and was gradually overtaken as global energy hegemon by the US.

pp. v–xii

13

THE COAL QUESTION; AN INQUIRY CONCERNING THE PROGRESS OF THE NATION, AND THE PROBABLE EXHAUSTION OF OUR COAL-MINES

William Jevons

Source: William Jevons, *The Coal Question; An Inquiry concerning the Progress of the Nation, and the Probable Exhaustion of our Coal-mines* (1866)

PREFACE

I AM desirous of prefixing to the second edition of the following work a few explanations which may tend to prevent misapprehension of its purpose and conclusions.

The expression "exhaustion of our coal mines," states the subject in the briefest form, but is sure to convey erroneous notions to those who do not reflect upon the long series of changes in our industrial condition which must result from the gradual deepening of our coal mines and the increased price of fuel. Many persons perhaps entertain a vague notion that some day our coal seams will be found emptied to the bottom, and swept clean like a coal-cellar. Our fires and furnaces, they think, will then be suddenly extinguished, and cold and darkness will be left to reign over a depopulated country. It is almost needless to say, however, that our mines are literally inexhaustible. We cannot get to the bottom of them; and though we may some day have to pay dear for fuel, it will never be positively wanting.

I have occasionally spoken in the following pages of "the end," of the "instability of our position," and so forth. When considered in connexion with the context, or with expressions and qualifications in other parts of the volume, it will be obvious that I mean not the end or overturn of the nation, but the end of the present progressive condition of the kingdom. If there be a few expressions which go beyond this, I should regard them as speculative only, and should not maintain them as an essential part of the conclusions.

Renewed reflection has convinced me that my main position is only too strong and true. It is simply that we cannot long progress as we are now doing. I give the

DOI: 10.4324/9781003194651-18

usual scientific reasons for supposing that coal must confer mighty influence and advantages upon its rich possessor, and I show that we now use much more of this invaluable aid than all other countries put together. But it is impossible we should long maintain so singular a position; not only must we meet some limit within our own country, but we must witness the coal produce of other countries approximating to our own, and ultimately passing it.

At a future time, then, we shall have influences acting against us which are now acting strongly with us. We may even then retain no inconsiderable share of the world's trade, but it is impossible that we should go on expanding as we are now doing. Our motion must be reduced to rest, and it is to this change my attention is directed. How long we may exist in a stationary condition I, for one, should never attempt to conjecture. The question here treated regards the length of time that we may go on rising, and the height of prosperity and wealth to which we may attain. Few will doubt, I think, after examining the subject, that we cannot long rise as we are now doing.

Even when the question is thus narrowed I know there will be no want of opponents. Some rather hasty thinkers will at once cut the ground from under me, and say that they never supposed we should long progress as we are doing, nor do they desire it. I would make two remarks in answer.

Firstly, have they taken time to think what is involved in bringing a great and growing nation to a stand? It is easy to set a boulder rolling on the mountain-side; it is perilous to try to stop it. It is just such an adverse change in the rate of progress of a nation which is galling and perilous. Since we began to develop the general use of coal, about a century ago, we have become accustomed to an almost yearly expansion of trade and employment. Within the last twenty years everything has tended to intensify our prosperity, and the results are seen in the extraordinary facts concerning the prevalence of marriage, which I have explained in pp. 197–200, and to which I should wish to draw special attention. It is not difficult to see, then, that we must either maintain the expansion of our trade and employment, or else witness a sore pressure of population and a great exodus of our people.

The fact is, that many of my opponents simply concede the point I am endeavouring to prove without foreseeing the results, and without, again, giving any reasons in support of their position.

Secondly, I do not know why this nation should not go on rising to a pitch of greatness as inconceivable now as our present position would have been inconceivable a century ago. I believe that our industrial and political genius and energy, used with honesty, are equal to anything. It is only our gross material resources which are limited. Here is a definite cause why we cannot always advance.

Other opponents bring a more subtle objection. They say that the coal we use affords no measure of our industry. At a future time, instead of exporting coal, or crude iron, we may produce elaborate and artistic commodities depending less on the use of coal than the skill and taste of the workman. This change is one which I anticipated (see p. 347). It would constitute a radical change in our industry. We have no peculiar monopoly in art, and skill, and science as we now have in coal.

That by art and handicraft manufactures we might maintain a moderate trade is not to be denied, but all notions of manufacturing and maritime supremacy must then be relinquished. Those persons very much mistake the power of coal, and steam, and iron, who think that it is now fully felt and exhibited; it will be almost indefinitely greater in future years than it now is. Science points to this conclusion, and common observation confirms it. These opponents, then, likewise concede what I am trying to show, without feeling how much they concede. They do not seem to know which is the sharp edge of the argument.

A further class of opponents feel the growing power of coal, but repose upon the notion that economy in its use will rescue us. If coal become twice as dear as it is, but our engines are made to produce twice as much result with the same coal, the cost of steam-power will remain as before. These opponents, however, overlook two prime points of the subject. They forget that economy of fuel leads to a great increase of consumption, as shown in the chapter on the subject; and, secondly, they forget that other nations can use improved engines as well as ourselves, so that our comparative position will not be much improved.

It is true that where fuel is cheap it is wasted, and where it is dear it is economised. The finest engines are those in Cornwall, or in steam-vessels plying in distant parts of the ocean. It is credibly stated, too, that a manufacturer often spends no more in fuel where it is dear than where it is cheap. But persons will commit a great oversight here if they overlook the cost of an improved and complicated engine, which both in its first cost, and its maintenance, is higher than that of a simple one. The question is one of capital against current expenditure. It is well known that nothing so presses upon trade as the necessity for a large capital expenditure; it is so much more risked, so much more to pay interest on, and so much more abstracted from the trading capital. The fact is, that a wasteful engine pays better where coals are cheap than a more perfect but costly engine. Bourne, in his "Treatise on the Steam Engine," expressly recommends a simple and wasteful engine where coals are cheap.

The state of the matter is as follows: – Where coal is dear, but there are other reasons for requiring motive power, elaborate engines may be profitably used, and may partly reduce the cost of the power.

But if coal be dear in one place and cheap in another, motive power will necessarily be cheaper where coal is cheap, because there the option of using either simple or perfect engines is enjoyed. It is needless to say that any improvement of the engine which does not make it more costly will readily be adopted, especially by an enterprising and ingenious people like the Americans.

I take it, therefore, that if there be any strong cause exclusive of the possession of coal which will tend to keep manufactures here, economy of fuel and a large employment of capital may neutralise in some degree the increased cost of motive power. But so far as cheap fuel and power is the exciting cause of manufactures, these must pass to where fuel is cheapest, especially when it is in the hands of persons as energetic and ingenious as ourselves.

Finally, I may mention the argument of Mr. Vivian, that the art of coal mining will advance so that coal may be drawn from great depths without any material increase of cost. The very moderate rise of price as yet experienced, apparently supports this view, and for my own part I entertain no doubt that a mine might, if necessary, be driven to the depth of 5,000 feet. The cost at which it must be done, however, is quite another matter. The expenditure on the shaft increases in a far higher ratio than its depth; the influence of this expenditure is more than can be readily estimated, because it is risked in the first instance, and in not a few cases is wholly lost; and not only must the capital itself be repaid, but considerable amounts of compound and simple interest must be met, in order that the undertaking shall be profitable. Were the depth of mines so slight an inconvenience as Mr. Vivian would make it appear, I think we should have more deep mines. It is now forty years since the Monkwearmouth Pit was commenced, and I believe that only one deeper pit has since been undertaken, that at Dukinfield, seventeen years ago. We cannot wonder that there are so few deep pits, when we consider that it required twenty years' labour to complete the Monkwearmouth pit, in consequence of the serious obstacles encountered (see p. 83). The Dukinfield Deep Pit, begun in June, 1849, was more fortunate, and reached the expected coal at a depth of 2,150 feet in March, 1859.

. . .

pp. xxiii–xxvi

It is a melancholy fact which no Englishman dare deny or attempt to palliate, that the whole structure of our wealth and refined civilization is built upon a basis of ignorance and pauperism and vice, into the particulars of which we hardly care to inquire. We are not entirely responsible for this. It is the consequence of tendencies which have operated for centuries past. But we are now under a fearful responsibility that, in the full fruition of the wealth and power which free trade and the lavish use of our resources are conferring upon us, we should not omit any practicable remedy. If we allow this period to pass without far more extensive and systematic exertions than we are now making, we shall suffer just retribution.

It is not hard to point out what kind of measures are here referred to. The ignorance, improvidence, and brutish drunkenness of our lower working classes must be dispelled by a general system of education, which may effect for a future generation what is hopeless for the present generation. One preparatory and indispensable measure, however, is a far more general restriction on the employment of children in manufacture. At present it may almost be said to be profitable to breed little slaves and put them to labour early, so as to get earnings out of them before they have a will of their own. A worse premium upon improvidence and future wretchedness could not be imagined.

Mr. Baker, the Inspector of Factories in South Staffordshire, has given a deplorable account of the way in which women and children are employed in the brickyards; and in the South Wales ironworks I have myself seen similar scenes, which would be incredible if described. Dr. Morgan holds that our manufacturing population is becoming degenerate; and it must be so unless, as our manufacturing

THE COAL QUESTION

system grows, corresponding restrictions are placed upon the employment of infant labour.

It will be said that we cannot deprive parents of their children's earnings. If we cannot do it now, we can never do it; and wretched, indeed, must be a kingdom which depends for subsistence upon infant labour. But we can do it to the ultimate advantage of all, and we are bound to do it from regard to the children themselves: and anything which we may lose or spend now in education and loss of labour will be repaid many times over by the increased efficiency of labour in the next generation.

Reflection will show that we ought not to think of interfering with the free use of the material wealth which Providence has placed at our disposal, but that our duties wholly consist in the earnest and wise application of it. We may spend it on the one hand in increased luxury and ostentation and corruption, and we shall be blamed. We may spend it on the other hand in raising the social and moral condition of the people, and in reducing the burdens of future generations. Even if our successors be less happily placed than ourselves they will not then blame us.

To some it might seem that no good can come from contemplating the weakness of our national position. Discouragement and loss of prestige could alone apparently result. But this is a very superficial view, and the truth, I trust, is far otherwise. Even the habitual contemplation of death injures no man of any strength of mind. It rather nerves him to think and act justly while it is yet day. As a nation we have too much put off for the hour what we ought to have done at once. We are now in the full morning of our national prosperity, and are approaching noon. Yet we have hardly begun to pay the moral and the social debts to millions of our countrymen which we must pay before the evening.

. . .

pp. 370–375

CHAPTER XVIII: CONCLUDING REFLECTIONS

MY work is completed in pointing out the necessary results of our present rapid multiplication when brought into comparison with a fixed amount of material resources. The social and political consequences to ourselves and to the world of a partial exhaustion of our mines are of an infinitely higher degree of uncertainty than the event itself, and cannot be made the subject of argument. But feeling as we must do that they will be of an untoward character, it is impossible to close without a few further remarks upon the truly solemn question – Are we wise in allowing the commerce of this country to rise beyond the point at which we can long maintain it?

To say the simple truth, will it not appear evident, soon after the final adoption of Free Trade principles, that our own resources are just those to which such principles ought to be applied last and most cautiously? To part in trade with the surplus yearly interest of the soil may be unalloyed gain, but to disperse so lavishly the cream of our mineral wealth is to be spendthrifts of our capital – to part with that which will never come back.

And after all commerce is but a means to an end, the diffusion of civilization and wealth. To allow commerce to proceed until the source of civilization is weakened and overturned is like killing the goose to get the golden egg. Is the immediate creation of material wealth to be our only object? Have we not hereditary possessions in our just laws, our free and nobly developed constitution, our rich literature and philosophy, incomparably above material wealth, and which we are beyond all things bound to maintain, improve, and hand down in safety? And do we accomplish this duty in encouraging a growth of industry which must prove unstable, and perhaps involve all things in its fall?

But the more there is said on the one side of this perplexing question, the more there is to say on the other side. We can hardly separate the attributes and performances of a kingdom, and have some without the others. The resplendent genius of our Elizabethan age might never have been manifested but in a period equally conspicuous for good order, industrial progress, and general enterprise. The early Hanoverian period, on the other hand, was as devoid of nobility as it was stationary in wealth and population. A clear and vigorous mind is to be looked for in a wholesome state of the body. So in our Victorian age we may owe indirectly to the lavish expenditure of our material energy far more than we can readily conceive. No part, no function of a nation is independent of the rest, and in fearlessly following our instincts of rapid growth we may rear a fabric of varied civilization, we may develop talents and virtues, and propagate influences which could not have resulted from slow restricted growth however prolonged.

The wish surely could never rise into the mind of any Englishman that Britain should be stationary and lasting as she was, rather than of growing and worldwide influence as she is. To secure a safe smallness we should have to go back, and strangle in their birth those thoughts and inventions which redeemed us from dullness and degeneration a century ago. Could we desire that Savery and Newcomen had abandoned their tiresome engines, that Darby had slept before the iron ran forth, that the Duke had broken before Brindley completed his canal, that Watt had kept to his compasses and rules, or Adam Smith burnt his manuscript in despair? Such experiments could not have succeeded, and such writings been published, among a free and active people in our circumstances, without leading to the changes that have been. Thence necessarily came the growth of manufactures and of people; thence the inexplicable power with which we fought and saved the Continent; thence the initiation of a Free-trade policy by Pitt, the growth of a middle class, and the rise of a series of statesmen – Canning, Huskisson, Peel, Cobden, and Gladstone – to represent their views and powers.

Our new industry and civilization had an obscure and unregarded commencement; it is great already, and will be far greater yet before it is less. It is questionable whether a country in any sense free can suffer such a grand movement to begin without suffering it to proceed its own length. One invention, one art, one development of commerce, one amelioration of society follows another almost as effect follows cause. And it is well that our beneficial influence is not bounded by our narrow wisdom or our selfish desires. Let us stretch our knowledge and our foresight to the furthest, yet we act by powers and towards ends of which we are scarcely conscious.

In our contributions to the arts, for instance, we have unintentionally done a work that will endure for ever. In whatever part of the world fuel exists, whether wood, or peat, or coal, we have rendered it the possible basis of a new civilization. In the ancient mythology, fire was a stolen gift from heaven, but it is our countrymen who have shown the powers of fire, and conferred a second Promethean gift upon the world. Without undue self-gratulation, may we not say in the words of Bacon? – "The introduction of new inventions seemeth to be the very chief of all human actions. The benefits of new inventions may extend to all mankind universally, but the good of political achievements can respect but some particular cantons of men; these latter do not endure above a few ages, the former for ever. Inventions make all men happy without either injury or damage to any one single person. Furthermore, new inventions are, as it were, new erections and imitations of God's own works."

When our great spring is here run down, our fires half burnt out, may we not look for an increasing flame of civilization elsewhere? Ours are not the only stores of fuel. Britain may contract to her former littleness, and her people be again distinguished for homely and hardy virtues, for a clear intellect and a regard for law, rather than for brilliancy and power. But our name and race, our language, history, and literature, our love of freedom and our instincts of self-government, will live in a world-wide sphere. We have already planted the stocks of multiplying nations in most parts of the earth, and, in spite of discouraging tendencies, it is hardly for us to doubt that they will prove a noble offspring.

The alternatives before us are simple. Our empire and race already comprise one-fifth of the world's population; and by our plantation of new states, by our guardianship of the seas, by our penetrating commerce, by the example of our just laws and firm constitution, and above all by the dissemination of our new arts, we stimulate the progress of mankind in a degree not to be measured. If we lavishly and boldly push forward in the creation and distribution of our riches, it is hard to over-estimate the pitch of beneficial influence to which we may attain in the present. *But the maintenance of such a position is physically impossible. We have to make the momentous choice between brief greatness and longer continued mediocrity.*

Editorial Headnote

1803 (Wick)–1888

John Cleghorn was an ironmonger and town councillor from Wick, Caithness, in the far north of Scotland who also made a mark speaking and writing on a range of issues in geology and natural history. He is generally held to have coined the term 'overfishing' in this address to the British Association for the Advancement of Science. Little is known of his background and scientific contributions beyond this notable achievement. In a short obituary, a local newspaper referred to him as the author of 'the fished up theory' (Aberdeen Weekly News 1888).

Cleghorn believed that the herring population in the Forth estuary and beyond was close to extinction and that other fish stocks in the wider North Sea (then known as the German Ocean) could follow. He cites Gilbert White in support of his reasoning, illustrating the reverence to which 'England's first Ecologist' was held. The figures he uses to support his assertions are shocking but well supported and appear credible. Perhaps inevitably, however, this line of argument was widely criticized by most within the fishing industry and Cleghorn was often vilified by fishermen in his hometown for seeming to challenge their means of making a living.

The theory of overfishing came to most notably be opposed by Thomas Huxley – the subject of the next section – who, as we shall see, considered sea fish stocks to be inexhaustible. Royal Commissions set up to examine the proposition essentially reinforced this viewpoint. As Cleghorn notes, the prevailing wisdom was that deteriorations in catch could be attributed to natural fluctuations in stock rather than progressive decline. Over time, however, the evidence for overfishing stacked up and scientific opinion gradually shifted to support Cleghorn, with British scientist Ray Lankester most notably taking up the mantle of acting in the name of sustainability (Ferguson-Cradler 2021). Outside of Britain, the influential German ichthyologist (fish biologist) Friedrich Heincke most notably used and further defined the concept of overfishing in an 1894 article examining North Sea fisheries (Heincke 1894). As outlined in Volume II Part 2, North Sea overfishing ultimately became the starting point for international legal measures to conserve marine stocks. However, the problem of overfishing remains pressing today in an enduring – and, indeed, worsening – collective goods or tragedy of the commons problem.

14

ON THE FLUCTUATIONS IN THE HERRING FISHERIES

John Cleghorn

Source: John Cleghorn, *On the fluctuations in the herring fisheries* (1854)

Read before the Statistical Section of the British Association for the Advancement of Science at Liverpool, on the 25th of September, 1854

THE Herring Trade is so important a branch of national industry, and is characterized by fluctuations so ruinous to those engaged in it, that it appears to me any facts that may throw light on its changes would interest the association and tend to the more successful prosecution of the fishing.

Popularly little is known of the natural history of the herring, and to this cause is to be imputed the uncertainty and loss that is so prominent a feature in its history. As specimens of the jumble of uncertainty that characterises the popular opinions on this important department of the subject, I beg to submit the following: –

To account for the disappearance of the herring from some of the islands on the west coast, the Secretary of the Commissioners for the British Herring Fishery says, in his report for 1844, p. 7, "That the only rational manner in which this phenomenon can be accounted for is, by supposing that it may have arisen from the cutting of the sea-weed for the manufacture of kelp on the shores of the bays and inlets where the fish came regularly from the neighbouring deeps for the purpose of spawning, which thus deprived them of the means of attachment and protection." In the report for 1848, the Commissioners say, "All fishings are fluctuating in their character, and liable to alternate diminution and increase; the deficiency alluded to can excite but little surprise." In the "North British Daily-Mail," a Wick correspondent writes, as follows, in July last. "There are still no herrings worth speaking of. We are nearly 8,000 crans short of last year. It is worth remarking, that in 1834, twenty years ago, our fishing was a complete failure, and that the preceding year's catch was more abundant than any that went before it. Last year our fishing exceeded all preceding years, and now it looks as if this season were to be a counterpart of 1834. Have we in these twenty years seen a cycle in the natural history of the herring? We know they visit our coast for food fitted to enable them to mature their milt and roe, Is the food of the herring this year deficient? It looks like it.

DOI: 10.4324/9781003194651-19

115

DISCOVERING NATURE

Mr. Hogarth has the salmon fishing at Castlehill, on the Pentland Firth, and was there in his yacht about a month ago. Mr. Stewart, the factor there, was on board, and Mr. Hogarth said to him, I can see, from the state of these salmon there, that we will have a poor fishing this year. – Mr. Stewart. Why think you so? – Mr Hogarth. I see they have been hungered. The salmon fishing has turned out just as Mr. Hogarth predicted. In the natural history of the salmon and the herring there are many points of analogy.

"At present Wick is the chief seat of the fishing here, and the produce has been," says the "John O' Groat Journal," "95,680 crans," or barrels. On comparing this with that of 1825 we are 14,000 barrels short, and, as compared with 1830, we are 57,000 barrels less. It is the smallest fishing since 1840, and it is 61,000 barrels short of last year. Various surmises are afloat as to the cause of this deficiency, but the generally received opinion is, that the whole falling off is owing to two rough nights, on which the boats did not put to sea while great shoals of herrings were on the coast. That this is an erroneous or very partial view of the matter, I infer, because at all the stations between Nosshead and Cape Wrath the fishing has been a complete failure, and the same may be said of Orkney and Shetland, while for the whole of Scotland the shortcoming is, perhaps, one-third of last year.

The cause, then, is general, and to arrive at correct conclusions as to this cause we must, I apprehend, make ourselves acquainted with the "life and conversation," as Gilbert White says, of the herring. Without entering into the minutiae of their lives, I would notice that in his "Natural History of Selborne," White says, "The two great motives which regulate the proceedings of the brute creation are love and hunger – the one incites them to perpetuate their kind, the latter induces them to preserve individuals." In obedience to those laws the herring congregates on our coasts, for there only they find food fitted to mature their milt and roe, and a sea bottom appropriate for receiving their spawn, consequently they are brought within the scope of those agents employed for their capture. Let us see what those agents are. 10,974 boats, 41,045 sailors employing 81,934,330 square yards of netting, an extent of netting that would cover an area of 261 square miles; and if the nets were extended lineally they would reach a distance of 4,741 miles.

May we not have drawn over liberally on our shoals of herring? With such appliances may we not have overfished the sea? That a river or lake may be over-fished, or that the whales between the tropics and at the poles may have their numbers so thinned that the fishing would cease to pay, will be readily conceded; but nobody here ever dreams of imputing the failures in the herring fishing to our having overdone it. The Commissioners for the British fisheries, in their Report for 1850, hint that overfishing has told on the cod and ling, for they say at page 3, "By the statements of the fishermen generally, it appears that the boats are almost everywhere obliged to go further from the land than formerly before they find fish; and hence it is assumed either that the fish have changed their runs on account of the fishing that has been carried on, or that the fishing grounds near the shore have been overfished. Of this there is no doubt that much longer voyages are now undertaken in connection with the cod fishing. Expeditions of smacks and other vessels to Davis Straits to fish cod have, in recent years, been established with varied success. An attempt to increase the supplies of fish has been set on foot in another direction. Two English smacks made different trips to Iceland, landing their fish, as they brought them, home, at Stornoway, in Lewis."

The truth is, the cod and ling fishing in the German Ocean is now not worth the prosecuting. Is it true that a river or a lake may be overfished, that we may extirpate the whole or so thin their numbers, that they may not be worth seeking, that even the cod and ling may be considered rare fish in their old haunts, and yet with our 81,934,330 square yards of netting make no sensible impression on the shoals of herrings? Let us see what has happened.

At the beginning of the present century the chief seats of the herring fishing were on the west coast. "Half a century ago," say the Commissioners, "the hopes of those engaged in the national fisheries seemed to be confined to the Firth of Forth and the lochs of the west coast of Scotland." The west coast waters were fished till fishing them ceased to pay.

From inquiries I have made into the statistics of the herring fishing on the west coast stations and those on the east coast that have been long fished, they present a steady progression in the quantities of herring caught up to a culminating point, then violent perturbations and final extinction as curing districts. Other waters are tried and found to pay – the same scenes are again enacted and with like results. The periods through which these changes move are varied by local causes. An extensive and sheltered seaboard, sheltered from violent tides, fitted for the resort of the herring, and with few stations fitted for the reception of boats, protracts the period towards extinction, while extensive accommodation for boats shortens the period. The conservative agencies at work are storms, and the strict observance of Sunday during the fishing season, the boats not going to sea on Saturday or Sunday nights, for then a portion, at least, of the shoals have time to deposit their spawn.

The British Association, by directing attention to the British herring fishery, will lend important assistance towards the saving of our fishing and the making it a perennial source of wealth to the nation.

Editorial Headnote

1825 (Ealing)–1885

Thomas Huxley was a biologist and anthropologist best known in his day as a strong proponent of evolution.

Huxley was from a middle-class family that fell on hard times. As a consequence, his schooling was limited, and he was largely self-educated. As a young man, he took on medical apprenticeships whilst studying privately in his spare time until he was able to secure a place to study anatomy at the University of London. He then worked as a surgeon in the navy, before embarking on an academic career.

Huxley worked extensively with other scientists, most notably Charles Darwin and John Tyndall. In 1864, he founded the influential 'X Club' of scientists who looked to find ways to collaborate and professionalize British science. He even became widely known as 'Darwin's Bulldog' for his staunch public defences of his mentor's work. His most famous such defence of evolution came in a widely publicized 1860 Oxford Union debate with Bishop Samuel Wilberforce, a creationist and a staunch opponent of Darwinism (Encyclopedia Britannica).

Huxley's advocacy for science and reason saw him create an enduring legacy by coining the term agnosticism to denote the distinction between what is knowable and what is not. He became an important figure in the rapid development of state education by advising on the content of school curricula. In 1881, he was appointed inspector of fisheries by the government, and it is in that context that he made this speech at the 1883 Fisheries Exhibition. Huxley suffered from the ill effects of London smog and retired to Eastbourne, where he died of a heart attack two years after giving this speech. His grandson was the renowned novelist Aldous Huxley.

As is evident in the speech, Huxley was sceptical about the notion of overfishing, as argued by John Cleghorn. As can be seen, he acknowledges that humans can deplete foods, including salmon fisheries. However, he considers sea fish to be so plentiful as to be inexhaustible. His cornucopian argument was countered at the exhibition by Edwin Lankester, a protégé of Cleghorn: "If man removes a large proportion of these fish from the areas which they inhabit, the natural balance is upset" (Lankester 1884).

Out of this classic debate on resource depletion came a common desire for a greater understanding of the science and economics of fisheries. The Marine Biological Association was founded the following year at the suggestion of Lankester with Huxley appointed as its first president. More research and statistical analysis on overfishing emerged as a result of this. Joseph Chamberlain, minister of the Board of Trade at the time, gave governmental backing to this venture.

DISCOVERING NATURE

Recognition of overfishing gradually grew and fed into international diplomacy at the dawn of the twentieth century. In 1903, the International Council for the Exploration of the Seas was established to collate information on overfishing to help manage resources. Today, however, in spite of its almost universal acceptance as a scientific fact, overfishing remains a global problem yet to be overcome.

pp. 81–90

15

INAUGURAL ADDRESS. FISHERIES EXHIBITION, LONDON

Thomas Huxley

Source: Thomas Huxley, *Inaugural Address. Fisheries Exhibition, London* (1883)

These few remarks must suffice to indicate the wide field of interesting research which fisheries offer to the philosophical historian; and I pass on to speak of the fisheries from the point of view of our present practical interests.

The supply of food is, in the long run, the chief of these interests. Every nation has its anxiety on this score, but the question presses most heavily on those who, like ourselves, are constantly and rapidly adding to the population of a limited area, and who require more food than that area can possibly supply. Unlike these circumstances, it is satisfactory to reflect that the sea which shuts us in, at the same time opens up its supplies of food of almost unlimited extent.

The produce of the sea around our coasts bears a far higher proportion to that of the land than is generally imagined. The most frequented fishing grounds are much more prolific of food than the same extent of the richest land. Once in a year, an acre of good land carefully tilled produces a ton of corn, or two or three hundredweight of meat or cheese. The same area at the bottom of the sea in the best fishing grounds yields a greater weight of food to the persevering fisherman every week in the year. Five vessels belonging to the same source in a single night's fishing brought in 17 tons weight of fish – an amount of wholesome food equal in weight to that of 50 cattle or 500 sheep. The ground which these vessels covered during the night's fishing could not have exceeded an area of 50 acres.

. . .

The fishing industry being thus important and thus ancient, it is singular that it can hardly be said to have kept pace with the rapid improvement of almost every other branch of industrial occupation in modern times. If we contrast the progress of fishery with that of agriculture, for example, the comparison is not favourable to fishery.

Within the last quarter of a century, or somewhat more, agriculture has been completely revolutionized, partly by scientific investigations into the conditions under which domestic animals and cultivated plants thrive; and partly by the application of mechanical contrivances, and of steam as a motive power, to agricultural processes.

DOI: 10.4324/9781003194651-20

The same causes have produced such changes as have taken place in fishery, but progress has been much slower. It is now somewhat more than twenty years since I was first called upon to interest myself especially in the sea fisheries; and my astonishment was great when 1 discovered that the practical fishermen, as a rule, knew nothing whatever about fish, except the way to catch them.

In answer to questions relating to the habits, the food, and the mode of propagation of fishes – points, be it observed, of fundamental importance in any attempt to regulate fishing rationally – I usually met with vague and often absurd guesses in the place of positive knowledge. The Royal Commission, of which I was a member in 1864 and 1865, was appointed chiefly on account of the allegation by the line fishermen that the trawlers destroyed the spawn of the white fish-cod, haddock, whiting, and the like. But, in point of fact, the 'spawn', which was produced in support of this allegation, consisted of all sorts of soft marine organisms, except fish. And if the men of practice had then known what the men of science have since discovered, that the eggs of cod, haddock, and plaice float at the top of the sea, they would have spared themselves and their fellow-fishermen, the trawlers, a great deal of unnecessary trouble and irritation. Thanks to the labours of Sars in the Scandinavian Seas, of the German Fishery Commission in the Baltic and North Sea, and of the United States Fishery Commission in American waters, we now possess a great deal of accurate information about several of the most important of the food fishes, and the foundations of a scientific knowledge of the fisheries have been laid. But we are still very far behind scientific agriculture; and, as to the application of machinery and of steam to fishery operations, it may be said that, in this country, a commencement has been made, but hardly more.

This relative backwardness of the fishing industry greatly impressed my colleagues and myself in the course of the inquiries of the Royal Commission to which I have referred; and I beg permission to quote some remarks on this subject which are to be found in our Report.

"When we consider the amount of care which has been bestowed on the improvement of agriculture, the national societies which are established for promoting it, and the scientific knowledge and engineering skill which have been enlisted in its aid, it seems strange that the sea fisheries have hitherto attracted so little of the public attention. There are few means of enterprise that present better chances of profit than our sea fisheries, and no object of greater utility could be named than the development of enterprise, skill, and mechanical ingenuity which might be elicited by the periodical exhibitions and publications of an influential society specially devoted to the British Fisheries."

. . .

But on looking over the list of allotted subjects, I find there is yet one important topic unappropriated – unless it belongs to Mr. Shaw. Lefevre, in which case I hope that my former colleague will forgive my depredations – and that is the question, WHETHER FISHERIES ARE EXHAUSTIBLE; AND IF SO, WHETHER ANYTHING CAN BE DONE TO PREVENT THEIR EXHAUSTION?

It so happens that I have had occasion to devote very particular attention to these questions, and to express definite opinions about them. And as these opinions seem to me to have been more often attacked than understood, I am glad to have the opportunity of briefly, but I hope clearly, submitting them, with the grounds on which they are based, to your judgment.

Are fisheries exhaustible? That is to say, can all the fish which naturally inhabit a given area be extirpated by the agency of man?

I do not think that this question can be answered categorically. There are fisheries and fisheries.

I have no doubt whatever that some fisheries may be exhausted. Take the case of a salmon river, for example. It needs no argument to convince any one who is familiar with the facts of the case that it is possible to net the main stream, in such a manner, as to catch every salmon that tries to go up and every smolt that tries to go down. Not only is this true, but daily experience in this country unfortunately proves that pollutions may be poured into the upper waters of a salmon river of such a character and in such quantity as to destroy every fish in it.

In this case, although man is only one of many agents which are continually effecting the destruction of salmon in all stages of its existence – although he shares the work with otters and multitudes of other animals, and even with parasitic plants – yet his intelligence enables him, whenever he pleases, to do more damage than all the rest put together; in fact, to extirpate all the salmon in the river and to prevent the access of any others.

Thus, in dealing with this kind of exhaustible fishery, the principle of the measures by which we may reasonably expect to prevent exhaustion is plain enough. Man is the chief enemy, and we can deal with him by force of law. If the stock of a river is to be kept up, it must be treated upon just the same principles as the stock of a sheep farm.

If an Australian sheep farmer is to be successful in his business he knows very well what he has to do. He must see that his sheep have a sufficient supply of food, he must take care that a sufficient breeding stock is preserved, and he must protect his sheep from all enemies but himself. He must defend his sheep, young and old, not only against the ravages of the wild dog, against infectious diseases, and against parasites but it is sometimes a very serious matter to protect them against the competition of other herbivorous animals, such as kangaroos, which appropriate the food destined for the sheep. And it is no easy matter to carry out an efficient system of protection. The destruction of the wild dogs may lead to the over multiplication of the kangaroos, and the destruction of the kangaroos may lead the wild dogs to devote their energies too seriously to the sheep. If the sheepowner does not take care what he is about, his very sheep dogs may become disseminators of the staggers among his flock. Moreover, the sheepowner must not let the butcher take more than a certain percentage of his sheep for boiling down, or the stock will be unduly diminished. It is only by incessant attention to all these points that a sheep farmer is successful; and, let him be as attentive as he likes, every now and then some variation in those conditions which are beyond his control – a sudden flood or a long drought, or the straying of a diseased sheep from another run – may bring him to ruin.

Now, if you will consider the action of the conservators of a salmon river, you will see that they, at any rate, strive to do for the salmon that which a careful shepherd does for his sheep. Obstacles in the way of free access to the breeding grounds are removed by the construction of fish passes; the breeding stock is protected by the annual close time; animals which prey on the fish, or compete dangerously with them, are kept down; or the salmon are placed at an advantage by artificially stocking the river. Finally, the destructive agency of man, who plays the part of the butcher, is limited by removal of pollution – by the prohibition of taking parr and smolts – by the restrictions on the character and on the size of meshes of nets; and, indirectly, by the license duty on nets and rods.

Whether the state of the law is such as to permit the work of the conservator to be carried out sufficiently, or not, is a point which will, 1 doubt not, be fully discussed by-and-by. All I desire to show is that in principle, the measures adopted by the conservators, if they are to be efficient, must be identical with those of the sheep farmer.

And the analogy is complete, for when the conservator has done all he can, droughts, parasites, and other natural agents which are beyond human control, may nullify his efforts. In the case of the salmon, as in that of the sheep, careful and intelligent protection may promote the prosperity of the stock to any conceivable extent; but it cannot ensure that prosperity, nor prevent immense fluctuations in the yield from year to year.

A salmon fishery then (and the same reasoning applies to all river fisheries) can be exhausted by man because man is, under ordinary circumstances, one of the chief agents of destruction; and, for the same reason, its exhaustion can usually be prevented, because man's operations may be controlled and reduced to any extent that may be desired by force of law.

And now arises the question, Does the same reasoning apply to the sea fisheries? Are there any sea fisheries which are exhaustible, and, if so, are the circumstances of the case such that they can be efficiently protected? I believe that it may be affirmed with confidence that, in relation to our present modes of fishing, a number of the most important sea fisheries, such as the cod fishery, the herring fishery, and the mackerel fishery, are inexhaustible. And I base this conviction on two grounds, first, that the multitude of these fishes is so inconceivably great that the number we catch is relatively insignificant; and, secondly, that the magnitude of the destructive agencies at work upon them is so prodigious, that the destruction effected by the fisherman cannot sensibly increase the death-rate.

At the great cod-fishery of the Lofoten Islands, the fish approach the shore in the form of what the natives call "cod mountains" – vast shoals of densely-packed fish, 120 to 180 feet in vertical thickness. The cod are so close together that Professor Sars tells us "the fishermen, who use lines, can notice how the weight, before it reaches the bottom, is constantly knocking against the fish." And these shoals keep coming in one after another for two months, all along the coast.

A shoal of codfish of this kind, a square mile in superficial extent, must contain, at the very least, 120,000,000 fish. But it is an exceptionally good season if the Lofoden fishermen take 30,000,000 cod, and not more than 70,000,000 or 80,000,000 are taken by all the Norwegian fisheries put together. So that one fair shoal of all that approach the coast in the season must be enough to supply the whole of the codfish taken by the Norwegian fisheries, and leave a balance of 40,000,000 or 50,000,000 over.

The principal food of adult cod appears to be herring. If we allow only one herring to each codfish per diem, the cod in a square mile of shoal will consume 840,000,000 herring in a week. But all the Norwegian fisheries put together do not catch more than half that number of herring. Facts of this kind seem to me to justify the belief that the take of all the cod- and herring-fisheries, put together, does not amount to 5 per cent. of the total number of the fish. But the mortality from other sources is enormous. From the time the fish are hatched, they are attacked by other marine animals. The great shoals are attended by hosts of dog-fish, pollack, cetaceans and birds, which prey upon them day and night, and cause a destruction infinitely greater than that which can be effected by the imperfect and intermittent operations of man.

I believe, then, that the cod fishery, the herring fishery, the pilchard fishery, the mackerel fishery, and probably all the great sea fisheries, are inexhaustible; that is to say, that nothing we do seriously affects the number of the fish. And any attempt to regulate these fisheries seems consequently, from the nature of the case, to be useless.

There are other sea fisheries, however, of which this cannot be said.

Take the case, for example, of the oyster fisheries, so far as it concerns beds which are outside the three-mile limit of the territorial jurisdiction of this country. Theoretically, at any rate, an oyster bed can be dredged clean. In practice, of course, it ceases to be worthwhile to dredge long before this limit is reached. But we may assume, for the sake of argument, that an oyster bed may be thus stripped. In this case the oyster bed is in the same position as a salmon river. The operations of man bear a very large proportion to the sum of destructive agencies at work, and it may seem that restriction by force of law should be as useful in the one case as in the other.

But it must not be forgotten that the efficacy of salmon protection depends on its completeness. What would be the value of the Salmon Acts if they contained only two provisions – the first that there shall be an annual close time, and the second that no parr or smolts shall be captured? Is it not obvious that there would be as good as no protection at all, inasmuch as every salmon that tried to ascend the river might be captured during the open season, and then, of course, there would be neither breeding-fish nor smolts to protect?

And yet this is all that the restrictions on oyster fishing enforced in this country have ever aimed at.

At one time, we enforced an annual close time, and we said that oysters below a certain size should not be taken; but I am at a loss to divine how the strictest enforcement of these regulations could prevent any one from stripping a bed bare of every adult oyster during the open season. But the interference with the removal of oysters below a certain size is so obviously a measure in the interest of dogwhelks and star-fish, and against mall, that we have given that up, and now we only insist upon the four months' close time; which appears to me to be just as rational as it would be to prohibit the catching of salmon in December, January, and February, and to permit the destruction of young and old by all imaginable means, and to any extent, during the rest of the year.

The only protection of oysters which can possibly be efficient is some such system as that pursued in Denmark, and in France – where the beds are the property of the State – where an estimate is made of the quantity of oysters in a bed – and where fishing is permitted only to the extent justified by that estimate.

How far the results of such a system of protection of oyster beds justify its adoption is a question which I will not at present attempt to discuss; but I think it must be perfectly clear to every one acquainted with the circumstances of our deep-sea oyster beds, that it is utterly impracticable to apply any such system to them. Who is to survey these beds? Who is to watch them? Who is to see that the dredgers do not take more than their allotted share? Who is to prevent fishermen sailing under the flag of a nation with which we have no fishery convention from disregarding our regulations?

Thus I arrive at the conclusion – first, that oyster fisheries may be exhaustible; and, secondly, that for those which lie outside the territorial limit no real protection is practically possible. In the case of the oyster fisheries which lie inside the territorial limit the case is different. Here the State can grant a property in the beds to corporations or to individuals whose interest it will become to protect them efficiently. And this I think is the only method by which fisheries can be preserved.

I have selected the oyster fisheries as those sea fisheries for the possible exhaustion of which there is most to be said. I have no doubt that those who take tip the subjects of trawling and of the shell fisheries will discuss the question in relation to those fisheries. All I desire to remark is, that if any of these fisheries should prove to be exhaustible, and in course of exhaustion, close time and the restriction of the size of fish taken cannot save them, unless those measures are accompanied by the limitation of the number of fish taken during the open season. And in the case of trawling, I am quite unable to imagine how such a limitation could be practically enforced.

I have ventured to dwell upon this topic of the exhaustibility of fisheries at some length, because it is of great importance, not only to the consumer, but to the fisherman. It is to currant opinion on this subject that we owe fishery legislation. Now every legislative restriction means the creation of a new offence. In the case of fishery it means that a simple man of the people, earning a scanty livelihood by hard toil, shall be liable to fine or imprisonment for doing that which he and his fathers before him have, up to that time, been free to do.

If the general interest clearly requires that this burden should be put upon the fishermen – well and good. But if it does not – if, indeed, there is any doubt about the matter – I think that the man who has made the unnecessary law deserves a heavier punishment than the man who breaks it.

Editorial Headnote

1808 (East Lothian)–1895

John Croumbie Brown was a missionary, botanist and one of the key pioneers of forestry management in Britain.

Brown was from a religious family, a grandson of the renowned Presbyterian theologian John Croumbie Brown. After studying at the University of Aberdeen and also being ordained, he set out on a missionary and clerical career, including postings in St Petersburg, Russia, and Cape Town, South Africa. He developed an interest in botany during this time and gave lectures in his time off from church duties. Consequently, he retrained in this discipline when he came back to Aberdeen in 1849 whilst still serving as a pastor. In 1853, he became a lecturer in botany at Aberdeen University whilst researching his doctorate in the subject (Nobbs 1956). In 1863, he then returned to Cape Town, this time as a fully fledged botanist.

This published piece is taken from Brown's April 1877 speech to the Town Council of Edinburgh and the Royal Scottish Arboricultural Society. In the speech, he advocates the establishment of a forest school and an arboretum for the city. In doing so, he draws extensively on his international expertise to support his arguments. Brown had been a colonial botanist at Cape Town from 1863, prior to his return to Scotland, and had also carried out research in other countries. He is at pains to point out that Britain has much to learn from other countries when it comes to forest management, including Germany and India. Indeed, he notes that most European countries have already established national forestry management programmes. He also observes that concerns about deforestation have been apparent for many centuries. Reference is made to the research of Hugh Cleghorn, another important Scottish forestry management pioneer, who five years earlier had become the first inspector general of forests in India.

Brown published widely on several aspects of forestry management, as well as on other matters of botany and on theology. He was also a fellow of the Royal Geographical Society. His appeal for a forestry school did have a quick impact. The University of Edinburgh established a lectureship on this subject and an International Forestry Exhibition took place in the city in 1884. The first person to take up the new forestry lectureship in 1889 was William Somerville, profiled in the next section.

pp. 225–227

16

ON FOREST SCHOOLS

John Croumbie Brown

Source: John Croumbie Brown, *On Forest Schools* (1878)

In April last I addressed to the Right Honourable the Lord Provost, the Magistrates, and the Town Councillors of Edinburgh; to the office-bearers of the Scottish Arboricultural Society; to the promoters of the purchase of ground at Inverleith to be transferred to Government for the formation of an Arboretum, and all others whom it may concern, a letter supplying detailed information in regard to schools of forestry on the Continent of Europe, and advocating the creation of a school of forestry in connection with the Arboretum in Edinburgh.

It was extensively distributed among members of the Scottish Arboricultural Society. Had I had the means of doing so, the letter, or one somewhat similar, would have been sent to all; and I gladly avail myself of the permission which has been given to me to address you on the subject, in the hope that you may now, or at some future time, take part in discussing what may be the best means of securing for young foresters an education corresponding to that enjoyed by their brethren on the Continent of Europe.

In prosecution of this purpose I shall supply some additional information in regard to existing schools of forestry, and state some points on which desiderated information is solicited from the Association.

The schools of forestry on the Continent of Europe are educational institutions in which provision has been made for leading candidates for employment as foresters through a protracted course of study similar to what is required in Scotland as a preparation for the so-called learned professions of law, medicine, and divinity. They may be considered as a necessary requirement of the system of forest management introduced on the Continent of Europe in the beginning of the present century, and also as a means of advancing the Forst-Wissenschaft or Forest Science of the day, and of promoting its application to the treatment of forests, so as to secure the greatest benefit from the system of forest economy considered the best adapted to the circumstances and condition and requirements of any particular case.

Some three hundred years ago it was perceived by Sully, the distinguished minister of Henry IV, that France was being ruined by the destruction of her forests. I almost quote his own words; and a hundred years later there was passed in 1666 a

DOI: 10.4324/9781003194651-21

129

famous ordinance to regulate the exploitation of these. The evil was not confined to France, and for a hundred and fifty years, in France and elsewhere, various measures were devised and adopted with a view to averting the catastrophe; but it was found that these could at best only retard the destructive process. At length Cotta and Hartig devised what is known in Germany as the Fachicerke methode of forest exploitation, the aim of which is to secure simultaneously, and without prejudice to each other, a sustained production of wood and timber, a progressive amelioration of the state of the forests, and a natural reproduction of these by self-sown seed.

To carry out this method of forest management, educated foresters are necessary; and I lay on the table for reference, if required, an account of the school of forestry in Vallombrosa, in Italy, by Dr Cleghorn, which appeared in the volume of Transactions of the Scottish Arboricultural Society for 1877; successive numbers of the Journal of Forestry for this year, containing programmes of study followed at Carlsruhe in the grand duchy of Baden, at Hohenheim in Wurtemberg, at the Escurial in Spain, and sheets provided in advance in view of this meeting – containing an account of that at Evois in Finland; also the letter referred to by me in the outset, subsequently published by Messrs Oliver & Boyd of this city, entitled "The Schools of Forestry in Europe: a Plea for the Creation of a School of Forestry in connection with the Arboretum at Edinburgh," in which is given a detailed resume of the programme of study followed at the school of forestry at Nancy, in France, a translation of the regulations issued by the King of Sweden for the management of the forest school at Stockholm, information in regard to the schools of forestry in Austria and Poland, and translations for the Forest Code of Russia in relation to the forest schools of Russia; and with these I lay on the table programmes of study followed at the schools of forestry at St Petersburg and at Lissino, at Neustadt Eberswalde in Prussia, at Miinden in Hanover, at Tharand in Saxony, at Giessen in Hesse-Darmstadt, at Aschafienburg in Bavaria, and at Stockholm in Sweden, most of them with translations in manuscript.

. . .

p. 227

Statistics illustrative of the pecuniary benefit of these schools to the several countries in which they have been established cannot be introduced now, but the magnitude of this may be otherwise indicated. In India, as in France and in Germany, it was found that the forests were being destroyed, that the destruction of these was entailing privations and sufferings upon the people, and that more disastrous consequences were looming in the distance. After careful deliberation, it was determined that a body of forest officials, educated at schools of forestry on the Continent of Europe, should be procured. The arrangements made are detailed in the letter to which I have referred.

The expense was considerable, and it may be considered that this was a bold measure, but the results have justified the steps taken. By progressive amelioration of their condition, forests have risen greatly in value and have been vastly extended, and the revenue from forests has been increased by hundreds of thousands of pounds. According to Resolution of Government of India, Financial Department, No. 2012, dated 11th March 1871, the latest to which I happen to have access, the estimated charges for the following year 1871–72, as settled in the Public Works Department, and as modified in the Financial Department, were 45,11,000 rupees (£451,100), and the receipts, 57,32,200 rupees (£573,220), showing a surplus of revenue over expenditure of 12,21,200 rupees (£122,120). I learn that in the year 1873–74 the forest revenue was £700,000, and the expenditure £414,000 odds, leaving a surplus of £285,000, both revenue and expenditure being about double what they were in 1864–65, ten years previously. It may facilitate recollection if I state that the expenditure one year was reported vaguely as £200,000, and the returns, £400,000. All which had been accomplished not by an impoverishing of the forests, but by a progressive amelioration of these and an increase of their pecuniary value in something like a corresponding ratio.

. . .

p. 230

The Governments of almost every country on the Continent of Europe – Denmark, Holland, Belgium, and perhaps Greece, being apparently the only exceptions – under the influence of students of forestry, have deemed it expedient to make provision for the instruction of officers in their forest service in all of the subjects embraced in that curriculum. The British Government of India have deemed it expedient to do the same, in so far as existing arrangements permit of this being done, and have found their advantage in the result; and in view of this I raise the question, May not something similar, but adapted to meet the requirements of our conditions, be done by us.

. . .

p. 232

It seems to me that the facility for locomotion supplied by railways, combined with the fact that the local expense of board, etc., is very much the same everywhere, has somewhat modified the views once entertained in regard to the location of a school of forestry, in, I shall not say "a cottage," but a palace, "near a wood" – for in such some of the schools of forestry on the Continent have been located. I may be allowed to state in this connection that, on the publication of my plea for the creation of a school of forestry in connection with the proposed Arboretum, one of my correspondents, Professor Blomqvist, director of the school of forestry at Evois, in Finland, wrote to me on this point, calling my attention to views expressed at a convention of State foresters, etc., at Freiburg, when it was said to be unanimously agreed that a university was the proper place for the study of forest science.

It is in connection with the consideration of the requirements of our Colonies that I have moved in this matter; I look upon India as a dependency like in some of its requirements to a colony; and I should be glad if access to a highly remunerative career were opened up to working foresters in the forest service of that country, believing that what thus brought gain to them would bring corresponding gain to the countries obtaining their services. But it is natural that the national

Arboricultural Society should look primarily to our national requirements. And anticipating as I do greater difficulties in securing from the first a body of students, than in securing the establishment of a school of forestry in the country, I would submit for consideration the expediency of the association selecting for discussion at the meeting of the Society in 1878, the following questions relating to points on which information is greatly desiderated and earnestly solicited:

1. What course of study at a school of forestry would best meet the requirements of young foresters intending to practise forestry in Scotland?
2. By what measures can students be procured to attend a school of forestry in Scotland for the prosecution of such studies?
3. In what way could students, at a school of forestry in Scotland, most efficiently spend the vacation in acquiring information from observations to be made by them in woods, plantations, and forests in Scotland?

Editorial Headnote

1860 (Lanarkshire)–1932

William Sommerville was a Scots agriculturalist and forestry management expert central to early British efforts in developing sustainable woodland management.

Somerville worked on his father's farm and then embarked on an academic career specializing in forestry. Utilizing funding generated by John Croumbie Brown's advocacy, he became the first lecturer in forestry at Edinburgh University before later becoming a professor of agriculture and forestry at the University of Newcastle-upon-Tyne. He subsequently took on similar posts at Oxford and Cambridge in a wide-ranging and successful academic career. Somerville was also widely published on a range of forestry matters. An obituary to him in Nature alluded to his abilities to transcend the academic and practical agricultural and arboreal worlds: "When Somerville went to Newcastle in 1891, his knowledge of the subjects then interesting Scottish farmers and his German training in scientific methods enabled him both to grasp quickly those questions on which farmers in the north of England required exact information and to devise field experiments of a kind likely to give the information needed" (Nature 1932: 389–390).

In this speech, Somerville calls for the extension of the Forest Schools initiative pioneered in Edinburgh, which kick-started his career. He also commends recent progress that has been made with afforestation schemes (cultivating new forests). At the same time, however, he notes that Britain lags well behind other countries in terms of woodland cover and in combatting long-term deforestation.

Somerville had been appointed head of the Royal Commission on Coast Erosion, the Reclamation of Tidal Lands and Aforestation, whose second report came out shortly before this speech. However, the recommendations of that commission, which were in line with Somerville's views here, were not acted upon aside from the initiation of a few small-scale schemes. Eventually, however, Britain fell into line with other states and introduced systematic national forestry management in the wake of the passing of the Forestry Act in 1919. The Great War had made it plain that Britain was over-reliant on timber imports and that, in particular, Germany was much better stocked. Put in stark national security terms, the case for afforestation was now compelling. Somerville was made Knight of the British Empire (KBE) in 1926 on his retirement. He died of pneumonia six years later in Oxford.

17

FORESTRY IN SOME OF ITS ECONOMIC ASPECTS

William Somerville

Source: William Somerville, *Forestry in Some of its Economic Aspects* (1909)

By Professor WILLIAM SOMERVILLE, M.A., D.Sc. [Read before the Royal Statistical Society, 16th February, 1909. Mr. NOEL A. Humphreys, I.S.O., in the Chair.]

pp. 40–3

THE subject of Forestry, in one aspect or another, has been attracting an increasing amount of attention during the past twenty-five years. In 1885 a Select Committee of the House of Commons was appointed "to consider whether, by the establishment of a Forest School, or otherwise, our woodlands could be rendered more "remunerative." The final report was presented in 1887, and contained the following conclusions:

That facilities for education should be provided.

That the management of our woodlands left much to be desired.

That on public and national grounds timber cultivation on a more scientific system should be encouraged.

That, apart from any immediate pecuniary benefits, there would be considerable social and economic advantages in an extensive system of planting in many parts of the kingdom.

That a Forest Board be established to organise forestry education, to make provision for examinations, and to prepare an official syllabus and textbook. The report and minutes of evidence had the effect of stirring up interest, and of directing some attention to the subject, but no specific results ensued.

The Board of Agriculture, chiefly as the outcome of persistent representations made to the President on the occasion of his annual visits to Scotland, appointed a Departmental Committee in 1902, which reported in the same year. Their principal recommendations were:

DOI: 10.4324/9781003194651-22

DISCOVERING NATURE

That one of the State forests in England should be made a demonstration area, and that a property should be acquired in Scotland for the same purpose.

That education in forestry should be developed in Oxford and Cambridge, and at local centres.

That estate duties, so far as timber is concerned, should be modified.

That the owners of locomotives should be compelled to take measures to prevent sparks getting into woodlands and so of causing fires.

That the Board of Agriculture should repeat the inquiry of 1895 concerning the area of woodlands, and that the character of the timber crop should be ascertained in greater detail.

That the attention of corporations and municipalities should be drawn to the desirability of planting with trees the catchment areas of their water supplies.

With the exception of the proposal in regard to estate duties it is satisfactory to know that these recommendations have been carried out. The State forests in England are being subjected to much improved management, a demonstration area of 12,500 acres has been obtained in Scotland, forestry education has been introduced in both Oxford and Cambridge, and has been provided to a modest extent at several local centres (Bangor, Newcastle-on-Tyne, Cirencester, Wye, Glasgow, Aberdeen), the "Sparks" Act has been passed, the Board of Agriculture has repeated and extended its inquiry as to the extent and character of our woodlands, and corporations and municipalities have been stimulated to plant the catchment areas of their water supplies.

In 1907 the Department of Agriculture and Technical Instruction in Ireland appointed a departmental committee to inquire into the question of afforestation in that country, and their report was entirely favourable to large extension through State agency. A start has been made in the direction of acquiring forest land, and land that may with advantage be planted, but whether the full recommendations will be carried out has not yet been determined.

Lastly, there remains to be mentioned the inquiry that has recently been concluded by the Royal Commission on Coast Erosion and Afforestation in terms of the reference "whether in connection with unclaimed lands or otherwise it is desirable to make an experiment in afforestation as a means of increasing employment during periods of depression in the labour market, and if so by what authority and under what conditions such experiments should be conducted." In their report the Commission recommend that Forest Commissioners be appointed to determine the specific areas that may with advantage be afforested – amounting, it is estimated, to 9,000,000 acres – and that the work should proceed at the rate of 150,000 acres annually, at a cost for land, labour and material, of 2,000,000*l.* a year. Seeing that this is a reproductive work it is recommended that it should be financed by loan, the annual interest, together with administrative charges, amounting in the first year to £90,000, and rising to over £3,000,000 in the fortieth year, after which, till the eightieth year, the woods would be more than

FORESTRY IN SOME OF ITS ECONOMIC ASPECTS

self-supporting. Thereafter there would be a clear revenue of over £21,000,000, which would represent about 33 per cent. On the whole of the charges of creation and maintenance accumulated till the eightieth year at 3 per cent. compound interest, less the intermediate returns (thinnings) similarly accumulated. It is suggested that land be acquired by voluntary negotiation where possible, but that compulsory powers be obtained and exercised if necessary. Owners of land falling within a statutory definition of "suitability" would be exempted from the operations of the Act, provided they were prepared to afforest the area within a reasonable time, and in a manner satisfactory to the Forestry Commissioners. Aforestation on the scale contemplated would mean the employment during the winter months of some 18,000 men, who, it is suggested, should be selected on their merits, and not from eleemosynary considerations. Aforestation is thus no panacea for unemployment, though, to the extent indicated, it would react on the general situation.

A subject that has received such a large amount of official attention during recent years, and which has been so favourably reported on by one select and two departmental committees, and by a Royal Commission, must have merits that are intrinsically attractive; and I therefore propose to discuss very shortly some of the social and economic aspects in which forestry, in its widest sense, may be regarded.

In respect of the relative area that is occupied by wood in the principal countries of Europe, we find that the United Kingdom stands at the bottom of the list with 4 per cent., and Sweden at the top with nearly 52 per cent. In Great Britain there has been an increase of 42,127 acres, or 15 per cent. between 1895 and 1905. Only in one county, Elgin (15.1 per cent.), does the percentage of woodland exceed 15 per cent., and only in other seven does it exceed 10 per cent (Kent, Surrey, Sussex, Hants, Clackmannan, Kincardine, Nairn). In four counties of the mainland of Great Britain the percentage is below 2 (Cambridge, Anglesey, Caithness, Sutherland), while in Ireland there are only five counties (Down, Queen's, Tipperary, Waterford, Wicklow) where the percentage exceeds 2. Should 9,000,000 acres be afforested, as recommended by the Royal Commission, the percentage of wooded area in the United Kingdom would be raised from 4 to 15–16, placing this country above Denmark, the Netherlands, and Italy, though still below all the other important countries of Europe. In Scotland, where it is suggested two-thirds of the total area would be situated the percentage would be raised from 4.6 to 35.4, which would make that country one of the best-wooded in Europe.

. . .

p. 47

Speaking generally, and with very few exceptions, the land that it is suggested may with advantage be afforested is at present grazed by mountain sheep. Even below the upper limit of profitable tree-growth in this country – 1,500 feet – it is seldom that such land can support throughout the year more than one sheep to two acres. The tangible produce that finds its way to market is the four months' old lambs, minus such female lambs as are necessary to maintain the flock at its numerical strength, plus a proportion of the ewes – the "draft" or "cast" ewes. In addition to this meat there is the yield of wool, of which the annual supply for the class of sheep in question may be put at 4 lb. per head, or 2 lb. per acre.

The Royal Commission that have recently reported went in considerable detail into the relationship of afforestation to meat production, and they arrived at the conclusion that the weight of meat, calculated as mutton, that would be displaced by the extensive planting of the class of land indicated, would amount at most to 15 lb. per acre per annum. The weight of meat that would be displaced by the afforestation of 9,000,000 acres would therefore aggregate 60,000 tons per annum; and, utilising the figures of the Milk and Meat Committee of this Society, the Commission pointed out that the meat displaced would amount to 4.81 per cent of our total home-grown produce, or 2.67 per cent of our annual consumption.

. . .

pp. 53–54

The Royal Commission on Coast Erosion and Afforestation took much evidence on the subject of the trend of prices and quality of timber, and the report and volume of evidence prove conclusively that while prices have been steadily rising during the past twenty years, and markedly so during the past ten, the quality has been persistently falling. A rise therefore of 20 per cent. in the price, for instance, of first quality Baltic yellow deal is, in itself, sufficiently serious, but the aspect of the case becomes still more serious when it is found that timber classed as "Grade I" to-day, would, some ten years ago, have been classed no higher than "Grade III."

Of the four countries on which we chiefly depend for our timber imports, it would appear that we cannot cherish the expectation that either the United States or Canada can long maintain their supplies. While there is uncertainty about Russia (including Siberia) the probability would seem to be favourable to that country maintaining her exports for a long period. As regards the fourth of these countries, Sweden, we have it on the authority of the Central Bureau of Statistics that, in 1900, 106,000,000 cubic feet were annually being withdrawn from her forests beyond what is annually produced. If this be so it would appear that a curtailment of supplies from that country must soon be expected. Time does not permit of the subject being pursued further, though the fact is not overlooked that relief may, to some extent, be found in the direction of the displacement of wood by concrete, iron, and similar substitutes. Much may also be done to prevent and control forest fires, which in the past have perhaps consumed as much timber as has fallen to the woodman's axe. Then, again, nations that have hitherto recklessly exploited their forests are now taking some steps to secure regeneration, and, in the course of time, such action will have its effect on supplies.

If material extension of afforestation is to take place in this, or, in fact, in any country, it can only be through the direct agency of the State. The planting of trees has appealed with great force to individuals, who have formed or extended woodlands to give shelter, afford sport, and improve the amenities of their estates. As often as not woods have been formed to gratify a taste of much the same character as that which induces a man of means to buy pictures, or establish a herd of pedigree shorthorns. The timber that private woodlands yield is of service in the upkeep of the estate, and the revenue resulting from the sale may be substantial as well as attractive. Few landowners care to see woodland reverting to rough pasture, so that one may say that it is seldom that the proportion of woodland on an estate is not maintained. But substantial extension of afforestation on an estate is comparatively rare. Of course there are exceptions, as in the case of the witness who came before the Committee of 1902, and testified that he himself had extended his woodlands by 12,000 acres. But afforestation can never appeal to the individual as a purely commercial undertaking. This, it seems to me, is inherent in the circumstances of the case, for when a scheme of planting is contemplated the landowner has to face two considerations, either of which may make him pause, and both of which will almost certainly make him stop. In the first place the necessary land has to be withdrawn from some other form of utilisation, and this means the loss of immediate income. In the second place, capital has to be found for the sylvicultural operations, and this must be accompanied by suspension of interest, or it must entail the payment of interest on borrowed capital. The individual may be quite convinced of the soundness of the investment, and of the ultimately remunerative character of the undertaking, but present necessities are much more potent than future advantages, and especially is this the case where the advantages are quite certain to be reaped by some other individual. In the case of the State, however, the matter appears in an entirely different light. An undertaking whose returns may be deferred for even a century need not deter her from taking action. A century, where an individual is concerned, is overwhelming; a century in the life of a nation is insignificant. To what depths of pessimism must a nation have descended if it dare not postulate an existence of a hundred years! In point of fact a crop of certain kinds of timber may be reaped in half this time, but even this restricted period has no attraction for the individual. On account, therefore, of the necessarily deferred character of the returns of forestry, the State is pre-eminently qualified to undertake the work. But on other grounds also the State makes an excellent forester. Continuity of management, comprehensive working plans, and maintenance of supplies at a steady level can only be satisfactorily secured in State forests. Whether large extension of afforestation in this country is desirable or not is open to argument, but if the desirability of such extension be admitted, the conclusion, it seems to me, cannot be avoided, that the State alone can accomplish the result.

1.3

POLLUTION

Editorial Headnote

1820 (London)–1873

Henry William Fuller was a physician and writer best known for his research on rheumatism but profiled here for his contribution to the appreciation of pesticide poisoning, which would eventually become an important cause of environmentalism. Fuller was the son of a surgeon and educated in medicine at Cambridge and St Georges Hospital in London, from where he wrote this letter to The Lancet. Fuller's insights here on arsenic poisoning, hence, represented a departure from his specific area of expertise.

The Marsh Test Fuller refers to here had been developed in 1836 and greatly improved the means of detecting small traces of arsenic (although it was not completely reliable). One imagines, however, that Fuller's methodology of deliberately poisoning a cat would fall foul of the medical ethics expectations for publication in The Lancet today! This also, perhaps, serves to illustrate how animal rights thinking has progressed over the last century and a half.

The toxic qualities of arsenic were well appreciated in the Victorian era. It was used for pest control in kitchens and its murderous potential as a poison were well known. Nevertheless, as the letter outlines, there did not appear to be any great fears about the chemical's toxic characteristics persisting in remnants left in food or the air after its application as a pesticide. The very deadliness of arsenic led to its adoption in insecticide formulations or for the redeployment of existing arsenical products. For example, Paris Green, an arsenic compound used for paint and pigments – particularly for colouring wallpaper – was very popular across Europe since first being marketed in 1814. That it was poisonous soon became apparent in several cases of illness and death of people inhabiting houses with fashionable bright green wallcoverings. There have even been suggestions that this was the long-term cause of Napoleon Bonaparte's death on St Helena (King 2001). Paris Green subsequently fell out of favour as a dye, but it came to be re-marketed as an insecticide when US farmers in the 1860s found its toxic qualities to be highly effective against Colorado beetles, a prominent potato pest.

The sale of Arsenic products was restricted by an Act of 1851, but this did not prohibit their use. A number of major food-poisoning scandals, including a notorious case of seventy people being killed in 1900 as a result of drinking traces of arsenic in beer that was being used in brewing sugars, made this apparent. Eventually, the 1851 act was repealed by the 1933 Pharmacy and Poisons Act, which more clearly prohibited the use of arsenic. Over a century after Fuller had written this letter chemical insecticides then became the key catalyst for the emergence of political ecology, owing to controversy over the use of synthetic organochlorine chemicals highlighted by Rachel Carson in the US (Carson 1962).

18

ON THE USE OF THE ARSENIC IN AGRICULTURE – POISONING BY ARSENIC, AND SYMPTOMS OF CHOLERA – THE POSSIBLE EFFECT OF THE GAME LAWS

Henry W. Fuller

Source: Henry W. Fuller, *On the Use of the Arsenic in Agriculture – Poisoning by Arsenic, and Symptoms of Cholera – The Possible Effect of the Game Laws* (1848)

For some months past, in certain parts of Hampshire, partridges have been found dead in the fields, presenting a very remarkable appearance. Instead of lying prostrate on their sides, as is usually the case with dead birds, they have been found sitting with their heads erect and their eyes open, presenting all the semblance of life. This peculiarity, which for some time had attracted considerable attention among sportsmen in the neighbourhood, led to no practical result until about ten days ago when a covey of ten birds having been found nestled together in this condition, two of the birds, together with the seeds taken from the crops of the remaining eight, were sent up to London for examination I was requested to undertake the investigation, and the result of my experiments I will now briefly detail.

I first examined the seeds taken from the crops of the birds, and detected, as I anticipated, a large quantity of arsenic. I will not take up your valuable space by detailing the various steps of my analysis; suffice it to say that by Reinsch's process I speedily obtained a very thick incrustation of metallic arsenic; that I then applied the reduction test; and subsequently Marsh's test, and the tests of the ammonio-nitrate of silver and the ammonio-sulphate of copper, each of which gave its characteristic result. Having thus ascertained the presence of arsenic in the food of the partridges, I proceeded to examine the birds themselves. They were plum and in good condition, but the oesophagus was in both cases highly inflamed, and presented no trace of ulceration, but they were remarkably empty and clean, almost as if they had been washed with water. May not this have been the result of diarrhoea? I now, at the suggestion of my friend, Mr. Stone, proceeded

DOI: 10.4324/9781003194651-24

to ascertain whether the flesh of birds so poisoned might not itself prove poisonous when eaten, and with this view I carefully cut the flesh off the breast and legs of one of the birds, and gave it, together with the liver, to a fine healthy cat. She ate it with avidity, but in about half an hour she began to vomit, and vomited almost incessantly for nearly twelve hours, during the whole of which time she evidently suffered excessive pain. After this, nothing would induce her to eat any more partridge. I kept her without food for twenty-four hours, but in vain; she resolutely refused to touch an atom more of the bird. This being the case, I gave her some beef and some milk, which she eagerly swallowed, proving beyond doubt that her instinct, and not her want of appetite, induced her to forego the dainty meal which had just been offered her. I now felt satisfied, from my observation of the symptoms induced in the cat, borne out as they were by many facts we are acquainted with respecting the action of poisons, that the arsenic which the partridges had swallowed had been absorbed in sufficient quantity into the system to render the flesh of the birds poisonous, and to induce poisonous effects in any one partaking of it. However, I was anxious to leave nothing to hypothesis and as the cat had so soon rejected by vomiting the greater part of the bird she had eaten, and pertinaciously refused to repeat the experiment, by again partaking of the poisoned food, I was obliged to have recourse to chemical analysis with the view of ascertaining with certainty the existence or non-existence of arsenic in the flesh itself. I therefore cut the flesh off one side of the breast of the other partridge, and after about an hour's boiling, I obtained by Reinsch's process a thin incrustation of metallic arsenic, thus demonstrating beyond question that the previous experiments had left little room for doubting. I was now anxious to ascertain the source of the poison, and a very little inquiry seemed to satisfy me on this point. I will not stop to go into many details which, though in themselves exceedingly interesting, have no direct bearing upon the question at issue. I will simply mention the leading facts – viz., that in Hampshire, Lincolnshire, and many other parts of the country, the farmers are now in the habit of steeping their wheat in a strong solution of arsenic previous to sowing it, with the view of preventing the ravages of the wire-worm on the seed, and of the smut on the plant when grown; that this process is found to be eminently successful, and is therefore daily becoming more and more generally adopted; that, even now, many hundreds weight of arsenic are yearly sold to agriculturalists for this express purpose; that although the seed is poisonous when sown, its fruit is in no degree affected by the poison; that wherever this plan has been extensively carried out, pheasants and partridges have been poisoned by eating the seed, and the partridges have been almost universally found sitting in the position I have already described; and lastly, that the men employed in sowing the poisonous seed, not unfrequently present the earlier symptoms which occur in the milder cases of poisoning by arsenic. This last fact I give on the authority of Dr. Heale, who up to the last two or three years practised at Staines, and has repeatedly had men under his care, suffering from symptoms due to this cause.

Now, the facts just enumerated suggest several most important points for consideration, it is notorious that many of the dealers in game are supplied through the agency of poachers and others who have a direct pecuniary interest in supplying them with the largest possible number of birds. It is certain, moreover, that if men of this sort were to find a covey of partridges in a field, dead, but fresh and in good condition, they would not hesitate to send them with the remainder of their booty to the poulterer, who would as certainly, without suspicion, sell them to his customers. And after the experiments above detailed, there can be no reasonable grounds for doubting that these birds, when eaten, would produce disagreeable and injurious – not to say poisonous – effects on those who partake of them. It is obvious, therefore, that in all cases of supposed cholera, or of suspicions belly-ache, occurring at this season of the year, we shall do well to make particular inquiry as to whether our patient has recently partaken of pheasants or partridges purchased at a poulterer's; and it is further manifest, that in all oases of poisoning or suspected poisoning by arsenic, the fact of the persons having lately eaten of partridges and pheasants must form an important element in the inquiry, and must tend to cast a suspicion on the evidence adduced to prove a criminal intent in the administration of the poison. So that, in a medico-legal point of view, the question is one of the gravest import.

Secondly. – If it should prove, on further inquiry, that the practice of steeping seed wheat in arsenic is, even indirectly, productive of injurious effects on our population, it may become, in those days of sanitary reform, a matter for the anxious consideration of the legislature, whether they should not adopt some measures to prevent the continuance of such a custom.

Thirdly. – As in the event of a practice so destructive of game becoming universal, pheasants and partridges, in their wild state at least, must, at no distant day, become extinct in this country, it is a question whether landlords may not henceforth be induced to insert a cause in their leases, prohibiting the use of arsenic on their farms; while, on the other hand it may be a question with those who are already weary of the protracted debates on the game laws, whether they should not allow them to die a natural death, by the gradual but inevitable destruction of the game it is the object of these laws to preserve.

I am. Sir, your obedient servant,
Henry William Fuller,
Assistant Physician to, and lecturer on Medical
Jurisprudence at, St. George's Hospital.
Half Moon Street, Piccadilly, Dec, 1848.

Editorial Headnote

1813 (York)–1858

John Snow was a physician and pioneering epidemiologist with two towering achievements from both fields: advancing the understanding of anaesthesia and explaining the spread of the disease cholera. This secondary pioneering contribution to public health and the understanding of pollution is highlighted here.

Snow came from a working-class background and took up a medical apprenticeship in Newcastle upon Tyne at the age of 14, during which time he encountered the horrific effects of cholera in British cities. The particularly deadly 1830–1 cholera epidemic and the fact that its thousands of victims tended to be the poor, particularly influenced him. He moved to London in 1836 to take up work as a physician and, on again encountering cholera, became a sceptic of the miasma 'bad air' theory then held to explain the diffusion of the disease through the atmosphere. Another major epidemic in 1849 provided the backdrop for his writing the groundbreaking *On the Mode of Communication of Cholera*. As the extract from this book shows, Snow was convinced that cholera was spread via river water since cases tended to be concentrated in riverside locations and not spread evenly, as might be assumed if transmitted via the air. He notes that Dumfries and Maxwelltown, where sewage is known to flow into the river supplying the towns' drinking water, have abnormally high incidences.

Five years after the publication of this book, through mapping the spread of epidemics in London, Snow found a striking correlation with water pumps so proving its aquatic transmission. Closing selected water pumps quickly led to a decline in cholera cases in the immediate vicinity. A second edition of the book included a detailed analysis of these findings and built a compelling case for the disease's transmission via drinking water. His evidence was not initially taken seriously (bacteria had not yet been discovered) but eventually proved incontrovertible, transforming public health and saving thousands of lives.

Snow was a teetotal vegetarian for most of his life but, on contracting a renal disorder, decided he may as well take up meat and wine. However, he died after a stroke aged just 45. The John Snow Society is named in his honour and there are many other memorials to his remarkable short life. Perhaps the most apt is a plaque at the spot on Broad (now Broadwick) Street, London, where the first water pump from which he removed the handle to stop usage was located (Hempel 2006).

pp. 4–12

19

ON THE MODE OF COMMUNICATION OF CHOLERA

John Snow

Source: John Snow, *On the Mode of Communication of Cholera* (1849)

It is not the intention of the writer to go over the much debated question of the contagion of cholera. An examination of the history of that malady, from its first appearance, or at least recognition, in India in 1817, has convinced him, in common with a great portion of the medical profession, that it is propagated by human intercourse. Its progress along the great channels of that intercourse, and the very numerous instances, both in this country and abroad, in which cholera dates its commencement in a town or village previously free from it to the arrival and illness of a person coming from a place in which the disease was prevalent, seem to leave no room for doubting its communicability.

It is quite true that a great deal of argument has been employed on the opposite side, and that many eminent men hold an opposite opinion; but, besides the objection that negative evidence ought not to overthrow that of a positive kind, the instances that are believed to oppose the proofs of communication are reasoned upon in the opinion that cholera, if conveyed by human intercourse, must be contagious in the same way that the eruptive fevers are considered to be, viz., by emanations from the sick person into the surrounding air, which enter the system of others by being inhaled, and absorbed by the blood passing through the lungs. There is, however, no reason to conclude, a priori, that this must be the mode of communication of cholera; and it must be confessed that it is difficult to imagine that there can be such a difference in the predisposition to be affected or not by an inhaled poison, as would enable a great number to breathe it without injury in a pretty concentrated form (the immunity not having been earned by a previous attack, as in the case of measles, &c), whilst others should be killed by it when millions of times diluted. The difficulties that beset this view are of the same kind, but not so great, as those which surround the hypothesis of a cholera poison generally diffused in the air, and not emanating from the sick.

Reasoning by analogy from what is known of other diseases, we ought not to conclude that cholera is propagated by an effluvium. In all known diseases in which the blood is poisoned in the first instance, general symptoms, such as rigors,

DOI: 10.4324/9781003194651-25

151

headache, and quickened pulse, precede the local symptoms; but it has always appeared, from what the writer could observe, that in cholera the alimentary canal is first affected, and that all the symptoms not referable to that part are consecutive, and apparently the result of the local affection. In those cases in which vertigo, lassitude, and depression precede the evacuations from the bowels, there is no reason to doubt that exudation of the watery part of the blood, which is soon copiously discharged, is already taking place from the mucous membrane; whilst in the cases in which the purging comes on more gradually, there is often so little feeling of illness that the patient cannot persuade himself that he has the cholera, or – apply for remedies until the disease is far advanced, this being a circumstance which increases the mortality. The quantity of fluid lost by purging and vomiting, taking into consideration the previous state of the patient, the suddenness of the attack, and the circumstance that the loss is not replaced by absorption, has seemed sufficient, in all the cases witnessed by the writer, to account, by the change it must occasion in the quantity and composition of the blood,[1] for the collapse, difficulty of breathing, and, in short, for all the symptoms, without assuming that the blood is poisoned, until it become so by the retention of matters which ought to pass off through the kidneys, the functions of which are, however, suspended by the thickened state of the blood, which will scarcely allow it to pass through the capillaries.

It is generally assumed that the blood becomes so altered by the cholera poison, that its watery and saline parts begin to exude by the mucous membrane of the alimentary canal; but it is more consonant with experience, both therapeutical and pathological, to attribute the exudation to some local irritant of the mucous membrane; no instance suggesting itself to the writer in which a poison in the blood causes irritation of, and exudation from, a single surface, as in cholera; for the sweating, as the patient approaches to collapse, is only what takes place in other eases from loss of blood, during fainting, and in any state in which the force of the circulation is greatly reduced.

Having rejected effluvia and the poisoning of the blood in the first instance, and being led to the conclusion that the disease is communicated by something that acts directly on the alimentary canal, the excretions of the sick at once suggest themselves as containing some material which, being accidentally swallowed, might attach itself to the mucous membrane of the small intestines, and there multiply itself by the appropriation of surrounding matter, in virtue of molecular changes going on within it or capable of going on, as soon as it is placed in congenial circumstances. Such a mode of communication of disease is not without precedent. The ova of the intestinal worms are undoubtedly introduced in this way. The affections they induce are amongst the most chronic, whilst cholera is one of the most acute; but duration does not of itself destroy all analogy amongst organic processes. The writer, however, does not wish to be misunderstood as making this comparison so closely as to imply that cholera depends on veritable animals, or even animalcules, but rather to appeal to that general tendency to the continuity of molecular changes, by which combustion, putrefaction, fermentation, and the various processes in organized beings, are kept up.

ON THE MODE OF COMMUNICATION OF CHOLERA

Whilst it is matter almost of certainty that intestinal worms are in this way communicated, it is never possible to trace the communication from one person to another: hence, if this be the mode of the propagation of cholera, there must often be great difficulty in detecting it. That a portion of the ejections or dejections must often be swallowed by healthy persons is, however, a matter of necessity. The latter even are voided with such suddenness and force that the clothes and bedding scarcely fail to become soiled, and being almost devoid of colour and odour, the presence of the evacuations is not always recognised; hence they become attached unobserved to the hands of the person nursing the patient, and are unconsciously swallowed, unless care be taken to wash the hands before partaking of food: or if the person waiting on the sick have to prepare food for the rest of the family, as often happens, the material of communication here suggested has a wider field in which to operate; and where the patient, or those waiting on him, are occupied in the preparation or vending of provisions, the disease may be conveyed to a distance, and into quarters having apparently no communication with the sick.

All the observers who have recorded their opinions on the subject, agree in attributing a great influence to want of personal cleanliness in increasing the prevalence and fatality of cholera. Dr. Lichtenstadt, in a work on Cholera published in 1831, states, "that at Berditscher, in Volhynia, a place of a few thousand inhabitants, no less than 900 were attacked in thirty-one days. Amongst 764 of these were 658 Jews, and only 106 Christians, although the Jewish population is far from being proportionally so great; and among the Christians the deaths were 61.3 per cent., while among the Jews they were 90.7 per cent. The only reason assigned by the reporter for these extraordinary differences is the excessive disregard of cleanliness among the Jewish inhabitants." The first appearance of cholera in many of the towns of this country in 1832 was in the courts and alleys to which vagrants resort for a night's lodging, where it often lingered for some time before spreading to the more cleanly part of the people.

The views here explained open up to consideration a most important way in which the cholera may be widely disseminated, viz., by the emptying of sewers into the drinking water of the community; and, as far as the writer's inquiries have extended, he has found that in most towns in which the malady has prevailed to an unusual extent this means of its communication has existed. The joint town of Dumfries and Maxwelltown, not usually an unhealthy place, has been visited by the cholera both in 1832 and at the close of last year with extreme severity. On the last occasion the deaths were 317 in Dumfries, and 114 in Maxwelltown, being 431 in a population of 14,000. The inhabitants drink the water of the Nith, a river into which the sewers empty themselves, their contents floating afterwards to and fro with the tide. Glasgow, which has been visited so severely with the malady, is supplied, as I understand, with water from the Clyde, by means of an establishment situated a little way from the town, and higher up the stream, and the water is professed to be filtered; but as the Clyde is a tidal river in that part of its course, the contents of the sewers must be washed up the stream, and, whatever care may be taken to get the supply of water when the tide is down, it cannot be altogether free from contamination. In the epidemic of seventeen years ago, the cholera was much more prevalent in the south and east districts of London, which are supplied with water from the Thames and the Lea, where these rivers are much contaminated by the sewers, than in the other parts of the metropolis differently supplied. And this is precisely what has occurred again, as will be shown further on.

The opinions now made known have been entertained by the author since the latter part of last year, and were mentioned by him to several medical gentlemen in the winter, – amongst others, to Dr. Garrod and Dr. Parkes; but he hesitated to publish them, thinking the evidence in their favour of so scattered and general a nature as not be likely to make a ready and easy impression. Within the last few days, however, some occurrences have come within his knowledge which seem to offer more direct proof, and have induced him to take the present course.

'Snow's Water Pump', London
Source: https://openverse.org/image/0f3b35c6-65c6-4ca1-93d2-b6e554e38f46?q=%22john%20snow%22%20pump

NOTE

1 The valuable analyses of Dr. Garrod have recently fully confirmed what had been stated in the former visitation of Europe by the cholera, viz., that the solid contents of the blood of patients labouring under this disease are greatly increased in proportion to the water a state of the blood that is not met with in any other malady.

Editorial Headnote

1817 (Glasgow)–1884

Robert Angus Smith was a chemist who became known as the 'Father of Acid Rain' for his groundbreaking research on this form of pollution, which, nearly a century later, became a central cause of political ecologists on the international stage.

Smith initially enrolled at Glasgow University at a young age to study divinity but dropped out and took up work as a private science tutor. When the family whose child he was tutoring emigrated from Scotland to Germany he accompanied them and subsequently completed a PhD in Chemistry at the University of Giessen in 1841.

On returning to the UK from Germany, Smith went to work as a chemist in rapidly industrializing Manchester. Here he became acutely aware of the polluting effects of the burning of sulphur-rich coal. In 1844, in a letter to the Manchester Guardian, he wrote:

> Coming in from the country last week on a beautiful morning, when the air was unusually clear and fresh, I was surprised to find Manchester was enjoying the atmosphere of a dark December day. . . . The gloominess of uncleanness is everywhere around us.
>
> (Smith 1844)

Smith became the Queen's Inspector of Alkali Works on the basis of the 1863 Alkali Act, which initiated limits on industrial emissions, and held this post until his death. The book sets out clearly his evidence for the phenomenon of acid rain, which he had actually proven some twenty years earlier. The case he makes for the presence of sulfuric acid in rainwater, and its variation in relation to location, was incontrovertible and paved the way for new scientific understanding of and legal action on pollution.

For a scientist, it is perhaps surprising that Smith was also interested in spiritualism and the occult. He kept this interest private for fear of undermining his scientific credibility (Reed 2014). He was also known for his love of the countryside. On his death, an obituary in Nature said of him:

> To keep the air in our towns fresh and wholesome, to restore the water of our streams to its pristine clearness, to preserve the freshness and verdure of the fields and woods, to sweeten the atmosphere of the crowded dwellings in cities, – this was the kind of work to which Smith dedicated his life, and at which he laboured to the very last.
>
> (Thorpe 1884)

DISCOVERING NATURE

Smith is buried where he made his name in Salford, and a Royal Society of Chemistry plaque at the site of his laboratory in nearby Manchester commemorates his huge contribution to the understanding of pollution.

pp. 225–228

20

AIR AND RAIN: THE BEGINNINGS OF A CHEMICAL CLIMATOLOGY

Robert Angus Smith

Source: Robert Angus Smith, *Air and rain: the beginnings of a chemical climatology* (1872)

RAIN

Rain has generally been considered as water simply, and its beneficial effects on man have been indefinitely summed up in the idea of refreshing. This, again, connects itself in our minds with temperature and moisture, whilst the purification of the air by washing has had little attention. If there is life and death in the air, we must believe the same of the rain, which collects solids and liquids, not omitting gases and vapours. These contents show themselves to chemical analysis and the microscope, so that distinctions between the air of different places may be known without the dangerous test on health. As this volume is a collection of early work in great part, it will be consistent to begin with my ideas when first finding practically how complicated the substance we call rain really is. It does not appear that I considered them new in principle, although new in some of their relations.

As I said before, I have nothing which I can call actually new to bring forward here, but it does still present some novel feature. The air was not examined as such, because I had not proper convenience for the experiments, and I was compelled therefore, merely to examine the rain. All the rain was found to contain sulphuric acid in proportion as it approached the town, and with the increase of acid the increase also of organic matter. The existence of albuminous compounds may be traced in the rain, however carefully collected, and the still further vestiges of living creatures, minute animalcules, may be found also. These creatures are sufficient of themselves to show the existence of phosphates, whilst sulphates and lime may be readily obtained. In examining the Thames water, I often found that the readiest way of collecting the phosphates and magnesia was to wait for the animalcules to do it. When the residue of the rain is burnt, an abundant evolution of ammonia may be obtained; but I have not ascertained the amount, because it varies much, and I do not well feel able to collect all the ammoniacal salts which may have existed in the rain, as so much loss is caused by evaporation, even if an acid is present. All results hitherto obtained must have been approximative and

DOI: 10.4324/9781003194651-26

too low. This organic matter, however, is capable of decomposing and of forming ammonia when it falls upon the ground, and of furnishing food to all kinds of plants. There is enough therefore to grow plants scantily, although experience shows that there is not enough to produce a crop of any value. I do not regard it, however, as the object of nature to manure the land by rain (this and other remarks would be modified were I to give present opinions); one more important and practical is to purify the air; and there is enough of evidence to show us that places entirely without organic matter may become covered with it, and also to show us that plants nourished even by rain-water only may be made to grow (that is, without the soil to feed them). This shows also the possibility of large quantities of impure matter being kept afloat in the air; indeed, it is scarcely possible to obtain the vapour of water without some such impure matter. The organic matter found in the rain seems to be in perfect solution, and no doubt the more decomposed portion of it at least is entirely so, but an exception must be made of that which is alive.

It becomes clear from the experiments that rain-water in town districts, even a few miles distant from a town, is not a pure water for drinking; and that, if it could be got direct from the clouds in large quantities, we must still resort to collecting it on the ground in order to get it pure. The impurities of rain are completely removed by filtration through the soil; when that is done there is no more nauseous taste of oil or of soot, and it becomes perfectly transparent. The presence of free sulphuric acid in the air sufficiently explains the fading of colours in prints and dyed goods, the rusting of metals, and the rotting of blinds, It has been observed that the lowest portions of projecting stones in buildings were more apt to crumble away than the upper; as the rain falls down and lodges there, and by degrees evaporates, the acid will be left and the action on the stone much increased.

I do not mean to say that all the rain is acid; it is often found with so such ammonia in it as to overcome the acidity; but in general, I think, the acid prevails in the town. But, even if alkaline when it falls, it becomes acid on standing, and especially on boiling down, as the ammonia in these cases is separated from its acid.

A specimen taken in Greenheys fields, half a mile from the extreme south-west of Manchester, wind blowing west, had a peculiarly oily and bitter taste when freshly caught. A person to whom I gave some of it to taste supposed it had been put into a glass in which castor oil had been put. I had collected the water in a large meat-dish, which had been very carefully cleaned, and was then set on a stand about two feet from the ground during the rain. Thinking it possible that some fatty matter might have been adhering to the vessel in spite of all my care, and not being inclined to believe that such an amount of impurity could be found in that place, I used a platinum basin, which was carefully cleaned, and, to prevent all mistakes as to organic matter, kept red-hot for some time. There was, however, no difference to be perceived from that collected in the larger vessel. The rain was very alkaline and contained scarcely a trace of carbonic acid.

Boiling removes all taste, and standing alone removes the taste of the oily matter and leaves only the taste of smoke. The smoke here shows that it was not out of the range of chimneys, although the wind was west.

The taste was that of the flattest and most insipid water, which could not be drunk with pleasure, independently of the nauseous taste.

Editorial Headnote

1791 (Surrey)–1867

Michael Faraday was a world-renowned physicist and chemist who made huge contributions to the understanding of electromagnetism, including producing the first dynamo and formulating the laws of electrolysis. His contributions to the appreciation of pollution are less well known but, nevertheless, considerable and it is this that is profiled here.

Faraday was from a family of modest means and had a fairly limited formal education. As a young man, he worked as an assistant to the prominent chemist Humphry Davy, accompanying him on a scientific tour of Europe from 1813–15. In his early career as a scientist, it was in chemistry that he made his name, although he subsequently became most renowned for his work in physics (Encyclopedia Britannica).

Faraday was deeply religious and spent some time in the 1830s working as a deacon in the Sandemanian sect of the Church of Scotland but always maintained a high profile as a scientist and was much in demand. He was commissioned to work on many government projects, including environmental topics such as air pollution and mining safety. His ethical convictions, however, led him to refuse to assist the government with designing chemical weapons for the Crimean War (Croddy & Wirtz 2005).

In this letter, Faraday added his considerable clout to a growing campaign to act on the all-too-obvious pollution levels in the River Thames. The country's most eminent chemist describing the river as a "fermenting sewer" could scarcely be dismissed as journalistic hyperbole. However, with a government mindful of the significant costs of remedying this and Snow's evidence that diseases like cholera were transmitted via water only just starting to be accepted, the campaign was initially resisted. The appalling stench that pervaded through the Houses of Parliament was initially acted on only so far as to douse chlorine of lime on the curtains to counter it and for some parliamentarians to wear pegs on their noses.

Three years later the government finally acted on pollution in the Thames when a hot summer prompted an acceleration of the problem and 'the Great Stink' of 1858. As a consequence, the engineer Joseph Bazalgette was commissioned to construct a major integrated sewage system for London, still in operation today. Cholera rates in London soon plummeted and countless thousands of lives were saved by this action. At around the same time as Bazalgette began laying London's sewers, Faraday's brilliant mind began to start failing him and he retired to a Hampton Court residence provided to him by Queen Victoria. Whilst grateful for this recognition of his public service, he did, however, refuse a knighthood and remained the modest Mr Faraday until his death in 1867. He is buried in Highgate Cemetery.

21

OBSERVATIONS ON THE FILTH OF THE THAMES

Michael Faraday

Source: Michael Faraday, *Observations on the Filth of the Thames* (1855)

SIR,

I traversed this day by steam-boat the space between London and Hangerford Bridges between half-past one and two o'clock; it was low water, and I think the tide must have been near the turn. The appearance and the smell of the water forced themselves at once on my attention. The whole of the river was an opaque pale brown fluid. In order to test the degree of opacity, I tore up some white cards into pieces, moistened them so as to make them sink easily below the surface, and then dropped some of these pieces into the water at every pier the boat came to; before they had sunk an inch below the surface they were indistinguishable, though the sun shone brightly at the time; and when the pieces fell edgeways the lower part was hidden from sight before the upper part was under water. This happened at St. Paul's Wharf, Blackfriars Bridge, Temple Wharf, Southwark Bridge, and Hungerford; and I have no doubt would have occurred further up and down the river. Near the bridges the feculence rolled up in clouds so dense that they were visible at the surface, even in water of this kind.

The smell was very bad, and common to the whole of the water; it was the same as that which now comes up from the gully-holes in the streets; the whole river was for the time a real sewer. Having just returned from out of the country air, I was, perhaps, more affected by it than others; but I do not think I could have gone on to Lambeth or Chelsea, and I was glad to enter the streets for an atmosphere which, except near the sink-holes, I found much sweeter than that on the river.

I have thought it a duty to record these facts, that they may be brought to the attention of those who exercise power or have responsibility in relation to the condition of our river; there's nothing figurative in the words I have employed, or any approach to exaggeration; they are the simple truth. If there be sufficient authority to remove a putrescent pond from the neighbourhood of a few simple dwellings, surely the river which flows for so many miles through London ought not to be allowed to become a fermenting sewer. The condition in which I saw the

DOI: 10.4324/9781003194651-27

DISCOVERING NATURE

Thames may perhaps be considered as exceptional, but it ought to be an impossible stat, instead of which I fear it is rapidly becoming the general condition. If we neglect this subject, we cannot expect to do so with impunity; nor ought we to be surprised if, ere many years are over, a hot season give us sad proof of the folly of our carelessness.

I am, Sir,
Your obedient servant,
M. FARADAY.
Royal Institution, July 7

Editorial Headnote

South Wales had the worst river pollution in the country at the time of this meeting and subsequent press report. This was a combination of the usual problem of human effluent being deposited there added to the accumulation of waste from the particularly intensive industrialization of the region. Rural Sanitary Authorities (RSAs), such as the Cardiff Union branch described in this news report, had been set up after the 1872 Public Health Act extended already-existing legal anti-pollution measures for metropolitan areas to surrounding regions. An 1875 Public Health Act then extended the authority of the RSAs for policing their regions. In the context of rivers, this meant that such authorities were responsible for implementing the 1876 Rivers Pollution Prevention Act. The Cardiff RSA was responsible for forty-five parishes across Glamorgan – north of Cardiff – and a small part of West Monmouthshire. Much of this area at the time was still farmland but in the early stages of rapid industrialization and urbanization (Waddington 2018).

The report of the RSA meeting paints a bleak picture of raw sewage, industrial ashes and untreated toxic wastes entering directly into the region's waterways. Given this area's rapidly rising population and levels of industrialization, it was also a major undertaking to seek to counter the public health consequences of this. The press in South Wales and elsewhere tended to point the finger at RSAs for neglecting their duties as effectively as their metropolitan counterparts and being a paper tiger in the face of greedy captains of industry. Historian Waddington, however, convincingly argues that this was an inaccurate and lazy narrative: "For the Authority and for rural communities the presence of industrial pollutants in rivers was not a 'necessary' evil, but a source of alarm and focus of intervention" (Waddington 2018: 39). As the report shows, the RSA was not shy about naming and shaming those guilty of wilful pollution and could not be accused of downplaying levels of river contamination in Glamorgan. It did levy many fines against businesses that flouted the River Pollution Act and other public health standards but had a very tough job to do given the scale of what it was up against.

In 1894, the Cardiff RSA was merged into Cardiff Rural District Council as local governance evolved. Pollution continued to blight Glamorgan for some time, due to the further industrialization of the region, but the commensurate growth of legislation gradually improved public health standards through the twentieth century.

22

'POLLUTION OF GLAMORGANSHIRE RIVERS'

Cardiff Rural Sanitary Authority

Source: Cardiff Rural Sanitary Authority, 'Pollution of Glamorganshire Rivers' (1878)

The annual meeting of this authority was held at the offices of the clerk Mr W. P. Stephenson. There were present Messrs. R. O. Jones, T. W. Booker, Meyrick, G. Phillips, J. Watson, T. Moore, T. Williams, Rev. AV. W. Harries, and W. Bruce.

On the motion of Alderman C. W. David, seconded by Mr T. W. Booker, Mr R.O. Jones was unanimously re-elected chairman of the authority for the ensuing year. Mr JONES, on taking the chair, said that he was much obliged to the members for re-electing him. He would endeavour to perform the duties devolving upon him, as well as the time at his disposal would permit. He thanked the members also for the support he had received from them in the past.

The Medical Officer, Dr Granger, reported that the death-rate of the district for the past month was higher than the rate of the previous month, being 18 per thousand, while for March the death-rate was 17 per 1000. This increase had resulted not from any increase of disease in the district, but from a large number of inquests held, and from eight deaths of persons who were over 70 years of age. The sanitary condition of the district was fairly good. The total number of deaths was 28, the total number of births 40.

A letter was read from the manager of the Melingriffith and Pentyrch Works, with reference to a report by Mr Williams, one of the inspectors of nuisances, to the authority, respecting the deposit of ashes and injurious matter from these works in the River Taff. In the case referred to by the inspector, the deposit was made by some of the workmen against their express orders, and, if known, the parties would be severely punished. With respect to the deposit of ashes on the bank of the Taff, near the Melingriffith Works, that had been their custom for more than a century. and they considered they had a prescriptive right to do so. At the same time it did not interfere with the flow of water in the river, and it was only when the freshes were high that any of the ashes were washed away. He also contended that the ashes were perfectly innoxious. If the authority took steps to prevent their putting the ashes at this place, it would cost them several hundreds of pounds a year in providing a place for their deposit.

DOI: 10.4324/9781003194651-28

Mr Booker considered that the inspector, before making his report, should have seen their manager, and the injurious matter thrown into the river would have been at once stopped. He also considered that the saying clause in the Act freed them from any liability in throwing the solid injurious matter on to the bank.

The CHAIRMAN was of opinion that the question at issue was the fact of throwing cinders on the bank. There was a doubt whether even that would not be prevented by the Act, as Mr Booker admitted that the freshes washed away some of the ashes, and, therefore, the heap must, to some extent, interfere with the stream. He suggested that information should be laid before the magistrates, and when the case was decided upon, whoever it was against whom decided, should apply for a case, and take the matter to a superior court, when the question raised by Mr Booker would be decided.

The Clerk was instructed to take the case before the magistrates, and get up evidence on the case.

RIVERS POLLUTION

Mr Williams, one of the inspectors of nuisances, reported that, according to instructions he had received at the last meeting, he had proceeded to find out the chief causes of the polluted state of the river Taff, and followed the course of the river from Tongwynlais to Pontypridd. At Tongwynlais he found a small sewer, which was constructed about eighteen months ago by the Pontypridd Rural Sanitary Authority. The sewage from this river is discharged into the Tongwynlais brook; which forms the boundary of Cardiff and Pontypridd Unions. This brook flows into the Glamorgan Canal. At Walnut Tree and Taffs Well he found innumerable small but very offensive drains discharging their contents on the side of the river at Nantoarra, a small sewer belonging to the Pontypridd Rural Sanitary Authority discharging itself into the river. At Pontypridd and Treforest he found that the urban sanitary authority there use the rivers Taff and Rhondda as a common receptacle for all the accumulated filth of this district. Drains without number are to be found like festering ulcers on the sides of both livers, discharging their pestifereus contents into the already turbid streams. Here he found that the urban sanitary authority had recently constructed a 15-inch sewer in the village of Llangitfma, and through which they convey a large quantity of sewage directly into the river Taff. This authority also causes all the solid refuse collected within their district to be tipped into the stream. From Pontypridd he followed the river Rhondda to Treberbert. The first infringement he found was the tipping of ashes into the stream by the Great Western Colliery Company. At the Hafod Colliery, which is situated on the Llanwonno side of the river, they tip the whole of the rubbish brought out of the works into the river Rhondda. The respective owners of Llwyncelyn, Cymmer, Dinas, and Llwynpia collieries tip their ashes into the river. At Dinas he found a sewer, belonging to the Pontypridd Rural Sanitary Authority, and with which all the houses there are connected, discharging its contents into the stream. From this point the district on each side is under the control of the Ystrad Urban Sanitary Authority, and the polluted state of the river in this district is entirely due to the enormous quantity of sewage which is discharged into it from all directions through the public sewers, private drains, and open gutters. The Ffrwdamos brook, which forms the boundary between the district of the newly-constituted urban sanitary authority and that of the rural sanitary authority of the Pontypridd Union had been literally converted into an open sewer. The Ystrad side of this brook is studded with privies. The liquid house refuse of hundreds of houses built on each side is discharged into the brook through as many private drains, so that the liquid flowing along its bed partakes, by the time it reaches the river Rhondda, more of the character of sewage diluted with water than a stream of water contaminated with sewage. At Ystrad, Treorky, and Treherbert he found the river Rhondda most seriously polluted by the sewage which is carried into it at each of those places by means of the public sewers and open channels. He said he had not attempted to describe in detail all the objectionable matter brought from almost every point into the river. The authority would be better able to estimate the alarming extent to which this river is polluted when it is stated that the Rhondda Valley at the present time contains a population of 40,000, and the river Rhondda is the only channel through which the sewage from so vast a multitude is removed. With respect to the river Rummey, he had inspected this river to the Bedwas Bridge. At Machett, he found a quantity of ashes tipped into it from the Machett Tin Works. About a mile higher up a large tin-plate and ironworks, known as the Waterloo Tin-plate and Ironworks, have been lately constructed. Here he found a poisonous water, which was produced in the washing of tin, and which is discharged into the river without any attempt being made to purify it. He considered this source of pollution a very grave one, and one which, if allowed to exist, would cause a great amount of mischief. From Bedwas Bridge he followed the course of the Parrot Brook as far as Caerphilly. This brook receives all the sewage from the town of Caerphilly. The sewage was brought into it through a sewer belonging to the Pontypridd Rural Sanitary Authority. The mouth of this sewer is about 400 yards below the town. He was informed by the farmers living in the neighbourhood of Machen that the river above Bedwas Bridge was badly polluted at times by a liquid discharged in to it from certain chemical works situated at Maesycwmmer. and which liquid on such occasions renders the water in the river so offensive that the cattle glazing on its banks would not partake of it.

The CHAIRMAN said the report was a very disagreeable one. He suggested that a copy of it should be sent to the several rural and sanitary authorities interested in it. and that their attention should be called to the statements made in it. A copy of it should be also sent to the Local Government Board.

This was agreed to.

Mr Waring produced his scheme for the drainage of the city of Llandaff into some fields by the side of the river Taff. The plans were approved of, and

Mr Waring was directed to send a detailed estimate of the cost to the Local Government Board for their approval. He also produced a Plan for the supply of the parish of St. Nicholas with water at a cost of £1,300, but he was directed to test the supply of water from a spring before the next meeting, at a cost not exceeding £10. This was all the business.

Editorial Headnote

1820 (County Carlow)–1893

John Tyndall was an Irish physicist and pioneer of climate science. He was from a poor Southern Irish Protestant family but still managed to receive a relatively good education. On leaving school, he initially worked for the Ordnance Survey, first in Ireland and then in England, before taking up science teaching. He then decided to embark on an academic and scientific career.

Like Robert Angus Smith, Tyndall studied for a PhD in chemistry in Germany working under the supervision of the eponymous Robert Bunsen. He was a friend and associate of Michael Faraday, whom he worked alongside at the Royal Institution of London as a professor in natural philosophy. He also wrote the first biography of Faraday. Furthermore, he was a close friend of Thomas Huxley – working with him in the scientific 'X Club' – and was, similarly, greatly influenced by Charles Darwin. With Huxley, he was a strong advocate of secularism in his writing and speeches, as well as advancing the cause of scientific education. Amongst his scientific accomplishments is giving his name to the Tyndall Effect, which describes how sunlight is diffused by dust and molecules in the atmosphere. As well as progressing the understanding of climate, this served as the basis for answering the age-old question, 'Why is the sky blue?' (Encyclopedia Britannica).

In 1859, Tyndall proved that carbon dioxide, along with other gasses and water vapour, had a 'greenhouse effect' in the Earth's atmosphere. These substances were shown to absorb heat, meaning that it was not just the Sun's direct infrared radiation that warmed the planet. This explained an existing conundrum as to why the Earth's atmosphere was warmer than could be rationally accounted for through the direct effects of sunlight alone. These findings formed the basis for the full appreciation of global warming or climate change over a century later.

Tyndall died of an accidental overdose of choral hydrate intended to treat his insomnia after retiring to live with his wife in Haselmere. He is buried there. Britain's foremost research institute on the subject, the Tyndall Centre for Climate Change, at the University of East Anglia in Norwich, is suitably named in his honour.

23

ON RADIATION THROUGH THE EARTH'S ATMOSPHERE

John Tyndall

Source: John Tyndall, *On Radiation Through the Earth's Atmosphere* (1863)

Nobody ever obtained the idea of a line from Euclid's definition, The idea is obtained from a real physical line drawn by a pen or pencil, and therefore possessing width, the notion of width being afterwards dropped by a process of abstraction. So also with regard to physical phenomena: we conceive the invisible by means of proper images derived from the visible, and purify our conceptions afterwards. Definiteness of conception, even though at some expense to delicacy, is of the greatest utility in dealing with physical phenomena. Indeed it may be questioned whether a mind in physical research can at all enjoy peace without having made clear to itself some possible way of imaging those operations which lie beyond the boundaries of sense, and in which sensible phenomena originate.

It is well known that our atmosphere is mainly composed of the two elements oxygen and nitrogen. These elementary atoms may be figured as small spheres scattered thickly in the space which immediately surrounds the earth. They constitute about 99½ per cent. of the atmosphere. Mixed with these atoms we have others of a totally different character; we have the molecules, or atomic groups, of carbonic acid, of ammonia, and of aqueous vapour. In these substances diverse atoms have coalesced to form little systems of atoms. The molecules of aqueous vapour, for example, consist each of two atoms of hydrogen united to one of oxygen; and they mingle as little triads among the monads of oxygen and nitrogen, which constitute the great of the atmosphere.

A medium embraces our atoms; within our atmosphere exists a second and a finer atmosphere, in which the atoms of oxygen and nitrogen hang like suspended grains. This finer atmosphere unites not only atom with atom, but star with star; and the light of all suns, and of all stars, is in reality a kind of motion propagated through this interstellar medium. This image must be clearly seized, and then we have to advance a step. We must not only figure our atoms suspended in this medium, but we must figure them vibrating in it. In this motion of the atoms consists what we call their heat. 'What is heat in us,' Locke perfectly expressed it, 'is in the body heated nothing but motion.' We must figure this motion communicated

DOI: 10.4324/9781003194651-29

DISCOVERING NATURE

to the medium in which the atoms swing, and sent through it with inconceivable velocity, Motion in this form, unconnected with ordinary matter, but speeding through the interstellar medium, receives the name of Radiant Heat; and if competent to excite the nerves of vision, we call it Light.

Aqueous vapour is an invisible gas. If vapour be permitted to issue horizontally with considerable force from a tube connected with a small boiler, the track of the cloud produced by the precipitation of the vapour is seen. What is seen, however, is not vapour, but vapour condensed to water. Beyond the visible end of the jet the cloud resolves itself again into true vapour. A lamp placed under the jet cuts the cloud sharply off, and when the flame is placed near the efflux orifice the cloud entirely disappears. The beat of the lamp completely prevents precipitation. This same vapour may be condensed and congealed on the surface of a vessel containing a freezing mixture, from which it may be scraped in quantities sufficient to form a small. When a luminous beam is sent through a large receiver placed on an air-pump, a single stroke of the pump causes the precipitation of the vapour a cloud within. This, illuminated by the beam, produces upon a screen behind a richly coloured halo, due to diffraction by the little cloud.

The waves of heat from our earth pass through our atmosphere towards space. These waves meet in their passage the atoms of oxygen and nitrogen, and the molecules of aqueous vapour. Thinly scattered as these latter are, we might naturally think meanly of them as barriers to the waves of heat. We might imagine that the wide spaces between the vapour molecules would be an open door for the of the undulations; and that if those waves were at all intercepted, it would be by the substances which form 99½ per cent. of the whole atmosphere. It had, however, been found that this small modicum of aqueous vapour intercepts fifteen times the quantity of beat stopped by the whole of the air in which it was diffused. It was afterwards found that the dry air then experimented with was not perfectly pure, and that the purer the air became the more it approached the character of a vacuum and the greater, by comparison, became the action of the aqueous vapour. The vapour was found to act with 30, 40, 50, 60, 70 times the energy of the air in which it was diffused; and no doubt was entertained that the aqueous vapour of the air which filled the Royal Institution theatre, during the delivery of this discourse, quenched 90 or 100 times the quantity of radiant heat absorbed by the main body of the air of the room.

Looking at the single atoms, for every 200 of oxygen and nitrogen there is about 1 molecule of aqueous vapour. This 1, then, is 80 times more powerful than the 200; and hence, comparing a single atom of oxygen or nitrogen with a single molecule of aqueous vapour, we may infer that the action of the latter is 16,000 times that of the former. This is very astonishing result, and it naturally excited opposition, based on the philosophic reluctance to accept a fact of such import before testing it to the uttermost. From such opposition a discover, if it be worth the name, emerges with its fibre strengthened; the human character gathers force from the healthy antagonisms of active life. It was urged that the result was on the face of it improbable; that there were, moreover, many ways of accounting for

174

it, without ascribing so enormous a comparative action to aqueous vapour. For example, the cylinder which contained the air in which these experiments were made, stopped at its ends by Plata of rock-salt, on account of their transparency to radiant heat. Now rock-salt is hygroscopic; it attracts the moisture of the atmosphere. Thus, a layer of brine readily forms on the surface of plate of rock-salt; and it is well that brine is very impervious to the rays of heat. Breathing for a moment on a polished plate of rock-salt, the brilliant colours of thin plates (soap bubble colours) flash forth, these being caused by the film of moisture which over-spread the salt. Such a film, it was contended, is formed when undried air is sent into the cylinder; it was, therefore, the absorption of a layer of brine that was instead of the absorption of aqueous vapour.

This objection was met in two ways: First by showing that the plates of salt when subjected to the strictest examination show no trace of a film of moisture. Secondly, by abolishing the plates of salt altogether, and obtaining the same results in a cylinder open at both ends.

It next surmised that the effect was due to the impurity of the laboratory air, and the suspended carbon particles were pointed to as to be cause of the capacity to heat. This objection was met by bringing air from Hyde Park, Hampstead Heath, Primrose Hill, Epsom Downs, a field near Newport in the Isle of Wight, St, Catharine's Down, and the sea-beach near Black Gang Chine. The aqueous vapour of the air from these localities intercepted at least 70 times the amount of radiant heat absorbed by the air in which the vapour was diffused. Experiments made with dry smoky air proved that the atmosphere of West London, even when an east wind pours over it the smoke of the city, exerts only a fraction of the destructive powers exercised by the transparent and impalpable aqueous vapour diffused in the air.

The cylinder which contained the air through which the calorific rays passed being polished within, the rays striking the interior surface were reflected from it to the thermo-electric pile. The following objection was raised: – You permit moist air to enter your cylinder; a portion of this moisture is condensed as a liquid film upon the interior surface of your tube; its reflective power is thereby diminished; less heat therefore reaches the pile, and you incorrectly ascribe to the absorption of aqueous vapour an effect which is really due to diminished reflexion of the interior surface of your tube.

But why should the aqueous vapour so condense? The tube within is warmer than the air without, and against its inner surface the rays of heat are impinging. There can be no tendency to condensation under such circumstances.[1] Further, let 5 inches of undried air be sent into the tube – that is, one-sixth of the amount which it can contain. These 5 inches produce their proportionate absorption. The driest day, on the driest portion of the earth's surface, would make no approach to the dryness of our cylinder when it contains only 5 inches of air. Make it 10, 15, 20, 25, 30 inches: you obtain an absorption exactly proportional to the quantity of vapour present. It is next to a physical impossibility that this could be the case if the effect were due to condensation. But lest a doubt should linger in the mind, not only were the plates of rock-salt abolished, but the cylinder itself dispensed with.

DISCOVERING NATURE

Humid air was displaced by dry, and dry air by humid in the free atmosphere; the absorption of the Aqueous vapour was here manifest, in all the other cases.

No doubt, therefore, can exist of the opacity of this substance to the rays of obscure heat; and particularly such rays are emitted by the earth after it has been warmed by the sun. It is perfectly that more than 10 per cent. of the terrestrial radiation from the soil of England is stopped within 10 feet of the surface of the soil. This one fact is sufficient to show the immense influence which this newly-discovered property of aqueous vapour must exert on the phenomena of meteorology.

This aqueous vapour is a blanket more necessary to the vegetable life of England than clothing is to man. Remove for a single summer-night the aqueous vapour from the air which this and you would assuredly destroy every plant capable of being destroyed by a freezing temperature. The warmth of our fields and gardens would pour itself unrequited into space and the sun would upon island held fast in the iron grip of frost. The aqueous vapour constitutes a local dam, by which the temperature at the earth's surface is deepened: the dam, however, finally overflows, and we give to space all that we receive from the sun.

The sun raises the vapours of the equatorial ocean; they rise, but for a time a vapour screen spreads above and around them. But the higher they rise, the more they come into the presence of pure space, and when, by their levity, they have penetrated the vapour screen, which lies close to the earth's what must occur?

It has been said that, compared molecule with atom, the absorption of a molecule of vapour is 16,000 times that of air. Now the power to absorb and the power to radiate are perfectly reciprocal and proportionate. The atom of aqueous vapour will therefore radiate with 16,000 times the energy of an atom of air. Imagine then this powerful radiant in the presence of space and with no screen above it to check its radiation. Into space it pours its heat, chills itself, condenses, and the torrents the consequence. The expansion of the air, no doubt, also refrigerate it; but in accounting for the deluges, the chilling of the vapour by its own radiation must play a most important part. The rain quits the ocean as vapour; it returns to it as water. How are the stores of beat set free by the change from the vaporous to the liquid disposed of? Doubtless in great part they are wasted by radiation into space. Similar remarks apply to the cumuli of our latitudes. The warmed air, charged with vapour, rises in columns, to penetrate the vapour screen which hugs the earth; in the presence of space, the bead of each pillar wastes its heat by radiation, condenses to a cumulus, which constitutes the visible capital of an invisible column of saturated air.

Numberless other meteorological phenomena receive their solution, by reference to the radiant and absorbent properties of aqueous vapour. It is the absence of this screen, and the consequent copious waste of heat, that causes mountains to be so much chilled when the sun is withdrawn. Its absence in Central Asia renders the winter there almost unendurable; in the Sahara the dryness of the air is sometimes such that, though during the day 'the soil is fire and the wind is flame,' the chill at night is painful to bear. In Australia, also, the thermometric range is enormous, on account of the absence of this qualifying agent. A clear day, and a dry day, moreover, are very different things. The atmosphere may possess great visual clearness while it is charged with aqueous vapour, and on such occasions great chilling cannot occur by terrestrial radiation. Sir John Leslie and others have been perplexed by the varying indications of their instruments on days equally bright – but all these anomalies are completely accounted for by reference to this newly-discovered property of transparent aqueous vapour. Its presence would check the earth's loss; its absence, without sensibly altering the transparency of the air, would open wide a door for the escape of the earth's heat into infinitude.

NOTE

1   This was saying too much. Professor Magnus has proved the existence of a kind of condensation under the conditions named.

Editorial Headnote

1835 (London)–1898

Ernest Hart was an eminent eye surgeon, long-time editor of the British Medical Journal, chair of the National Health Society, and, in the extract that follows, is speaking principally in his capacity as a founder of the Smoke Abatement Institution. His father was a dentist, and he had a comfortable upbringing in London. Hart trained as a medic, at St George's Hospital, after failing to procure a scholarship at Cambridge University due to its anti-Semitic rules and proceed to have a good career as a surgeon (Nature 1898). It is as a campaigner and socially conscious journalist, however, that he is best remembered.

Hart served as a Poor Law inspector in the 1860s and became a firm advocate of social reform. His research led to the creation of Metropolitan Asylum Boards by the government which improved the care of the insane. Hart was also a passionate advocate of vaccinations against smallpox and other diseases and published a book rebuking anti-vaccination sentiment, The Truth About Vaccination: An Examination and Refutation of the Assertions of the Anti-Vaccinators (1880).

As detailed in the extract, Hart worked with Octavia Hill of the Kyrle Society in forming the Smoke Abatement Committee (which later changed its name to Institution). As he notes in this lecture, awareness of – and even some action against – urban smog actually dated back many centuries. The Smoke Abatement Committee sponsored several well-attended exhibitions showcasing smoke-prevention technologies and lobbied the government for a Royal Commission on urban smoke pollution and a bill regulating emissions from newly built houses (via Lord Strathedan & Campbell). Both of these initiatives were unsuccessful but, in the long run, Hart and the institution did much to advance the cause of legislating against urban pollution. Hart died of the effects of diabetes in his fifties, which had previously caused him to have a leg amputated. An obituary in the British Medical Journal states:

> IN the sphere of public health and preventive medicine Mr. Ernest Hart has been one of the foremost leaders of the reforms which have been secured during the past quarter of a century. At the commencement of his career the public mind had not yet fully grasped the great principles of sanitation, although the persistent efforts of the earlier reformers Southwood Smith, Chadwick, Simon, and others-were beginning to take effect. Mr. Hart brought his keen intellect to bear on the glaring evils of the time, and by a persistent attack on one blot after another he let light into many of the dark corners of our social life. He had the not too

179

common gift of seizing the most favourable opportunity for securing attention to glaring evils, and he had the tact and courage to persevere until the reforms he had in view were attained.

(BMJ 1898: 177)

pp. 3–9

24

SMOKE ABATEMENT: A LECTURE DELIVERED IN THE LECTURE ROOM OF THE INTERNATIONAL HEALTH EXHIBITION

Ernest Hart

Source: Ernest Hart, *Smoke abatement: a lecture delivered in the lecture room of the International Health Exhibition* (July 21, 1884)

There are so many sides upon which the question of smoke abatement may be considered, and there is so much to be said both from an historic point of view and from the point of view of present action, that it is impossible that I should treat all parts of the theme in the short half hour to which these lectures are in mercy to their audiences usually confined. I shall not therefore to-day say much upon one aspect of the subject on which it is, however, extremely and essentially necessary that there should be some public enlightenment, I mean the subject of combustion generally, but I shall refer to the present and past position of smoke abatement as an administrative and legislative, rather than as a purely scientific movement. I have son1e hopes that other members of the Smoke Abatement Institution; specially well qualified to deal with the scientific part of the question, such as Professor Chandler Roberts, or Captain Douglas Galton, will, at a later date, deal with the technical side of the question.

The question is not a new one in this country, but has a history extending back nearly 600 years. We find that in the year 1306, when coal had come into considerable demand in London, Parliament complained of the injurious effects to health and property arising from the use of coal, and the king adopted an effectual means of checking the evils arising from smoke, for he absolutely prohibited the use of coal. Later on, in the reign of Elizabeth, a motion was introduced into Parliament to prohibit the use of coal on account of the noxious vapours and smoke arising from it, which were considered very prejudicial to the health, especially of persons who were unaccustomed to it.

From this time the minds of public and scientific men were occasionally exercised in protesting against the evils of smoke production and in devising suitable means for its abatement. But it will only be necessary to allude to Sir Hugh Platt

DOI: 10.4324/9781003194651-30

181

in 1594, to Evelyn's eloquent protest in his *Fumifugium* in 1661, to Benjamin Franklin's efforts in 1745, to those of James Watt in 1795, and Count Rumford in the first decade of the present century, in their well-sustained warfare against smoke and its attendant evils. In 1819 the national importance of the smoke question was admitted in a very practical way by the appointment of a Select Committee of the House of Commons, "to inquire how far persons using steam engines and furnaces could erect them in a manner Jess prejudicial to public health and comfort." The Committee reported that" so far as they had hitherto proceeded they confidently hope that the nuisance, so universally and so justly complained of, may at least be considerably diminished, if not altogether removed." In 1843, another Select Committee "inquired into the means and expediency of preventing the nuisance of smoke arising from fires or furnaces." The list of witnesses examined by the committee comprised the honoured name of Farraday, and, as the report points out, "they received the most gratifying assurances of the confident hope entertained by several of the highest scientific authorities examined by them that the black smoke proceeding form fires and private dwellings, and all other places, may eventually be entirely prevented." They concluded by recommending "that a Bill should be brought into Parliament to prohibit the production of smoke from furnaces and steam engines." In May 1845 yet another Select Committee of the House reported "that in the present state of knowledge and experience upon the subject, it is not desirable to extend the provisions of an Act beyond furnaces used for the generation of steam."

In August 1845, Sir Henry de la Beche and Dr. Lyon Playfair reported to Lord Canning "that it cannot for a moment be questioned that the continued emission of smoke is an unnecessary consequence of the combustion of fuel, and that, as an abstract statement, it can be dispensed with." They added, however, "it is useless to expect, in the present state of our knowledge, that any Jaw can be practically applied to the fireplaces of common houses, which, in a large town like London, contribute very materially to the pollution of the atmosphere."

It was not, however, till 1880 that a substantial attempt was made, by the National Health Society at my instance and with the co-operation of Miss Octavia Hill on behalf of the Kyrle Society to organise public opinion and scientific research; nor was it till the formation of our Smoke Abatement Committee in 1880 that any substantial effort was made to ascertain what the present state of our knowledge of the subject generally really is. An interesting series of reports published from time to time mark the stage of progress which has now been reached, and I shall have occasion later on to show how abundant have been the results of the labours of this Committee during the three years that we have been at work; one result of their work is shown in this Exhibition and elsewhere by the large number of persons, representing all classes and interests, who are now fully sensible of the importance of the subject; and, further, there is abundant and satisfactory evidence, in London and in the chief provincial towns, of anxiety to adopt any improved appliances for burning fuel, or any smokeless forms of fuel, when their merits have been fairly proved.

The Smoke Abatement Exhibition which we organised in 1881 in part of these buildings placed at our disposal for the purpose by the Royal Commissioners, with the approval of the authorities at South Kensington, stimulated and encouraged inventors, manufacturers, and others, and aroused a healthy spirit of competition in the production of smoke abating appliances. At the Smoke Abatement Exhibition, buildings were fitted up for the purpose of testing the efficiency of grates, stoves and other appliances suited for domestic use; and trials of various fuels and boiler appliances were also provided in the Exhibition buildings, in the Royal Albert Hall, and at certain factories where facilities were afforded. This series of mechanical and physical tests were conducted by Mr. D. Kinnear Clarke, C.E., and the chemical investigations on the effluent gases of the flue by Professor Chandler Roberts, F.R.S. The results obtained by these gentlemen and by their competent assistants were of a unique kind, and no pains were spared to ensure their completeness. The results are preserved in a permanent form in the Report of the Smoke Abatement Committee of 1882, published by Messrs. Smith, Elder & Co. It would be well if architects and others officially concerned, and all persons whose duty it is to determine on the question of rates, were to consult that report. Quite recently I found that two of my friends had placed themselves in the hands of eminent architects and asked them to fit up suitable grates for the prevention of smoke. In one case the gentleman who stands in the foremost rank of his profession frankly avowed himself ignorant of the subject and under some unhappy inspiration chose for this new mansion the class of grates which was shown by the test at the Smoke Abatement Exhibition to produce the very worst results, and in the other case the architect, who was one of the most eminent architects in the kingdom, said he did know all about the subject, and yet, strange to say, he chose the same grate, which proved that he had never even looked at the results which had been obtained, and was still in a state of dense ignorance of the results actually achieved, and of the facts proved. Only two days ago I met in this Exhibition a gentleman who is the architect and adviser for one of the largest building estates in the kingdom, and I found he had never read this report or ascertained what were the results arrived at upon the subject. He asked me, "Have you come to any result-what can I advise, is there any grate at all which will lessen smoke? Have you got any result?" He was so great a man that I did not like to tell him the results had been under his eyes for some time, so I promised to take him over the present Exhibition and point out some of the results of the Smoke Abatement Exhibition of 1881, and to bring under his attention some of the successes which had been attained. That is not very encouraging, but I can only hope that as we have made those results available to the public, and as our opinion can be brought to bear upon these learned gentlemen – learned in their own profession and able to appreciate, although regardless at present of the results obtained by others – that they will give attention to those results. I am bound to say that I consider it not altogether creditable to the Royal Society of Architects or to any of the great architectural societies, that some one of their members has not abstracted and criticised for the use of these societies the practical results which have been obtained by these physical and chemical tests, and that architects as a body seem at present to be quite unaware of their extent and importance, and to have learned none of the lessons which are clearly set out. I venture upon this somewhat strongly worded expression of opinion because, with the great respect which I have for those gentlemen, I believe that practically at the present moment it lies very much in their hands whether the information and the conclusions which we have obtained shall be buried, or whether they shall be vital and progressive and lead to the great results they are capable of leading to, especially with respect to new houses. I think it little less than a scandal that, notwithstanding the promises which have been made to us by the heads of many of the Government Departments, no systematic steps have yet been made, and more particularly by the Department of which my distinguished and able friend Mr. Shaw-Lefevre is the head, to apply these results. Some time ago trials were carried on at the Arsenal and very good results obtained, of which the First Lord of the Admiralty must have had cognizance, and yet no steps have been taken to make the results available either for the Institution or the Arsenal, to which it was promised they should be made available, nor to any of the ships of her Majesty's Navy. When I had the honour of going through the Exhibition with that most intelligent and distinguished lady the Empress Eugenie, I found she was not only extremely interested in the question from. the domestic and sanitary point of view, but she at once said, "This is a matter of great importance to ships of war, and that is what interests me. When a steamer is seen at a distance the first thing you see, and the first thing which gives notice to an enemy which approaches, is the steam coming from its funnel." She said, "I feel interested in this for the sake of the war vessels as well as for the sake of the ordinary abuse in the production of dense smoke in steamers which traverse the rivers of our great towns." I am bound to refer to these instances, owing to the indifference shown to the results already obtained, because I believe that nothing but a strong public opinion brought to bear upon the heads of departments, and upon the respective technical professors, and the respective professional men employed in the construction of houses and the sanitation of cities will make the results which we have obtained fructify, or will lead to the progress of which the first elements are undoubtedly already prac-tically furnished in this most valuable report.

In the remarks which follow, I propose to deal: 1, with the objections which have been raised to the prosecution of the movement; 2, to trace the steps which have been taken in collecting evidence as to the extent to which the evil exists, and the possibility of abating it; and to indicate the individual efforts which appear to be demanded by the evidence adduced; 3, to offer a brief statement as to the results which have been attained and are within reach.

Some objections have been made to the movement on the ground that it is not a new one, and that the public have the evils arising from smoke so fully brought before them as to render unnecessary the formation of a society for the purpose. It is true, as we have already seen, that the movement is not a new one, as it existed in a crude form from a very early period. Royal proclamations prohibited the production of smoke, and various appliances for preventing its production were devised, but until the formation of the Smoke Abatement Committee, over which I have had the honour to preside, In virtue of my labours in initiating it, the subject had never been treated as one of public importance, and even national interest, nor had the description of the extent and character of the evils associated with the production of smoke been brought in a clear and definite way before the public.

. . .

pp. 14–15

During the five years, 1868–73, the average death-rate from disses of the respiratory organs was 2.27 per 1,000 in Westmoreland (one of the healthiest counties in England) and 2.51 in North Wales.

For the whole of England and Wales it was 3.54; for Salford, 5.12; and for the Registration district of Manchester, 6.10. Taking, however, the township of Manchester alone, it appears that in 1874, the last for which returns have been published by the RegistrarGeneral, the death-rate from these diseases amounted to 7.7 or three times the average of healthy districts, and more than double the general average for town and country districts – healthy and unhealthy. If, therefore, the rate could be reduced to the average for all England, there would be an annual saving of more than 700 lives in Manchester alone. In 1873 the deaths in Westmoreland from diseases of the respiratory organs were 13.7 per cent of the total deaths from all causes; in North Wales also 13.7 per cent; in all England and Wales 17.2 per cent; in Birmingham, 18.2; in Liverpool, 18.7; in Sheffield, 21.0; and in Manchester, 21.6 per cent; but excluding the out townships, the rates in the township of Manchester alone amounted to 23.2 per cent. It appears, therefore, that Manchester suffers more from diseases of respiratory organs than any other town or city in England; and it may be safely affirmed that if no means can be found of reducing the number of deaths from this class of diseases, it is hopeless to expect that any material improvement can be made in the general state of the public health, or any sensible reduction effected in the general death-rate of the city. All authorities who have investigated the question are agreed that, in the case of manufacturers, future legislation should deal with the sulphurous acid given off as from the combustion of coal in large furnaces, as a noxious vapour, and that a large part of the injury close to vegetation and to public buildings in the neighbourhood of such factories is due to the production of sulphurous acid.

. . .

pp. 25–27

Until the Smoke Abatement Committee was formed and a centre was established to which general interest in the subject could converge, the public were never adequately informed of the extent of the evil nor aroused to the necessity for concerted effort to abate it. No machinery by which the evil could be seriously grappled with had been provided, but in saying this, I do not disparage the efforts of those who have gone before, who are entitled to be considered as pioneers. They warned us against the evils of smoke, and even in some cases provided means for avoiding it to a great extent. The legislation which they initiated had the effect of reducing the smoke of certain districts, yet in spite of individual and isolated efforts, the excessive production of smoke has increased, growing with the growth of our cities, and the strides of our industrial progress. Self interest has, it must be borne in mind, done much within the last three or four years to check the evil, as was recently stated at Glasgow.

The future progress of the cause must depend mainly on the extent to which the public interest is awakened to recognition of the necessity and desirability of change, and on the choice of the time at which this influence is brought to bear. If public support is prompt in encouraging and extending the movement now in active existence, scientific ingenuity and commercial interests will naturally be stimulated to continue efforts in an increasing ratio to supply public demand.

It is only by enlisting general public interest, now fairly awakened by the smoke-abatement movement, that present results have been attained, and we may now, without incurring the ridicule· which at first attached to our efforts, reasonably indulge the hope of ultimate success in abolishing a smoke-laden atmosphere. I would quote the eloquent words of Sir Frederic Leighton, who said at the Mansion House, "If each individual would say, 'My fireplace shall smoke no longer,' the millenium would have come." The means exist and are accessible to all, and I am satisfied that London is now sensibly less smoky than when we began to work.

In conclusion, I may say that I do not believe that the Bill which has been brought in by Lord Stratheden and Campbell is destined to very serious consideration at present in Parliament, because it has been brought in under circumstances which, highly honourable as they are to the noble lord who has introduced the Bill, are not the circumstances under which an important measure of this sort ought to be brought in. It has not been brought in with the active aid of the leaders of any party, or with the assistance which we had a right to expect of the Home Office; and at the present time, valuable as is the proposed Bill for eliciting public opinion, I fear that it is powerless as regards legislation. We must look to the leaders and people, to those who are in authority and power, not to allow a measure of this sort to be bandied about in the House as a measure in which they have no interest, in the manner in which the House is apt to deal with mere crotchets that can be delayed from year to year. We claim for the measure of Lord Stratheden and Campbell official recognition by the Government, and we claim for it a reference to a Select Committee or to a Royal Commission which shall impartially investigate the facts that we can place before the Committee. We have arrived at a stage when, as we say, great progress has been made and great possibilities are open, and we ask for an official investigation into the statements made – not alone by myself, but by a committee including the official adviser of the Government at the Royal Mint, the Lecturer on Metallurgy, and the great master of the science of combustion in this country, Professor Chandler Roberts, and on statements made by Mr. Kinnear Clark, and by Captain Douglas Galton, as well as by Dr. Frankland, and other high scientific authorities. All I have tried this evening to do, I know very imperfectly, but I hope earnestly, has been to promote a great public cause, which up to the present has been wholly carried on by private effort. We shall continue to carry the cause on though there are limits beyond which unaided private enterprise should not be solely relied upon. We believe that we have now reached that limit and that Government should step in to help us to solve this important question, and to give effect to the reforms which have been achieved.

Editorial Headnote

1859 (Preston)–1932

John William Graham was a mathematician, scientist, theologian and political reformer. He was a Quaker and attended Friends' Schools before attending university at University College London and Cambridge. He then embarked on a teaching career in mathematics, which led him to become an influential principal of Dalton Hall (a forerunner of Manchester University established by the Quakers) in 1897. It is in this capacity that Graham wrote the book extracted here, urging reform to combat urban smoke pollution.

Graham was part of the Quaker Renaissance that sought for their faith to evolve away from evangelical preaching to modernize and, in particular, embrace new scientific thinking and engage in movements seeking political reform. John Pease, profiled in Volume II Part 1 for his contributions to advancing animal welfare legislation, had been a pioneer of this movement and become the first Quaker to enter parliament. Like Pease, Graham took up the cause of animal rights and was a prominent anti-vivisection campaigner. He also stood for election for the Liberals, although he was unsuccessful.

Combatting urban pollution was one of several political causes Graham engaged with in civil society, and it became a focus of his work in his later life. He was chairman of the Smoke Abatement League from 1909 to 1925 (Dales 2020).

Graham's reverence for John Ruskin (profiled in Volume I Part 2) is evident in this passage and elsewhere in the book. He also name-checks William Morris and Thomas Carlyle for their community-mindedness, both of whom are also profiled in the next part of this volume. In 1904, a Ruskin exhibition had taken place at Manchester, featuring Ruskin himself along with many of his 'Pre-Raphaelite' protégés, at which Graham paid tribute to his work in critiquing industrialization. Graham went on to write The Harvest of Ruskin, elaborating on this thesis (Graham 1920). In spite of his liberalism, we can see that Graham criticizes laissez-faire economics and sees greed and individualism as responsible for the social evil of pollution. He does not, however, wholly oppose industrialization so much as the reason that it needs to be regulated in the public interest. He also argues that this would not be so difficult a task, just a case of overcoming greed and complacency: 'It will be a task for the future social historian to explain why the English of our time were content to live in dirty and gloomy air'.

pp. 1–5

25

THE DESTRUCTION OF DAYLIGHT.
A STUDY IN THE SMOKE PROBLEM

John Graham

Source: John Graham, *The Destruction of Daylight. A Study in the Smoke Problem* (1907)

CHAPTER 1

Smoke

Before the days of modern cities smoke could be sent up into the clean air without harm. The sky was relatively so vast that the atmosphere was not seriously dirtied before the carbon and the sulphur acids descended along with the rain harmlessly again to the earth. But the air can no longer be kept clean without regulation. There have been added to the domestic fires of our crowded towns pillars of black cloud which the manufacturers pour into the air as if the air were their own. Similarly there were ages when men were few, and the happy hunting grounds of earth and water were free to all: these have long passed into the stage of private property or special right in a way in which the indivisible and unfenceable air can never pass.

But land and water have reached a third stage, in which the community, by legislation, by taxation and by manifold bye-laws of local bodies, has in the public interest asserted its paramount and original rights. Everything points to a tendency to strengthen the hold of the State upon the land. This third stage has to be reached for the atmosphere without passing through the second as the time has long ago come when the community can no further neglect to guard or to resume its indefeasible inheritance of pure air, as a necessity not perhaps of mere life, but of health and ordinary happiness. We live more close to the air than we do to the land or the water; we bathe in it all the time it not only affects our clothes and our skins but we breathe it with all its impurities into those delicate passages of the lungs which were made for the abode of its pureness only. To foul the air is to condemn us all in the most intimate fashion to dirt and darkness and to a sad universal ugliness.

Sunlight among the foliage of green trees or dappling the pure stream – sunshine on grass or on distant hills – clear gleams after rain – golden settings and risings – these are the lovely things of the earth. On sunshine depends the beauty of all

DOI: 10.4324/9781003194651-31

glorious animals and plants, of the peacock butterfly and the daisy of the field. We too are creatures of sunshine by nature and inheritance; to be deprived of light is to us a species of starvation and imprisonment. The town dweller of to-day has in fact ceased to expect to live in sunshine; but he is descended from ploughmen and milkmaids, who for countless generations before the factory system arose, lived open to the sun. Our organisms, which have been developed through these generations to meet this environment, still need it, and must plainly suffer for want of sunshine. We know too well the pale children of our streets, the weakly delicate young women of our towns. Why do they differ from country children with their robust limbs and tanned faces? Why are they denied the happy health of the company one meets at a village flower show? Food and wages and Sanitation are probably better in the towns. The atmosphere is largely responsible for the difference, aggravating all overcrowding; and the atmosphere is made what it is by smoke.

On a single page of the Manchester Guardian this morning a particularly careful observer states that really clear summer days in Cheshire are fewer of recent years, due to the extension of manufactories and an increased output of smoke; and a Philistine correspondent objects to the building of a new Art Gallery because you cannot observe objects of art on more than 15 per cent. of the days in a year. (This conclusion is, of course, nonsense, for is there not electric light?)

We are told by Charles Booth that Londoners do not survive as Londoners beyond the third generation, but some of our great cities are smokier and less healthy than London through burning a smokier coal, The race is being made weak, bloodless, and depressed; for about four-fifths of our people live in towns under a smoke cloud. Sir Thomas Barlow says concerning health: "Recent investigations have shown that the value of direct sunlight is absolutely untold."

Dr. Tatham, the Medical Officer of Health for Manchester, stated in his report in 1890 that the working life of people in Manchester township, which is the central part of the city, and not worse than many other towns, was curtailed by ten years. They are worn out ten years before their time. The average expectation of life among men from 1881–90 was stated by him to be for England and Wales 43.66 years; for the country districts 51.48 years; for Manchester 28.78 years. Our people lose 30 per cent of their lives, says Dr. Tatham. What days of weariness and pain, what encroachment of weakness and ill-health in the prime of life, – all this means. The acids of smoke and its carbon particles operate upon the lungs for years before they finally destroy them.

. . .

pp. 141–146

CHAPTER XI

Final

This book has been written in a restrained style, and depends for its effect on the eloquence of its facts. I close with a few words to the makers of smoke.

THE DESTRUCTION OF DAYLIGHT. A STUDY IN THE SMOKE PROBLEM

Although an economical method of combustion is likely to pay in the long run, a reform doubtless means a fresh investment of capital on apparatus, or on providing new boiler room, or installing a gas or electric plant. This will not be done without compulsion in all cases. But there can be no genuine ground of complaint by a firm who overwork their boilers and thereby make smoke. Restriction will only put them on the level of their competitors who work their boilers normally. There will be no added burden on the trade as a whole in such a case.

In any case the public welfare is here so important and in such need of safeguard that I think the public is justified in insisting that for ease in their businesses – businesses, it happens, in which most of our very wealthy men have been, or are, engaged, and have become wealthy thereby – men shall not be allowed to spoil the lives of Englishmen in general. Reforms of this kind always produce some hardship and much outcry, but time justifies them. They are in the regular time of progress. I believe that this is really the most curable of all our great national evils. It is not much complicated with other evils; it is not a deep-seated organic disease of the body politic, like poverty or unemployment, or low wages; not deeply ingrained in vicious natures like drink or gambling; not a traditional barbarism like war; it is just a piece of criminal negligence that could be cured in twelve months to our economic advantage, if the public conscience were awake and the magistrates ready to support public opinion. The engineers have done their part; there is a mechanical device to suit every one; but England goes on choking in gloomy fogs and breathing soot. It is altogether an error to say that "Dirt is cheap." Dirt is dear.

It will be a task for the future social historian to explain why the English of our time were content to live in dirty and gloomy air. He will probably explain that it was a survival of the worship of that careless god Laisaez Faire, under whose easy rule much wealth had been collected; that they who had made the wealth were the chief sinners, and though they were not bad or cruel the exercise of thought was a great effort to them, and their thoughts were already crowded with other affairs. They passively resisted the law, and the English people have always been patient, and also very busy; they even deceived themselves into the belief that a smoky chimney was a sign of active prosperity, and that "where there's reek there's brass." We have inherited smoke from that noble but chaotic period when philanthropy was individualistic – when the franchise and free trade and the abolition of tests and taxes occupied Bright and Gladstone and Cobden. But it is time we gave heed rather to Kingsley and Ruskin, Morris and Carlyle, with their greater sense of the community, and their claim upon the State to regulate individualism. The pile of the feudal castle has given way to the greater pile of the modem factory. Every class in every age in whose control lie the means of production and consequent power over others, needs watching for the public weal. No class has ever been fit to be entrusted with imfettered power; and the modem manufacturing firm or capitalist, wise and good as he often is individually, is no exception to that rule. In what I have said I have been obliged to treat a most excellent class of the community as though they were public enemies, whereas we

193

DISCOVERING NATURE

know that they are neither better nor worse than the rest of us; that they are men who are bearing great responsibilities, and often honestly wishful to benefit their workpeople. Therefore I wish to guard myself against any undue personal severity in what I have said with regard to this serious public evil. It is always the case that the few who are wealthy and powerful tend to form a system of conduct which, without any personal ill-will or voluntary tyranny, presses hardly upon the poor. We admire the feudal castles of the days gone by, but they, alas, were the centres of tyranny and terror to the serfs who tilled the ground around them. These huge factories surrounded by working people's houses are politically different from that feudalism, but it is still as necessary to maintain and defend the common rights of the public to health and happiness as ever it was in the days of the feudal masters of England. Those old barons too had the duties of their chivalry. They wielded power for the rescue of the weak. To-day knightly service must be rendered under the quieter name of public duty. Those in danger of oppression are not the aristocratic dames nor the dispossessed heirs, but the workmen and work-girls of the nation. Their health, joy, and beauty, our modem knighthood must surely guard from the sulphurous smoke of their own mills. We would fain persuade the better-minded mill owners that to make smoke is disgraceful, inconsistent with self-respect and good will, and we want a public opinion determined to coerce the careless and selfish ones with an effective law.

REFERENCES

Aberdeen Weekly News (1888) October 20th: 5.

Anker, P (2002) *Imperial Ecology: Environmental Order in the British Empire 1895–1945*, Cambridge USA: Harvard University Press.

Arrhenius, S. (1896) 'On the Influence of Carbonic Acid in the Air Upon the Temperature of the Ground'. London, Edinburgh and Dublin Philosophical Magazine and Journal of Science (5th Series) vol. 41: 237–275.

Beatson A. (1816) *Tracts Relative To The Island Of St. Helena: Written During A Residence Of Five Years*, London: Bulmer.

Beinart, W. & Hughes, L. (2007). *Environment and Empire*, Oxford: Oxford University Press.

BMJ (1898) 'Obituary. Ernest Hart, M.R.C.S, D.C.L.' *British Medical Journal Jan 15: 175–186 www.bmj.com/content/bmj/1/1933/175.full.pdf* (accessed 12.6.2022)

Brown, J.C. (1878) 'On Forest Schools', *Transactions of the Royal Scottish Arboricultural Society*, 8: 225–232.

Burchell, W. (1822) *Residence in Cape Town and Rambles in the Vicinity*, Hurst, Reese, Orme & Brown.

Caldwell, C. (1830) *Thoughts on the Original Unity of the Human Race*, New York: Bliss.

Carson, R. (1962) *Silent Spring*, Harmondsworth UK: Penguin.

Clarke, A. (2004) *Oxford Dictionary of National Biography*, Oxford: Oxford University Press.

Cleghorn J. (1855) 'On the fluctuations in the herring fisheries'. *Journal of the Statistical Society of London* 18 (3): 240–242.

Cleverely, L. (1987) *W.J. Burrell. Special Agent or Naturalist? A Short Biography*, Edenvale, S. Africa: Prestige.

Dales, J. (2020) *The Quaker Renaissance and Liberal Quakerism in Britain, 1895–1930: Seeking a Real Religion*, Leiden & Boston: Brill.

Darwin, C. (1859) *On the origin of species by means of natural selection, or the preservation of favoured races in the struggle for life*. London: John Murray.

Darwin, C. (1969). (Barlow, N. ed)., *The Autobiography of Charles Darwin 1809–1882*, London: Collins.

Dominick, R. (1992) The Environmental Movement in Germany: Prophets and Pioneers 1871–1971, Chichester: Wiley.

Driver, F. (1988) 'Moral Geographies: Social Science and the Urban Environment in Mid-Nineteenth Century England', *Transactions of the Institute of British Geographer* 13(3): 275–287.

Ehrlich, P. (1968) *The Population Bomb*, New York: Ballantine.

Faraday, M. (1855) 'Observations on the Filth of the Thames', letters, *The Times*, July 7, 1855.

Farr, W (1877) Economic Value of Population Registrar – General's 39th Annual Report London: Sanitary Institute, Reproduced in: *Population and Development Review* 27(3) (Sep.): 565–571.

Ferguson-Cradler, G. (2021) 'The Overfishing Problem: Natural and Social Categories in Early Twentieth-Century Fisheries Science', *Journal of the History of Biology* 54, 719–738.

Fisher, W. (1894) 'Afforestation in the British Isles'. *Nature* 49: 601–603.

Fuller, H. (1848) 'On the Use of the Arsenic in Agriculture-Poisoning by Arsenic, and Symptoms of Cholera-The Possible Effect of the Game Laws', *The Lancet* 2: 648.

Gilbert White's house (2022) https://gilbertwhiteshouse.org.uk/gilbert-white/ (accessed 29.09.2022)

Graham, J. (1907) *The Destruction of Daylight. A Study in the Smoke Problem*. London: George Allen.

Graham, J. (1920) *The Harvest of Ruskin*, London: Allen & Unwin.

Grove, R. (1995) *Green Imperialism: Colonial Expansion, Tropical Island Gardens and the Origins of Environmentalism*. Cambridge: Cambridge University Press.

Guardian (2018) www.theguardian.com/books/2018/may/11/gilbert-white-fourth-most-published-book-in-english-language-natural-history-and-antiquities-of-selborne-to-go-online (accessed 25/11/2022)

Haeckel, E. (1866) *Generelle Morphologie der Organismen*, Berlin: Verlag von Georg Reimer.

Hardin, G. (1968) 'The Tragedy of the Commons', *Science*, 162: 1243–8.

Hart, E. (1884) *Smoke abatement: a lecture delivered in the lecture room of the International Health Exhibition, July 21st, 1884*, London: William Clowes and Sons.

Heincke, F. (1894) 'Die Ueberfischung der Nordsee und Schutzmaßregeln dagegen'. *Sonder Ausdruck Aus Den Mittheilungen Der Sektion Für Küsten- Und Hochsee-Fischerei* 3: 1–24.

Hempel, S. (2006) *The Medical Detective John Snow, Cholera and the Mystery of the Broad Street Pump* London: Granta.

Jeremy, D. (1973) 'British Textile Technology Transmission to the United States: The Philadelphia Region Experience, 1770–1820', *The Business History Review*, Spring, 1973, 47(1): 24–52.

Jevons, W. (1866) The Coal Question; *An Inquiry concerning the Progress of the Nation, and the Probable Exhaustion of our Coal-mines,* 2nd edition, revised, London: Macmillan.

Jstor (2022) Roxburgh, William (1751–1815) on JSTOR (accessed 25.02.2021)

Kelly, J., Scarpino, V., Berry, H., Syvitski, J., & Meybeck, M. (eds) University of California Press.

King, V. (2001) 'Arsenic' *History Magazine*, October/November.

Lankester, E. (1884) The scientific results of the exhibition. International Fisheries Exhibition, 1883, *Literature*, 4, 443–446.

Lloyd, W.F. (1980) 'On the Checks to Population', reproduced in: *Population and Development Review*, Sep., 6(3): 473–496.

Luckin, B. (2003) 'The Heart and Home of Horror': The Great London Fogs of the Late Nineteenth Century, *Social History*, 28(1) (Jan): 31–48.

REFERENCES

Macloed, R. (1971) 'The Support of Victorian Science: The Endowment of Research Movement in Great Britain, 1868–1900', *Minerva*, April 1971, 9(2) (April): 197–230.

Malthus, T. (1798) *An Essay on the Principle of Population, as it Affects the Future Improvement of Society with Remarks on the Speculations of Mr. Godwin, M. Condorcet, and Other Writers*, London: Johnson.

Nature (1871) *August 17th.*

Nature (1898) 57: 251–252.

Nature (1907) 75: 179–181.

Nature (1932) 129: 389–390.

Nature (1933) 'The Iron and Steel Industry', *Nature* 131, 335–336 (1933).

Newton, A. (1861) 'Abstract of Mr. J. Wolley's researches in Iceland respecting the gare-fowl or great auk (*Alca impennis*, linn.)', *Ibis 3*, 374–399. https://archive.org/stream/zoologist20lond/zoologist20lond_djvu.txt (accessed 12.12.2021)

Nobbs, P. (1956) 'A pioneer of botany and forestry at the Cape of Good Hope'. *Journal of the South African Forestry Association* 27: 86–89.

O'Brien, P. (2022). Was the British industrial revolution a conjuncture in global economic history? *Journal of Global History, 17*(1), 128–150.

Osbourne, P. *Oxford Dictionary of National Biography*, Oxford: Oxford University Press.

Parkins, W. & Adkins, P., (2018) "Introduction: Victorian Ecology and the Anthropocene", *19: Interdisciplinary Studies in the Long Nineteenth Century* 26. doi: https://doi.org/10.16995/ntn.818

Prichard, J.C. (1855) *The natural history of man: comprising inquiries into the modifying influence of physical and moral agencies on the different tribes of the human family* (4th ed), London: Wilson and Ogilvy.

Reed, P. (2014) Acid Rain and the Rise of the Environmental Chemist in Nineteenth Century Britain. The Life and Work of Robert Angus Smith, London: Ashgate.

Rackham, O. (1986) *The History of the Countryside*, London: Dent.

Roderick, G. & Stephens., M. (1982) "Scientific Education in England and Germany in the Second Half of the Nineteenth Century." *The Irish Journal of Education/Iris Eireannach an Oideachais* 16(1): 62–83.

Roxburgh, W. (1795) *Letter to Joseph Banks* https://transcripts.sl.nsw.gov.au/page/letter-received-banks-william-roxburgh-25-april-1795-series-2054-no-0001 (accessed 13.12.2021)

Roxburgh, W. (1820) *Flora Indica. Or Descriptions of Indian Plants*, (Ed. W. Carey), Serampore: Mission Press.

Simon, J. (1981) *The Ultimate Resource*, Princeton: Princeton University Press.

Smith, R.A. (1872) *Air and rain: the beginnings of a chemical climatology*, London: Longmans, Green, and Co.,

Smith, R.A. (1844) *Manchester Guardian* November 2nd.

Somerville, W. (1909) 'Forestry in Some of its Economic Aspects' *Journal of the Royal Statistical Society*, 72(1) (Mar. 1909): 40–63.

Snow, J. (1849) *On the Mode of Communication of Cholera*. London: John Churchill.

South Wales Daily News (1878) 'Pollution of Glamorganshire Rivers'

May 9 1878: 3 South Wales Daily News – Welsh Newspapers (library.wales) (accessed 30.09.2022)

Stanford (2015) 'William Jevons', *Stanford Encyclopedia of Philosophy* https://plato.stanford.edu/entries/william-jevons/ (accessed 25.23.2022)

Stewart, R. and Warner, B (2012) 'William John Burchell: The Multi-skilled Polymath' *South African Journal of Science*: 108.

Tansley A. (1914) 'Presidential Address' *Journal of Ecology*, 2(3) (Sep., 1914), pp. 194–202.

Thorpe, T. (1884) 'Robert Angus Smith', *Nature* 30: 104–105.

The Times (1854) August 1st.

Tyndall, J. (1863) 'On radiation through the earth's atmosphere', *The London, Edinburgh, and Dublin Philosophical Magazine and Journal of Science*, 25:167: 200–206.

Von Humboldt, A. & Bonpland, A. (1819) *Personal Narrative of Travels to the Equinocital Regions of America: During the Years 1799–1800*, volume *4*, London: Longman.

Waddington, K. (2018). 'Vitriol in the Taff: River Pollution, Industrial Waste, and the Politics of Control in late Nineteenth-Century Rural Wales', *Rural History*, *29*(1): 23–44.

White, G. (1789) *The Natural History and Antiquities of Selborne in the County of Southampton: with Engravings and an Appendix*, London: White & sons.

Wilkening, K. (2004) Acid Rain Science and Policy in Japan: A History of Knowledge and Action Toward Sustainability. Cambridge: MIT.

Williams, J. (1789) *The Natural History of the Mineral Kingdom*, Edinburgh: Ruddiman.

Wool, D. (2001) 'Charles Lyell – "the father of geology" – as a forerunner of modern ecology', *Oikos* 94: 385–391.

Part 2

ROMANTICIZING NATURE
Environmental Conservation as a Nationalistic Artistic and Political Movement in Nineteenth-Century Britain

CHRONOLOGY OF ENVIRONMENTAL CONSERVATION AS A NATIONALISTIC AND ARTISTIC MOVEMENT IN THE NINETEENTH CENTURY

1798   William Wordsworth and Thomas Coleridge's *Lyrical Ballads* launches the romantic movement

1826   Zoological Society of London established

1830   William Cobbett's *Rural Rides* published

1836   Charles Dickens's first novel *Pickwick Papers* published

1841   Young England political grouping formed.

1843   Wordsworth becomes Poet Laureate

1848   Pre-Raphaelite Brotherhood formed

1850   Tennyson becomes Poet Laureate

1865   Commons Preservation Society formed

1867   Scots émigré John Muir undertakes his 1,000-mile wilderness walk in the US

1869   Sea Birds Preservation Act sponsored by Percy Duke of Northumberland

1876   William Morris launches the Society for the Protection of Ancient Buildings

1878   Anna Sewell's *Black Beauty* published

1879   Manchester Corporation Waterworks Act establishes that environmental effects can be considered in authorizing damming of Thirlmere

1883   Lake District Defence Society launched by John Ruskin

1883   Thomas Hardy's *The Dorsetshire Labourer* published

1884   Disused Burial Grounds Act restricts sale after campaign led by Octavia Hill and Lord Brabazon.

1885   Selborne Society founded

1888   Alfred Tennyson made president of the Selborne Society

1890   Sequoia and Yosemite National Parks established in the US by John Muir

1896   Light Railways Act makes it obligatory for environmental impacts to be assessed

1898   Coal Smoke Abatement Society founded by Lord Meath and artist William Blake Richmond

1899   Wicken Fen becomes Britain's first nature reserve

1912   Society for the Promotion of Nature Reserves launched

DOI: 10.4324/9781003194651-33

VOLUME I PART 2 INTRODUCTION

The rise of environmental conservationism in the nineteenth century was, in some ways, a facet of the emergent phenomenon of nationalism. Along with major scientific advances, industrialization in nineteenth-century Britain and elsewhere manifested itself in the rise of nationalism as modernizing societies came to become more aware of their and other national identities through state socialization (such as via state education or conscription) and communications advances. People came to have more of a sense of who they were and were not in identity terms than in previous ages. Although it is too abstract a concept to precisely date, it is generally accepted that national identity essentially evolved from the nineteenth century when greater numbers of ordinary people, better able to travel and communicate, began to become more aware of people from other countries and were hence able to perceive of their own societies as having certain distinguishing characteristics (Anderson 1991; Smith 1991). Prior to this age, the vast majority of a population would never meet people from other countries and know very little about them so any sense of 'self' and 'other' could not really form. Whilst organized states existed in the medieval and ancient world, very few of their inhabitants could meaningfully identify as nationals of those states. For instance, people living along the Nile valley thousands of years ago paid taxes and used currencies organized by the pharaohs, but they could not be said to have Egyptian identities since hardly any of them had any reference point for what might link them and millions of others in North-East Africa and distinguish them as a collectivity from Greeks, Romans, Persians or any other peoples. By the nineteenth century, however, many 'ordinary' Britons had some means of differentiating themselves from other Europeans and elites had greater means and motivations to encourage this. Uniting all of a country's people to work and fight together necessitated 'nation-building': finding ways to bind them together and build loyalty.

This construction of national identities often came to particularly feature the glorification of the domestic landscape and a romanticization of traditional rural culture. Thus, the environment came to be valued by state elites and nationalists to a much greater degree than seen before. Hence, the political right and aristocracy came to be more clearly associated with the advance of the politics of conservation in Britain, as well as in Germany, Scandinavia and elsewhere in the

DOI: 10.4324/9781003194651-34

203

industrializing world of the late nineteenth century. In spite of peasants becoming mobilized by insecurities in the face of food and land shortages, conservation became chiefly an elitist 'top-down' movement, quite distinct from the more bottom-up 'new middle class' environmentalist social movement that later emerged from the 1960s. The aristocracy could claim to be the saviours of peasant lives and culture in the course of seeking to save themselves from the 'new middle class' of the nineteenth century: urban Liberal industrialists.

In England, this 'environmental nationalism' chiefly manifested itself around the preservation of lakes and village greens threatened by industrialization whilst in other countries different natural resources came to symbolize the nation. In Germany, for instance, deforestation was the key concern since German national identity idealized the ancient Teutonic tribes of the Black Forest and other woodlands. For the English, 'the green and pleasant land' came to be defined more in terms of lakes, pastures and the verdant rural landscape in general. The Scots and Welsh looked more to the mountains that defined their countryside and differentiated them from England, more in line with, for instance, Norwegian or Italian nationalists seeking to solidify their emerging countries at around the same time. The 'Emerald Isle' of Irish national identity is somewhat analogous to the English focus on pasture, lakes and coastline.

Lowenthal notes that the construction of 'Englishness' – like other national identities – was very much a late nineteenth-century phenomenon.

> The now hallowed visual cliche – the patchwork of meadow and pasture, the hedgerows and copses, the immaculate villages nestling among small tilled fields – is in fact quite recent; only after the pre-Raphaelites did the recognisably 'English' landscape become an idealised medieval vision, all fertile, secure, small-scale, seamed with associations.
>
> (Lowenthal 1991: 213)

Such a consensus on these defining characteristics of the English landscape – along with the lionizing of key historical and mythical figures such as Alfred the Great, Robin Hood and King Arthur – was far less apparent in the seventeenth or eighteenth century. At that time, far fewer Britons were being taught or reading about such iconic figures or sites. Kumar similarly asserts that the 'moment of Englishness' came just before the dawn of the twentieth century (Kumar 2000: 592). Prior to this 'moment' there was a lack of consensus across the country on national heroes or symbols in the way that we have had since the nineteenth century. This reflects the general subjectivity of national identity but is particularly so in Britain because the country lacks the obvious figures or events associated with a particular defining historical moment – such as achieving independence – that most nations have. There is no date for Britons comparable to 1789 for the French or 1776 for the US Americans.

In the US and other white-settler states, independence and national unity also came to be expressed via nature. The pioneering spirit underpinning this form of nationalism was very landscape-focused, often equating human colonization with the conquest of nature in a positive sense. The landscapes of North America, Australia and New Zealand were, at one level, revered for their purity and openness but, on another, viewed as dangerous wildernesses in need of taming. A missionary zeal underpinned colonial settlers so that 'nature was treated as an obstacle to be overcome, an uncivilized place of darkness to be filled with the light of God's teaching' (Kaufman 1998: 669). We can see this in the words of British émigré John Muir in extolling the godly virtues of the pristine American countryside. Muir was a huge figure in environmentalism, influencing the groundbreaking conservational policies of President Theodore Roosevelt and pioneering the idea of national parks and setting up one of the world's first conservation nongovernmental organizations, The Sierra Club. However, Muir has become a controversial figure as his idealisation of nature was also racist. Whilst eulogising the mountains, trees and animals of America, he refers to the native peoples of that country as: 'ugly', 'hideous' and having 'no right place in the landscape' (Muir 1894: 46). Here again, then, conservationism is a product of elitism, nationalism and imperialism.

AESTHETES AND CONSERVATION

British art in the nineteenth century took a romantic turn, and this came to feed into environmental nationalism. Prominent intellectuals of the age railed against the ugly sides of industrialization and social modernization that were manifesting themselves across a country at the forefront of this 'progress' and advocated a return to pre-industrial labour values and aesthetics. John Ruskin's promotion of Britain's Pre-Raphaelite painters, William Morris's 'Arts and Crafts' movement and the celebration of traditional rural life in the poetry of Tennyson, Wordsworth and Coleridge and novels of Austen, Hardy and Eliot all equated Englishness with the shrinking traditional countryside rather than its booming cities. The Pre-Raphaelite Brotherhood was a label applied to a group of painters (and poets and critics) in 1848, including John Millais and Dante Gabriel Rossetti, who eschewed modern styles and desired to return art to the era of the early Italian Renaissance. An important part of this movement was embracing an appeal made by Ruskin for artists to '[g]o to Nature in all singleness of heart, and walk with her laboriously and trustingly, having no other thought but how best to penetrate her meaning, rejecting nothing, selecting nothing, and scorning nothing' (Ruskin 1843: 418). As becomes evident in reading the selected extracts here and surveying art and literature of this age more generally, this reverence for nature became tied up with the nationalism of celebrating the traditional English countryside. Englishness and Britishness, far from being celebrated for coming to politically or economically dominate the world, were being seen as threatened by the forces of industrialization and urbanization Britain had given birth to.

Charles Dickens, profiled in Volume II Part 1, because of his more overtly political sentiments, remains the strongest literary voice contrasting British economic growth with its urban decay. Much of this artistic movement, however, was not nationalistic in terms of romanticizing peasantry in a social context. As is evident in their extracts here and in many of their other works, Morris and Hardy championed the cause of rural artisans in a practical, humanistic way. Morris's Arts and Crafts movement, certainly, was politically utopian and socially reformist but aesthetically desired a return to a pre-industrial golden age. These conservationists were aesthetes insofar as seeing beauty as having value in terms of engendering human improvement, but they also valued artisan craftsmanship and the empowerment of the poor. Many of the nineteenth century's best-known literary figures based much of their work on the preservation of rural life and landscape against urbanization and industrialization.

However, nineteenth-century scientific and academic progress was not necessarily anathema to the cause of environmental conservation and sometimes came to blend with aesthetic sentiment. Lloyd's 'tragedy of the commons', set out in this volume part, found expression in Britain in the Commons Preservation Society, established in 1865 by Robert Hunter, who later set up the still-influential conservationist group the National Trust. This movement resisting the enclosure of common lands, such as village greens, woodlands and footpaths, actually dated back to the seventeenth century when this phenomenon began but was mobilized into a prominent national campaign by the likes of Hunter and Olivia Hill, profiled in this volume part. In 1883 the artistic and literary giant John Ruskin established the Lake District Defence Society, which succeeded in restricting much rail construction in England's most picturesque countryside. Ruskin, Morris and others also lent their support to the commons preservation movement, and this form of collaboration between aesthete conservationists was a prominent phenomenon of the time, as can be seen throughout this volume part.

A spin-off of Ruskin's anti-rail campaigning coalesced around a proposal to transform Lakeland's Thirlmere into a reservoir to serve the burgeoning Manchester metropolis, and this became a cause célèbre. Many local businessmen supported the damming project because of the likely economic boost to the region, but one exception was local aesthete William Somervell. Somervell was an associate of Ruskin and produced the pamphlet in which his anti-rail protest extracted here was published. Somervell mobilized popular support to restrict the reservoir project through the Thirlmere Defence Association (TDA) and lobbied parliament over a bill authorizing the Manchester Corporation to proceed. Luminaries lined up to support the TDA including Octavia Hill, William Morris, Thomas Carlyle – all profiled here – along with the poet Matthew Arnold and pre-Raphaelite sculptor Thomas Woolner. The campaign failed to stop the damming and conversion of Thirlmere into a reservoir but, nonetheless, the principle that aesthetics could trump economic interests was established in the run-up to the 1879 Act of Parliament that authorized this. At the parliamentary committee stage of the bill, it was recognized that 'the public at large has also an inheritance in the beautiful scenery of these mountains and lakes', and the much-delayed act set a precedent that such projects needed to take on board the natural costs (Ritvo 2009: 105).

VOLUME I PART 2 INTRODUCTION

These campaigns against the despoilment of beautiful lakes, woodlands and pastures were at heart aesthetic, but for some of the protestors, they came to represent part of a wider radical socio-economic critique of industrialization and capitalism. As is illustrated in several of the transcripts, some, like Wordsworth, Coleridge, Ruskin and Carlyle, were aesthetes but actually socially, as well as environmentally, conservative. For others, like Morris and his protégé Edward Carpenter, however, these protests resisting industrialization were very much socio-economic and they were pioneering an early incarnation of eco-socialism: critiquing capitalism as a whole as the root cause of environmental degradation.

CONSERVING NATURE AND THE ARISTOCRACY

On the other side of the political continuum from radicals such as Morris or Carpenter, the evolution of scientific and economic thought in nineteenth-century Britain also came to inform social conservatives. The logic of Malthus, Darwin and Lloyd also prompted concern from elites that they could be threatened by industrialization. The nation's and the Empire's resources could come to be exhausted and the traditional social order could be threatened by urbanization and pollution. The leading Conservative politician of the age, Benjamin Disraeli, pioneered the Young England movement which, very much in keeping with the logic of the tragedy of the commons, equated the importance of property rights with the responsible stewardship of the land by the aristocracy. In a similar vein, Forestry Schools came to be established by German gentry, which later merged into the influential Congress of German Foresters in 1872 as part of their national unification process. Pontin refers to this correlating of environmental with social conservatism as the 'patrician estate stewardship paradigm' (Pontin 2014: 766). Whilst serving their own interests, there was some substance to the notion of the landed gentry as conservationists if we consider their tenants were usually under a legal obligation to conserve woodlands and hedgerows in their small holdings.

More clearly ecocentric, whilst still a product of agrarian romanticism and patrician conservatism, was the emergence of policy for the preservation of birds in the nineteenth century which enjoyed the patronage of the aristocracy. As discussed in this volume part, the advance of naturalism played a big role in this, but it was a cause very much latched onto by the landed gentry. In Britain, the Sea Birds Preservation Act of 1869 – featured in Volume II Part 1 – was sponsored by Percy Duke of Northumberland. The Wild Birds Protection Act 1880 and later the launch of the Society for the Protection of Birds (SPB) resulted from concerns at the possible extinction of birds favoured for hunting and plumage in hats was led by wealthy women Emily Williamson and Eliza Phillips. Similarly, in Germany the Bird Protection Bill of 1890 had the regal backing of the Hohenzollern family.

For the aristocracy, industrialization meant more than the loss of countryside; it represented an existential threat. As Woods expresses, 'the nobility of the country gentry was portrayed as a reflection of the nobility of the countryside' (Woods 2005: 29). As is developed in Volume II Part 1, conservation became a key

207

dimension of political conservatism as part of the cause of sustaining the natural order. It represented part of the chivalrous duties and responsibilities of noble Lords as guardians of the countryside. Sociologically this represented some of the last vestiges of feudalism. A new agrarian elite was emerging with farmers as well as industrialists and merchants empowered by the social change. As is apparent in the words of literary figures such as Austen and Hardy and political figures such as Disraeli and Cobbett, the demise of feudalism was seen as something to lament rather than regard as progress. The Duke of Wellington (profiled in Volume II Part 2) in 1833 lamented:

> The revolution is made, that is to say, that power is transferred from one class of society, the gentlemen of England, professing the faith of the Church of England, to another class of society, the shop-keepers, being dissenters from the Church, many of them Socinians, others atheists.
>
> (Jennings 1884)

Much of the politics of nature conservation hence became ultra-conservative in a social sense. As well as elitism, there are strong elements of racial supremacy in the words of Disraeli, Cobbett, Muir and, particularly, Carlyle. Disraeli, although notably not of Anglo-Saxon stock, laments the political usurpation of this ethnic group by the Normans eight centuries ago and sees urbanization as a continuation of this alien-led process. Cobbett and Carlyle similarly extol Anglo-Saxon virtues as synonymous with the traditional English countryside threatened by urban 'others' such as the Jews. On a wider level, Cobbett and Carlyle also viewed the enslavement of black Africans in the empire as part of the natural order and comparable to the keeping of cattle in a rural setting.

Elitist conservation, however, could still be progressive in an environmental sense. With the expansion and consolidation of the Empire in the nineteenth century, some British aristocrats came to internationalize their stewardship of nature duties to include the preservation of Asian and African animals. As discussed in Volume II Part 2, for some, this was an extension of the desire to preserve 'big game' for the survival of hunting rather than the species themselves. However, the likes of Raffles, Russell and Rothschild were more scientifically informed and initiated the idea of zoological parks and nature reserves with a clearer biodiversity agenda. The referent object of nineteenth-century aristocratic conservation was, at one level, themselves, but it was also, at another, nature.

CONSERVATION AND FEAR OF THE FUTURE

Political conservatism is, at heart, the ideology of fearing that change is often for the worse rather than the better or, 'if it aint broke don't fix it'. The Industrial Revolution had been the making of Britain's unprecedented global power but there was also fear that the social changes it was unleashing could break this. In the nineteenth century, environmental determinism came to inform national policies to a much greater degree than before, and in Britain, this particularly manifested itself in the consideration of imperial sustainability. Lord Meath added to the concern about the dwindling of key natural resources, discussed in later this part, by positing that urbanization was leading to the physical degeneration of young Britons, with potentially dire consequences for British global supremacy. Early defeats in the Boer War seemed to corroborate this assertion. Meath's theory was not without foundation. Recent research has demonstrated a correlation between height and pollution levels amongst men born in the 1890s (Bailey, Hatton & Inwood 2018). As we can see, even some young Liberals, such as Masterton and Wilson, rallied to this cause of embracing sustainability in order to sustain the British Empire. This wave of 'naturalistic nationalism' (Kaufman 1998) paved the way for the environment to be raised in prominence in the power politics of war and imperialism, as is explored in Volume II Part 2.

In line with this political pessimism, a more radical conservationist turn in literature came towards the close of the long nineteenth century with the rise of more apocalyptic storytelling inspired by fears of the consequences of the industrial revolution. Hay's *The Doom of the Great City*, prophesizing London's destruction in an environmental catastrophe, was, at one level, a trashy Victorian equivalent of contemporary disaster movies but, on another level, clearly a result of creeping social anxiety about urban pollution. Of the many writers to develop this new genre of shock science fiction, undoubtedly the most enduring has been H.G. Wells. Wells, however, far from viewing technological development as sowing the seeds of humanity's doom considered that science could save humans from themselves and was the answer to the threat of imminent environmental collapse. As is illustrated, however, his utopianism receded as the horrors of the early twentieth century unfolded.

The elitist, statist and nationalistic environmentalism of the nineteenth century is quite distinct ideologically from the transnational, socially oriented political ecology that later emerged in the late twentieth century. Nevertheless, this was still environmentalism. Aristocrats and aesthetes using landscape to invoke the English or British nation often did still serve the interests of nature. Nationalism is complex and multi-faceted. The nation is a highly subjective concept, a 'we feeling' meaning different things to different people. It is also a highly emotive and powerful concept, and so a diverse array of politicians and artists have and continue to wrap themselves in the flag. The nationalism of acting on behalf of the nation hence can sometimes be socially radical but, at other times, socially conservative. Reverence for the old order in the face of change and the glorification of the traditional countryside and rural life makes environmental conservation a natural cause for political and artistic conservatism. The more radical and less elitist second wave of environmentalism from the 1960s sometimes leads us to lose sight of this.

2.1

AESTHETES AND CONSERVATION

Editorial Headnote

1772 (Devon)–1834

Samuel Taylor Coleridge was a poet, journalist and literary critic who was a pivotal figure in the romantic artistic movement that grew in nineteenth-century Britain. He was from a wealthy Devonian family – the youngest of fourteen siblings from his father's two marriages. His father, John, was a headmaster and vicar and Coleridge remained a devout Christian throughout his life. Coleridge was only eight when his father died, and he was sent to a boarding school in London, where his love of poetry and learning across disciplines was honed. He went to study at Cambridge but dropped out due to financial difficulties and enlisted in the army for a spell under an assumed name before turning to poetry (Encyclopedia Britannica).

Coleridge had a long friendship with fellow poet William Wordsworth (he moved to the Lake District to be close to him for several years), and together they founded the romantic movement initiated with their co-authored 'Lyrical Ballads', which included 'The Rime of the Ancient Mariner', perhaps his best-known poem. He travelled widely, including spending much time in Germany – together with Wordsworth – where he came to be influenced by the liberal philosophy of Immanuel Kant and other idealists. Politically, the young Coleridge was a radical utopian Liberal who was supportive of the French Revolution and the abolition of slavery and advocated cooperative living (in egalitarian communes he termed 'pantisocracies').

'The Raven' was written by Coleridge at around the same time as the much-better-known 'Rime of the Ancient Mariner'. Although deeper meanings can be attributed, at face value, this is a simple morality tale warning of the perils of human actions that are oblivious to their environmental consequences. The disasters that unfold after a sailor kills an albatross in the 'Rime of the Ancient Mariner' paint a similar picture. As such these were ecocentric calls for people to think and act beyond calculations of human utility. The romanticization of nature that defined these and other of Coleridge's works – such as 'The Nightingale' (1798) and 'Frost at Midnight' (1798) – reflected his conviction that humanity should be at one with other life forms. Extolling the beauty of nature in this way represented an antidote to seeing the wild as brutal and dangerous, intensified by the rise of pandemics in the nineteenth century and the onset of the Little Ice Age (Pontin 2014: 775–776). Coleridge's liberalism equated human liberty with nature and the natural order, expressed particularly in relation to the French Revolution in 'France: An Ode' (1798).

In later life, Coleridge moderated his politics, but an eco-centric conviction was maintained. He moved far from the pantisocracy in declaring that in 1799, 'government is good in which property is secure' and upholding the power of traditional landowners (Coleridge 1850: 331). He also became an advocate for elitism, calling on a 'Clerisy' of religiously informed intellects to safeguard the nation from the excesses of commercialism. This social conservatism, however, was still informed by a love of nature. In line with the aristocrat conservationists later discussed, Coleridge came to the conclusion that the landed gentry were a bastion against unfettered industrialization.

Coleridge suffered from depression and illness and had a long-standing opium addiction. He moved to Highgate in his forties under the care of a personal physician, but it was there that he died and is now buried (Encyclopedia Britannica).

26

'THE RAVEN'

Samuel Taylor Coleridge

Source: Samuel Taylor Coleridge, 'The Raven' (1791)

Under the arms of a goodly oak-tree,
There was of Swine a huge company,
They were making a rude repast,
Grunting as they crunched the mast.
Then they trotted away: for the wind grew high –
One acorn they left, ne more mote you spy.
Next came a Raven, who lik'd not such folly:
He belong'd, I believe, to the witch MELANCHOLY!
Blacker was he than blackest jet,
Flew low in the rain; his feathers were wet.
He pick'd up the acorn and buried it strait,
By the side of a river both deep and great.
Where then did the Raven go?
He went high and low –
O'er hill, o'er dale, did the black Raven go!
Many Autumns, many Springs
Travell'd he with wand'ring wings;
Many Summers, many Winters –
I can't tell half his adventures.
At length he return'd, and with him a she,
And the acorn was grown a large oak tree.
They built them a nest in the topmost bough,
And young ones they had, and were happy enow.
But soon came a Woodman in leathern guise:
His brow like a pent-house hung over his eyes.
He'd an axe in his hand, and he nothing spoke,
But with many a hem! and a sturdy stroke,
At last he brought down the poor Raven's own oak.
His young ones were kill'd, for they could not depart,
And his wife she did die of a broken heart!
The boughs from off it the Woodman did sever;

DOI: 10.4324/9781003194651-36

ROMANTICIZING NATURE

And they floated it down on the course of the River;
They sawed it in planks, and its bark they did strip,
And with this tree and others they built up a ship.
The ship it was launch'd; but in sight of the land,
A temptest arose which no ship could withstand.
It bulg'd on a rock, and the waves rush'd in fast –
The auld Raven flew round and round, and caw'd to the blast.
He heard the sea-shriek of their perishing souls!
They be sunk! O'er the top-mast the mad water rolls.
The Raven was glad that such fate they did meet –
They had taken his all, and REVENGE WAS SWEET!

Editorial Headnote

1770 (Cockermouth)–1850

Wordsworth was a poet – one of the most revered England has produced – and a pioneer of the romantic movement. He was brought up in a Lakeland mansion (his father was a prominent lawyer) and graduated in English at Cambridge University. Although always ultimately returning to the Lake District, Wordsworth travelled widely and lived in France as a young man where he witnessed and was inspired by the early stages of revolution.

Wordsworth worked together closely with Coleridge, launching the romantic movement with their joint venture 'Lyrical Ballads' in 1798, which included one of his most revered works, 'Lines Written a Few Miles Above Tintern Abbey'. Poetically, he and his fellow romantics favoured and advocated eschewing flowery prose and using common English to maximize their reach. The romantic movement idealized nature and placed emotion above rationalism and so lamented the loss of many forms of medieval art and thought to the Enlightenment and Industrialization. Conservation was hence a natural cause for Wordsworth to embrace and, along with John Ruskin and other romantics, he came to involve himself in campaigns such as blocking the construction of rail lines into his beloved Lakeland. Wordsworth used his fame to personally kick-start this campaign by submitting to the London Morning Post 'Sonnet on the Projected Kendal and Windermere Railway'.

> Is then no nook of English ground secure
> From rash assault? Schemes of retirement sown
> In youth, and mid the busy world kept pure
> As when the earliest flowers of hope were blown,
> Must perish; – how can they this blight endure?
> And must he too the ruthless change bemoan
> Who scorns a false utilitarian lure
> Mid his paternal fields at random thrown?
> Baffle the threat, bright Scene, from Orrest-head
> Given to the pausing traveller's rapturous glance:
> Plead for thy peace, thou beautiful romance
> Of nature; and, if human hearts be dead,
> Speak, passing winds; ye torrents, with your strong
> And constant voice, protest against the wrong.

(Wordsworth 1844)

This particular campaign did not succeed in blocking the Kendal-to-Windermere rail line, but it did serve as an inspiration to Ruskin and others who proved more successful in later similar campaigns.

Like his great friend Coleridge, Wordsworth was a political radical as a young man and was inspired by the French Revolution and the republican liberalism of Rousseau. At the same time, though, he was always religiously conservative. Like Coleridge, Wordsworth is also generally held to have politically mellowed – and perhaps dulled – with age (Bate 2020). The Excursion was written in this later, less liberal phase of his life and has a clear message of respect for tradition and a rejection of revolution (Beenstock 2016: 103). The chosen extract is part of one of nine books that make up a very long poem which represented a series of philosophical monologues. Despite the move towards social conservatism, Wordsworth maintains an eco-centric radicalism in the work. In particular, he rails against industrialization and urbanization, lamenting 'such outrage done to nature' and 'her violated rights'. This message hence preempted the 'rights to nature' movement still in its infancy today in seeking to criminalize 'ecocide', the deliberate damage of the environment.

Wordsworth's popularity waned in his later years, and he came to receive much literary criticism. However, his de-radicalization won him favour in elite circles, and he became Queen Victoria's Poet Laureate in 1843, a post he held until his death – of pleurisy – seven years later.

Pp. 359–386

27

THE EXCURSION

William Wordsworth

Source: William Wordsworth, *The Excursion* (1814)

THE PARSONAGE (Book 8)

The pensive Sceptic of the lonely Vale
To those acknowledgments subscribed his own
With a sedate compliance, which the Priest
Failed not to notice inly pleased, and said,
"If Ye, by whom invited I commenced
Those Naratives of calm and humble life,
Be satisfied, 'tis well, – the end is gained;
And, in return for sympathy bestowed
And patient listening, thanks accept from me.
– Life, Death, Eternity! momentous themes
Are these – and might demand a Seraph's tongue,
Were they not equal to their own support;
And therefore no incompetence of mine
Could do them wrong. The universal Forms
Of human nature, in a Spot like this,
Present themselves, at once, to all Men's view:
Ye wished for act and circumstance, that make
The Individual known and understood;
And such as my best judgment could select
From what the Place afforded have been given;
Though apprehensions crossed me, in the course
Of this self-pleasing exercise, that Ye
My zeal to his would liken, who, possessed
Of some rare gems, or pictures finely wrought,
Unlocks his Cabinet, and draws them forth
One after one, – soliciting regard
To this – and this, as worthier than the last,
Till the Spectator, who a while was pleased
More than the Exhibitor himself, becomes

Weary and faint, and longs to be released.
– But let us hence! my Dwelling is in sight,
And there –"
At this the Solitary shrunk
With backward will; but, wanting not address
That inward motion to disguise, he said
To his Compatriot, smiling as he spake;
– "The peaceable Remains of this good Knight
Would be disturbed, I fear, with wrathful scorn,
If consciousness could reach him where he lies
That One, albeit of these degenerate times,
Deploring changes past, or dreading change
Foreseen, had dared to couple, even in thought,
The fine Vocation of the sword and lance
With the gross aims and body-bending toil
Of a poor Brotherhood who walk the earth
Pitied, and where they are not known, despised.
– Yet, by the good Knight's leave, the two Estates
Are graced with some resemblance. Errant Those,
Exiles and Wanderers – and the like are These;
Who, with their burthen, traverse hill and dale,
Carrying relief for Nature's simple wants.
– What though no higher recompence they seek
Than honest maintenance, by irksome toil
Full oft procured! Yet Such may claim respect,
Among the Intelligent, for what this course
Enables them to be, and to perform.
Their tardy steps give leisure to observe;
While solitude permits the mind to feel;
And doth instruct her to supply defects
By the division of her inward self,
For grateful converse: and to these poor Men,
(As I have heard you boast with honest pride)
Nature is bountiful, where'er they go;
Kind Nature's various wealth is all their own.
Versed in the characters of men; and bound,
By tie of daily interest, to maintain
Conciliatory manners and smooth speech;
Such have been, and still are in their degree,
Examples efficacious to refine
Rude intercourse; apt Instruments to excite,
By importation of unlooked-for Arts,
Barbarian torpor, and blind prejudice;
Raising, through just gradation, savage life

THE EXCURSION

To rustic, and the rustic to urbane.
– Within their moving magazines is lodged
Power that comes forth to quicken and exalt
The affections seated in the Mother's breast,
And in the Lover's fancy; and to feed
The sober sympathies of long tried Friends.
– By these Itinerants, as experienced Men,
Counsel is given; contention they appease
With healing words; and in remotest Wilds
Tears wipe away, and pleasant tidings bring;
Could the proud quest of Chivalry do more?"

"Happy," rejoined the Wanderer, "They who gain
A panegyric from your generous tongue!
But, if to these Wayfarers once pertained
Aught of romantic interest, 'tis gone;
Their purer service, in this realm at least,
Is past for ever. – An inventive Age
Has wrought, if not with speed of magic, yet
To most strange issues. I have lived to mark
A new and unforeseen Creation rise
From out the labours of a peaceful Land,
Wielding her potent Enginery to frame
And to produce, with appetite as keen
As that of War, which rests not night or day,
Industrious to destroy! With fruitless pains
Might One like me now visit many a tract
Which, in his youth, he trod, and trod again,
A lone Pedestrian with a scanty freight,
Wished for, or welcome, wheresoe'er he came,
Among the Tenantry of Thorpe and Vill;
Or straggling Burgh, of ancient charter proud,
And dignified by battlements and towers
Of some stern Castle, mouldering on the brow
Of a green hill or bank of rugged stream.
The foot-path faintly marked, the horse-track wild,
And formidable length of plashy lane,
(Prized avenues ere others had been shaped
Or easier links connecting place with place)
Have vanished, – swallowed up by stately roads
Easy and bold, that penetrate the gloom
Of England's farthest Glens. The Earth has lent
Her waters, Air her breezes; and the Sail
Of traffic glides with ceaseless interchange,

Glistening along the low and woody dale,
Or on the naked mountain's lofty side.
Meanwhile, at social Industry's command,
How quick, how vast an increase! From the germ
Of some poor Hamlet, rapidly produced
Here a huge Town, continuous and compact,
Hiding the face of earth for leagues – and there,
Where not a Habitation stood before,
The Abodes of men irregularly massed
Like trees in forests – spread through spacious tracts,
O'er which the smoke of unremitting fires
Hangs permanent, and plentiful as wreaths
Of vapour glittering in the morning sun.
And, wheresoe'er the Traveller turns his steps,
He sees the barren wilderness erased,
Or disappearing; triumph that proclaims
How much the mild Directress of the plough
Owes to alliance with these new-born Arts!
– Hence is the wide Sea peopled, – and the Shores
Of Britain are resorted to by Ships
Freighted from every climate of the world
With the world's choicest produce. Hence that sum
Of Keels that rest within her crowded ports,
Or ride at anchor in her sounds and bays;
That animating spectacle of Sails
Which through her inland regions, to and fro
Pass with the respirations of the tide,
Perpetual, multitudinous! Finally,
Hence a dread arm of floating Power, a voice
Of Thunder, daunting those who would approach
With hostile purposes the blessed Isle,
Truth's consecrated residence, the seat
Impregnable, of Liberty and Peace.

And yet, O happy Pastor of a Flock
Faithfully watched, and by that loving care
And heaven's good providence preserved from taint!
With You I grieve, when on the darker side
Of this great change I look; and there behold,
Through strong temptation of those gainful Arts,
Such outrage done to Nature as compels
The indignant Power to justify herself;
Yea to avenge her violated rights

THE EXCURSION

For England's bane. – When soothing darkness spreads
O'er hill and vale," the Wanderer thus expressed
His recollections, "and the punctual stars,
While all things else are gathering to their homes,
Advance, and in the firmament of heaven
Glitter – but undisturbing, undisturbed,
As if their silent company were charged
With peaceful admonitions for the heart
Of all-beholding Man, earth's thoughtful Lord;
Then, in full many a region, once like this
The assured domain of calm simplicity
And pensive quiet, an unnatural light,
Prepared for never-resting Labour's eyes,
Breaks from a many-windowed Fabric huge;
And at the appointed hour a Bell is heard –
Of harsher import than the Curfew-knoll
That spake the Norman Conqueror's stern behest,
A local summons to unceasing toil!
Disgorged are now the Ministers of day;
And, as they issue from the illumined Pile,
A fresh Band meets them, at the crowded door, –
And in the Courts – and where the rumbling Stream,
That turns the multitude of dizzy wheels,
Glares, like a troubled Spirit, in its bed
Among the rocks below. Men, Maidens, Youths,
Mother and little Children, Boys and Girls,
Enter, and each the wonted task resumes
Within this Temple – where is offered up
To Gain – the Master Idol of the Realm,
Perpetual sacrifice. Even thus of old
Our Ancestors, within the still domain
Of vast Cathedral or Conventual Church,
Their vigils kept; where tapers day and night
On the dim altar burned continually,
In token that the House was evermore
Watching to God. Religious Men were they;
Nor would their Reason, tutored to aspire
Above this transitory world, allow
That there should pass a moment of the year,
When in their land the Almighty's Service ceased.

Triumph who will in these profaner rites
Which We, a generation self-extolled,

As zealously perform! I cannot share
His proud complacency; yet I exult,
Casting reserve away, exult to see
An Intellectual mastery exercised
O'er the blind Elements; a purpose given,
A perseverance fed; almost a soul
Imparted – to brute Matter. I rejoice,
Measuring the force of those gigantic powers,
Which by the thinking Mind have been compelled
To serve the Will of feeble-bodied Man.
For with the sense of admiration blends
The animating hope that time may come
When strengthened, yet not dazzled, by the might
Of this dominion over Nature gained,
Men of all lands shall exercise the same
In due proportion to their Country's need;
Learning, though late, that all true glory rests,
All praise, all safety, and all happiness,
Upon the Moral law. Egyptian Thebes;
Tyre by the margin of the sounding waves;
Palmyra, central in the Desart, fell;
And the Arts died by which they had been raised.
– Call Archimedes from his buried Tomb
Upon the plain of vanished Syracuse,
And feelingly the Sage shall make report
How insecure, how baseless in itself,
Is that Philosophy, whose sway is framed
For mere material instruments: – how weak
Those Arts, and high Inventions, if unpropped
By Virtue. – He with sighs of pensive grief,
Amid his calm abstractions, would admit
That not the slender privilege is theirs
To save themselves from blank forgetfulness!"

Editorial Headnote

1809 (Somersby, Lincs.)–1892

Lord Alfred Tennyson was and is one of Britain's best-known poets. He served as Poet Laureate throughout most of Queen Victoria's reign.

Tennyson was from a comfortably off but not aristocratic family. His father was an Anglican clergyman and served the church locally in a number of capacities. Tennyson went to grammar school in Lincolnshire and then studied English at Cambridge University. However, he left university before completing his degree on the death of his father.

Tennyson loved nature and was well known as a conservationist, as evidenced by him being chosen to be the first president of the Selborne Society (highlighted in in Part 1 of this volume) in 1888 and remaining in this position until his death. He was not only a romantic, in a similar vein to Wordsworth and Coleridge, but also very much a rationalist. He was a Christian and an aesthete but emergent thinking in science also informed his writing, as is evident in this poem lamenting the early death of his university friend and fellow poet Arthur Henry Hallam. In this work, new thinking in geology is drawn on in order to try to put questions of life and death into perspective. Tennyson reasons that nature is tough – 'red in tooth and claw' – but, nonetheless, must be embraced. Death is part of life and lives go on after death. Notions of evolution are hinted at (prior to its official popularization by Darwin) in citing the interconnectedness of nature as a means of coping with grief and understanding death and humanity's place in the world.

Tennyson's tenure with the Selborne Society saw it move in a more educational and less political direction, perhaps partly reflecting his scientific leanings. The society later came to be somewhat eclipsed by and estranged from the Society for the Protection of Birds (see Volume II Part 1), in spite of their common lineage. In 1908, the Selborne Society even opposed some aspects of the RSPB-sponsored Importation of Plumage Bill in 1908 on the grounds of it impeding scientific research (whilst supporting it overall) (Clarke 2005).

Tennyson succeeded Wordsworth as Poet Laureate in 1850 and five years later penned perhaps his best-known verse, 'The Charge of the Light Brigade', in reference to this now notorious episode in the Crimean War a year earlier. He accepted a peerage from Gladstone in 1883 and took up a seat in the House of Lords the following year. He is buried at Poet's Corner in Westminster Abbey and is also commemorated by a monument on the Isle of Wight, where he lived in later life.

28

'IN MEMORIAM A.H.H.'

Alfred Tennyson

Source: Alfred Tennyson, 'In Memoriam A.H.H.' (1849)

I

I held it truth, with him who sings
To one clear harp in divers tones,
That men may rise on stepping-stones
Of their dead selves to higher things.

But who shall so forecast the years
And find in loss a gain to match?
Or reach a hand thro' time to catch
The far-off interest of tears?

Let Love clasp Grief lest both be drown'd,
Let darkness keep her raven gloss:
Ah, sweeter to be drunk with loss,
To dance with death, to beat the ground,

Than that the victor Hours should scorn
The long result of love, and boast,
'Behold the man that loved and lost,
But all he was is overworn.'

II

Old Yew, which graspest at the stones
That name the under-lying dead,
Thy fibres net the dreamless head,
Thy roots are wrapt about the bones.

DOI: 10.4324/9781003194651-38

ROMANTICIZING NATURE

The seasons bring the flower again,
And bring the firstling to the flock;
And in the dusk of thee, the clock
Beats out the little lives of men.

O, not for thee the glow, the bloom,
Who changest not in any gale,
Nor branding summer suns avail
To touch thy thousand years of gloom:

And gazing on thee, sullen tree,
Sick for thy stubborn hardihood,
I seem to fail from out my blood
And grow incorporate into thee.

III

O Sorrow, cruel fellowship,
O Priestess in the vaults of Death,
O sweet and bitter in a breath,
What whispers from thy lying lip?

'The stars,' she whispers, 'blindly run;
A web is wov'n across the sky;
From out waste places comes a cry,
And murmurs from the dying sun:

'And all the phantom, Nature, stands –
With all the music in her tone,
A hollow echo of my own, –
A hollow form with empty hands.'

And shall I take a thing so blind,
Embrace her as my natural good;
Or crush her, like a vice of blood,
Upon the threshold of the mind?

. . .

LIV

Oh yet we trust that somehow good
Will be the final goal of ill,
To pangs of nature, sins of will,
Defects of doubt, and taints of blood;

'IN MEMORIAM A.H.H.'

That nothing walks with aimless feet;
That not one life shall be destroy'd,
Or cast as rubbish to the void,
When God hath made the pile complete;

That not a worm is cloven in vain;
That not a moth with vain desire
Is shrivell'd in a fruitless fire,
Or but subserves another's gain.

Behold, we know not anything;
I can but trust that good shall fall
At last – far off – at last, to all,
And every winter change to spring.

So runs my dream: but what am I?
An infant crying in the night:
An infant crying for the light:
And with no language but a cry.

LV

The wish, that of the living whole
No life may fail beyond the grave,
Derives it not from what we have
The likest God within the soul?

Are God and Nature then at strife,
That Nature lends such evil dreams?
So careful of the type she seems,
So careless of the single life;

That I, considering everywhere
Her secret meaning in her deeds,
And finding that of fifty seeds
She often brings but one to bear,

I falter where I firmly trod,
And falling with my weight of cares
Upon the great world's altar-stairs
That slope thro' darkness up to God,

I stretch lame hands of faith, and grope,
And gather dust and chaff, and call

LVI

'So careful of the type?' but no.
From scarped cliff and quarried stone
She cries, 'A thousand types are gone:
I care for nothing, all shall go.

'Thou makest thine appeal to me:
I bring to life, I bring to death:
The spirit does but mean the breath:
I know no more.' And he, shall he,

Man, her last work, who seem'd so fair,
Such splendid purpose in his eyes,
Who roll'd the psalm to wintry skies,
Who built him fanes of fruitless prayer,

Who trusted God was love indeed
And love Creation's final law –
Tho' Nature, red in tooth and claw
With ravine, shriek'd against his creed –

Who loved, who suffer'd countless ills,
Who battled for the True, the Just,
Be blown about the desert dust,
Or seal'd within the iron hills?

No more? A monster then, a dream,
A discord. Dragons of the prime,
That tare each other in their slime,
Were mellow music match'd with him.

O life as futile, then, as frail!
O for thy voice to soothe and bless!
What hope of answer, or redress?
Behind the veil, behind the veil.

. . .

CXVIII

Contemplate all this work of Time,
The giant labouring in his youth;
Nor dream of human love and truth,
As dying Nature's earth and lime;

But trust that those we call the dead
Are breathers of an ampler day
For ever nobler ends. They say,
The solid earth whereon we tread

In tracts of fluent heat began,
And grew to seeming-random forms,
The seeming prey of cyclic storms,
Till at the last arose the man;

Who throve and branch'd from clime to clime,
The herald of a higher race,
And of himself in higher place,
If so he type this work of time

Within himself, from more to more;
Or, crown'd with attributes of woe
Like glories, move his course, and show
That life is not as idle ore,

But iron dug from central gloom,
And heated hot with burning fears,
And dipt in baths of hissing tears,
And batter'd with the shocks of doom

To shape and use. Arise and fly
The reeling Faun, the sensual feast;
Move upward, working out the beast,
And let the ape and tiger die.

CXIX

Doors, where my heart was used to beat
So quickly, not as one that weeps

I come once more; the city sleeps;
I smell the meadow in the street;

I hear a chirp of birds; I see
Betwixt the black fronts long-withdrawn
A light-blue lane of early dawn,
And think of early days and thee,

And bless thee, for thy lips are bland,
And bright the friendship of thine eye;
And in my thoughts with scarce a sigh
I take the pressure of thine hand.

CXX

I trust I have not wasted breath:
I think we are not wholly brain,
Magnetic mockeries; not in vain,
Like Paul with beasts, I fought with Death;

Not only cunning casts in clay:
Let Science prove we are, and then
What matters Science unto men,
At least to me? I would not stay.

Let him, the wiser man who springs
Hereafter, up from childhood shape
His action like the greater ape,
But I was born to other things.

CXXI

Sad Hesper o'er the buried sun
And ready, thou, to die with him,
Thou watchest all things ever dim
And dimmer, and a glory done:

The team is loosen'd from the wain,
The boat is drawn upon the shore;
Thou listenest to the closing door,
And life is darken'd in the brain.

Bright Phosphor, fresher for the night,
By thee the world's great work is heard

'IN MEMORIAM A.H.H.'

Beginning, and the wakeful bird;
Behind thee comes the greater light:

The market boat is on the stream,
And voices hail it from the brink;
Thou hear'st the village hammer clink,
And see'st the moving of the team.

Sweet Hesper-Phosphor, double name
For what is one, the first, the last,
Thou, like my present and my past,
Thy place is changed; thou art the same.

CXXII

Oh, wast thou with me, dearest, then,
While I rose up against my doom,
And yearn'd to burst the folded gloom,
To bare the eternal Heavens again,

To feel once more, in placid awe,
The strong imagination roll
A sphere of stars about my soul,
In all her motion one with law;

If thou wert with me, and the grave
Divide us not, be with me now,
And enter in at breast and brow,
Till all my blood, a fuller wave,

Be quicken'd with a livelier breath,
And like an inconsiderate boy,
As in the former flash of joy,
I slip the thoughts of life and death;

And all the breeze of Fancy blows,
And every dew-drop paints a bow,
The wizard lightnings deeply glow,
And every thought breaks out a rose.

CXXIII

There rolls the deep where grew the tree.
O earth, what changes hast thou seen!

There where the long street roars, hath been
The stillness of the central sea.

The hills are shadows, and they flow
From form to form, and nothing stands;
They melt like mist, the solid lands,
Like clouds they shape themselves and go.

But in my spirit will I dwell,
And dream my dream, and hold it true;
For tho' my lips may breathe adieu,
I cannot think the thing farewell.

CXXIV

That which we dare invoke to bless;
Our dearest faith; our ghastliest doubt;
He, They, One, All; within, without;
The Power in darkness whom we guess;

I found Him not in world or sun,
Or eagle's wing, or insect's eye;
Nor thro' the questions men may try,
The petty cobwebs we have spun:

If e'er when faith had fall'n asleep,
I heard a voice 'believe no more'
And heard an ever-breaking shore
That tumbled in the Godless deep;

A warmth within the breast would melt
The freezing reason's colder part,
And like a man in wrath the heart
Stood up and answer'd 'I have felt.'

No, like a child in doubt and fear:
But that blind clamour made me wise;
Then was I as a child that cries,
But, crying, knows his father near;

And what I am beheld again
What is, and no man understands;
And out of darkness came the hands
That reach thro' nature, moulding men.

Editorial Headnote

1819 (London)–1900

John Ruskin was a prominent art critic and author who came to embrace polemical writing on various matters of conservation. Ruskin was an only child of wealthy parents, and his father was a successful wine merchant. His parents were artistic and deeply religious and educated him at home in line with this before he went on to study at Kings College London and Oxford University.

Ruskin became the first Slade Professor of Fine Art at Oxford and strongly championed romantic British artists such as JMW Turner and the pre-Raphaelites. He was associated with the advocacy of medievalism in art and architecture in the face of the advance of modernism and industrialization. In doing so Ruskin's romanticism and pantheism saw him align with Wordsworth, Coleridge and other prominent artistic figures of the age.

Ruskin became increasingly interested in social issues and, on the death of his father, used much of his inheritance on causes such as resisting the encroachment of new railway lines into the countryside. In the late 1850s, he formed a close friendship with the conservative thinker Thomas Carlyle (profiled later) which further politicized him and deepened his rejection of modernism and the free trade of liberalism.

Ruskin became increasingly mentally unstable and volatile in his later years and was the subject of greater public criticism. Famously, in 1878, he was the subject of libel action by the US artist James Whistler for his highly negative reviews of his work: a case widely held to have ruined both men's careers. Whistler won his case but was awarded only a farthing in damages, leaving him broke. Ruskin's previously strong reputation was damaged as he came to be seen by many as old-fashioned and vindictive. He resigned from the Slade later that year after a mental breakdown. He retired to the Lake District, where he was to die just after the turn of the century.

The proposed extension of the rail line into Windermere in the 1870s was blocked by Ruskin's campaign (after Wordsworth had failed to block the original Kendal–Windermere line in the 1840s). Ruskin was joined in his ongoing campaign to resist further encroachment of train lines into the Lake District by the Kyrle Society and Commons Preservation Society and had further successes in blocking lines from Keswick to Buttermere and from the coast to Ennerdale. The movement also spawned the Derwent Water and Borrowdale Defence Committee in 1882, featuring his protégé the vicar and poet Hardwicke Rawnsley. Building on this the Lake District Defence Society (LDDS) was established the following year to 'protect the Lake District from those injurious encroachments which are from time to time attempted from purely commercial or speculative motives, without regard to its claim as a national recreation ground' (Ranlett 1983: 202). A key ally in this campaign was the Liberal politician James Bryce (profiled in Volume II Part 1) who advocated for the LDDS in parliament in particular campaigns and in the entering into law of the 1896 Light Railways Act imposing environmental restrictions on future train developments.

The preface of this extract starts with a strong statement on the general environmental malaise of the time in citing a 'frenzy of avarice . . . drowning our sailors, suffocating our miners, poisoning our children and blasting the cultivable surface of England into a treeless waste of ashes'. We also see how the Middle Ages are idealized and urban living demonized not only in aesthetic but in moral terms. However, Ruskin is not persuaded by arguments of rail travel as giving greater access to beauty for those trapped in urban squalor. Elitism more than a desire for social reform is evident in lamenting the possibility of Grasmere being turned into a tacky holiday resort or Helvellyn being trampled over by drunks from the cities.

pp. 125–132

29

A PROTEST AGAINST THE EXTENSION OF RAILWAYS IN THE LAKE DISTRICT

John Ruskin

Source: John Ruskin, *A Protest Against the Extension of Railways in the Lake District* (1876)

PREFACE

The evidence collected in the following pages, in support of their pleading, is so complete, and the summary of his cause given with so temperate mastery by Mr. Somervell, that I find nothing to add in circumstance, and little to re-enforce in argument. And I have less heart to the writing even of what brief preface so good work might by its author's courtesy be permitted to receive from me, occupied as I so long have been in efforts tending in the same direction, because, on that very account, I am far less interested than my friend in this local and limited resistance to the elsewhere fatally victorious current of modern folly, cruelty, and ruin. When the frenzy of avarice is daily drowning our sailors, suffocating our miners, poisoning our children, and blasting the cultivable surface of England into a treeless waste of ashes, what does it really matter whether a flock of sheep, more or less, be driven from the slopes of Helvellyn, or the little pool of Thirlmere filled with shale, or a few wild blossoms of St. John's vale lost to the coronal of English spring? Little to anyone; and – let me say this, at least, in the outset of all saying – nothing to me. No one need charge me with selfishness in any word or action for defense of these mossy hills. I do not move, with such small activity as I have yet shown in the business, because I live at Coniston (where no sound of the iron wheels by Dunmail Raise can reach me), nor because I can find no other place to remember Wordsworth by, than the daffodil margin of his little Rydal marsh. What thoughts and work are yet before me, such as he taught, must be independent of any narrow associations. All my own dear mountain grounds and treasure-cities, Chamouni, Interlachen, Lucerne, Geneva, Venice, are long ago destroyed by the European populace; and now, for my own part, I don't care what more they do; they may drain Loch Katrine, drink Loch Lomond, and blow all Wales and Cumberland into a heap of slate shingle; the world is wide enough yet to find me some refuge during the days appointed for me to stay in it. But it is no less my duty, in

DOI: 10.4324/9781003194651-39

the cause of those to whom the sweet landscapes of England are yet precious, and to whom they may yet teach what they taught me, in early boyhood, and would still if I had it now to learn, – it is my duty to plead with what earnestness I may, that these sacred sibylline books may be redeemed from perishing.

But again, I am checked, because I don't know how to speak to the persons who need to be spoken to in this matter.

Suppose I were sitting, where still, in much-changed Oxford, I am happy to find myself, in one of the little latticed cells of the Bodleian Library, and my kind and much-loved friend, Mr. Coxe, were to come to me with news that it was proposed to send nine hundred excursionists through the library every day, in three parties of three hundred each; that it was intended they should elevate their minds by reading all the books they could lay hold of while they stayed; – and that practically scientific persons accompanying them were to look out for and burn all the manuscripts that had any gold in their illuminations, that the said gold might be made of practical service; but that he, Mr. Coxe, could not, for his part, sympathize with the movement, and hoped I would write something in deprecation of it! As I should then feel, I feel now, at Mr. Somervell's request that I would write him a preface in defense of Helvellyn. What could I say for Mr. Coxe? Of course, that nine hundred people should see the library daily, instead of one, is only fair to the nine hundred, and if there is gold in the books, is it not public property? If there is copper or slate in Helvellyn, shall not the public burn or hammer it out – and they say they will, of course – in spite of us? What does it signify to them how we poor old quiet readers in this mountain library feel? True, we know well enough, – what the nine hundred excursionist scholars don't – that the library can't be read quite through in a quarter of an hour; also, that there is a pleasure in real reading, quite different from that of turning pages; and that gold in a missal, or slate in a crag, may be more precious than in a bank or a chimney-pot. But how are these practical people to credit us, – these, who cannot read, nor ever will; and who have been taught that nothing is virtuous but care for their bellies, and nothing useful but what goes into them?

Whether to be credited or not, the real facts of the matter, made clear as they are in the following pages, can be briefly stated for the consideration of any candid person.

The arguments in favor of the new railway are in the main four, and may be thus answered.

1.   "There are mineral treasures in the district capable of development."

Answer. It is a wicked fiction, got up by whosoever has got it up, simply to cheat shareholders. Every lead and copper vein in Cumberland has been known for centuries; the copper of Coniston does not pay; and there is none so rich in Helvellyn. And the main central volcanic rocks, through which the track lies, produce neither slate nor hematite, while there is enough of them at Llanberis and Dalton to roof

AGAINST THE EXTENSION OF RAILWAYS IN THE LAKE DISTRICT

and iron-grate all England into one vast Bedlam, if it honestly perceives itself in need of that accommodation.

2.   "The scenery must be made accessible to the public."

Answer. It is more than accessible already; the public are pitched into it head-foremost, and necessarily miss two-thirds of it. The Lake scenery really begins, on the south, at Lancaster, where the Cumberland hills are seen over Morecambe Bay; on the north, at Carlisle, where the moors of Skiddaw are seen over the rich plains between them and the Solway. No one who loves mountains would lose a step of the approach, from these distances, on either side. But the stupid herds of modern tourists let themselves be emptied, like coals from a sack, at Windermere and Keswick. Having got there, what the new railway has to do is to shovel those who have come to Keswick to Windermere, and to shovel those who have come to Windermere to Keswick. And what then?

3.   "But cheap and swift transit is necessary for the working population, who otherwise could not see the scenery at all."

Answer. After all your shrieking about what the operatives spend in drink, can't you teach them to save enough out of their year's wages to pay for a chaise and pony for a day, to drive Missis and the Baby that pleasant twenty miles, stopping when they like, to unpack the basket on a mossy bank? If they can't enjoy the scenery that way, they can't any way; and all that your railroad company can do for them is only to open taverns and skittle grounds round Grasmere, which will soon, then, be nothing but a pool of drainage, with a beach of broken gingerbeer bottles; and their minds will be no more improved by contemplating the scenery of such a lake than of Blackpool.

4.   What else is to be said? I protest I can find nothing, unless that engineers and contractors must live. Let them live, but in a more useful and honorable way than by keeping Old Bartholomew Fair under Helvellyn, and making a steam merry-go-round of the lake country.

There are roads to be mended, where the parish will not mend them, harbors of refuge needed, where our deck-loaded ships are in helpless danger; get your commissions and dividends where you know that work is needed, not where the best you can do is to persuade pleasure-seekers into giddier idleness.

. . .

p. 264

The arguments brought forward by the promoters of the railway may thus be summarily answered. Of those urged in the following pamphlet in defense of the country as it is, I care only myself to direct the reader's attention to one, the certainty, namely, of the deterioration of moral character in the inhabitants of every district penetrated by a railway. Where there is little moral character to be lost, this argument has small weight. But the Border peasantry of Scotland and England, painted with absolute fidelity by Scott and Wordsworth (for leading types out of this exhaustless portraiture, I may name Dandie Dinmont and Michael), are hitherto a scarcely injured race, whose strength and virtue yet survive to represent the body and soul of England before her days of mechanical decrepitude and commercial dishonor. There are men working in my own fields who might have fought with Henry the Fifth at Agincourt without being discerned from among his knights; I can take my tradesmen's word for a thousand pounds; my garden gate opens on the latch to the public road, by day and night, without fear of any foot entering but my own, and my girl-guests may wander by road, or moorland, or through every bosky dell of this wild wood, free as the heather bees or squirrels.

What effect, on the character of such a population, will be produced by the influx of that of the suburbs of our manufacturing towns, there is evidence enough, if the reader cares to ascertain the facts, in every newspaper on his morning table.

And now one final word concerning the proposed beneficial effect on the minds of those whom you send to corrupt us.

I have said I take no selfish interest in this resistance to the railroad. But I do take an unselfish one. It is precisely because I passionately wish to improve the minds of the populace, and because I am spending my own mind, strength, and fortune, wholly on that object, that I don't want to let them see Helvellyn while they are drunk. I suppose few men now living have so earnestly felt – none certainly have so earnestly declared – that the beauty of nature is the blessedest and most necessary of lessons for men; and that all other efforts in education are futile till you have taught your people to love fields, birds, and flowers. Come then, my benevolent friends, join with me in that teaching. I have been at it all my life, and without pride, do solemnly assure you that I know how it is to be managed. I cannot indeed tell you, in this short preface, how, completely, to fulfill so glorious a task. But I can tell you clearly, instantly, and emphatically, in what temper you must set about it. Here are you, a Christian, a gentleman, and a trained scholar; there is your subject of education – a Godless clown, in helpless ignorance. You can present no more blessed offering to God than that human creature, raised into faith, gentleness, and the knowledge of the works of his Lord. But observe this – you must not hope to make so noble an offering to God of that which doth cost you nothing! You must be resolved to labor, and to lose, yourself, before you can rescue this overlabored lost sheep, and offer it alive to its Master. If then, my benevolent friend, you are prepared to take out your two pence, and to give them to the hosts here in Cumberland, saying – "Take care of him, and whatsoever thou spendest more, I will repay thee when I come to Cumberland myself," on these terms – oh my benevolent friends, I am with you, hand and glove, in every effort you wish to make for the enlightenment of poor men's eyes. But if your motive is, on the contrary, to put two pence into your own purse, stolen between the Jerusalem and Jericho of Keswick and Ambleside, out of the poor drunken traveler's pocket; – if your real object, in your charitable offering, is, not even to lend unto the Lord by giving to the poor, but to lend unto the Lord by making a dividend out of the poor; – then, my pious friends, enthusiastic Ananias, pitiful Judas, and sanctified Korah, I will do my best in God's name, to stay your hands, and stop your tongues.

Brantwood, 22nd June, 1876.

John Ruskin (by Millais)
Source: https://openverse.org/image/0aeb361d-e4cd-4e4e-b118-808380a158fb?q=%22john%20ruskin%22

Editorial Headnote

1819 (Nuneaton)–1880

George Eliot was the pen name of Mary Ann Evans, a prolific, influential and enduring novelist, poet and journalist. Her works were and are particularly revered for their social realism and the glorification of the countryside.

Eliot was from a middle-class Midlands family, and as a child, she attended a religiously austere boarding school. As a young woman, however, she associated with social reformers and distanced herself from the church, causing a rift with her pious and conservative father. The rift was repaired and, when Eliot's father died in 1849, he left her an inheritance, which she used to travel and looked to initiate a writing career. In 1851, after a couple of years travelling around Europe, she moved to London to work on The Westminster Review, a reformist journal founded by Jeremy Bentham. This proved successful and opened the door for her to begin publishing novels, starting with Adam Bede in 1859. She went on to write a further six novels, including The Mill on the Floss in 1860 and, in the following year, the one extracted here, Silas Marner.

A negative portrayal of industrialization provides a continual underlying context to Silas Marner, as well as in many of Eliot's other novels. There is a recurring theme of environmental determinism: people's lives being moulded by their circumstances. In this story, an early nineteenth-century weaver man is excommunicated for a crime he did not commit by a religious sect in Lantern Yard, a district of a large northern English town. Silas subsequently travels south and resettles in the Midlands village of Raveloe, where, after a number of years, he comes to adopt a young orphaned girl he names Eppie. They form a close bond, and Eppie helps him rebuild his life. In the selected extract, the two of them visit Lantern Yard, and the rural idyll of Raveloe is contrasted with the urban decay and depravity of where Silas used to live: 'a dark, ugly place'. The story then ends happily back in Raveloe. The author's own move to London from rural Warwickshire to advance her career is generally held to have helped inform this.

George Eliot died in 1880, shortly after marrying for the first time. She had previously caused some scandal by living with but not marrying her partners and attracted criticism again with this marriage in that her husband was considerably younger than her. She is buried at Highgate Cemetery and has a commemorative stone at Poet's Corner in Westminster Abbey (Encyclopedia Britannica).

pp. 485–490

30

SILAS MARNER

George Eliot

Source: George Eliot, *Silas Marner* (1861)

CHAPTER 21

The next morning, when Silas and Eppie were seated at their breakfast, he said to her –

"Eppie, there's a thing I've had on my mind to do this two year, and now the money's been brought back to us, we can do it. I've been turning it over and over in the night, and I think we'll set out to – morrow, while the fine days last. We'll leave the house and everything for your godmother to take care on, and we'll make a little bundle o' things and set out."

"Where to go, daddy?" said Eppie, in much surprise.

"To my old country – to the town where I was born – up Lantern Yard. I want to see Mr. Paston, the minister: something may ha' come out to make 'em know I was innicent o' the robbery. And Mr. Paston was a man with a deal o' light – I want to speak to him about the drawing o' the lots. And I should like to talk to him about the religion o' this country – side, for I partly think he doesn't know on it."

Eppie was very joyful, for there was the prospect not only of wonder and delight at seeing a strange country, but also of coming back to tell Aaron all about it. Aaron was so much wiser than she was about most things – it would be rather pleasant to have this little advantage over him. Mrs. Winthrop, though possessed with a dim fear of dangers attendant on so long a journey, and requiring many assurances that it would not take them out of the region of carriers' carts and slow waggons, was nevertheless well pleased that Silas should revisit his own country, and find out if he had been cleared from that false accusation.

"You'd be easier in your mind for the rest o' your life, Master Marner," said Dolly – "that you would. And if there's any light to be got up the yard as you talk on, we've need of it i' this world, and I'd be glad on it myself, if you could bring it back."

So on the fourth day from that time, Silas and Eppie, in their Sunday clothes, with a small bundle tied in a blue linen handkerchief, were making their way through the streets of a great manufacturing town. Silas, bewildered by the changes thirty years had brought over his native place, had stopped several persons in

DOI: 10.4324/9781003194651-40

ROMANTICIZING NATURE

succession to ask them the name of this town, that he might be sure he was not under a mistake about it.

"Ask for Lantern Yard, father – ask this gentleman with the tassels on his shoulders a – standing at the shop door; he isn't in a hurry like the rest," said Eppie, in some distress at her father's bewilderment, and ill at ease, besides, amidst the noise, the movement, and the multitude of strange indifferent faces.

"Eh, my child, he won't know anything about it," said Silas; "gentlefolks didn't ever go up the Yard. But happen somebody can tell me which is the way to Prison Street, where the jail is. I know the way out o' that as if I'd seen it yesterday."

With some difficulty, after many turnings and new inquiries, they reached Prison Street; and the grim walls of the jail, the first object that answered to any image in Silas's memory, cheered him with the certitude, which no assurance of the town's name had hitherto given him, that he was in his native place.

"Ah," he said, drawing a long breath, "there's the jail, Eppie; that's just the same: I aren't afraid now. It's the third turning on the left hand from the jail doors – that's the way we must go."

"Oh, what a dark ugly place!" said Eppie. "How it hides the sky! It's worse than the Workhouse. I'm glad you don't live in this town now, father. Is Lantern Yard like this street?"

"My precious child," said Silas, smiling, "it isn't a big street like this. I never was easy i' this street myself, but I was fond o' Lantern Yard. The shops here are all altered, I think – I can't make 'em out; but I shall know the turning, because it's the third."

"Here it is," he said, in a tone of satisfaction, as they came to a narrow alley. "And then we must go to the left again, and then straight for'ard for a bit, up Shoe Lane: and then we shall be at the entry next to the o'erhanging window, where there's the nick in the road for the water to run. Eh, I can see it all."

"O father, I'm like as if I was stifled," said Eppie. "I couldn't ha' thought as any folks lived i' this way, so close together. How pretty the Stone – pits 'ull look when we get back!"

"It looks comical to me, child, now – and smells bad. I can't think as it usened to smell so."

Here and there a sallow, begrimed face looked out from a gloomy doorway at the strangers, and increased Eppie's uneasiness, so that it was a longed – for relief when they issued from the alleys into Shoe Lane, where there was a broader strip of sky.

"Dear heart!" said Silas, "why, there's people coming out o' the Yard as if they'd been to chapel at this time o' day – a weekday noon!"

Suddenly he started and stood still with a look of distressed amazement, that alarmed Eppie. They were before an opening in front of a large factory, from which men and women were streaming for their midday meal.

"Father," said Eppie, clasping his arm, "what's the matter?"

But she had to speak again and again before Silas could answer her.

"It's gone, child," he said, at last, in strong agitation – "Lantern Yard's gone. It must ha' been here, because here's the house with the o'erhanging window – I know that – it's just the same; but they've made this new opening; and see that big factory! It's all gone – chapel and all."

"Come into that little brush – shop and sit down, father – they'll let you sit down," said Eppie, always on the watch lest one of her father's strange attacks should come on. "Perhaps the people can tell you all about it."

But neither from the brush – maker, who had come to Shoe Lane only ten years ago, when the factory was already built, nor from any other source within his reach, could Silas learn anything of the old Lantern Yard friends, or of Mr. Paston the minister.

"The old place is all swep' away," Silas said to Dolly Winthrop on the night of his return – "the little graveyard and everything. The old home's gone; I've no home but this now. I shall never know whether they got at the truth o' the robbery, nor whether Mr. Paston could ha' given me any light about the drawing o' the lots. It's dark to me, Mrs. Winthrop, that is; I doubt it'll be dark to the last."

"Well, yes, Master Marner," said Dolly, who sat with a placid listening face, now bordered by grey hairs; "I doubt it may. It's the will o' Them above as a many things should be dark to us; but there's some things as I've never felt i' the dark about, and they're mostly what comes i' the day's work. You were hard done by that once, Master Marner, and it seems as you'll never know the rights of it; but that doesn't hinder there being a rights, Master Marner, for all it's dark to you and me."

"No," said Silas, "no; that doesn't hinder. Since the time the child was sent to me and I've come to love her as myself, I've had light enough to trusten by; and now she says she'll never leave me, I think I shall trusten till I die."

CONCLUSION

There was one time of the year which was held in Raveloe to be especially suitable for a wedding. It was when the great lilacs and laburnums in the old-fashioned gardens showed their golden and purple wealth above the lichen-tinted walls, and when there were calves still young enough to want bucketfuls of fragrant milk. People were not so busy then as they must become when the full cheese-making and the mowing had set in; and besides, it was a time when a light bridal dress could be worn with comfort and seen to advantage.

Happily the sunshine fell more warmly than usual on the lilac tufts the morning that Eppie was married, for her dress was a very light one. She had often thought, though with a feeling of renunciation, that the perfection of a wedding-dress would be a white cotton, with the tiniest pink sprig at wide intervals; so that when Mrs. Godfrey Cass begged to provide one, and asked Eppie to choose what it should be, previous meditation had enabled her to give a decided answer at once.

Seen at a little distance as she walked across the churchyard and down the vil-lage, she seemed to be attired in pure white, and her hair looked like the dash of gold on a lily. One hand was on her husband's arm, and with the other she clasped the hand of her father Silas.

"You won't be giving me away, father," she had said before they went to church; "you'll only be taking Aaron to be a son to you."

Dolly Winthrop walked behind with her husband; and there ended the little bridal procession.

There were many eyes to look at it, and Miss Priscilla Lammeter was glad that she and her father had happened to drive up to the door of the Red House just in time to see this pretty sight. They had come to keep Nancy company to-day, because Mr. Cass had had to go away to Lytherley, for special reasons. That seemed to be a pity, for otherwise he might have gone, as Mr. Crackenthorp and Mr. Osgood certainly would, to look on at the wedding – feast which he had ordered at the Rainbow, naturally feeling a great interest in the weaver who had been wronged by one of his own family.

"I could ha' wished Nancy had had the luck to find a child like that and bring her up," said Priscilla to her father, as they sat in the gig; "I should ha' had something young to think of then, besides the lambs and the calves."

"Yes, my dear, yes," said Mr. Lammeter; "one feels that as one gets older. Things look dim to old folks: they'd need have some young eyes about 'em, to let 'em know the world's the same as it used to be."

Nancy came out now to welcome her father and sister; and the wedding group had passed on beyond the Red House to the humbler part of the village.

Dolly Winthrop was the first to divine that old Mr. Macey, who had been set in his arm-chair outside his own door, would expect some special notice as they passed, since he was too old to be at the wedding – feast.

"Mr. Macey's looking for a word from us," said Dolly; "he'll be hurt if we pass him and say nothing – and him so racked with rheumatiz."

So they turned aside to shake hands with the old man. He had looked forward to the occasion, and had his premeditated speech.

"Well, Master Marner," he said, in a voice that quavered a good deal, "I've lived to see my words come true. I was the first to say there was no harm in you, though your looks might be again' you; and I was the first to say you'd get your money back. And it's nothing but rightful as you should. And I'd ha' said the "Amens", and willing, at the holy matrimony; but Tookey's done it a good while now, and I hope you'll have none the worse luck."

In the open yard before the Rainbow the party of guests were already assembled, though it was still nearly an hour before the appointed feast time. But by this means they could not only enjoy the slow advent of their pleasure; they had also ample leisure to talk of Silas Marner's strange history, and arrive by due degrees at the conclusion that he had brought a blessing on himself by acting like a father to a lone motherless child. Even the farrier did not negative this sentiment: on the contrary, he took it up as peculiarly his own, and invited any hardy person present to contradict him. But he met with no contradiction; and all differences among the company were merged in a general agreement with Mr. Snell's sentiment, that when a man had deserved his good luck, it was the part of his neighbours to wish him joy.

As the bridal group approached, a hearty cheer was raised in the Rainbow yard; and Ben Winthrop, whose jokes had retained their acceptable flavour, found it agreeable to turn in there and receive congratulations; not requiring the proposed interval of quiet at the Stone-pits before joining the company.

Eppie had a larger garden than she had ever expected there now; and in other ways there had been alterations at the expense of Mr. Cass, the landlord, to suit Silas's larger family. For he and Eppie had declared that they would rather stay at the Stone-pits than go to any new home. The garden was fenced with stones on two sides, but in front there was an open fence, through which the flowers shone with answering gladness, as the four united people came within sight of them.

"O father," said Eppie, "what a pretty home ours is! I think nobody could be happier than we are."

Editorial Headnote

1834 (Walthamstow–1896

William Morris was a popular and influential textile designer, novelist and socialist activist.

Morris was from a wealthy middle-class family and was educated at Marlborough College and then Oxford University, where he studied classics. Aesthetically, he revered medievalism and championed traditional forms of the arts. A family visit to the Great Exhibition in 1851 when he was a teenager is often said to have been a formative moment in his life as he hated the celebration of modernity and factory production that it represented (MacCarthy 1994: 121).

In his early career as a painter and designer, Morris befriended and promoted many of the pre-Raphaelites who sought to revive classical art, such as Dante Gabriel Rosetti. He also founded the Society for the Preservation of Ancient Buildings (SPAB) in 1877 to oppose the excessive and unsympathetic restoration of churches and other historical structures. The SPAB came to work with the National Trust and proved highly influential in its conservation work; it is still prominent today and is still guided by a manifesto Morris co-wrote with the architect Philip Webb. Morris and Webb also worked together in founding the influential Arts and Crafts movement which advocated a revival of pre-mechanical styles and methods of design and linked him with other prominent critics such as John Ruskin and Thomas Carlyle. This movement was more than aesthetic and had a social dimension in aiming to preserve and gain an appreciation of traditional craftspeople in the face of a mechanizing world seen as soulless.

Morris, however, was quite a different conservationist than most of his fellow aesthetes railing against industrialization at the time. In this extract from Under an Elm-Tree, a notably militant conservationist message can be seen. Making reference to a 'countryside worth fighting for' and likening this struggle to Alfred the Great's battles to save England from the Danes is a stronger message than the typical lament of romantic conservationists of the day. Morris is also far more socially radical than the likes of Ruskin or Wordsworth in referring to 'capitalist robbers' and arguing that agricultural labourers have been reduced to 'slaves' by industrialization. Morris, in fact, became a fully fledged proponent of socialism, as he freely advocates here. Socially, there was nothing conservative about Morris. If anything, he was a revolutionary rather than a romantic. His belief that modernization and capitalism needed to be toppled in order to save the environment was a precursor to the late twentieth-century eco-anarchism of the likes of Bookchin (1971). Morris summed up his life succinctly: 'Apart from the desire to produce beautiful things the leading passion in my life has been and is hatred of modern civilization' (Briggs 1962: 34). The William Morris Society was set up in his honour to advance his causes in 1955 – with a branch in the US – and has certainly succeeded in keeping his name and causes alive.

pp. 212–213

31

UNDER AN ELM-TREE; OR, THOUGHTS IN THE COUNTRY-SIDE

William Morris

Source: William Morris, *Under an Elm-Tree; or, Thoughts in the Country-Side* (1889)

Midsummer in the country – here you may walk between the fields and hedges that are as it were one huge nosegay for you, redolent of bean-flowers and clover and sweet hay and elder-blossom. The cottage gardens are bright with flowers, the cottages themselves mostly models of architecture in their way. Above them towers here and there the architecture proper of days bygone, when every craftsman was an artist and brought definite intelligence to bear upon his work. Man in the past, nature in the present, seem to be bent on pleasing you and making all things delightful to your senses; even the burning dusty road has a look of luxury as you lie on the strip of roadside green, and listen to the blackbirds singing, surely for your benefit, and, I was going to say as if they were paid to do it, but I was wrong, for as it is they seem to be doing their best.

And all, or let us say most things, are brilliantly alive. The shadowy bleak in the river down yonder, which is – ignorant of the fate that Barking Reach is preparing for its waters – sapphire blue under this ruffling wind and cloudless sky, and barred across here and there with the pearly white-flowered water-weeds, every yard of its banks a treasure of delicate design, meadowsweet and dewberry and comfrey and bed-straw – from the bleak in the river, amongst the labyrinth of grasses, to the starlings busy in the new shorn fields, or about the grey ridges of the hay, all is eager, and I think all is happy that is not anxious.

What is that thought that has come into one's head as one turns round in the shadow of the roadside elm? A country-side worth fighting for if that were necessary, worth taking trouble to defend its peace. I raise my head, and betwixt the elm-boughs I see far off a grey buttressed down rising over the sea of green and blue-green meadows and fields, and dim on the flank of it over its buttresses can see a quaint figure made by cutting the short turf away from the chalk of the hillside; a figure which represents a White Horse according to the heraldry of the period, eleven hundred years ago. Hard by that hill-side the country people of the day did verily fight for the peace and loveliness of this very country where I lie, and coming back from their victory scored the image of the White Horse as a

DOI: 10.4324/9781003194651-41

253

token of their valour, and, who knows? perhaps as an example for their descendants to follow.

For a little time it makes the blood stir in me as I think of that, but as I watch the swallows flitting past me betwixt hedge and hedge, or mounting over the hedge in an easy sweep and hawking over the bean-field beyond, another thought comes over me. These live things I have been speaking of, bleak and swallows and starlings and blackbirds, are all after their kind beautiful and graceful, not one of them is lacking in its due grace and beauty; but yesterday as I was passing by a hay-field there was an old red-roan cart-horse looking seriously but good-humouredly at me from a gap in the hedge, and I stopped to make his acquaintance; and I am sorry to say that in spite of his obvious merits he was ugly, Roman-nosed, shambling, ungainly: yet how useful he had been – for others. Also the same day (but not in the same field) I saw some other animals, male and female, with whom also I made acquaintance, for the male ones at least were thirsty. And these animals, both male and female, were ungraceful, unbeautiful, as ungainly as the roan cart-horse; yet they were obviously useful, for they were making hay before my eyes. Then I bethought me that as I had seen starlings in Hertfordshire that were of the same race as the Thames side starlings, so I had seen or heard of featherless two-legged animals of the same race as the thirsty creatures in the hay-field; they had been sculptured in the frieze of the Parthenon, painted on the ceiling of the Sistine Chapel, imagined in literature as the heroes and heroines of romance; nay, when people had created in their minds a god of the universe, creator of all that was, is, or shall be, they were driven to represent him as one of that same race to which the thirsty haymakers belonged; as though supreme intelligence and the greatest measure of gracefulness and beauty and majesty were at their highest in the race of those ungainly animals.

Under the elm-tree these things puzzle me, and again my thoughts return to the bold men of that very country-side, who, coming back from Ashdown field, scored that White Horse to look down for ever on the valley of the Thames; and I thought it likely that they had this much in common with the starlings and the bleak, that there was more equality amongst them than we are used to now, and that there would have been more models available amongst them for Woden than one would be like to find in the Thames-side meadows.

Under the elm-tree I don't ask myself whether that is owing to the greater average intelligence of men at the present day, and to the progress of humanity made since the time of the only decent official that England ever had, Alfred the Great, to wit; for indeed the place and time are not favourable to such questions, which seem sheer nonsense amidst of all that waste of superabundant beauty and pleasure held out to men who cannot take it or use it, unless some chance rich idler may happen to stray that way. My thoughts turn back to the haymakers and their hopes, and I remember that yesterday morning I said to a bystander, 'Mr So-and-so (the farmer) is late in sending his men into the hay-field'.

Quoth he, 'You see, sir, Mr So-and-so is short-handed'.

'How's that?' said I, pricking up my Socialist ears.

UNDER AN ELM-TREE; OR, THOUGHTS IN THE COUNTRY-SIDE

'Well, sir,' said he, 'these men are the old men and women bred in the village, and pretty much past work; and the young men with more work in them, they do think that they ought to have more wages than them, and Mr So-and-so, he won't pay it. So you see, he be short-handed.'

As I turned away, thinking over all the untold, untellable details of misery that lay within this shabby, sordid story, another one met my ears. A labourer of the village comes to a farmer and says to him that he really can't work for 9s. a week any more, but must have 10s. Says the farmer, 'Get your 10s. somewhere else then'. The man turns away to two month's lack of employment, and then comes back begging for his 9s. slavery.

Commonplace stories of unsupported strikes, you will say. Indeed they are, if not they would be easily remedied; the casual tragedy cut short; the casual wrong-doer branded as a person out of humanity. But since they are so commonplace-

What will happen, say my gloomy thoughts to me under the elm tree, with all this country beauty so tragically incongruous in its richness with the country misery which cannot feel its existence? Well, if we must still be slaves and slaveholders, it will not last long; the Battle of Ashdown will be forgotten for the last commercial crisis; Alfred's heraldry will yield to the lions of the half crown. The architecture of the crafts-gildsmen will tumble down, or be 'restored' for the benefit of the hunters of picturesque, who, hopeless themselves, are incapable of understanding the hopes of past days, or the expression of them. The beauty of the landscape will be exploited and artificialized for the sake of the villa-dweller's purses where it is striking enough to touch their jaded appetites; but in quiet places like this it will vanish year by year (as indeed it is now doing) under the attacks of the most grovelling commercialism.

Yet think I to myself under the elm-tree, whatever England, once so beautiful, may become, it will be good enough for us if we set no hope before us but the continuance of a population of slaves and slave-holders for the country which we pretend to love, while we use it and our sham love for it as a stalking-horse for robbery of the poor at home and abroad. The worst outward ugliness and vulgarity will be good enough for such sneaks and cowards.

Let me turn the leaf and find a new picture, or my holiday is spoilt; and don't let some of my Socialist friends with whom I have wrangled about the horrors of London, say, 'This is all that can come of your country life'. For as the round of the seasons under our system of landlord farmer and labourer produces in the country pinching parsimony and dullness, so does the 'excitement of intellectual life' in the cities produce the slum under the capitalist system of turning out and selling market wares not for use but for waste. Turn the page I say. The hayfield is a pretty sight this month seen under the elm, as the work goes forward on the other side of the way opposite to the bean-field, till you look at the haymakers closely. Suppose the haymakers were friends working for friends on land which was theirs, as many as were needed, with leisure and hope ahead of them instead of hopeless toil and anxiety, need their useful labour for themselves and their neighbours cripple and disfigure them and knock them out of the shape of men fit to represent the Gods and Heroes? And if under such conditions a new Ashdown had to be fought (against capitalist robbers this time), the new White Horse would look down on the home of men as wise as the starlings in their equality, and so perhaps as happy.

Editorial Headnote

1793 (Helpstone, Northamptonshire [now Cambridgeshire])–1864

John Clare was a romantic poet who celebrated England's peasantry and nature.

Clare was from a poor rural family and became an agricultural labourer from a young age. He proceeded to work in a number of lowly paid jobs and was at one time in receipt of poor relief. However, he pursued his passion for poetry in his spare time and in 1820 managed to secure a publisher for his 'Poems Descriptive of Rural Life and Scenery'. Clare was one of several 'peasant poets' briefly elevated into the literary spotlight at the time as representing authentic voices from the increasingly romanticized English countryside. As we have seen, the popular romantic poets of the age, such as Wordsworth, as well as wanting to celebrate nature, wished to eschew elitism and communicate more directly with the masses. However, after some initial interest and notoriety, Clare's literary career never really took off, and he periodically returned to labouring in the fields. His acclaim as a poet was to come posthumously.

The particular context of this poem by Clare, and others he wrote, such as 'To a Fallen Elm', was the Enclosures. The early nineteenth century saw an escalation of a phenomenon apparent since the seventeenth century of selling off common land for conversion into farms. Between 1809 and 1820, the rich common land countryside around Helpstone he had played in as a boy was sold off in enclosure acts and transformed into fenced-off farmsteads. Marshes were drained, woodlands felled, scrublands cleared and rivers canalized. Hugely profitable arable land was created in this way but with major environmental and human costs. As well as the landscape, local lifestyles were radically transformed. For instance, traditional festivals and holidays, such as 'Plough Monday' at the start of the agricultural year, were ended. The renowned contemporary ecologist George Monbiot describes that the land around Helpstone 'now ranks among the most dismal and regularised tracts of countryside in Europe' (Monbiot 2012).

As can be seen, Clare's poetry maintains rural vernacular, something that was part of his early appeal. For instance, the 'mouldywharps' referred to are moles. The loss of these and other animals, as well as trees, streams and even low hills, are depicted in both sorrowful and graphic terms in the elegy. In mourning the loss of his childhood landscape, however, it is evident that Clare's lament is far more than romantic nostalgia. The enclosures are portrayed as hostile and aggressive acts akin to the conquests of Napoleon Bonaparte. The depiction of his and his fellow villagers' oneness with nature and how this is destroyed by 'the spoiler and self-interest' is a political and ecological message still with great resonance today.

Clare suffered from ill health all his life, and in his forties, his mind began to fail him. In 1837, five years after penning the poem profiled here, he was committed to a lunatic asylum. He managed to escape institutionalization for a while and lived until his seventies but never recovered. Ultimately, however, Clare came to leave a significant legacy as a chronicler of environmental change. The literary biographer Jonathan Bate has said of him: 'No one has ever written more powerfully of nature' (Bate 2003). In 2005, the John Clare Trust restored his old cottage in Helpstone and opened it to the public as a museum and shop.

32

'REMEMBRANCES'

John Clare

Source: John Clare, 'Remembrances' (1832)

Summer pleasures they are gone like to visions every one
And the cloudy days of autumn and of winter cometh on
I tried to call them back but unbidden they are gone
Far away from heart and eye and for ever far away
Dear heart and can it be that such raptures meet decay
I thought them all eternal when by Langley Bush I lay
I thought them joys eternal when I used to shout and play
On its bank at 'clink and bandy' 'chock' and 'taw' and ducking stone
Where silence sitteth now on the wild heath as her own
Like a ruin of the past all alone

When I used to lie and sing by old eastwells boiling spring
When I used to tie the willow boughs together for a 'swing'
And fish with crooked pins and thread and never catch a thing
With heart just like a feather- now as heavy as a stone
When beneath old lea close oak I the bottom branches broke
To make our harvest cart like so many working folk
And then to cut a straw at the brook to have a soak
O I never dreamed of parting or that trouble had a sting
Or that pleasures like a flock of birds would ever take to wing
Leaving nothing but a little naked spring

When jumping time away on old cross berry way
And eating awes like sugar plumbs ere they had lost the may
And skipping like a leveret before the peep of day
On the rolly polly up and downs of pleasant swordy well
When in round oaks narrow lane as the south got black again
We sought the hollow ash that was shelter from the rain
With our pockets full of peas we had stolen from the grain
How delicious was the dinner time on such a showry day
O words are poor receipts for what time hath stole away
The ancient pulpit trees and the play

DOI: 10.4324/9781003194651-42

ROMANTICIZING NATURE

When for school oer 'little field' with its brook and wooden brig
Where I swaggered like a man though I was not half so big
While I held my little plough though twas but a willow twig
And drove my team along made of nothing but a name
'Gee hep' and 'hoit' and 'woi'- O I never call to mind
These pleasant names of places but I leave a sigh behind
While I see the little mouldywharps hang sweeing to the wind
On the only aged willow that in all the field remains
And nature hides her face where theyre sweeing in their chains
And in a silent murmuring complains

Here was commons for the hills where they seek for freedom still
Though every commons gone and though traps are set to kill
The little homeless miners- O it turns my bosom chill
When I think of old 'sneap green' puddocks nook and hilly snow
Where bramble bushes grew and the daisy gemmed in dew
And the hills of silken grass like to cushions to the view
When we threw the pissmire crumbs when we's nothing else to do
All leveled like a desert by the never weary plough
All vanished like the sun where that cloud is passing now
All settled here for ever on its brow

I never thought that joys would run away from boys
Or that boys would change their minds and forsake such summer joys
But alack I never dreamed that the world had other toys
To petrify first feelings like the fable into stone
Till I found the pleasure past and a winter come at last
Then the fields were sudden bare and the sky got overcast
And boyhoods pleasing haunts like a blossom in the blast
Was shrivelled to a withered weed and trampled down and done
Till vanished was the morning spring and set that summer sun
And winter fought her battle strife and won

By Langley bush I roam but the bush hath left its hill
On cowper green I stray tis a desert strange and chill
And spreading lea close oak ere decay had penned its will
To the axe of the spoiler and self interest fell a prey
And cross berry way and old round oaks narrow lane
With its hollow trees like pulpits I shall never see again
Inclosure like a Buonaparte let not a thing remain
It levelled every bush and tree and levelled every hill
And hung the moles for traitors – though the brook is running still
It runs a naked brook cold and chill

'REMEMBRANCES'

O had I known as then joy had left the paths of men
I had watched her night and day besure and never slept agen
And when she turned to go O I'd caught her mantle then
And wooed her like a lover by my lonely side to stay
Aye knelt and worshipped on as love in beautys bower
And clung upon her smiles as a bee upon her flower
And gave her heart my poesys all cropt in a sunny hour
As keepsakes and pledges to fade away
But love never heeded to treasure up the may
So it went the common road with decay

Editorial Headnote

1838 (Wisbech, Cambridgeshire)–1912

Octavia Hill was a social reformer best remembered for being a co-founder of the hugely influential National Trust.

Hill had a limited formal education but was from a family committed to social justice and this very much guided her life. Her father's lucrative corn business collapsed when she was a young girl, leading him to abandon his family. Consequently, Olivia's mother took control of the family and moved them to a more modest life in the London suburb of Finchley. Here, Hill worked with her mother in a 'Ragged School', a Christian socialist cooperative where young, impoverished girls were taught to make toys to sell. Through her mother's connections, Hill became a long-term friend of John Ruskin, who provided her with crucial financial backing for her early campaigns such as the redevelopment of housing in Marylebone, North London. Ruskin, however, declined to back Hill in her 1873 campaign to save Swiss Cottage Fields from being built on, since he had come to see the London suburbs as a lost cause. Consequently, she shifted her allegiance to Lord Meath and James Bryce (profiled elsewhere) (Mallett 1995). Hill's sister, Miranda, was also a conservation campaigner and was instrumental in the establishment of the Kyrle Society which Octavia also worked alongside Robert Hunter and William Morris (both also profiled elsewhere).

Hill was a passionate advocate of social housing and open spaces in cities. She coined the still-important term Green Belt and campaigned against construction on London open spaces, such as Hampstead Heath and Parliament Hill. An important culmination of Hill's cooperation with Meath was the 1884 Disused Burial Grounds Act, under which the sale of burial grounds to building constructors was restricted. Probably Hill's greatest legacy, however, was to be one of the three founders of the National Trust, alongside the poet Hardwicke Rawnsley and lawyer Robert Hunter. The Octavia Hill Society was founded in 1992 in her honour centred on a museum at her birthplace in Wisbech.

In the selected extract of Hill's work, we again see rural idyll contrasted sharply with urban ugliness, both environmental and human. However, it is also evident that Hill is more socially conscious than her friend and ally Ruskin in wanting to help the poor rather than keep them away. The Bank Holiday hordes she describes as pouring out of London are a sad result of the shrinking of open spaces for people to visit. She cites Lefevre's (profiled in Volume II Part 1) estimate of four-fifths of such common lands having been taken over in the past century. Similarly, she is also less romantic about feudalism than many other conservationists of the time. Hill was a reformer lamenting aristocratic privilege and the practice of putting profit over the environment.

pp. 3–16

33

OUR COMMON LAND

Octavia Hill

Source: Octavia Hill, *Our Common Land* (1877)

I. OUR COMMON LAND

Probably few persons who have a choice of holidays select a Bank holiday, which falls in the spring or summer, as one on which they will travel, or stroll in the country, unless, indeed, they live in neighbourhoods very far removed from large towns. Every railway station is crowded; every booking-office thronged; every seat – nay, all standing room – is occupied in every kind of public conveyance; the roads leading out of London for miles are crowded with every description of vehicle – van, cart, chaise, gig – drawn by every size and sort of donkey, pony, or horse; if it be a dusty day, a great dull unbroken choking cloud of dust hangs over every line of road.

Yet in spite of all this, and in spite of the really bad sights to be seen at every public-house on the road, in spite of the wild songs and boisterous behaviour, and reckless driving home at night, which show how sadly intoxication is still bound up with the idea and practical use of a holiday to hundreds of our people, how much intense enjoyment the day gives! how large a part of this enjoyment is unmixed good! And the evil is kept in check very much. We may see the quiet figure of the mounted policeman as we drive home, dark in the twilight, dark amidst the dust, keeping order among the vehicles, making the drunken drivers mind what they are doing. He keeps very tolerable order. And then these days in the country ought to lessen the number of drunkards every year; and more and more we shall be able to trust to the public opinion of the quiet many to preserve order.

And watch, when at last the open spaces are reached towards which all these lines of vehicles are tending – be it Epping, or Richmond, or Greenwich, or Hampstead – every place seems swarming with an undisciplined, but heartily happy, crowd. The swings, the roundabouts, the donkeys, the stalls, are beset by dozens or even hundreds of pleasure-seekers, gay and happy, though they are not always the gentlest or most refined. Look at the happy family groups – father, and mother, and children, with their picnic dinners neatly tied up in handkerchiefs; watch the joy of eager children leaning out of vans to purchase for a halfpenny the wonderful pink paper streamers which they will stick proudly in their caps; see the merry little

DOI: 10.4324/9781003194651-43

265

things running untiringly up and down the bank of sand or grass; notice the affectionate father bringing out the pot of ale to the wife as she sits comfortably tucked up in shawls in the little cart, or treating the children to sweetmeats; sympathise in the hearty energy of the great rough lads who have walked miles, as their dusty boots well show; their round, honest faces have beamed with rough mirth at every joke that has come in their way all day; they have rejoiced more in the clamber to obtain the great branches of may than even in the proud possession of them, though they are carrying them home in triumph. To all these the day brings unmixed good.

Now, have you ever paused to think what Londoners would do without this holiday, or what it would be without these open spaces? Cooped up for many weeks in close rooms, in narrow streets, compelled on their holiday to travel for miles in a crowded stream, first between houses, and then between dusty high hedges, suddenly they expand into free uncrowded space under spreading trees, or on to the wide Common from which blue distance is visible; the eye, long unrefreshed with sight of growing grass, or star-like flowers, is rejoiced by them again. To us the Common or forest looks indeed crowded with people, but to them the feeling is one of sufficient space, free air, green grass, and colour, with a life without which they might think the place dull. Every atom of open space you have left to these people is needed; take care you lose none of it; it is becoming yearly of more vital importance to save or increase it.

There is now a Bill for regulating inclosure before the House of Commons. Mr. Cross has said what he trusts will be its effect if it becomes law; but those who have been watching the history of various inclosures, and the trials respecting special Commons, are not so hopeful as Mr. Cross is as to the effect this Bill would have. It makes indeed good provisions for regulating Commons to be kept open for the public when a scheme for regulation is applied for. But the adoption of such a scheme depends in large part on the lord of the manor. Will he in nine cases out of ten ever even apply for a scheme for regulating a Common, when he knows that by doing so he shuts out from himself and his successors for ever the possibility of inclosing it, and appropriating some part of it? Do any provisions for regulating, however excellent, avail anything when no motive exists which should prompt the lord of the manor to bring the Common under them? and, as the Bill stands, it cannot be so brought without his consent.

Secondly, the Bill provides that urban sanitary authorities can purchase rights which will enable them to keep open any suburban Common, or may accept a gift of the same. But then a suburban Common is defined as one situated within six miles of the outside of a town of 5,000 inhabitants. Now, I hardly know how far out of a large town Bank-holiday excursionists go, but I know they go every year farther and farther. I am sure that a Common twelve, nay, twenty, miles off from a large town is accessible by cheap trains to hundreds of excursionists all the summer, to whom it is an inestimable boon. Again, is the privilege of space, and light, and air, and beauty not to be considered for the small shopkeeper, for the hard-working clerk, who will probably never own a square yard of English land, but who cares to take his wife and children into the country for a fortnight in the summer? Do you not know numbers of neighbourhoods where woods, and Commons, and fields used to be open to pedestrians, and now they must walk, even in the country, on straight roads between hedges? The more that fields and woods are closed, the more does every atom of Common land, everywhere, all over England, become of importance to the people of every class, except that which owns its own parks and woods. "On the lowest computation," says the Report of the Commons Preservation Society, "5,000,000 acres of Common land have been inclosed since Queen Anne's reign; now there are but 1,000,000 acres left.[1] The right of roving over these lands has been an immense boon to our people; it becomes at once more valued and rarer year by year. Is it impossible, I would ask lawyers and statesmen, to recognise this right as a legal one acquired by custom, and not to be taken away? Mr. Lefevre suggested this in a letter to *The Times*. He says:

The right of the public to use and enjoy Commons (which they have for centuries exercised), it must be admitted, is not distinctly recognised by law, though there is a remarkable absence of adverse testimony on the subject. The law, however, most fully recognises the right of the village to its green, and allows the establishment of such right by evidence as to playing games, &c., but it has failed as yet to recognise the analogy between the great town and its Common, and the village and its green, however complete in fact that analogy may be. But some of these rights of Common, which are now so prized as a means of keeping Commons open, had, if legal theory is correct, their origin centuries ago in custom. For long they had no legal existence, but the courts of law at last learned to recognise custom as conferring rights. The custom has altered in kind; in lieu of cattle, sheep, and pigs turned out to pasture on the Commons, human beings have taken their place, and wear down the turf instead of eating it. I can see no reason why the law, or, if the courts are too slow to move, the Legislature, should not recognise this transfer and legalise this custom. Again, it is probable that Commons belonged originally much more to the inhabitants of a district than to the lord. Feudal theory and its subsequent development – English Real Property Law – have ridden rather roughly over the facts and the rights of the case. The first placed the lord of the manor in his position as lord, giving him certain privileges, and coupling with them many responsibilities. The second gradually removed these responsibilities, and converted into a property what was at first little more than an official trust. If these considerations are beyond the scope of the law courts, they are proper for Parliament. One step has been made. It has been proved that it is not necessary to purchase Commons for the public, but that ample means of protecting them from inclosure exist. It is also obvious that the rights which constitute these means are now in practice represented by a public user of Commons for recreation. The Legislature should, I venture to think, recognise this user as a legal right.

If the Legislature would do this, Commons all over England might be kept open, which, I venture to think, would be a great gain. Hitherto the right to keep Commons open has been maintained, even in the neighbourhood of towns, by legal questions affecting rights of pasturage, of cutting turf, or carting gravel. This is all very well if it secures the object, but it is on the large ground of public policy, for the sake of the health and enjoyment of the people, that the conscience of the nation supports the attempt to keep them open; it cares little for the defence of obsolete and often nearly valueless customs, and it would be very well if the right acquired by use could be recognised by law, and the defence put at once on its real grounds.

I have referred to the opinion expressed by lawyers and members of Parliament that the opportunity of applying for schemes for regulation provided by the Bill now before the House will not be used at all largely, owing to the necessity of the consent of those owning two-thirds value of the Common, and of the veto possessed by the lord of the manor. They tell me also (and it certainly appears to me that both statements are evident on reading the Bill) that unless Mr. Cross consents to insert a clause forbidding all inclosures except under this Act, the passing of it will be followed by a large number of high-handed inclosures under old Acts, or without legal right. For unless the right of some independent body like the public who use the space can be recognised as having a voice in opposing illegal inclosures, what chance have the rural Commons? The agricultural labourers, often tenants-at-will of a powerful landlord, can be ejected and their rights immediately cancelled; moreover, they do not know the law, they have few to advise them, to plead their cause, or to spend money on expensive lawsuits. Mr. Lefevre says in the same letter quoted above, "I would at least ask them to declare all inclosures not authorised by Parliament to be primâ facie illegal and to remove the necessity of litigation by persons actually themselves commoners, by authorising any public body, or public-spirited individual, to interfere in the case of any such inclosures, and put the lord to strict proof of his right."

And do not let us be too ready to see the question dealt with as a matter of mere money compensation. It is much to be feared lest the short-sighted cupidity of one generation of rural commoners may lose a great possession for future times. This danger is imminent because we are all so accustomed to treat money value as if it were the only real value! Can we wonder if the eyes of poor men are often fixed rather on the immediate money value to themselves than on the effect of changes for their descendants? Should we stand by, we who ought to see farther, and let them part with what ought to be a possession to the many in the future? A few coals at Christmas, which rapidly come to be looked upon as a charity graciously accorded by the rich, or the recipients of which are arbitrarily selected by them, may in many cases be blindly accepted by cottagers in lieu of Common rights. Is the influence of such doles so healthy that we should wish to see them taking the place of a Common right over a little bit of English soil? The issue at a nominal charge of orders to cut turf or furze by a lord of the manor has been known gradually to extinguish the right to do so without his leave. Is the influence of the rich and powerful so slight that we should let it be thus silently strengthened? Is the knowledge just brought so prominently before us that one quarter of the land in England is owned by only seven hundred and ten persons so satisfactory that we will stand by and see quietly absorbed those few spots which are our common birthright in the soil? It is not likely that farms or estates will diminish in size; and the yeoman class is, I suppose, passing away rapidly. With the small holdings, is there to pass away from our people the sense that they have any share in the soil of their native England? I think the sense of owning some spaces of it in common may be healthier for them than even the possession of small bits by individuals, and certainly it now seems more feasible. Lowell tells us that what is free to all is the best of all possessions:

> 'Tis heaven alone that is given away,
> 'Tis only God may be had for the asking;
> There is no price set on the lavish summer,
> And June may be had by the poorest comer.

Hugh Miller, too, points out how intimately the right to roam over the land is connected with the love of it, and hence with patriotism. He says, speaking of his first visit to Edinburgh: "I threw myself, as usual, for compensatory pleasures, on my evening walks, but found the inclosed state of the district, and the fence of a rigorously-administered trespass-law, serious drawbacks; and ceased to wonder that a thoroughly cultivated country is, in most instances, so much less beloved by its people than a wild and open one. Rights of proprietorship may exist equally in both; but there is an important sense in which the open country belongs to the proprietors and to the people too. All that the heart and intellect can derive from it may be alike free to peasant and aristocrat; whereas the cultivated and strictly fenced country belongs usually, in every sense, to only the proprietor; and as it is a much simpler and more obvious matter to love one's country as a scene of hills, and streams, and green fields, amid which nature has often been enjoyed, than as a definite locality, in which certain laws and constitutional privileges exist, it is rather to be regretted than wondered at that there should be often less true patriotism in a country of just institutions and equal laws, whose soil has been so exclusively appropriated as to leave only the dusty high-roads to its people, than in wild open countries, in which the popular mind and affections are left free to embrace the soil, but whose institutions are partial and defective." So writes at least one man of the people; and whether we estimate the relative value of just laws or familiar and beloved scenes quite as he does, or not, I think we must all feel there is deep truth in what he says.

Let us then press Government, while there is still time, that no bit of the small portion of uninclosed ground, which is the common inheritance of us all as English men and women, shall be henceforth inclosed, except under this Bill; which simply means that each scheme shall be submitted to a Committee of the House, and considered on its merits.

Surely this is a very reasonable request. Do not let us be satisfied with less. Do not let us deceive ourselves as to the result of this Bill if it pass unamended.

Octavia Hill Woodlands at Toy's Hill Kent
Source: Octavia Hill Woodland in the dark | Openverse

NOTE

1   The amount remaining uninclosed and subject to Common-rights is variously estimated; a report of the Inclosure Commissioners in 1874 putting it at about 2,600,000 for England and Wales, while the recent return of landowners, prepared by the Local Government Board, makes the uninclosed area little more than 1,500,000 acres.

Editorial Headnote

1820 (Great Yarmouth)–1878

Black Beauty was Anna Sewell's only published work but remains very well known today as a tale of life from the perspective of a horse. She died only a few months after its publication of a long-standing illness. Sewell was paid a one-off fee by Jarrolds of Norwich for the work which became an instant success and has stood the test of time as a book and the basis of a subsequent popular TV series.

Sewell was born into a poor Quaker family in Norfolk who moved to London when she was young. She was also in poor health for most of her life, having been crippled by a serious fall in childhood. Difficulty in walking led her to spend more time driving horse-drawn carriages, including taking her father across London to work from an early age. Thus, she grew up in the company of horses and not only learned to love them but also became aware of how badly they were often treated. Sewell's mother was an author of religious books for children, and as a young woman, Anna assisted her in editing these, which helped prepare her for later taking to writing herself.

Black Beauty was one of the first English novels to be written from the perspective of an animal and remains probably the best-known book in this genre. Sewell wrote the book as a guide to good horse husbandry, and it did prove influential in that regard. In this course of this, though, the book advocated kindness to horses as a moral and religious duty. In the first extracted chapter, it is notable that the boy ill-treating his horse is also shown to be a school bully and suggested to be ungodly. In line with how legislation protecting animals at the time was evolving, a key concern of advocates for this was the corrupting effect of such behaviour on the human perpetrators. However, Sewell's use of the horse's perspective helped advance the debate beyond this. In the second of the two extracts here, Black Beauty highlighted the cruelty inherent in the popularity of the time for using 'bearing reins' – to keep the horse's head high for appearances' sake. This made a big impact, and the practice subsequently came to be phased out. The book features a commendation from the Royal Society for the Prevention of Cruelty to Animals in its preface.

Sewell died of either hepatitis or tuberculosis and at least lived to see her book begin to sell well. She is buried at a Quaker burial ground in Buxton, Norfolk, and commemorated in many ways including by a museum at her birthplace in Great Yarmouth and a fountain in Norwich (Encyclopedia Britannica).

pp. 60–62

34

BLACK BEAUTY

Anna Sewell

Source: Anna Sewell, *Black Beauty* (1878)

PART 1, CHAPTER 13: THE DEVIL'S TRADE MARK

One day when John and I had been out on some business of our master's, and were returning gently on a long, straight road, at some distance we saw a boy trying to leap a pony over a gate; the pony would not take the leap, and the boy cut him with the whip, but he only turned off on one side. He whipped him again, but the pony turned off on the other side. Then the boy got off and gave him a hard thrashing, and knocked him about the head; then he got up again and tried to make him leap the gate, kicking him all the time shamefully, but still the pony refused. When we were nearly at the spot the pony put down his head and threw up his heels, and sent the boy neatly over into a broad quickset hedge, and with the rein dangling from his head he set off home at a full gallop. John laughed out quite loud. "Served him right," he said.

"Oh, oh, oh!" cried the boy as he struggled about among the thorns; "I say, come and help me out."

"Thank ye," said John, "I think you are quite in the right place, and maybe a little scratching will teach you not to leap a pony over a gate that is too high for him," and so with that John rode off. "It may be," said he to himself, "that young fellow is a liar as well as a cruel one; we'll just go home by Farmer Bushby's, Beauty, and then if anybody wants to know you and I can tell 'em, ye see." So we turned off to the right, and soon came up to the stack-yard, and within sight of the house. The farmer was hurrying out into the road, and his wife was standing at the gate, looking very frightened.

"Have you seen my boy?" said Mr. Bushby as we came up; "he went out an hour ago on my black pony, and the creature is just come back without a rider."

"I should think, sir," said John, "he had better be without a rider, unless he can be ridden properly."

"What do you mean?" said the farmer.

"Well, sir, I saw your son whipping, and kicking, and knocking that good little pony about shamefully because he would not leap a gate that was too high for him. The pony behaved well, sir, and showed no vice; but at last he just threw up his heels and tipped the young gentleman into the thorn hedge. He wanted me to help him out, but I hope you will excuse me, sir, I did not feel inclined to do so. There's no bones broken, sir; he'll only get a few scratches. I love horses, and it riles me to see them badly used; it is a bad plan to aggravate an animal till he uses his heels; the first time is not always the last."

During this time the mother began to cry, "Oh, my poor Bill, I must go and meet him; he must be hurt."

"You had better go into the house, wife," said the farmer; "Bill wants a lesson about this, and I must see that he gets it; this is not the first time, nor the second, that he has ill-used that pony, and I shall stop it. I am much obliged to you, Manly. Good-evening."

So we went on, John chuckling all the way home; then he told James about it, who laughed and said, "Serve him right. I knew that boy at school; he took great airs on himself because he was a farmer's son; he used to swagger about and bully the little boys. Of course, we elder ones would not have any of that nonsense, and let him know that in the school and the playground farmers' sons and laborers' sons were all alike. I well remember one day, just before afternoon school, I found him at the large window catching flies and pulling off their wings. He did not see me and I gave him a box on the ears that laid him sprawling on the floor. Well, angry as I was, I was almost frightened, he roared and bellowed in such a style. The boys rushed in from the playground, and the master ran in from the road to see who was being murdered. Of course I said fair and square at once what I had done, and why; then I showed the master the flies, some crushed and some crawling about helpless, and I showed him the wings on the window sill. I never saw him so angry before; but as Bill was still howling and whining, like the coward that he was, he did not give him any more punishment of that kind, but set him up on a stool for the rest of the afternoon, and said that he should not go out to play for that week. Then he talked to all the boys very seriously about cruelty, and said how hard-hearted and cowardly it was to hurt the weak and the helpless; but what stuck in my mind was this, he said that cruelty was the devil's own trade-mark, and if we saw any one who took pleasure in cruelty we might know who he belonged to, for the devil was a murderer from the beginning, and a tormentor to the end. On the other hand, where we saw people who loved their neighbors, and were kind to man and beast, we might know that was God's mark."

"Your master never taught you a truer thing," said John; "there is no religion without love, and people may talk as much as they like about their religion, but if it does not teach them to be good and kind to man and beast it is all a sham – all a sham, James, and it won't stand when things come to be turned inside out."

. . .

pp. 127–130

BLACK BEAUTY

PART 2, CHAPTER 28: A JOB HORSE AND HIS DRIVERS

Hitherto I had always been driven by people who at least knew how to drive; but in this place I was to get my experience of all the different kinds of bad and ignorant driving to which we horses are subjected; for I was a "job horse", and was let out to all sorts of people who wished to hire me; and as I was good-tempered and gentle, I think I was oftener let out to the ignorant drivers than some of the other horses, because I could be depended upon. It would take a long time to tell of all the different styles in which I was driven, but I will mention a few of them.

First, there were the tight-rein drivers – men who seemed to think that all depended on holding the reins as hard as they could, never relaxing the pull on the horse's mouth, or giving him the least liberty of movement. They are always talking about "keeping the horse well in hand", and "holding a horse up", just as if a horse was not made to hold himself up.

Some poor, broken-down horses, whose mouths have been made hard and insensible by just such drivers as these, may, perhaps, find some support in it; but for a horse who can depend upon his own legs, and who has a tender mouth and is easily guided, it is not only tormenting, but it is stupid.

Then there are the loose-rein drivers, who let the reins lie easily on our backs, and their own hand rest lazily on their knees. Of course, such gentlemen have no control over a horse, if anything happens suddenly. If a horse shies, or starts, or stumbles, they are nowhere, and cannot help the horse or themselves till the mischief is done. Of course, for myself I had no objection to it, as I was not in the habit either of starting or stumbling, and had only been used to depend on my driver for guidance and encouragement. Still, one likes to feel the rein a little in going downhill, and likes to know that one's driver is not gone to sleep.

Besides, a slovenly way of driving gets a horse into bad and often lazy habits, and when he changes hands he has to be whipped out of them with more or less pain and trouble. Squire Gordon always kept us to our best paces and our best manners. He said that spoiling a horse and letting him get into bad habits was just as cruel as spoiling a child, and both had to suffer for it afterward.

Besides, these drivers are often careless altogether, and will attend to anything else more than their horses. I went out in the phaeton one day with one of them; he had a lady and two children behind. He flopped the reins about as we started, and of course gave me several unmeaning cuts with the whip, though I was fairly off. There had been a good deal of road-mending going on, and even where the stones were not freshly laid down there were a great many loose ones about. My driver was laughing and joking with the lady and the children, and talking about the country to the right and the left; but he never thought it worth while to keep an eye on his horse or to drive on the smoothest parts of the road; and so it easily happened that I got a stone in one of my fore feet.

Now, if Mr. Gordon or John, or in fact any good driver, had been there, he would have seen that something was wrong before I had gone three paces. Or

ROMANTICIZING NATURE

even if it had been dark a practiced hand would have felt by the rein that there was something wrong in the step, and they would have got down and picked out the stone. But this man went on laughing and talking, while at every step the stone became more firmly wedged between my shoe and the frog of my foot. The stone was sharp on the inside and round on the outside, which, as every one knows, is the most dangerous kind that a horse can pick up, at the same time cutting his foot and making him most liable to stumble and fall.

Whether the man was partly blind or only very careless I can't say, but he drove me with that stone in my foot for a good half-mile before he saw anything. By that time I was going so lame with the pain that at last he saw it, and called out, "Well, here's a go! Why, they have sent us out with a lame horse! What a shame!"

He then chucked the reins and flipped about with the whip, saying, "Now, then, it's no use playing the old soldier with me; there's the journey to go, and it's no use turning lame and lazy."

Just at this time a farmer came riding up on a brown cob. He lifted his hat and pulled up.

"I beg your pardon, sir," he said, "but I think there is something the matter with your horse; he goes very much as if he had a stone in his shoe. If you will allow me I will look at his feet; these loose scattered stones are confounded dangerous things for the horses."

"He's a hired horse," said my driver. "I don't know what's the matter with him, but it is a great shame to send out a lame beast like this."

The farmer dismounted, and slipping his rein over his arm at once took up my near foot.

"Bless me, there's a stone! Lame! I should think so!"

At first he tried to dislodge it with his hand, but as it was now very tightly wedged he drew a stone-pick out of his pocket, and very carefully and with some trouble got it out. Then holding it up he said, "There, that's the stone your horse had picked up. It is a wonder he did not fall down and break his knees into the bargain!"

"Well, to be sure!" said my driver; "that is a queer thing! I never knew that horses picked up stones before."

"Didn't you?" said the farmer rather contemptuously; "but they do, though, and the best of them will do it, and can't help it sometimes on such roads as these. And if you don't want to lame your horse you must look sharp and get them out quickly. This foot is very much bruised," he said, setting it gently down and patting me. "If I might advise, sir, you had better drive him gently for awhile; the foot is a good deal hurt, and the lameness will not go off directly."

Then mounting his cob and raising his hat to the lady he trotted off.

When he was gone my driver began to flop the reins about and whip the harness, by which I understood that I was to go on, which of course I did, glad that the stone was gone, but still in a good deal of pain.

This was the sort of experience we job horses often came in for.

Editorial Headnote

1839 (Bury St Edmunds)–1908

Louise de la Ramée – who went by the literary nom de plume Ouida – was a prolific novelist known mostly for swashbuckling romantic tales. Ouida was a nickname she adopted based on her own mispronunciation of her real first name as a young child.

Ouida's father was an émigré from France and a French teacher, and as a result, she spent some of her childhood in Paris and her whole life came to be marked by internationalism. She took up writing from an early age, and this became her lifelong career. After having some of her stories serialized in Bentley's Magazine, her first published novel was Granville De Vigo in 1860, and she proceeded to write many more, along with a number of short stories. Probably her best-known publication was Under Two Flags in 1867, set in France's Algerian colony.

Ouida moved to the picturesque countryside of Tuscany in Italy in her thirties and lived the rest of her life there. It was here that she wrote The Waters of Edera, something of a departure from her other novels in having a somewhat political message amongst the more typical themes of romance and intrigue. The book is, at one level at least, a tale of conservation in the face of the devastating ravages of industrialization, as is apparent in the following extract. For example. she notably makes reference to the 'gift of nature' in a gently ecological message. It is notable also that the river diversion is likened to the rape of a woman. This feminization of nature was common in nineteenth-century literature and, as we see in several of the selected extracts, women writers were prominent defenders of the environment. In the story, an idyllic Tuscan river is set to be diverted in order to create a factory. Three activists set out to resist this development but, ultimately, fail: two of them dying in the process and the third – a priest – abandoning the protest and returning to Rome. Carroll refers to Ouida as a proto-environmentalist, noting that, alongside her mildly ecological storytelling, she was a practical contributor to the emerging animal rights movement. She spoke out vociferously against the 1871 UK Dog Act, which authorized the killing of stray dogs deemed dangerous and was a founding member of the British Humanitarian League, which campaigned for animal protection (Carroll 2019: 150–151).

Ouida died in Italy and is buried there in Bagni di Lucca. However, she is also commemorated in England by a blue plaque on her one-time home in Hammersmith and a memorial in her birth town, Bury St Edmonds (Victoriaweb 2002).

pp. 38–41

35

THE WATERS OF EDERA

Louise de la Ramée (aka Ouida)

Source: Louise de la Ramée (aka Ouida), *The Waters of Edera* (1900)

"It must be a misprint; it must be a mistake for the Era of Volterra, or the Esino, north of Ancona," he said to himself, and he went to his book closet and brought out an old folio geography which he had once bought for a few pence on a Roman bookstall, spread it open before him, and read one by one the names of all the streams of the peninsula, from the Dora Baltea to the Giarretta. There was no other Edera river. Unless it were indeed a misprint altogether, the stream which flowed under his church walls was the one which was named in the news-sheet.

"But it is impossible, it is impossible!" he said so loudly, that his little dog awoke and climbed on his knee uneasily and in alarm. "What could the people do? What could the village do, or the land or the fisher folk? Are we to have drought added to hunger? Can they respect nothing? The river belongs to the valley: to seize it, to appraise it, to appropriate it, to make it away with it, would be as monstrous as to steal his mother's milk from a yearling babe!"

He shut the folio and pushed it away from him across the table. "If this is true," he said to himself, "if, anyhow, this monstrous thing be true, it will kill Adone!"

In the morning he awoke from a short perturbed sleep with that heavy sense of a vaguely remembered calamity which stirs in the awakening brain like a worm in the unclosing flower.

The morning-office over, he sought out the little news-sheet, to make sure that he had read aright; his servant had folded it up and laid it aside on a shelf, he unfolded it with a hand which trembled; the same lines stared at him in the warm light of sunrise as in the faint glimmer of the floating wick. The very curtness and coldness of the announcement testified to its exactitude. He did not any longer doubt its truth; but there were no details, no explanations: he pondered on the possibilities of obtaining them; it was useless to seek them in the village or the countryside, the people were as ignorant as sheep.

Adone alone had intelligence, but he shrank from taking these tidings to the youth, as he would have shrunk from doing him a physical hurt. The news might be false or premature; many projects were discussed, many schemes sketched out, many speculations set on foot which came to nothing in the end: were this thing true, Adone would learn it all too soon and read it on the wounded face of nature.

DOI: 10.4324/9781003194651-45

ROMANTICIZING NATURE

Not at least until he could himself be certain of its truth would he speak of it to the young man whose fathers had been lords of the river.

His duties over for the forenoon, he went up the three hundred stairs of his bell-tower, to the wooden platform, between the machicolations. It was a dizzy height, and both stairs and roof were in ruins, but he went cautiously, and was familiar with the danger. The owls which bred there were so used to him that they did not stir in their siesta as he passed them. He stood aloft in the glare of noon-day, and looked down on the winding stream as it passed under the ruined walls of Ruscino, and growing, as it flowed, clearer and clearer, and wilder and wilder, as it rushed over stones and boulders, foaming and shouting, rushed through the heather on its way towards the Marches. Under Ruscino it had its brown mountain colour still, but as it ran it grew green as emeralds, blue as sapphires, silver and white and gray like a dove's wings; it was unsullied and translucent; the white clouds were reflected on it. It went through a country lonely, almost deserted, only at great distances from one another was there a group of homesteads, a cluster of stacks, a conical cabin in some places where the woods gave place to pasture; here and there were the ruins of a temple, of a fortress, of some great marble or granite tomb; but there was no living creature in sight except a troop of buffaloes splashing in a pool.

Don Silverio looked down on its course until his dazzled eyes lost it from sight in the glory of light through which it sped, and his heart sank, and he would fain have been a woman to have wept aloud. For he saw that its beauty and its solitude were such as would likely enough tempt the spoilers. He saw that it lay fair and defenceless as a maiden on her bed.

He dwelt out of the world now, but he had once dwelt in it; and the world does not greatly change, it only grows more rapacious. He knew that in this age there is only one law, to gain; only one duty, to prosper: that nature is of no account, nor beauty either, nor repose, nor ancient rights, nor any of the simple claims of normal justice. He knew that if in the course of the river there would be gold for capitalists, for engineers, for attorneys, for deputies, for ministers, that then the waters of the Edera were in all probability doomed.

He descended the rotten stairs slowly, with a weight as of lead at his heart. He did not any longer doubt the truth of what he had read. Who, or what, shall withstand the curse of its time?

"They have forgotten us so long," he thought, with bitterness in his soul. "We have been left to bury our dead as we would, and to see the children starve as they might; they remember us now, because we possess something which they can snatch from us!"

He did not doubt any more. He could only wait: wait and see in what form and in what time the evil would come to them. Meantime, he said to himself, he would not speak of it to Adone, and he burned the news-sheet. Administrations alter frequently and unexpectedly, and the money-changers, who are fostered by them, sometimes fall with them, and their projects remain in the embryo of a mere prospectus. There was that chance.

He knew that, in the age he lived in, all things were estimated only by their value to commerce or to speculation; that there was neither space nor patience amongst men for what was, in their reckoning, useless; that the conqueror was now but a trader in disguise; that civilisation was but the shibboleth of traffic; that because trade follows the flag, therefore to carry the flag afar, thousands of young soldiers of every nationality are slaughtered annually in poisonous climes and obscure warfare, because such is the suprema lex and will of the trader. If the waters of Edera would serve to grind any grit for the mills of modern trade they would be taken into bondage with many other gifts of nature as fair and as free as they were. All creation groaned and travailed in pain that the great cancer should spread.

"It is not only ours," he remembered with a pang; on its way to and from the Valdedera the river passed partially through two other communes, and water belongs to the district in which it runs. True, the country of each of these was like that of this valley, depopulated and wild; but, however great a solitude any land may be, it is still locally and administratively dependent on the chief town of its commune. Ruscino and its valley were dependent on San Beda; these two other communes were respectively under a little town of the Abruzzo and under a seaport of the Adriatic.

The interest of the valley of the Edera in its eponymous stream was a large share; but it was not more than a share, in this gift of nature. If it came to any question of conflicting interests, Ruscino and the valley might very likely be powerless, and could only, in any event, be represented by and through San Beda; a strongly ecclesiastical and papal little place, and, therefore, without influence with the ruling powers, and consequently viewed with an evil eye by the Prefecture.

He pondered anxiously on the matter for some days, then, arduous as the journey was, he resolved to go to San Beda and inquire.

The small mountain city was many miles away upon a promontory of marble rocks, and its many spires and towers were visible only in afternoon light from the valley of the Edera. It was as old as Ruscino, a dull, dark, very ancient place with monasteries and convents like huge fortresses and old palaces still fortified and grim as death amongst them. A Cistercian monastery, which had been chiefly built by the second Giulio, crowned a prominent cliff, which dominated the town, and commanded a view of the whole of the valley of the Edera, and, on the western horizon, of the Leonessa and her tributary mountains and hills.

He had not been there for five years; he went on foot, for there was no other means of transit, and if there had been he would not have wasted money on it; the way was long and irksome; for the latter half, entirely up a steep mountain road. He started in the early morning as soon as Mass had been celebrated, and it was four in the afternoon before he had passed the gates of the town, and paid his respects to the Bishop. He rested in the Certosa, of which the superior was known to him; the monks, like the Bishop, had heard nothing. So far as he could learn when he went into the streets no one in the place had heard anything of the project to alter the course of the river. He made the return journey by night, so as to reach his church by daybreak, and was there in his place by the high altar when the bell tolled at six o'clock, and the three or four old people, who never missed an office, were kneeling on the stones.

He had walked over forty miles, and had eaten nothing except some bread and a piece of dried fish. But he always welcomed physical fatigue; it served to send to sleep the restless intellect, the gnawing regrets, the bitter sense of wasted powers and of useless knowledge, which were his daily company.

He had begged his friends, the friars, to obtain an interview with the Syndic of Sand Beda, and interrogate him on the subject. Until he should learn something positive he could not bring himself to speak of the matter to Adone: but the fact of his unusual absence had too much astonished his little community for the journey not to have been the talk of Ruscino. Surprised and disturbed like others, Adone was waiting for him in the sacristy after the first mass.

"You have been away a whole day and night and never told me, reverendissimo!" he cried in reproach and amazement.

"I have yet to learn that you are my keeper," said Don Silverio with a cold and caustic intonation.

Adone coloured to the roots of his curling hair.

"That is unkind, sir!" he said humbly; "I only meant that – that – "

"I know, I know!" said the priest impatiently, but with contrition. "You meant only friendship and good-will; but there are times when the best intentions irk one. I went to see the Prior of the Certosa, and old friend; I had business in San Beda."

Adone was silent, afraid that he had shown an unseemly curiosity; he saw that Don Silverio was irritated and not at ease, and he hesitated what words to choose.

His friend relented, and blamed himself for being hurried by disquietude into harshness.

"Come and have a cup of coffee with me, my son," he said in his old, kind tones. "I am going home to break my fast."

But Adone was hurt and humiliated, and made excuse of field work, which pressed by reason of the weather, and so he did not name to his friend and councillor the visit of the three men to the river.

Don Silverio went home and boiled his coffee; he always did this himself; it was the only luxury he ever allowed himself, and he did not indulge even in this very often. But for once the draught had neither fragrance nor balm for him. He was overtired, weary in mind as in body, and greatly dejected; even though nothing was known at San Beda he felt convinced that what he had read was the truth.

Editorial Headnote

1844 (Hove)–1926

Edward Carpenter was a poet and author. At the same time, he was a notable socialist, vegetarian, anti-vivisectionist, nudist, gay rights activist and early advocate of recycling.

Carpenter was from a middle-class Sussex family, was Cambridge-educated and entered the Church of England on graduating. In 1874, however, he switched from working for the church to an academic career, touring the country giving lectures – on a wide range of subjects – as part of a new university extension movement. This movement was an initiative to take higher education to 'the masses' and saw him teaching miners and other industrial workers around South Yorkshire. This work gave him a deeper appreciation of and respect for northern working-class life and shaped his passion for social reform. He was an admirer and follower of fellow aesthete and radical William Morris and became a founder member of the Labour Party. As the extract discusses, he was also a friend and influence on the great Russian novelist Leo Tolstoy. Carpenter also had correspondence with the legendary Indian nationalist Mahatma Gandhi, and Asian philosophy is known to have influenced his thinking on human oneness with nature.

Carpenter's best-known book was Civilisation: Its Cause and Cure, which he discusses in the following extract from his autobiography. Here he questions the scientific method, arguing that facts are not enough (including, despite his left leanings, the economic determinism of socialism). 'Laws' of science can come to be overturned; ideas and morals matter, as well as supposed facts. As such, his thinking here pre-empts post-positivist analysis, not widely advocated until the late twentieth century. One of the things Carpenter sees being undermined by science and rationality is a proper appreciation of humanity's place in the natural world. Calling on the "removal of those things which stand between us and Nature" constitutes a strong ecological message. This more radical commitment to conservationism, including animal rights, also pre-empts deep green ecologism of the contemporary age.

In 1883, Carpenter bought a small farm in Derbyshire, and there lived the 'simple life' he both craved and advocated until old age. His last few years, however, were spent in Guildford, where he is buried with his long-time partner George Merrill. A revival of interest in Carpenter's writing has occurred since the 1970s thanks to his then highly radical ideas on rights, research methodology and the environment coming to find much wider acceptance (Encyclopedia Britannica).

pp. 207–209

36

MY DAYS AND DREAMS

Edward Carpenter

Source: Edward Carpenter, *My Days and Dreams* (1916)

The attempt made a quarter of a century ago – in *Civilization: its Cause and Cure* – to define the characteristics of (modern) civilization, and to show the civilization-period as a distinct stage in social evolution, destined to pass away and to be succeeded by a later stage – of which later stage even now some of the features may be indicated – has never as far as I know been seriously taken up and worked out. The Socialists of course have certain views on the subject, but they are limited to the economic field, and do not by any means cover the whole ground; and various doctrinaire sets and sects are nibbling at the problem from different sides; but a real statement and investigation of the whole question, and a linking of it up to deepest spiritual facts, would obviously be absorbingly interesting. I first read the paper which bears the above name at the Fabian Society (? in 1888), and, needless to say, it was jeered at on all sides; but since then, somehow, a change has come, and even Sidney Webb and Bernard Shaw, who most attacked me at the time, have ceased to use the word 'Civilization' in its old optimistic and mid-Victorian sense. What we want now is a real summing-up and settling of what the word connotes – both from the historical point of view, and with regard to the future.

Another paper in the same book, which shocked a good many of my Cambridge friends, was my "Criticism of Modern Science." The Victorian age glorified modern Science – not only in respect of its patient and assiduous observation of facts, which every one allows, but also on account of the supposed Laws of Nature which it had discovered, and which were accounted immutable and everlasting. A light arising from some quite other source convinced me that this infallibility of the scientific "Laws" was an entire illusion. I had been brought up on mathematics and physical science. I had lectured for years on the latter. But now the reaction set in; and – rather rudely and crudely it must be confessed – I turned on my old teacher to rend her! I published in 1885, and in Manchester, a shilling pamphlet called Modern Science: A Criticism, and sent it round to my mathematical and scientific friends. I think most of them thought I had gone daft! But, after all, the whirligig of Time has brought its revenge, and the inevitable evolution of human

DOI: 10.4324/9781003194651-46

thought has done its work; and now, one may ask, where are the airy fairy laws and theories of the Science of the last century? The great stores of observations and facts are certainly there, and so are the marvellous applications of these things to practical life – but where are the immutable Laws? – where are the clean-cut systems of the families and species of plants and animals? where is Boyle's law of gases? where the stability of the planetary orbits? where the permanence and indestructibility of the atom? where is the theory of gravitation, where the theory of light, the theory of electricity? the law of supply and demand in Political Economy, of Natural Selection in Biology? of the fixity of the Elements in Chemistry, or the succession of the strata in Geology? All gone into the melting-pot – and quickly losing their outlines!

It is true that in the great brew which is being thus formed, rags and chunks of the old "Laws of Nature" are still discernible; but no one supposes they are there for long, and on all sides it is obvious that the scientific world is giving up the search for them, and the expectation (in the face of such things as radium, Hertzian waves, Karyokinesis and so forth) of ever reconstituting Science again on the old Victorian basis. These fixed 'Laws,' it is pretty evident, and their remaining debris, will melt away, till out of the seething brew something entirely different and unexpected emerges. And that will be? . . .

Yes, what indeed out of such a Cauldron might be expected to emerge – a strange and wonderful Figure, a living Form!

Yet the curious thing is that while this process of the dissolution of scientific theory is going on before our eyes, and on all sides, no one seems to be aware of it – at any rate no one sums it up, gives it outline and definition, or tackles its meaning and result. Tolstoy was pleased with the attacks on Modern Science contained in Civilization: its Cause and Cure, wrote to me about it, and had the chapter printed in Russian, with a preface by himself. But his point of view was that Science being a serious enemy to Religion anything which bombarded and crippled Science would help to free Religion. That was not my point of view. I do not regard Science – or rather Intellectualism – as the foe of Religion, but more as a stage which has to be passed through on the way to a higher order of perception or consciousness – which might possibly be termed Religion – only the word religion is too vague to be very applicable here.

Another airy castle which is obviously fading away before our eyes is that of the "Laws" of Morality. The whole structure of civilization-morality is being rapidly undermined. The moral aspects of Property, Commerce, Class-relations, Sex-relations, Marriage, Patriotism, and so forth, are shifting like dissolving views. Nietzsche has scorched up the old Christian altruism; Bernard Shaw has burned the Decalogue. Yet (in this country and according to our custom) we jog along and pretend not to see what is happening. No body of people faces out the situation, or attempts to foretell its future. The Ethical society professes to substitute Ethics for Religion, as a basis of social life; yet never once has it informed us what it means by Ethics! The Law courts go mumbling on over ancient measures of right and wrong which the man in the street has long ago discarded. Much less has any group attempted to foreshadow the new Morality, and concatenate it on to the great root-fact of existence. In my "Defence of Criminals a Criticism of Morality," (one of the Chapters in *Civilisation: its Cause and Cure*) I gave an outline and an indication of what was happening, and of the way out into the future; but that paper, as far as I know, has never been seriously discussed.

Neverthless under the surface new ideas are forming, the lines of the coming life are spreading. The book *Civilization* – first published by Sonnenschein, in 1889 – has had a good circulation, and been translated into many languages. Though somewhat hastily and crudely put together, yet owing to a certain elan about it, and probably largely owing to the fact that it gives expression to the main issues above-mentioned, it has been well received.

One idea, which runs all through the book – namely, that of there being three great stages of Consciousness: the simple consciousness (of the animal or of primitive man), the self-consciousness (of the civilized or intellectual man), and the mass-consciousness or cosmic consciousness of the coming man, is only roughly sketched there, but is developed more fully in *The Art of Creation*. It is of course deeply germane to *Towards Democracy*. And though we may not yet be in a position to define the conception very exactly, still it is quite evident, I think, that some such evolution into a further order of consciousness is the key to the future, and that many aeons to come (of human progress) will be ruled by it. Dr. Richard Bucke, by the publication (in 1901) of his book *Cosmic Consciousness* made a great contribution to the cause of humanity. The book was a bit casual, hurried, doctrinaire, un-literary, and so forth, but it brought together a mass of material, and did the inestimable service of being the first to systematically consider and analyse the subject. Strangely here again we find that his book – though always spreading and circulating about the world, beneath the surface – has elicited no serious recognition or response from the accredited authorities, philosophers, psychologists, and so forth; and the subject with which it deals is in such circles practically ignored – though in comparatively unknown coteries it may be warmly discussed. So the world goes on – the real expanding vital forces being always beneath the surface and hidden, as in a bud, while the accepted forms and conclusions are little more than a vari-coloured husk, waiting to be thrown off.

Relating itself closely and logically with the idea (1) of the three stages of Consciousness is that (2) of the Berkeleyan view of matter – the idea that matter in itself is an illusion, being only a film between soul and soul: called matter when the film is opaque to the perceiving soul, but called mind! when the latter sees through to the intelligence behind it. And these stages again relate logically to the idea (3) of the Universal or Omnipresent Self. *The Art of Creation* was written to give expression to these three ideas and the natural deductions from them.

The doctrine of the Universal Self is obviously fundamental; and it is clear that once taken hold of and adopted it must inevitably revolutionize all our views of Morality – since current morality is founded on the separation of self from self; and must revolutionize too all our views of Science. Such matters as the Transmutation of Chemical Elements, the variation of biological Species, the unity of

Health, the unity of Disease, our views of Political Economy and Psychology; Production for Use instead of for Profit, Communism, Telepathy; the relation between Psychology and Physiology, and so forth, must take on quite a new complexion when the idea which lies at the root of them is seized. This idea must enable us to understand the continuity of Man with the Protozoa, the relation of the physiological centres, on the one hand to the individual Man and on the other to the Race from which he springs, the meaning of Reincarnation, and the physical conditions of its occurrence. It must have eminently practical applications; as in the bringing of the Races of the world together, the gradual evolution of a Non-governmental form of Society, the Communalization of Land and Capital, the freeing of Woman to equality with Man, the extension of the monogamic Marriage into some kind of group-alliance, the restoration and full recognition of the heroic friendships of Greek and primitive times; and again in the sturdy Simplification and debarrassment of daily life by the removal of those things which stand between us and Nature, between ourselves and our fellows – by plain living, friendship with the Animals, open-air habits, fruitarian food, and such degree of Nudity as we can reasonably attain to.

These mental and social changes and movements and many others which are all around us waiting for recognition, will clearly, when they ripen, constitute a revolution in human life deeper and more far-reaching than any which we know of belonging to historical times. Even any one of them, worked out practically, would be fatal to most of our existing institutions. Together they would form a revolution so great that to call it a mere extension or outgrowth of Civilization would be quite inadequate. Rather we must look upon them as the preparation for a stage entirely different from and beyond Civilization. To tackle these things in advance, to prepare for them, study them, understand them is clearly absolutely necessary. It is a duty which – however burked or ignored for a time – will soon be forced upon us by the march of events. And it is a duty which cannot effectively be fulfilled piecemeal, but only by regarding all these separate movements of the human mind, and of society, as part and parcel of one great underlying movement – one great new disclosure of the human Soul.

My little covey of books, dating from *Towards Democracy*, has been hatched mainly for the purpose of giving expression to these and other various questions which – raised in my mind by the writing of *Towards Democracy* – demanded clearer statement than they could find there. *Towards Democracy* came first, as a Vision, so to speak, and a revelation – as a great body of feeling and intuition which I *had* to put into words as best I could. It carried with it – as a flood carries trees and rocks from the mountains where it originates – all sorts of assumptions and conclusions. Afterwards – for my own satisfaction as much as for the sake of others – I had to examine and define these assumptions and conclusions.

That was the origin of my prose writings – most of them – of *England's Ideal, Civilization, The Art of Creation, Love's Coming-of-Age, The Intermediate Sex, The Drama of Love and Death, Angels' Wings, Non-governmental Society* (a chapter in *Prisons's Police and Punishment*), *A Visit to a Ghani* (in *Adam's Peak to Elephanta*) and so forth. They, like the questions they deal with, have led a curious underground life in the literary world, spreading widely as a matter of fact, yet not on the surface. Like old moles they have worked away unseen and unobserved; yet in such a manner as to throw up heaps here and there and in the most unlikely places, and bring back friends to me on all sides – lovely and beautiful friends for whom I cannot sufficiently thank them.

Editorial Headnote

1838 (Dunbar)–1914

John Muir was a Scottish American naturalist and ecological pioneer.

Muir immigrated to Wisconsin with his family at the age of eleven but is said to have always maintained a Scots identity and accent. He studied chemistry at university but dropped out before graduating. An early career as an inventor was then abandoned in 1867 after a serious accident and he turned his attention to writing about and campaigning to preserve nature. Later that year, he gained a lot of publicity in carrying out a 1,000-mile walk from Kentucky to Florida which furthered his cause of promoting wildlife conservation.

Muir subsequently became a hugely influential conservationist campaigner who was pivotal in the adoption of National Parks in his adopted US from 1872 when Yellowstone became the world's first conservation area. Sequoia and Yosemite National Parks were later established in 1890 largely as a result of his personal work and campaigning. He also co-founded the Sierra Club to lobby for nature conservation in 1892 and served as the president of this pioneering and influential pressure group until his death. President Theodore Roosevelt visited Muir in 1903 during his term in office, and they camped together in Yosemite. The president, clearly an admirer of Muir, subsequently sanctioned the opening of five new National Parks in the US, along with many other conservation measures. Muir also became a US citizen in 1903.

The glorification of the countryside is evident in this passage – and all of Muir's works. Seeing God in nature and the pristine perfection of the wilderness free of the 'rubbish' and 'waste' of the urban environment is apparent. John Muir, however, was actually far more than a romantic conservationist, and his work also fiercely critiqued anthropocentricism: 'Why should man value himself as more than a small part of the one great unit of creation' (Muir 1916: 139). More than a conservationist Muir was a preservationist, believing in protecting nature from man rather than for him and, as such, can more clearly be linked to ecocentrism and contemporary political ecologists.

Controversies around some of Muir's views have persisted, particularly in relation to race. In 2020, the Sierra Club issued a statement acknowledging and apologizing for the fact that some of his printed opinions on Native and African Americans were blatantly racist (Sierra Club 2020). Nevertheless, he still remains a widely revered figure in the US, as well as back in his original homeland. John Muir Day was introduced in Scotland to mark the hundred-year anniversary of his death in 2014, and there is a museum dedicated to him in his hometown of Dunbar in Lothian (Encyclopedia Britannica).

pp. 149–158

37

MY FIRST SUMMER IN THE SIERRA

John Muir

Source: John Muir, *My First Summer in the Sierra* (1911)

CHAPTER 6

Mount Hoffman and Lake Tenaya

July 26

Ramble to the summit of Mt. Hoffman, eleven thousand feet high, the highest point in life's journey my feet have yet touched. And what glorious landscapes are about me, new plants, new animals, new crystals, and multitudes of new mountains far higher than Hoffman, towering in glorious array along the axis of the range, serene, majestic, snow-laden, sundrenched, vast domes and ridges shining below them, forests, lakes, and meadows in the hollows, the pure blue bell-flower sky brooding them all, – a glory day of admission into a new realm of wonders as if Nature had wooingly whispered, "Come higher." What questions I asked, and how little I know of all the vast show, and how eagerly, tremulously hopeful of some day knowing more, learning the meaning of these divine symbols crowded together on this wondrous page.

Mt. Hoffman is the highest part of a ridge or spur about fourteen miles from the axis of the main range, perhaps a remnant brought into relief and isolated by unequal denudation. The southern slopes shed their waters into Yosemite Valley by Tenaya and Dome Creeks, the northern in part into the Tuolumne River, but mostly into the Merced by Yosemite Creek. The rock is mostly granite, with some small piles and crests rising here and there in picturesque pillared and castellated remnants of red metamorphic slates. Both the granite and slates are divided by joints, making them separable into blocks like the stones of artificial masonry, suggesting the Scripture "He hath builded the mountains." Great banks of snow and ice are piled in hollows on the cool precipitous north side forming the highest perennial sources of Yosemite Creek. The southern slopes are much more gradual and accessible. Narrow slot-like gorges extend across the summit at right angles, which look like lanes, formed evidently by the erosion of less resisting beds. They are usually called "devil's slides," though they lie far above the region usually haunted by the devil;

DOI: 10.4324/9781003194651-47

293

for though we read that he once climbed an exceeding high mountain, he cannot be much of a mountaineer, for his tracks are seldom seen above the timberline.

The broad gray summit is barren and desolate-looking in general views, wasted by ages of gnawing storms; but looking at the surface in detail, one finds it covered by thousands and millions of charming plants with leaves and flowers so small they form no mass of color visible at a distance of a few hundred yards. Beds of azure daisies smile confidingly in moist hollows, and along the banks of small rills, with several species of eriogonum, silky-leaved ivesia, pentstemon, orthocarpus, and patches of *Primula suffruticosa*, a beautiful shrubby species. Here also I found bryanthus, a charming heathwort covered with purple flowers and dark green foliage like heather, and three trees new to me, – a hemlock and two pines. The hemlock (*Tsuga Mertensiana*) is the most beautiful conifer I have ever seen; the branches and also the main axis droop in a singularly graceful way, and the dense foliage covers the delicate, sensitive, swaying branchlets all around. It is now in full bloom, and the flowers, together with thousands of last season's cones still clinging to the drooping sprays, display wonderful wealth of color, brown and purple and blue. Gladly I climbed the first tree I found to revel in the midst of it. How the touch of the flowers makes one's flesh tingle! The pistillate are dark, rich purple, and almost translucent, the staminate blue, – a vivid, pure tone of blue like the mountain sky, – the most uncommonly beautiful of all the Sierra tree flowers I have seen. How wonderful that, with all its delicate feminine grace and beauty of form and dress and behavior, this lovely tree up here, exposed to the wildest blasts, has already endured the storms of centuries of winters!

The two pines also are brave storm-enduring trees, the mountain pine (*Pinus monticola*) and the dwarf pine (*Pinus albicaulis*). The mountain pine is closely related to the sugar pine, though the cones are only about four to six inches long. The largest trees are from five to six feet in diameter at four feet above the ground, the bark rich brown. Only a few storm-beaten adventurers approach the summit of the mountain. The dwarf or white-bark pine is the species that forms the timberline, where it is so completely dwarfed that one may walk over the top of a bed of it as over snow-pressed chaparral.

How boundless the day seems as we revel in these storm-beaten sky gardens amid so vast a congregation of onlooking mountains! Strange and admirable it is that the more savage and chilly and storm-chafed the mountains, the finer the glow on their faces and the finer the plants they bear. The myriads of flowers tingeing the mountain-top do not seem to have grown out of the dry, rough gravel of disintegration, but rather they appear as visitors, a cloud of witnesses to Nature's love in what we in our timid ignorance and unbelief call howling desert. The surface of the ground, so dull and forbidding at first sight, besides being rich in plants, shines and sparkles with crystals: mica, hornblende, feldspar, quartz, tourmaline. The radiance in some places is so great as to be fairly dazzling, keen lance rays of every color flashing, sparkling in glorious abundance, joining the plants in their fine, brave beauty-work, – every crystal, every flower a window opening into heaven, a mirror reflecting the Creator.

MY FIRST SUMMER IN THE SIERRA

From garden to garden, ridge to ridge, I drifted enchanted, now on my knees gazing into the face of a daisy, now climbing again and again among the purple and azure flowers of the hemlocks, now down into the treasuries of the snow, or gazing afar over domes and peaks, lakes and woods, and the billowy glaciated fields of the upper Tuolumne, and trying to sketch them. In the midst of such beauty, pierced with its rays, one's body is all one tingling palate. Who wouldn't be a mountaineer! Up here all the world's prizes seem nothing.

The largest of the many glacier lakes in sight, and the one with the finest shore scenery, is Tenaya, about a mile long, with an imposing mountain dipping its feet into it on the south side, Cathedral Peak a few miles above its head, many smooth swelling rock-waves and domes on the north, and in the distance southward a multitude of snowy peaks, the fountain-heads of rivers. Lake Hoffman lies shimmering beneath my feet, mountain pines around its shining rim. To the northward the picturesque basin of Yosemite Creek glitters with lakelets and pools; but the eye is soon drawn away from these bright mirror wells, however attractive, to revel in the glorious congregation of peaks on the axis of the range in their robes of snow and light.

Carlo caught an unfortunate woodchuck when it was running from a grassy spot to its boulder-pile home – one of the hardiest of the mountain animals. I tried hard to save him, but in vain. After telling Carlo that he must be careful not to kill anything, I caught sight, for the first time, of the curious pika, or little chief hare, that cuts large quantities of lupines and other plants and lays them out to dry in the sun for hay, which it stores in underground barns to last through the long, snowy winter. Coming upon these plants freshly cut and lying in handfuls here and there on the rocks has a startling effect of busy life on the lonely mountain-top. These little haymakers, endowed with brain stuff something like our own, – God up here looking after them, – what lessons they teach, how they widen our sympathy!

An eagle soaring above a sheer cliff, where I suppose its nest is, makes another striking show of life, and helps to bring to mind the other people of the so-called solitude, – deer in the forest caring for their young; the strong, well-clad, well-fed bears; the lively throng of squirrels; the blessed birds, great and small, stirring and sweetening the groves; and the clouds of happy insects filling the sky with joyous hum as part and parcel of the down-pouring sunshine. All these come to mind, as well as the plant people, and the glad streams singing their way to the sea. But most impressive of all is the vast glowing countenance of the wilderness in awful, infinite repose.

Toward sunset, enjoyed a fine run to camp, down the long south slopes, across ridges and ravines, gardens and avalanche gaps, through the firs and chaparral, enjoying wild excitement and excess of strength, and so ends a day that will never end.

July 27

Up and away to Lake Tenaya, – another big day, enough for a lifetime. The rocks, the air, everything speaking with audible voice or silent; joyful, wonderful, enchanting, banishing weariness and sense of time. No longing for anything now or hereafter as we go home into the mountain's heart. The level sunbeams are touching the fir-tops, every leaf shining with dew. Am holding an easterly course, the deep cañon of Tenaya Creek on the right hand, Mt. Hoffman on the left, and the lake straight ahead about ten miles distant, the summit of Mt. Hoffman about three thousand feet above me, Tenaya Creek four thousand feet below and separated from the shallow, irregular valley, along which most of the way lies, by smooth domes and wave-ridges. Many mossy emerald bogs, meadows, and gardens in rocky hollows to wade and saunter through, – and what fine plants they give me, what joyful streams I have to cross, and how many views are displayed of the Hoffman and Cathedral Peak masonry, and what a wondrous breadth of shining granite pavement to walk over for the first time about the shores of the lake! On I sauntered in freedom complete; body without weight as far as I was aware; now wading through starry parnassia bogs, now through gardens shoulder deep in larkspur and lilies, grasses and rushes, shaking off showers of dew; crossing piles of crystalline moraine boulders, bright mirror pavements, and cool, cheery streams going to Yosemite; crossing bryanthus carpets and the scoured pathways of avalanches, and thickets of snow-pressed ceanothus; then down a broad, majestic stairway into the ice-sculptured lake-basin.

The snow on the high mountains is melting fast, and the streams are singing bankfull, swaying softly through the level meadows and bogs, quivering with sun-spangles, swirling in pot-holes, resting in deep pools, leaping, shouting in wild, exulting energy over rough boulder dams, joyful, beautiful in all their forms. No Sierra landscape that I have seen holds anything truly dead or dull, or any trace of what in manufactories is called rubbish or waste; everything is perfectly clean and pure and full of divine lessons. This quick, inevitable interest attaching to everything seems marvelous until the hand of God becomes visible; then it seems reasonable that what interests Him may well interest us. When we try to pick out anything by itself, we find it hitched to everything else in the universe. One fancies a heart like our own must be beating in every crystal and cell, and we feel like stopping to speak to the plants and animals as friendly fellow-mountaineers. Nature as a poet, an enthusiastic workingman, becomes more and more visible the farther and higher we go; for the mountains are fountains – beginning places, however related to sources beyond mortal ken.

2.2

CONSERVING NATURE AND THE ARISTOCRACY

Editorial Headnote

1775 (Steventon, Hampshire)–1817

Jane Austen was an acclaimed novelist in her day and has remained so ever since. The six major novels she penned have rarely been out of print and have all been adapted into popular films, plays or television series.

Austen was from an upper-middle-class rural Hampshire family, and her father was a vicar of a country parish. Her sister Cassandra was her closest companion for all her life and neither of them married. Austen started writing as a teenager and continued for the rest of her short life. The novels Persuasion and Northanger Abbey were published posthumously, and her greatest acclaim came some years after her death in her forties of an unconfirmed illness.

Austen's novels reflected her life and have remained hugely popular and respected for their realism and wit. She pokes fun at many aspects of patriarchy and upper-middle-class culture but, in other ways, she is socially conservative. She was not overtly political in her novels or public life and various interpretations of her novels have been made. A running theme in her work, however, is a reverence for traditional rural life: 'English verdure' as she refers to here. In Emma and elsewhere, Austen ultimately upholds the virtues of good manners, the church, the landed gentry and the countryside and portrays urban living as a threat to these English traditions.

In this extract, the titular Emma Woodhouse describes the grounds of Donwell Abbey in Surrey, the home of George Knightly, a man she comes to love, so named to personify Englishness and nobility. Englishness hence is defined in rural terms and culture equated with nature (Bate 1999). In contrast, London is depicted in several of Austen's novels in far more negative terms, both environmentally and socially. Elsewhere in Emma, her father exclaims: "Ah! my poor dear child, the truth is, that in London it is always a sickly season. Nobody is healthy in London, nobody can be. It is a dreadful thing to have you forced to live there! so far off! – and the air so bad!" (Austen 1815: 92).

There seems little doubt that this juxtaposition of rural idyll and urban squalor was informed by Austen's visits to London. On one such trip to the capital, she wrote to Cassandra: 'Here I am once more in this scene of dissipation & vice, and I begin already to find my Morals corrupted' (Austen 1796).

pp. 326–329

38

EMMA

Jane Austen

Source: Jane Austen, *Emma* (1815)

CHAPTER 6

It was hot; and after walking some time over the gardens in a scattered, dispersed way, scarcely any three together, they insensibly followed one another to the delicious shade of a broad short avenue of limes, which stretching beyond the garden at an equal distance from the river, seemed the finish of the pleasure grounds. It led to nothing; nothing but a view at the end over a low stone wall with high pillars, which seemed intended, in their erection, to give the appearance of an approach to the house, which never had been there. Disputable, however, as might be the taste of such a termination, it was in itself a charming walk, and the view which closed it extremely pretty. The considerable slope, at nearly the foot of which the Abbey stood, gradually acquired a steeper form beyond its grounds; and at half a mile distant was a bank of considerable abruptness and grandeur, well clothed with wood; and at the bottom of this bank, favourably placed and sheltered, rose the Abbey Mill Farm, with meadows in front, and the river making a close and handsome curve around it.

It was a sweet view – sweet to the eye and the mind. English verdure, English culture, English comfort, seen under a sun bright, without being oppressive.

In this walk Emma and Mr. Weston found all the others assembled; and towards this view she immediately perceived Mr. Knightley and Harriet distinct from the rest, quietly leading the way. Mr. Knightley and Harriet! – It was an odd tete-a-tete; but she was glad to see it. – There had been a time when he would have scorned her as a companion, and turned from her with little ceremony. Now they seemed in pleasant conversation. There had been a time also when Emma would have been sorry to see Harriet in a spot so favourable for the Abbey Mill Farm; but now she feared it not. It might be safely viewed with all its appendages of prosperity and beauty, its rich pastures, spreading flocks, orchard in blossom, and light column of smoke ascending. – She joined them at the wall, and found them more engaged in talking than in looking around. He was giving Harriet information as to modes of agriculture, etc. and Emma received a smile which seemed to say, "These are my own concerns. I have a right to talk on such subjects, without being suspected of introducing Robert Martin." – She did not suspect him. It was too old a story. – Robert Martin had probably ceased to think of Harriet. – They took a few turns together along the walk. – The shade was most refreshing, and Emma found it the pleasantest part of the day.

The next remove was to the house; they must all go in and eat; – and they were all seated and busy, and still Frank Churchill did not come. Mrs. Weston looked, and looked in vain. His father would not own himself uneasy, and laughed at her fears; but she could not be cured of wishing that he would part with his black mare. He had expressed himself as to coming, with more than common certainty. "His aunt was so much better, that he had not a doubt of getting over to them." – Mrs. Churchill's state, however, as many were ready to remind her, was liable to such sudden variation as might disappoint her nephew in the most reasonable dependence – and Mrs. Weston was at last persuaded to believe, or to say, that it must be by some attack of Mrs. Churchill that he was prevented coming. – Emma looked at Harriet while the point was under consideration; she behaved very well, and betrayed no emotion.

The cold repast was over, and the party were to go out once more to see what had not yet been seen, the old Abbey fish-ponds; perhaps get as far as the clover, which was to be begun cutting on the morrow, or, at any rate, have the pleasure of being hot, and growing cool again. – Mr. Woodhouse, who had already taken his little round in the highest part of the gardens, where no damps from the river were imagined even by him, stirred no more; and his daughter resolved to remain with him, that Mrs. Weston might be persuaded away by her husband to the exercise and variety which her spirits seemed to need.

Mr. Knightley had done all in his power for Mr. Woodhouse's entertainment. Books of engravings, drawers of medals, cameos, corals, shells, and every other family collection within his cabinets, had been prepared for his old friend, to while away the morning; and the kindness had perfectly answered. Mr. Woodhouse had been exceedingly well amused. Mrs. Weston had been shewing them all to him, and now he would shew them all to Emma; – fortunate in having no other resemblance to a child, than in a total want of taste for what he saw, for he was slow, constant, and methodical. – Before this second looking over was begun, however, Emma walked into the hall for the sake of a few moments' free observation of the entrance and ground-plot of the house – and was hardly there, when Jane Fairfax appeared, coming quickly in from the garden, and with a look of escape. – Little expecting to meet Miss Woodhouse so soon, there was a start at first; but Miss Woodhouse was the very person she was in quest of.

"Will you be so kind," said she, "when I am missed, as to say that I am gone home? – I am going this moment. – My aunt is not aware how late it is, nor how long we have been absent – but I am sure we shall be wanted, and I am determined to go directly. – I have said nothing about it to any body. It would only be giving trouble and distress. Some are gone to the ponds, and some to the lime walk. Till they all come in I shall not be missed; and when they do, will you have the goodness to say that I am gone?"

EMMA

"Certainly, if you wish it; – but you are not going to walk to Highbury alone?"

"Yes – what should hurt me? – I walk fast. I shall be at home in twenty minutes."

"But it is too far, indeed it is, to be walking quite alone. Let my father's servant go with you. – Let me order the carriage. It can be round in five minutes."

"Thank you, thank you – but on no account. – I would rather walk. – And for me to be afraid of walking alone! – I, who may so soon have to guard others!"

She spoke with great agitation; and Emma very feelingly replied, "That can be no reason for your being exposed to danger now. I must order the carriage. The heat even would be danger. – You are fatigued already."

"I am," – she answered – "I am fatigued; but it is not the sort of fatigue – quick walking will refresh me. – Miss Woodhouse, we all know at times what it is to be wearied in spirits. Mine, I confess, are exhausted. The greatest kindness you can shew me, will be to let me have my own way, and only say that I am gone when it is necessary."

Emma had not another word to oppose. She saw it all; and entering into her feelings, promoted her quitting the house immediately, and watched her safely off with the zeal of a friend. Her parting look was grateful – and her parting words, "Oh! Miss Woodhouse, the comfort of being sometimes alone!" – seemed to burst from an overcharged heart, and to describe somewhat of the continual endurance to be practised by her, even towards some of those who loved her best.

"Such a home, indeed! such an aunt!" said Emma, as she turned back into the hall again. "I do pity you. And the more sensibility you betray of their just horrors, the more I shall like you."

Editorial Headnote

1763 (Farnham)–1835

William Cobbett was a political journalist and farmer very well known in his time for his outspoken views on a range of contemporary subjects, including the changing English landscape. He was the son of a farmer/innkeeper and not of noble stock but nevertheless lamented the demise of feudal England.

Cobbett was a soldier as a young man but soon turned to writing. He published prolifically and wrote the popular pamphlet 'Political Register' from 1802 right up until his death. Famously, he coined the well-known expression 'red herring' as a metaphor for the distraction of the press, in a story on using strong smells to confuse hunting hounds.

To research Rural Rides, Cobbett rode across the English countryside between 1822 and 1826, chronicling what he found. He was opposed to The Enclosures and concerned about rural depopulation and neglect. In the selected extract, he chastises the noblemen for failing to prevent rural decline and the encroachment of towns and factories on farms and common land. The divisiveness of urbanization is strikingly asserted here in suggesting that Surrey has come to contain both the best and the worst lands in England and even the world. Cobbett was, in many ways, a radical and a reformist and supported the 1832 Reform Act and Catholic emancipation. He was, however, also deeply reactionary and a romantic nationalist who wanted England to return to the good old days of lords and the servitude of serfdom. As the extract shows, for example, one aspect of his social conservatism was that he was deeply anti-Semitic. Jews are portrayed as part of a new greedy and corrupt urban elite ruining the country. Cobbett also publicly supported the slave trade. He was a controversial and outspoken figure even in his time and was imprisoned between 1810–12 for publishing objections to the flogging of militiamen in Ely for ill discipline.

Cobbett lived in the US from 1817–19 but remained a thorn in the side of the British government. He became particularly critical of the Tory administration of Lord Liverpool in the aftermath of the Peterloo Massacre of pro-democracy protestors in Manchester in 1819. He was again prosecuted in 1831 for supporting the rural riots that had unfolded in the south of England but was cleared after defending himself in court. After several unsuccessful bids, he was then finally elected into parliament in 1832. However, he was not a popular figure in Westminster and was in poor health and died of influenza just three years later (Encyclopedia Britannica).

pp. 93–95

39

RURAL RIDES

William Cobbett

Source: William Cobbett, *Rural Rides* (1830)

This county of Surrey presents to the eye of the traveller a greater contrast than any other county in England. It has some of the very best and some of the worst lands, not only in England, but in the world. We were here upon those of the latter description. For five miles on the road towards Guildford the land is a rascally common covered with poor heath, except where the gravel is so near the top as not to surfer even the heath to grow. Here we entered the enclosed lands, which have the gravel at bottom, but a nice light, black mould at top; in which the trees grow very well. Through bye-lanes and bridle-ways we came out into the London road, between Ripley and Guildford, and immediately crossing that road, came on towards a village called Merrow. We came out into the road just mentioned, at the lodge-gates of a Mr. Weston, whose mansion and estate have just passed (as to occupancy) into the hands of some new man. At Merrow, where we came into the Epsom road, we found that Mr. Webb Weston, whose mansion and park are a little further on towards London, had just walked out, and left it in possession of another new man. This gentleman told us, last year, at the Epsom meeting, that he was losing his income; and I told him how it was that he was losing it! He is said to be a very worthy man; very much respected; a very good landlord; but, I dare say, he is one of those who approved of yeomanry cavalry to keep down the; Jacobins and Levellers; "but who, in fact, as I always told men of this description, have put down themselves and their landlords; for without them this thing never could have been done. To ascribe the whole to contrivance would be to give to Pitt and his followers too much credit for profundity; but, if the knaves who assembled at the Crown and Anchor in the Strand, in 1793, to put down, by the means of prosecutions and spies, those whom they called "Republicans and Levellers;" if these knaves had said, "Let us go to work to induce the owners and occupiers of the land to convey their estates and their capital into our hands," and if the Government had corresponded with them in views, the effect could not have been more complete than it has, thus far, been. The yeomanry actually, as to the effect, drew their swords to keep the reformers at bay, while the tax-eaters were taking away the estates and the capital. It was the sheep surrendering up the dogs into the hands of the wolves.

DOI: 10.4324/9781003194651-50

Lord Onslow lives near Merrow. This is the man that was, for many years, so famous as a driver of four-in-hand. He used to be called Tommy Onslow. He has the character of being a very good landlord. I know he called me "a d—d Jacobin" several years ago, only, I presume, because I was labouring to preserve to him the means of still driving four-in-hand, while he, and others like him, and their yeomanry cavalry, were working as hard to defeat my wishes and endeavours. They say here, that, some little time back, his lordship, who has, at any rate, had the courage to retrench in all sorts of ways, was at Guildford in a gig with one horse, at the very moment when Spicer, the stockbroker, who was a chairman of the committee for prosecuting Lord Cochrane, and who lives at Esher, came rattling in with four horses and a couple of outriders! They relate an observation made by his lordship, which may, or may not, be true, and which, therefore, I shall not repeat. But, my lord, there is another sort of courage; courage other than that of retrenching, that would become you in the present emergency: I mean political courage, and especially the courage of acknowledging your errors; confessing that you were wrong, when you called the reformers Jacobins and levellers; the courage of now joining them in their efforts to save their country, to regain their freedom, and to preserve to you your estate, which is to be preserved, you will observe, by no other means than that of a reform of the Parliament. It is now manifest, even to fools, that it has been by the instrumentality of a base and fraudulent paper-money, that loan-jobbers, stock-jobbers, and Jews have got the estates into their hands. With what eagerness, in 1797, did the nobility, gentry and clergy rush forward to give their sanction and their support to the system which then began, and which has finally produced what we now behold! They assembled in all the counties, and put forth declarations, that they would take the paper of the bank, and that they would support the system. Upon this occasion the county of Surrey was the very first county; and, on the list of signatures, the very first name was Onslow! There may be sales and conveyances; there may be recoveries, deeds, and other parchments; but this was the real transfer; this was the real signing away of the estates.

. . .

pp. 187–190
Easton (Hampshire),
Wednesday Evening, 6th August.

This village of Easton lies at a few miles towards the north-east from Winchester. It is distant from Botley, by the way which I came, about fifteen or sixteen miles. I came through Durley, where I went to the house of farmer Mears. I was very much pleased with what I saw at Durley, which is about two miles from Botley, and is certainly one of the most obscure villages in this whole kingdom. Mrs. Mears, the farmer's wife, had made, of the crested dog's tail grass, a bonnet which she wears herself. I there saw girls platting the straw. They had made plat of several degrees of fineness; and they sell it to some person or persons at Fareham, who, I suppose, makes it into bonnets. Mrs. Mears, who is a very intelligent and clever woman, has two girls at work, each of whom earns per week as much (within a shilling) as her father, who is a labouring man, earns per week. The father has at this time only 7s. per week. These two girls (and not very stout girls) earn six shillings a week each: thus the income of this family is, from seven shillings a week, raised to nineteen shillings a week. I shall suppose that this may in some measure be owing to the generosity of ladies in the neighbourhood, and to their desire to promote this domestic manufacture; but if I suppose that these girls receive double compared to what they will receive for the same quantity of labour when the manufacture becomes more general, is it not a great thing to make the income of the family nineteen shillings a week instead of seven? Very little, indeed, could these poor things have done in the field during the last forty days. And, besides, how clean; how healthful; how everything that one could wish is this sort of employment! The farmer, who is also a very intelligent person, told me that he should endeavour to introduce the manufacture as a thing to assist the obtaining of employment, in order to lessen the amount of the poor-rates. I think it very likely that this will be done in the parish of Durley. A most important matter it is, to put paupers in the way of ceasing to be paupers. I could not help admiring the zeal as well as the intelligence of the farmer's wife, who expressed her readiness to teach the girls and women of the parish, in order to enable them to assist themselves. I shall hear, in all probability, of their proceedings at Durley, and if I do, I shall make a point of communicating to the Public an account of those interesting proceedings. From the very first, from the first moment of my thinking about this straw affair, I regarded it as likely to assist in bettering the lot of the labouring people. If it has not this effect, I value it not. It is not worth the attention of any of us; but I am satisfied that this is the way in which it will work. I have the pleasure to know that there is one labouring family, at any rate, who are living well through my means. It is I, who, without knowing them, without ever having seen them, without even now knowing their names, have given the means of good living to a family who were before half-starved. This is indisputably my work; and when I reflect that there must necessarily be, now, some hundreds of families, and shortly, many thousands of families, in England, who are and will be, through my means, living well instead of being half-starved, I cannot but feel myself consoled; I cannot but feel that I have some compensation for the sentence passed upon me by Ellenborough, Grose, Le Blanc, and Bailey; and I verily believe, that in the case of this one single family in the parish of Durley I have done more good than Bailey ever did in the whole course of his life, notwithstanding his pious Commentary on the Book of Common Prayer. I will allow nothing to be good, with regard to the labouring classes, unless it make an addition to their victuals, drink, or clothing. As to their minds, that is much too sublime matter for me to think about. I know that they are in rags, and that they have not a belly-full; and I know that the way to make them good, to make them honest, to make them dutiful, to make them kind to one another, is to enable them to live well; and I also know that none of these things will ever be accomplished by Methodist sermons, and by those stupid, at once stupid and malignant things, and roguish things, called Religious Tracts.

It seems that this farmer at Durley has always read the Register, since the first appearance of little *Two-penny Trash*. Had it not been for this reading, Mrs. Mears would not have thought about the grass; and had she not thought about the grass, none of the benefits above mentioned would have arisen to her neighbours. The difference between this affair and the spinning-jenny affairs is this: that the spinning-jenny affairs fill the pockets of "rich ruffians," such as those who would have murdered me at Coventry; and that this straw affair makes an addition to the food and raiment of the labouring classes, and gives not a penny to be pocketed by the rich ruffians.

From Durley I came on in company with farmer Mears through Upham. This Upham is the place where Young, who wrote that bombastical stuff, called "Night Thoughts," was once the parson, and where, I believe, he was born. Away to the right of Upham lies the little town of Bishop's Waltham, whither I wished to go very much, but it was too late in the day. From Upham we came on upon the high land, called Black Down. This has nothing to do with that Black-down Hill, spoken of in my last ride. We are here getting up upon the chalk hills, which stretch away towards Winchester. The soil here is a poor blackish stuff, with little white stones in it, upon a bed of chalk. It was a down not many years ago. The madness and greediness of the days of paper-money led to the breaking of it up. The corn upon it is miserable; but as good as can be expected upon such land.

At the end of this tract we come to a spot called Whiteflood, and here we cross the old turnpike road which leads from Winchester to Gosport through Bishop's Waltham. Whiteflood is at the foot of the first of a series of hills over which you come to get to the top of that lofty ridge called Morning Hill. The farmer came to the top of the first hill along with me; and he was just about to turn back, when I, looking away to the left, down a valley which stretched across the other side of the down, observed a rather singular appearance, and said to the farmer, "What is that coming up that valley? is it smoke, or is it a cloud?" The day had been very fine hitherto; the sun was shining very bright where we were. The farmer answered, "Oh, it's smoke; it comes from Ouselberry, which is down in that bottom behind those trees." So saying, we bid each other good day; he went back, and I went on. Before I had got a hundred and fifty yards from him, the cloud which he had taken for the Ouselberry smoke came upon the hill and wet me to the skin. He was not far from the house at Whiteflood; but I am sure that he could not entirely escape it. It is curious to observe how the clouds sail about in the hilly countries, and particularly, I think, amongst the chalk-hills. I have never observed the like amongst the sand-hills, or amongst rocks.

From Whiteflood you come over a series of hills, part of which form a rabbit-warren called Longwood warren, on the borders of which is the house and estate of Lord Northesk. These hills are amongst the most barren of the downs of England; yet a part of them was broken up during the rage for improvements; during the rage for what empty men think was an augmenting of the capital of the country. On about twenty acres of this land, sown with wheat, I should not suppose that there would be twice twenty bushels of grain! A man must be mad, or nearly mad, to sow wheat upon such a spot. However, a large part of what was enclosed has been thrown out again already, and the rest will be thrown out in a very few years. The down itself was poor; what, then, must it be as corn-land! Think of the destruction which has here taken place. The herbage was not good, but it was something; it was something for every year, and without trouble. Instead of grass it will now, for twenty years to come, bear nothing but that species of weeds which is hardy enough to grow where the grass will not grow. And this was "augmenting the capital of the nation." These new enclosure-bills were boasted of by George Rose and by Pitt as proofs of national prosperity! When men in power are ignorant to this extent, who is to expect anything but consequences such as we now behold.

Editorial Headnote

1804 (London)–1881

The prominent politician and novelist Benjamin Disraeli was from a comfortably well-off (but not aristocratic) family of Italian and Jewish descent and was privately educated. As a child, he converted to Christianity after his father had a dispute with his synagogue, which ultimately opened up a political career to him since Jews were not able to take up seats in parliament until the Jewish Relief Act of 1858.

Disraeli first entered parliament in 1837 as the Conservative MP for Maidstone, after several previous failures to do so as a maverick Independent. He turned against the Conservative leader Robert Peel after being overlooked for a cabinet position after their electoral win of 1841 and became the lead figure in a new 'Young England' movement that sought to revamp conservatism in a clearer anti-liberal direction. Disraeli came to use fictional novels – alongside flamboyant political speeches – as a means to criticize the 'Peelites' for being in league with the Liberals in embracing free trade (with the repeal of the Corn Laws). He also railed against them for ruining the countryside with industrialization, undermining the church and neglecting the poor. Peel resigned in 1846 in the face of growing opposition from within his party and Disraeli entered into government, initially as Chancellor of the Exchequer (under the Earl of Derby) and then twice as prime minister in 1868 and 1874–80.

Sybil was part of a trilogy of novels – preceded by *Coningsby* and followed by *Tancred* – used by the young politician to challenge the ascendancy of liberalism, employing romanticism and paternalism to revamp the brand of conservatism. Disraeli's Young England movement upheld the virtues of a responsible aristocracy and, in the process, critiqued the ethics of the newly emergent middle classes as well as those aristocrats who had lost their sense of social responsibility and divided the country into rich and poor. The still prominent label 'one nation conservatism', referring to the bridging of the rich–poor divide, originates from this novel.

In the following extract, Lord Marney's greed and indifference to the workers of the new town that bears his name is illustrated by contrasting urban squalor and pestilence with the rural idyll that once characterized the valley in which it sits. Here and elsewhere in Disraeli's trilogy, industrialization and Liberal reforms such as the New Poor Laws (in which the state took over the role of safeguarding unemployed workers from landowners) are vilified for breaking the traditional bonds between the aristocracy and peasantry. Young England was also a consciously nationalistic movement and a reverence for traditional Saxon values – eroded from the time of the Norman invasion – is evident in the following passage and elsewhere in Disraeli's trilogy. The decline of the Church of England was also lamented at a time when liberalism was freeing up Catholicism, Christian non-conformism and atheism to challenge its moral and political ascendancy. As such, the Young England movement romanticized traditional rural life and feudalism and rejected contemporary industrialization, modernization and what we would today label neoliberalism or globalization.

pp. 116–126

40

SYBIL

Benjamin Disraeli

Source: Benjamin Disraeli, *Sybil* (1845)

BOOK 2 CHAPTER 3

The situation of the rural town of Marney was one of the most delightful easily to be imagined. In a spreading dale, contiguous to the margin of a clear and lively stream, surrounded by meadows and gardens, and backed by lofty hills, undulating and richly wooded, the traveller on the opposite heights of the dale would often stop to admire the merry prospect, that recalled to him the traditional epithet of his country.

Beautiful illusion! For behind that laughing landscape, penury and disease fed upon the vitals of a miserable population!

The contrast between the interior of the town and its external aspect, was as striking as it was full of pain. With the exception of the dull high street, which had the usual characteristics of a small agricultural market town, some sombre mansions, a dingy inn, and a petty bourse, Marney mainly consisted of a variety of narrow and crowded lanes formed by cottages built of rubble, or unhewn stones without cement, and from age, or badness of the material, looking as if they could scarcely hold together. The gaping chinks admitted every blast; the leaning chimneys had lost half their original height; the rotten rafters were evidently misplaced; while in many instances the thatch, yawning in some parts to admit the wind and wet, and in all utterly unfit for its original purpose of giving protection from the weather, looked more like the top of a dunghill than a cottage. Before the doors of these dwellings, and often surrounding them, ran open drains full of animal and vegetable refuse, decomposing into disease, or sometimes in their imperfect course filling foul pits or spreading into stagnant pools, while a concentrated solution of every species of dissolving filth was allowed to soak through and thoroughly impregnate the walls and ground adjoining.

These wretched tenements seldom consisted of more than two rooms, in one of which the whole family, however numerous, were obliged to sleep, without distinction of age, or sex, or suffering. With the water streaming down the walls, the light distinguished through the roof, with no hearth even in winter, the virtuous mother in the sacred pangs of childbirth, gives forth another victim to our

DOI: 10.4324/9781003194651-51

ROMANTICIZING NATURE

thoughtless civilization; surrounded by three generations whose inevitable presence is more painful than her sufferings in that hour of travail; while the father of her coming child, in another corner of the sordid chamber, lies stricken by that typhus which his contaminating dwelling has breathed into his veins, and for whose next prey is perhaps destined, his new-born child. These swarming walls had neither windows nor doors sufficient to keep out the weather, or admit the sun or supply the means of ventilation; the humid and putrid roof of thatch exhaling malaria like all other decaying vegetable matter. The dwelling rooms were neither boarded nor paved; and whether it were that some were situate in low and damp places, occasionally flooded by the river, and usually much below the level of the road; or that the springs, as was often the case, would burst through the mud floor; the ground was at no time better than so much clay, while sometimes you might see little channels cut from the centre under the doorways to carry off the water, the door itself removed from its hinges: a resting place for infancy in its deluged home. These hovels were in many instances not provided with the commonest conveniences of the rudest police; contiguous to every door might be observed the dung-heap on which every kind of filth was accumulated, for the purpose of being disposed of for manure, so that, when the poor man opened his narrow habitation in the hope of refreshing it with the breeze of summer, he was met with a mixture of gases from reeking dunghills.

This town of Marney was a metropolis of agricultural labour, for the proprietors of the neighbourhood having for the last half century acted on the system of destroying the cottages on their estates, in order to become exempted from the maintenance of the population, the expelled people had flocked to Marney, where, during the war, a manufactory had afforded them some relief, though its wheels had long ceased to disturb the waters of the Mar.

Deprived of this resource, they had again gradually spread themselves over that land which had as it were rejected them; and obtained from its churlish breast a niggardly subsistence. Their re-entrance into the surrounding parishes was viewed with great suspicion; their renewed settlement opposed by every ingenious contrivance; those who availed themselves of their labour were careful that they should not become dwellers on the soil; and though, from the excessive competition, there were few districts in the kingdom where the rate of wages was more depressed, those who were fortunate enough to obtain the scant remuneration, had, in addition to their toil, to endure each morn and even a weary journey before they could reach the scene of their labour, or return to the squalid hovel which profaned the name of home. To that home, over which Malaria hovered, and round whose shivering hearth were clustered other guests besides the exhausted family of toil – Fever, in every form, pale Consumption, exhausting Synochus, and trembling Ague, – returned after cultivating the broad fields of merry England the bold British peasant, returned to encounter the worst of diseases with a frame the least qualified to oppose them; a frame that subdued by toil was never sustained by animal food; drenched by the tempest could not change its dripping rags; and was indebted for its scanty fuel to the windfalls of the woods.

316

SYBIL

The eyes of this unhappy race might have been raised to the solitary spire that sprang up in the midst of them, the bearer of present consolation, the harbinger of future equality; but Holy Church at Marney had forgotten her sacred mission. We have introduced the reader to the vicar, an orderly man who deemed he did his duty if he preached each week two sermons, and enforced humility on his congregation and gratitude for the blessings of this life. The high Street and some neighbouring gentry were the staple of his hearers. Lord and Lady Marney came, attended by Captain Grouse, every Sunday morning with commendable regularity, and were ushered into the invisible interior of a vast pew, that occupied half of the gallery, was lined with crimson damask, and furnished with easy chairs, and, for those who chose them, well-padded stools of prayer. The people of Marney took refuge in conventicles, which abounded; little plain buildings of pale brick with the names painted on them, of Sion, Bethel, Bethesda: names of a distant land, and the language of a persecuted and ancient race: yet, such is the mysterious power of their divine quality, breathing consolation in the nineteenth century to the harassed forms and the harrowed souls of a Saxon peasantry.

But however devoted to his flock might have been the Vicar of Marney, his exertions for their well being, under any circumstances, must have been mainly limited to spiritual consolation. Married and a father he received for his labours the small tithes of the parish, which secured to him an income by no means equal to that of a superior banker's clerk, or the cook of a great loanmonger. The great tithes of Marney, which might he counted by thousands, swelled the vast rental which was drawn from this district by the fortunate earls that bore its name.

The morning after the arrival of Egremont at the Abbey, an unusual stir might have been observed in the high Street of the town. Round the portico of the Green Dragon hotel and commercial inn, a knot of principal personages, the chief lawyer, the brewer, the vicar himself, and several of those easy quidnuncs who abound in country towns, and who rank under the designation of retired gentlemen, were in close and very earnest converse. In a short time a servant on horseback in the Abbey livery galloped up to the portico, and delivered a letter to the vicar. The excitement apparently had now greatly increased. On the opposite side of the way to the important group, a knot, larger in numbers but very deficient in quality, had formed themselves, and remained transfixed with gaping mouths and a Curious not to say alarmed air. The head constable walked up to the door of the Green Dragon, and though he did not presume to join the principal group, was evidently in attendance, if required. The clock struck eleven; a cart had stopped to watch events, and a gentleman's coachman riding home with a led horse.

"Here they are!" said the brewer.

"Lord Marney himself," said the lawyer.

"And Sir Vavasour Firebrace, I declare. I wonder how he came here," said a retired gentleman, who had been a tallow-chandler on Holborn Hill.

The vicar took off his hat, and all uncovered. Lord Marney and his brother magistrate rode briskly up to the inn and rapidly dismounted.

317

"Well, Snigford," said his lordship, in a peremptory tone, "this is a pretty business; I'll have this stopped directly."

Fortunate man if he succeed in doing so! The torch of the incendiary had for the first time been introduced into the parish of Marney; and last night the primest stacks of the Abbey farm had blazed a beacon to the agitated neighbourhood.

Editorial Headnote

1795 (Dumfriesshire)–1881

Thomas Carlyle was a mathematician turned historian and polemicist.

One notable contribution of Carlyle to the study of the relationship between humans and nature is etymological. He is believed to have coined the word environment to characterize the relationship between organisms – in the course of translating the works of Goethe into English (from the German word umgebung). Like Disraeli, Carlyle was from middle-class rather than aristocratic stock but similarly lamented the loss of the natural order of nobility and peasants having stewardship of the land that was occurring in the nineteenth century.

Carlyle was the son of a Calvinist minister and was educated at Edinburgh University. He became a distinguished mathematician before also turning his mind to history and political theory in a series of influential publications. Politically, Carlyle became known for highlighting the plight of the British working class in what he termed 'The Condition of England Question'. In Signs of the Times and later works, Carlyle cited the 'Mechanical Age' as culpable for heightened levels of urban poverty and squalor, as well as the general spiritual and moral decline of the nation. His reference to this as amounting to a 'war' against nature is overtly environmentalist. This line of thinking is known to have influenced Charles Dickens – who dedicated Hard Times to him – and the US philosopher Ralph Waldo Emerson, amongst others.

Carlyle's social conscience was born of a deep conservatism and a nationalistic romanticization of the past. As also is evident in the following extract, his political views were deeply illiberal, and he viewed industrialization as just one facet of liberal modernizing 'progress' ruining the country he loved. Hence, Carlyle also railed against democracy, free trade and individual rights for eroding the natural order of rule by elites and particularly heroic strongman figures. Even by the standards of the age, Carlyle's views were highly reactionary. He openly advocated a return to slavery after its abolition, viewing black Africans as having no more rights than cattle; was profoundly anti-Semitic; and was an Anglo-Saxon supremacist. It is not difficult to see why several historians view Carlyle as a proto-fascist, and it is known that the Nazi philosophy of Goebbels, which also revered peasant culture, was influenced by him (Kerry & Hill 2010: 99–103). The embrace of environmentalism by the political right is perhaps epitomized by the thinking of Thomas Carlyle.

pp. 99–104

41

SIGNS OF THE TIMES

Thomas Carlyle

Source: Thomas Carlyle, *Signs of the Times* (1858)

Were we required to characterise this age of ours by any single epithet, we should be tempted to call it, not an Heroical, Devotional, Philosophical, or Moral Age, but, above all others, the Mechanical Age. It is the Age of Machinery, in every outward and inward sense of that word; the age which, with its whole undivided might, forwards, teaches and practises the great art of adapting means to ends. Nothing is now done directly, or by hand; all is by rule and calculated contrivance. For the simplest operation, some helps and accompaniments, some cunning abbreviating process is in readiness. Our old modes of exertion are all discredited, and thrown aside. On every hand, the living artisan is driven from his workshop, to make room for a speedier, inanimate one. The shuttle drops from the fingers of the weaver, and falls into iron fingers that ply it faster. The sailor furls his sail, and lays down his oar; and bids a strong, unwearied servant, on vaporous wings, bear him through the waters. Men have crossed oceans by steam; the Birmingham Fire-king has visited the fabulous East; and the genius of the Cape were there any Camoens now to sing it, has again been alarmed, and with far stranger thunders than Gamas. There is no end to machinery. Even the horse is stripped of his harness, and finds a fleet fire-horse invoked in his stead. Nay, we have an artist that hatches chickens by steam; the very brood-hen is to be superseded! For all earthly, and for some unearthly purposes, we have machines and mechanic furtherances; for mincing our cabbages; for casting us into magnetic sleep. We remove mountains, and make seas our smooth highways; nothing can resist us. We war with rude Nature; and, by our resistless engines, come off always victorious, and loaded with spoils.

What wonderful accessions have thus been made, and are still making, to the physical power of mankind; how much better fed, clothed, lodged and, in all outward respects, accommodated men now are, or might be, by a given quantity of labour, is a grateful reflection which forces itself on every one. What changes, too, this addition of power is introducing into the Social System; how wealth has more and more increased, and at the same time gathered itself more and more into masses, strangely altering the old relations, and increasing the distance between

DOI: 10.4324/9781003194651-52

the rich and the poor, will be a question for Political Economists, and a much more complex and important one than any they have yet engaged with.

But leaving these matters for the present, let us observe how the mechanical genius of our time has diffused itself into quite other provinces. Not the external and physical alone is now managed by machinery, but the internal and spiritual also. Here too nothing follows its spontaneous course, nothing is left to be accomplished by old natural methods. Everything has its cunningly devised implements, its preestablished apparatus; it is not done by hand, but by machinery. Thus we have machines for Education: Lancastrian machines; Hamiltonian machines; monitors, maps and emblems. Instruction, that mysterious communing of Wisdom with Ignorance, is no longer an indefinable tentative process, requiring a study of individual aptitudes, and a perpetual variation of means and methods, to attain the same end; but a secure, universal, straightforward business, to be conducted in the gross, by proper mechanism, with such intellect as comes to hand. Then, we have Religious machines, of all imaginable varieties; the Bible-Society, professing a far higher and heavenly structure, is found, on inquiry, to be altogether an earthly contrivance: supported by collection of moneys, by fomenting of vanities, by puffing, intrigue and chicane; a machine for converting the Heathen. It is the same in all other departments. Has any man, or any society of men, a truth to speak, a piece of spiritual work to do; they can nowise proceed at once and with the mere natural organs, but must first call a public meeting, appoint committees, issue prospectuses, eat a public dinner; in a word, construct or borrow machinery, wherewith to speak it and do it. Without machinery, they were hopeless, helpless; a colony of Hindoo weavers squatting in the heart of Lancashire. Mark, too, how every machine must have its moving power, in some of the great currents of society; every little sect among us, Unitarians, Utilitarians, Anabaptists, Phrenologists, must have its Periodical, its monthly or quarterly Magazine; – hanging out, like its windmill, into the *popularis aura*, to grind meal for the society.

With individuals, in like manner, natural strength avails little. No individual now hopes to accomplish the poorest enterprise single-handed and without mechanical aids; he must make interest with some existing corporation, and till his field with their oxen. In these days, more emphatically than ever, "to live, signifies to unite with a party, or to make one." Philosophy, Science, Art, Literature, all depend on machinery. No Newton, by silent meditation, now discovers the system of the world from the falling of an apple; but some quite other than Newton stands in his Museum, his Scientific Institution, and behind whole batteries of retorts, digesters, and galvanic piles imperatively "interrogates Nature," who however, shows no haste to answer. In defect of Raphaels, and Angelos, and Mozarts, we have Royal Academies of Painting, Sculpture, Music; whereby the languishing spirits of Art may be strengthened, as by the more generous diet of a Public Kitchen. Literature, too, has its Paternoster-row mechanism, its Trade-dinners, its Editorial conclaves, and huge subterranean, puffing bellows; so that books are not only printed, but, in a great measure, written and sold, by machinery. National culture, spiritual benefit of all sorts, is under the same management. No Queen Christina,

SIGNS OF THE TIMES

in these times, needs to send for her Descartes; no King Frederick for his Voltaire, and painfully nourish him with pensions and flattery: any sovereign of taste, who wishes to enlighten his people, has only to impose a new tax, and with the proceeds establish Philosophic Institutes. Hence the Royal and Imperial Societies, the Bibliothèques, Glyptothèques, Technothèques, which front us in all capital cities; like so many well-finished hives, to which it is expected the stray agencies of Wisdom will swarm of their own accord, and hive and make honey. In like manner, among ourselves, when it is thought that religion is declining, we have only to vote half-amillion's worth of bricks and mortar, and build new churches. In Ireland it seems they have gone still farther, having actually established a "Penny-a-week Purgatory-Society"! Thus does the Genius of Mechanism stand by to help us in all difficulties and emergencies, and with his iron back bears all our burdens.

. . .

pp. 114–118

Again, with respect to our Moral condition: here also he who runs may read that the same physical, mechanical influences are everywhere busy. For the "superior morality," of which we hear so much, we too would desire to be thankful: at the same time, it were but blindness to deny that this "superior morality" is properly rather an "inferior criminality," produced not by greater love of Virtue, but by greater perfection of Police; and of that far subtler and stronger Police, called Public Opinion. This last watches over us with its Argus eyes more keenly than ever; but the "inward eye" seems heavy with sleep. Of any belief in invisible, divine things, we find as few traces in our Morality as elsewhere. It is by tangible, material considerations that we are guided, not by inward and spiritual. Self-denial, the parent of all virtue, in any true sense of that word, has perhaps seldom been rarer: so rare is it, that the most, even in their abstract speculations, regard its existence as a chimera. Virtue is Pleasure, is Profit; no celestial, but an earthly thing. Virtuous men, Philanthropists, Martyrs are happy accidents; their "taste" lies the right way! In all senses, we worship and follow after Power; which may be called a physical pursuit. No man now loves Truth, as Truth must be loved, with an infinite love; but only with a finite love, as it were par amours. Nay, properly speaking, he does not believe and know it, but only "think" it, and that "there is every probability!" He preaches it aloud, and rushes courageously forth with it, – if there is a multitude huzzaing at his back; yet ever keeps looking over his shoulder, and the instant the huzzaing languishes, he too stops short. In fact, what morality we have takes the shape of Ambition, or "Honour": beyond money and money's worth, our only rational blessedness is Popularity. It were but a fool's trick to die for conscience. Only for "character," by duel, or in case of extremity, by suicide, is the wise man bound to die. By arguing on the "force of circumstances," we have argued away all force from ourselves; and stand leashed together, uniform in dress and movement, like the rowers of some boundless galley. This and that may be right and true; but we must not do it. Wonderful "Force of Public Opinion"! We must act and walk in all points as it prescribes; follow the traffic it bids us, realise the sum of money, the degree of "influence" it expects of us, or we shall be lightly esteemed; certain mouthfuls of articulate wind will be blown at us, and this what mortal courage can front? Thus, while civil liberty is more and more secured to us, our moral liberty is all but lost. Practically considered, our creed is Fatalism; and, free in hand and foot, we are shackled in heart and soul with far straiter than feudal chains. Truly may we say, with the Philosopher," the deep meaning of the Laws of Mechanism lies heavy on us"; and in the closet, in the Marketplace, in the temple, by the social hearth, encumbers the whole movements of our mind, and over our noblest faculties is spreading a nightmare sleep.

These dark features, we are aware, belong more or less to other ages, as well as to ours. This faith in Mechanism, in the all-importance of physical things, is in every age the common refuge of Weakness and blind Discontent; of all who believe, as many will ever do, that man's true good lies without him, not within. We are aware also, that, as applied to ourselves in all their aggravation, they form but half a picture; that in the whole picture there are bright lights as well as gloomy shadows. If we here dwell chiefly on the latter, let us not be blamed: it is in general more profitable to reckon up our defects than to boast of our attainments.

Neither, with all these evils more or less clearly before us, have we at any time despaired of the fortunes of society. Despair, or even despondency, in that respect, appears to us, in all cases, a groundless feeling. We have a faith in the imperishable dignity of man; in the high vocation to which, throughout this his earthly history, he has been appointed. However it may be with individual nations, whatever melancholic speculators may assert, it seems a well-ascertained fact, that in all times, reckoning even from those of the Heraclides and Pelasgi, the happiness and greatness of mankind at large have been continually progressive. Doubtless this age also is advancing. Its very unrest, its ceaseless activity, its discontent contains matter of promise. Knowledge, education are opening the eyes of the humblest; are increasing the number of thinking minds without limit. This is as it should be; for not in turning back, not in resisting, but only in resolutely struggling forward, does our life consist.

Nay, after all, our spiritual maladies are but of Opinion; we are but fettered by chains of our own forging, and which ourselves also can rend asunder. This deep, paralysed subjection to physical objects comes not from Nature, but from our own unwise mode of viewing Nature. Neither can we understand that man wants, at this hour, any faculty of heart, soul or body, that ever belonged to him. 'He, who has been born, has been a First Man'; has had lying before his young eyes, and as yet unhardened into scientific shapes, a world as plastic, infinite, divine, as lay before the eyes of Adam himself. if Mechanism, like some glass bell, encircles and imprisons us; if the soul looks forth on a fair heavenly country which it cannot reach, and pines, and in its scanty atmosphere is ready to perish, – yet the bell is but of glass, 'one bold stroke to break the bell in pieces, and thou art delivered!' Not the invisible world is wanting, for it dwells in man's soul, and this last is still here. Are the solemn temples, in which the Divinity was once visibly revealed among us, crumbling away? We can repair them, we can rebuild them. The wisdom, the heroic worth of our forefathers, which we have lost, we

SIGNS OF THE TIMES

can recover. That admiration of old nobleness, which now so often shows itself as a faint dilettantism, will one day become a generous emulation, and man may again be all that he has been, and more than he has been. Nor are these the mere daydreams of fancy; they are clear possibilities; nay, in this time they are even assuming the character of hopes. Indications we do see in other countries and in our own, signs infinitely cheering to us, that Mechanism is not always to be our hard taskmaster, but one day to be our pliant, all-ministering servant; that a new and brighter spiritual era is slowly evolving itself for all man. But on these things our present course forbids us to enter.

Meanwhile, that great outward changes are in progress can be doubtful to no one. The time is sick and out of joint. Many things have reached their height; and it is a wise adage that tells us, "the darkest hour is nearest the dawn." Wherever we can gather indication of the public thought, whether from printed books' as in France or Germany, or from Carbonari rebellions and other political tumults, as in Spain, Portugal, Italy, and Greece, the voice it utters is the same. The thinking minds of all nations call for change. There is a deep-lying struggle in the whole fabric of society; a boundless grinding collision of the New with the Old. The French Revolution, as is now visible enough, was not the parent of this mighty movement, but its offspring. Those two hostile influences, which always exist in human things, and on the constant intercommunion of which depends their health and safety, had lain in separate masses, accumulating through generations, and France was the scene of their fiercest explosion; but the final issue was not unfolded in that country: nay, it is not yet anywhere unfolded. Political freedom is hitherto the object of these efforts; but they will not and cannot stop there. It is towards a higher freedom than mere freedom from oppression by his fellow-mortal, that man dimly aims. Of this higher, heavenly freedom, which is "man's reasonable service," all his noble institutions, his faithful endeavours and loftiest attainments, are but the body, and more and more approximated emblem.

On the whole, as this wondrous planet, Earth, is journeying with its fellows through infinite Space, so are the wondrous destinies embarked on it journeying through infinite Time, under a higher guidance than ours. For the present, as our astronomy informs us, its path lies towards Hercules, the constellation of Physical Power: but that is not our most pressing concern. Go where it will, the deep HEAVEN will be around it. Therein let us have hope and sure faith. To reform a world, to reform a nation, no wise man will undertake; and all but foolish men know, that the only solid, though a far slower reformation, is what each begins and perfects on himself.

Editorial Headnote

1840 (Dorset)–1928

Thomas Hardy was a prominent novelist and poet of his time who remains highly popular today, largely for his sympathetic depiction of country life.

Hardy grew up on the edge of Dorset heathland in a family of modest means. He exited education at the age of sixteen and became an apprentice to a local architect. His father was a stone mason, so this was a natural career path to take. In his twenties, whilst working as a draftsman in London, he acquired the means to finance a degree in architecture at Kings College. He then worked as an architect for a few years before switching to a writing career in 1872 when he earned a contract to write monthly instalments of his first publication 'A Pair of Blue Eyes' with Tinsley's Magazine. This paved the way for Hardy's first novel, Far From the Madding Crowd. In this and his subsequent works, Hardy situates the stories in the fictional county of Wessex – related to Dorset – and laments the loss of aspects of traditional rural life in the face of industrialization (Encyclopedia Britannica).

Politically, Hardy was liberal and influenced by John Stuart Mill, and it was the plight of the rural worker – the 'Hodge' – in the face of industrialization that troubled him more than the aesthetics of a changing countryside. In 1883, this was laid bare in the essay profiled here: his one noted work of non-fiction, 'The Dorsetshire Labourer', a polemic published in Longman's Magazine. This work directly addressed the impoverishment of agricultural labourers and the eviction of tenant farmers. Here, in spite of his liberal sensibilities, Hardy displayed a certain degree of conservative romanticism in lamenting the loss of the old social order. There is no doubt that his principal concern is the impoverished labourers, but he sees their fate as a consequence of abandoning 'centuries of serfdom' in which peasantry had the option of 'going to my Lord' in times of trouble.

Hardy returned to this theme, in more subtle forms, in his subsequent novels. Six years later in The Woodlanders, for instance, he depicts the ruin of the Wessex village of Little Hintock by the arrival of outsiders with little understanding of rural life. In this story, the trees of the local woodlands are thoughtlessly felled by these newcomers and sold off to people ignorant as to what they have bought. The villains of the piece are the new middle classes ignorant of the countryside and ruining it for short-term gain, a socially and environmentally conservative message (Hardy 1887).

Hardy was cremated and his ashes interred at Westminster Abbey, but his heart was preserved and buried in his beloved home village of Bockhampton in Dorset. A – likely baseless – rumour has persisted that, in a grim but environmental posthumous twist, Hardy's pet cat ate his heart (Tapper 1996).

pp. 252–269

42

'THE DORSETSHIRE LABOURER'

Thomas Hardy

Source: Thomas Hardy, 'The Dorsetshire Labourer' (1883)

It seldom happens that a nickname which affects to portray a class is honestly indicative of the individuals composing that class. The few features distinguishing them from other bodies of men have been seized on and exaggerated, while the incomparably more numerous features common to all humanity have been ignored. In the great world this wild colouring of so-called typical portraits is clearly enough recognised. Nationalities, the aristocracy, the plutocracy, the citizen class, and many others, have their allegorical representatives, which are received with due allowance for flights of imagination in the direction of burlesque.

But when the class lies somewhat out of the ken of ordinary society the caricature begins to be taken as truth. Moreover, the original is held to be an actual unit of the multitude signified. He ceases to be an abstract figure and becomes a sample. Thus when we arrive at the farm-labouring community we find it to be seriously personified by the pitiable picture known as Hodge; not only so, but the community is assumed to be a uniform collection of concrete Hodges.

This supposed real but highly conventional Hodge is a degraded being of uncouth manner and aspect, stolid understanding, and snaillike movement. His speech is such a chaotic corruption of regular language that few persons of progressive aims consider it worth while to enquire what views, if any, of life, of nature, or of society, are conveyed in these utterances. Hodge hangs his head or looks sheepish when spoken to, and thinks Lunnon a place paved with gold. Misery and fever lurk in his cottage, while, to paraphrase the words of a recent writer on the labouring classes, in his future there are only the workhouse and the grave. He hardly dares to think at all. He has few thoughts of joy, and little hope of rest. His life slopes into a darkness not 'quieted by hope'.

If one of the many thoughtful persons who hold this view were to go by rail to Dorset, where Hodge in his most unmitigated form is supposed to reside, and seek out a retired district, he might by and by certainly meet a man who, at first contact with an intelligence fresh from the contrasting world of London, would seem to exhibit some of the above-mentioned qualities. The latter items in the list, the mental miseries, the visitor might hardly look for in their

DOI: 10.4324/9781003194651-53

ROMANTICIZING NATURE

fulness, since it would have become perceptible to him as an explorer, and to any but the chamber theorist, that no uneducated community, rich or poor, bond or free, possessing average health and personal liberty, could exist in an unchangeable slough of despond, or that it would for many months if it could. Its members, like the accursed swine, would rush down a steep place and be choked in the waters. He could have learnt that wherever a mode of supporting life is neither noxious nor absolutely inadequate, there springs up happiness, and will spring up happiness, of some sort or other. Indeed, it is among such communities as these that happiness will find her last refuge on earth, since it is among them that a perfect insight into the conditions of existence will be longest postponed.

That in their future there are only the workhouse and the grave is no more and no less true than that in the future of the average well-to-do householder there are only the invalid chair and the brick vault.

. . .

If it were possible to gauge the average sufferings of classes, the probability is that in Dorsetshire the figure would be lower with the regular farmer's labourers – 'workfolk' as they call themselves – than with the adjoining class, the unattached labourers, approximating to the free labourers of the middle ages, who are to be found in the larger villages and small towns of the county – many of them, no doubt, descendants of the old copyholders who were ousted from their little plots when the system of leasing large farms grew general. They are, what the regular labourer is not, out of sight of patronage; and to be out of sight is to be out of mind when misfortune arises, and pride or sensitiveness leads them to conceal their privations.

. . .

Ten or a dozen of these families, with their goods, may be seen halting simultaneously at an out-of-the-way inn, and it is not possible to walk a mile on any of the high roads this day without meeting several. This annual migration from farm to farm is much in excess of what it was formerly. For example, on a particular farm where, a generation ago, not more than one cottage on an average changed occupants yearly, and where the majority remained all their lifetime, the whole number of tenants were changed at Lady Day just past, and this though nearly all of them had been new arrivals on the previous Lady Day. Dorset labourers now look upon an annual removal as the most natural thing in the world, and it becomes with the younger families a pleasant excitement. Change is also a certain sort of education. Many advantages accrue to the labourers from the varied experience it brings, apart from the discovery of the best market for their abilities. They have become shrewder and sharper men of the world, and have learnt how to hold their own with firmness and judgment. Whenever the habitually-removing man comes into contact with one of the old-fashioned stationary sort, who are still to be found, it is impossible not to perceive that the former is much more wide awake than his fellow-worker, astonishing him with stories of the wide world comprised in a twenty-mile radius from their homes.

They are also losing their peculiarities as a class; hence the humorous simplicity which formerly characterised the men and the unsophisticated modesty of the women are rapidly disappearing or lessening, under the constant attrition of lives mildly approximating to those of workers in a manufacturing town. It is the common remark of villagers immediately above the labouring class, who know the latter well as personal acquaintances, that 'there are no nice homely workfolk now as there used to be'. There may be, and is, some exaggeration in this, but it is only natural that, now different districts of them are shaken together once a year and redistributed, like a shuffled pack of cards, they have ceased to be so local in feeling or manner as formerly, and have entered on the condition of inter-social citizens, whose city stretches the whole county over. Their brains are less frequently than they once were 'as dry as the remainder biscuit after a voyage', and they vent less often the result of their own observations than what they have heard to be the current ideas of smart chaps in towns. The women have, in many districts, acquired the rollicking air of factory hands. That seclusion and immutability, which was so bad for their pockets, was an unrivalled fosterer of their personal charm in the eyes of those whose experiences had been less limited. But the artistic merit of their old condition is scarcely a reason why they should have continued in it when other communities were marching on so vigorously towards uniformity and mental equality. It is only the old story that progress and picturesqueness do not harmonise. They are losing their individuality, but they are widening the range of their ideas, and gaining in freedom. It is too much to expect them to remain stagnant and old-fashioned for the pleasure of romantic spectators.

But, picturesqueness apart, a result of this increasing nomadic habit of the labourer is, naturally, a less intimate and kindly relation with the land he tills than existed before enlightenment enabled him to rise above the condition of a serf who lived and died on a particular plot like a tree. During the centuries of serfdom, of copyholding tenants, and down to twenty or thirty years ago, before the power of unlimited migration had been clearly realised, the husbandman of either class had the interest of long personal association with his farm. The fields were those he had ploughed and sown from boyhood, and it was impossible for him, in such circumstances, to sink altogether the character of natural guardian in that of hireling. Not so very many years ago, the landowner, if he were good for anything, stood as a court of final appeal in cases of the harsh dismissal of a man by the farmer. 'I'll go to my lord' was a threat which overbearing farmers respected, for 'my lord' had often personally known the labourer long before he knew the labourer's master. But such arbitrament is rarely practicable now. The landlord does not know by sight, if even by name, half the men who preserve his acres from the curse of Eden. They come and go yearly, like birds of passage, nobody thinks whence or whither. This dissociation is favoured by the customary system of letting the cottages with the land, so that, far from having a guarantee of a holding to keep him fixed, the labourer has not even the stability of a landlord's tenant; he is only tenant of a tenant, the latter possibly a new comer, who takes strictly commercial views of his man and cannot afford to waste a penny on sentimental considerations.

Thus, while their pecuniary condition in the prime of life is bettered, and their freedom enlarged, they have lost touch with their environment, and that sense of long local participancy which is one of the pleasures of age. The old casus conscientice of those in power – whether the weak tillage of an enfeebled hand ought not to be put up with in fields which have had the benefit of that hand's strength – arises less frequently now that the strength has often been expended elsewhere. The sojourning existence of the town masses is more and more the existence of the rural masses, with its corresponding benefits and disadvantages. With uncertainty of residence often comes a laxer morality, and more cynical views of the duties of life. Domestic stability is a factor in conduct which nothing else can equal. On the other hand, new varieties of happiness evolve themselves like new varieties of plants, and new charms may have arisen among the classes who have been driven to adopt the remedy of locomotion for the evils of oppression and poverty – charms which compensate in some measure for the lost sense of home.

A practical injury which this wandering entails on the children of the labourers should be mentioned here. In shifting from school to school, their education cannot possibly progress with that regularity which is essential to their getting the best knowledge in the short time available to them. It is the remark of village school-teachers of experience, that the children of the vagrant workfolk form the mass of those who fail to reach the ordinary standard of knowledge expected of their age. The rural schoolmaster or mistress enters the schoolroom on the morning of the sixth of April, and finds that a whole flock of the brightest young people has suddenly flown away. In a village school which may be taken as a fair average specimen, containing seventy-five scholars, thirty-three vanished thus on the Lady Day of the present year. Some weeks elapse before the new comers drop in, and a longer time passes before they take root in the school, their dazed, unaccustomed mood rendering immediate progress impossible; while the original bright ones have by this time themselves degenerated into the dazed strangers of other districts.

That the labourers of the country are more independent since their awakening to the sense of an outer world cannot be disputed. It was once common enough on inferior farms to hear a farmer, as he sat on horseback amid a field of workers, address them with a contemptuousness which could not have been greatly exceeded in the days when the thralls of Cedric wore their collars of brass. Usually no answer was returned to these tirades; they were received as an accident of the land on which the listeners had happened to be born, calling for no more resentment than the blows of the wind and rain. But now, no longer fearing to avail himself of his privilege of flitting, these acts of contumely have ceased to be regarded as inevitable by the peasant. And while men do not of their own accord leave a farm without a grievance, very little fault-finding is often deemed a sufficient one among the younger and stronger. Such ticklish relations are the natural result of generations of unfairness on one side, and on the other an increase of knowledge, which has been kindled into activity by the exertions of Mr Joseph Arch.

. . .

A reason frequently advanced for dismissing these families from the villages where they have lived for centuries is that it is done in the interests of morality; and it is quite true that some of the 'liviers' (as these half-independent villagers used to be called) were not always shining examples of churchgoing, temperance, and quiet walking. But a natural tendency to evil, which develops to unlawful action when' excited by contact with others like-minded, would often have remained latent amid the simple isolated experiences of a village life. The cause of morality cannot be served by compelling a population hitherto evenly distributed over the country to concentrate in a few towns, with the inevitable results of overcrowding and want of regular employment. But the question of the Dorset cottager here merges in that of all the houseless and landless poor, and the vast topic of the Rights of Man, to consider which is beyond the scope of a merely descriptive article.

Editorial Headnote

1781 (Jamaica)–1826

Thomas Stamford Raffles was a colonial administrator turned conservationist.

Raffles was very much a child of the Empire, born on a trading ship captained by his father near the coast of Jamaica. He had a fairly limited education owing to family debts accruing and left boarding school to work as a clerk for the East India Company (EIC) from an early age. He rose quickly through the ranks at the EIC and was appointed assistant secretary in a new government established in Penang, Malaysia.

Raffles then went on to become Lieutenant-Governor of Java in 1811 after fighting in a short war that seized the island from the Dutch. This was at a time the French were establishing a military presence in the region and were seen to be threatening British interests in Asia. His detailed knowledge of the Indies had brought Raffles to the attention of the governor-general of India Lord Minto. This expertise was also recognized in the publication of his book The History of Java in 1817, which included accounts of the island's flora and fauna. He was subsequently knighted in the same year. Two years later, after taking on the role of lieutenant governor of Bencoolen after Java had been returned to the Dutch, Raffles then 'founded' Singapore as a port city. He negotiated the rights to establish a British settlement on the island after recognizing its great commercial potential.

Raffles was an imperialist but also a reformist liberal and worked with William Wilberforce – a neighbour in Mill Hill, north of London – in the slavery abolitionist movement. He himself had ended slavery and enacted reforms in his tenure on Java, to the displeasure of many in the EIC.

Raffles retired from colonial administration due to health problems but continued to pursue his interests in natural history. He founded the Zoological Society of London in 1826 – as discussed in his following speech – and became its first president. However, he died suddenly of apoplexy shortly after this, a day before his 45th birthday. The most obvious legacy of the society was the opening of the Zoological Gardens at Regents Park. London Zoo, as it became known, had at the time the biggest collection of animals in the world and the society vowed to be driven by species conservation in this endeavour. The society later also opened Whipsnade as the world's first safari park. Raffles notes that Britain is lagging behind other countries in this regard. Zoos had been established in Vienna and Paris as far back as the eighteenth century. The role of the nobility in pioneering wildlife conservation in this way is evidenced by the dignitaries listed in this report.

The vicar of Raffles's local parish at Hendon, Theodor Williams, who had profited from slavery, refused his burial inside the church because of his abolitionist sentiments. However, his tomb was later incorporated into the church when it was expanded in the 1920s. A statue in Westminster Abbey commemorates his life and, perhaps most famously, a luxury hotel in Singapore still bears his name.

43

LONDON ZOOLOGICAL SOCIETY

Thomas Stamford Raffles

Source: Thomas Stamford Raffles, *London Zoological Society* (1825)

For the general advancement of Zoological Science, it is proposed that a Society shall be established, the immediate object of which will be the collection of such living subjects of the Animal Kingdom as may be introduced and domesticated with advantage in this country.

For this purpose a collection of living animals belonging to the Society will be established in the vicinity of the metropolis; to which the Members of the Society will have access as a matter of right, and the public on such conditions as may be hereafter arranged.

It is proposed that the Society shall have a museum, as well as a library of all books connected with the subject; to which access will be given to the members and the public as above stated.

As it is impossible to attain all the objects of the Society on its first establishment, those of utility will engage its earliest attention, and the more scientific views will be attended to as the means of the Society admit.

The Society will be directed as other public Societies are – by a President, Council, and Officers, and regulated by laws to be established with the concurrence of the members of the Society.

A detailed Prospectus of the objects of this Society having been circulated privately last year, a corrected copy is annexed.

The Terms of Admission to the Society will be Three Pounds, and the Annual Subscription Two Pounds; or the whole to be compounded for on the usual terms.

A Committee of the following Noblemen and Gentlemen was originally nominated by a meeting of friends of the proposed Society in July last, and the Prospectus is published under their authority.

CHAIRMAN: SIR STAMFORD RAFFLES.

Duke of Somerset
Earl of Darnley
Earl of Egremont
Earl of Malmesbury

DOI: 10.4324/9781003194651-54

Viscount Gage
Bishop of Carlisle
Lord Stanley
Sir H. Davy
Sir Everard Home
E. Barnard, Esq.
H. T. Colebrooke, Esq.

Davies Gilbert, Esq.
Rev. Dr. Goodenough
Thos. Horsfield, Esq., M.D.
Rev. W. Kirby
T. A. Knight, Esq.
T. A. Knight, Jun., Esq.
W. Sharp MacLeay, Esq.
J. Sabine, Esq.
N. A. Vigors, Esq.
Chas. Baring Wall, Esq.

Zoology, which exhibits the nature and properties of animated beings, their analogies to each other, the wonderful delicacy of their structure, and the fitness of their organs to the peculiar purposes of their existence, must be regarded not only as an interesting and intellectual study, but as a most important branch of Natural Theology, teaching by the design and wonderful results of organization the wisdom and power of the Creator. In its relation to useful and immediate oeconomical purposes it is no less important. The different races of animals employed in social life, for labour, clothing, food, etc., are the direct objects of its attention; their improvement, the manner in which their number may be increased, the application of their produce, and its connection with various departments of industry and manufactures, are of the utmost importance to Man, in every stage of his existence, but most so in proportion as he advances in wealth, civilization, and refinement.

It has long been a matter of deep regret to the cultivators of Natural History, that we possess no great scientific establishments either for teaching or elucidating Zoology; and no public menageries or collections of living animals where their nature, properties and habits may be studied. In almost every other part of Europe, except in the metropolis of the British empire, something of this kind exists: but though richer than any other country in the extent and variety of our possessions, and having more facilities from our colonies, our fleets, and our varied and constant intercourse with every quarter of the globe, for collecting specimens and introducing live animals, we have as yet attempted little and effected almost nothing; and the student of Natural History, or the philosopher who wishes to examine animated nature, has no other resource but that of visiting and profiting by the magnificent institutions of neighbouring countries.

338

LONDON ZOOLOGICAL SOCIETY

In the hope of removing this opprobrium to our age and nation, it is proposed to establish a society bearing the same relation to zoology that the Horticultural does to botany, and upon a similar proposal and plan The great objects should be, the introduction of new varieties, breeds, and races of animals, for the purpose of domestication or for stocking our farm-yards, woods, pleasure-grounds, and wastes; with the establishment of a general zoological collection, consisting of prepared specimens in the different classes and orders, so as to afford a correct view of the Animal Kingdom at large, in as complete a series as may be practicable; and at the same time point out the analogies between the animals already domesticated, and those which are similar in character, upon which the first experiments may be made.

To promote these objects, a piece of ground should be provided in the neighbourhood of the metropolis, affording sufficient accommodation for the above purposes; with a suitable establishment so conducted as to admit of its extension on additional means being afforded.

As it is presumed that a number of persons would feel disposed to encourage an institution of this kind, it is proposed to make the Annual Subscription from each individual only Two Pounds, and the Admission Fee Three Pounds. The Members, of course, will have free and constant access to the Collections and Grounds, and might, at a reasonable price, be furnished with living specimens, or the ova of fishes and birds.

When it is considered how few amongst the immense variety of animated beings have been hitherto applied to the uses of Man, and that most of those which have been domesticated or subdued belong to the early periods of society, and to the efforts of savage or uncultivated nations, it is impossible not to hope for many new, brilliant, and useful results in the same field, by the application of the wealth, ingenuity, and varied resources of a civilized people.

It is well known with respect to most of the Animal Tribes, that domestication is a process which requires time; that the offspring of wild animals raised in a domestic state are more easily tamed than their parents; and that in a certain number of generations the effect is made permanent, and connected with a change, not merely in the habits but even in the nature of the animal. The inconveniences of migration may be, in certain cases, prevented, and the wildest animals, when supplied abundantly with food, may lose the instinct of locomotion, and their offspring acquire new habits; and it is known that a breed, fairly domesticated, is with difficulty brought back to its original state.

Should the Society flourish and succeed, it will not only be useful in common life, but would likewise promote the best and most extensive objects of the Scientific History of Animated Nature, and offer a collection of living animals, such as never yet existed in ancient or modern times. Rome, at the period of her greatest splendour, brought savage monsters from every quarter of the world then known, to be shown in her ampitheatres, to destroy or be destroyed as spectacles of wonder to her citizens. It would well become Britain to offer another, and a very different series of exhibitions to the population of her metropolis; namely,

339

animals brought from every part of the globe to be applied either to some useful purpose, or as objects of scientific research, not of vulgar admiration. Upon such an institution a philosophy of Zoology may be founded, pointing out the comparative anatomy, the habits of life, the improvement and the methods of multiplying those races of animals which are most useful to man, and thus fixing a most beautiful and important branch of knowledge on the permanent basis of direct utility.

Editorial Headnote

1858 (London)–1940

This book, The Game Animals of Africa by Richard Lydekker, was dedicated to the Duke of Bedford (Herbrand Russell), making reference to his contributions to the conservation of several species of African mammals. The work features many of his own photographs of his personal stock of such animals. Lydekker (1849–1915) was a prolific and well-respected writer on natural history and geology. He was part of the Geological Survey of India and catalogued many fossils which are still exhibited in the Natural History Museum.

Aristocratic politician and zoologist Herbrand Russell was the Eleventh Duke of Bedford, succeeding his elder brother in 1893. He was Oxford-educated and had a prominent military career, serving in several parts of the Empire and in World War I. He also held a number of diplomatic positions in a varied career. He was a successor to Raffles as president of the Zoological Society of London (1899–1936), during which time he oversaw many animal conservation initiatives.

Russell saved the milu (Pere David's Deer) from extinction by buying up all eighteen known survivors from European zoos in 1898 and breeding them on the grounds of his family home at Woburn Abbey. Nearly a century later, a number of this milu herd were then re-introduced into China (where they had become extinct in the nineteenth century). Russell also bred bison, lions, tigers and Prevalsky's horses (Europe's last wild species) at Woburn. It is also believed that he introduced grey squirrels to the UK, which are now widely considered a damaging invasive species, having come close to displacing the native red squirrel. Russell is known to have gifted several of these squirrels and released others into the wild – including in Regents Park, London. Muntjac deer are another invasive species, considered harmful to woodland ground flora by some, that can be traced to the conservation work of Russell. Many of these small deer, native to China, which are today common in the woodlands of South England, are descendants of escapees from Woburn in the early twentieth century (although the Zoological Society also had muntjac before Russell).

Russell's Grandson, the Thirteenth Duke of Bedford Ian Russell, transformed the animal collection into Woburn Safari Park in 1970 (in conjunction with the famed circus master Jimmy Chipperfield), after previously opening up the family home to the public.

In the selected extracts, Lydekker describes two species of animals – gnus and sable antelopes – that Russel made important contributions to preserving in the face of potential extinction through hunting.

In later life, Russell became president of the Cremation Society and, on his death, was himself cremated, with his ashes scattered at Bedford Chapel (Woburn Abbey 2022).

44

THE GAME ANIMALS OF AFRICA (DEDICATED TO HERBRAND RUSSELL)

Richard Lydekker

Source: Richard Lydekker, *The Game Animals of Africa (dedicated to Herbrand Russell)* (1908)

PREFACE

TO THE DUKE OF BEDFORD, K.G. WHO HAS DONE MUCH TO INCREASE
OUR KNOWLEDGE OF THE BIG GAME OF THE WORLD THIS VOLUME
BY HIS GRACE'S PERMISSION IS DEDICATED BY THE AUTHOR

. . .

pp. 132–134

Gnu

Like bulls, gnus are violently excited by red, and when hunting them the Boers at
the Cape were in the habit of hoisting a scarlet cloth at the top of a long pole. At
sight of this the gnus would, according to Pringle, a well-known and trustworthy
writer in the early part of last century, "caper about, lashing their flanks with their
long tails, and tearing up the ground with their hoofs as if violently excited, and
ready to rush down upon us; and then, all at once, when we were about to fire, they
would bound away, and again go prancing round us at a safer distance."

Reference has already been made to the association in the old days of gnus
and quaggas; it should be added that the party was completed by ostriches. Similarly the brindled gnu displays the same partiality for the company of the bonte-
quagga; the ostrich in this case, too, frequently forming a third member of the
apparently ill-assorted party.

In speed the gnu is well capable of holding its own among other members of
the African fauna; and as it has also great staying capacity, it is a difficult animal
to ride down. It had, however, a remarkable partiality for one particular piece of
country, so that if driven off one day, it might be found in its own haunts a short
time afterwards. Of late years the species appears to have obtained a very good
idea of the distance to which it is safe to allow a human being to approach; so that

DOI: 10.4324/9781003194651-55

343

on the Boer farms, before the war, it was almost impossible to procure a good head except by stalking.

Gnu venison (both that of the present and the brindled species) lacks the gamy taste characteristic of the flesh of so many South African antelopes, and is compared to very inferior beef. Calves, however, afford a somewhat more palatable dish. In old days gnu and quagga were chiefly shot by the Boer farmers as food for their Hottentot servants, they themselves eating more tasty venison, such as that of springbok, hartebeest, or gemsbok. The hides of the gnus were used for harness, whips, ropes, and other farm-gear. Even under this system the game in Cape Colony was soon decimated, but when skin-hunting became the vogue, the fate of the gnu was soon sealed.

Some twenty years ago Mr. Piet Terblans had, according to Mr. H. A. Bryden, more than a couple of hundred head of gnu on his farms, and there were at that time two other farms in the Orange River Colony on which the species was preserved. Even then the number of head living in South Africa was estimated at not more than 600 or 700, and it is now infinitely less. A few have been imported into Europe, where, as in the Duke of Bedford's park at Woburn, they have in some instances bred; and there is Mr. Rudd's herd in Cape Colony, of which mention has been already made. But the species is evidently doomed, and as a truly wild animal no longer exists. In captivity gnus display the same grotesque habits as in the wild state. In both conditions they frequently tear up the ground with their horns, to the no small detriment of the tips of those formidable weapons, which the old bulls know only too well how to use in attack. Gnus are, indeed, dangerous animals and should be approached with caution.

. . .

pp. 290–292

Sable Antelope

With this magnificent antelope, which runs the kudu hard as a claimant to be considered the finest representative of the whole tribe, we come to the typical genus of the subfamily *Hippotraginæ* (This genus includes the largest members of the group, and is characterised by the stout and heavily ridged horns rising at an obtuse angle to the plane of the face, and then sweeping backwards in a scimitar-like curve. A well-developed and often upright mane clothes the neck; the throat is more or less distinctly maned; the moderate tail is terminally tufted; the long pointed ears are characterised by their excessive size; and there are tufts of long white hair below the eyes. The sable coat of both sexes, white under-parts, gazelle-like face-markings, in which the white eye-stripe is continued downwards to join the white of the muzzle, the moderate size of the ears, the length of the mane, and the enormous horns of the bucks, render this antelope so easy of recognition that detailed description is superfluous. It will suffice, therefore, to state that the shoulder-height of the buck is about 54 inches (4½ feet); and that a single horn in the Florence Museum measures 61 inches in length, the next best specimen being

THE GAME ANIMALS OF AFRICA (DEDICATED TO HERBRAND RUSSELL)

52½ inches. The foxy-coloured calves show the same face-markings as their sable parents, and are thereby at once distinguishable from those of the roan antelope.

Blackness in animals is what naturalists term a specialised feature; and from this point of view (as is demonstrated by the fact that the young are chestnut or tan coloured) the sable antelope is a highly specialised creature. Its great specialisation in this respect is indicated by the fact that the sable livery is assumed by both sexes, instead of being, as in Mrs. Gray's and the white-eared kob, confined to the adult males. The species is, in fact, unique among antelopes in this particular. On the other hand, the retention of the gazelline face-markings common to the members of the gemsbuck or oryx group, the relatively moderate size of the ears, and the small development of the eye-tuft, point to the conclusion that the sable antelope is in these respects a far less specialised animal than its less handsomely coloured relative, the roan antelope.

Discovered in the year 1837 by the great hunter Sir Cornwallis Harris in the hills of the Magaliesberg district of the Transvaal, the sable antelope ranges thence northwards to Nyasaland and the neighbouring parts of south-eastern and eastern Africa. South of the Zambesi the range of the species appears, indeed, to have been confined to the eastern half of the continent, except for a western extension along the valley of the Limpopo and the southern bank of the Chobi. Northern Mashonaland seems to have been the district in which it most abounded, and where it is said to have been the commonest of all antelopes; but the eastern part of that country, and thence towards the coast, were also favourite localities. Northward of the Zambesi it was always less common, although the Batoka plateau is one of its present strongholds; and it was never abundant in the Mozambique province.

From ten to twenty is the usual number of individuals in a herd of sable antelope, although occasionally the total may be as many as forty or fifty, while in one herd the number has been estimated at eighty. Very rarely, however, is there more than a single adult bull in a herd, no matter how large. In the districts to the south of the Zambesi adult cows are nearly as black as the bulls, but to the northward of that river the former are stated to be in most cases reddish brown. With regard to the object of the black colouring of this and other sable species, it has been suggested that the dark livery is a "warning colour," Dr. E. Lonnberg has, however, pointed out that blackness in male animals may more probably be attributed to general vigour of development, and to the necessity for using up superfluous products in the organism. It is analogous, in fact, to the development of the comb in the cock, and the dark colour and curved lower jaw in the male salmon. When once firmly established in the male, the black livery may make its appearance, as a secondary development, in the female, as in the case of the present species.

The coat of the sable antelope is in best condition and darkest in colour immediately after the rainy season, when food has been abundant, the mane being then so long as to all partially to one side. But early in the dry season, that is to say towards the middle of June, the long hair on the neck begins to be shed, and by September there is little left except short brownish hair, with numerous bare patches; while the coat on other parts becomes scantier and duller. In fact, at this season the animals present a decidedly poor and untidy appearance, very different from their look a few months later, when they once more don their new spring coats. Sparsely forested, grassy upland districts form the favourite resorts of the sable antelope; and it is on this account that the species is so abundant in Matabili-land, Barotsiland, and Mashonaland. During the rains these antelopes are stated, however, to retire to thicker forest at lower elevations for the sake of shelter. And in some instances they may be found on rough, rocky ground, where they display considerable activity in ascending and descending bad places. Early spring, that is to say during the months of September and October, is the chief calving-season, although a few cows may produce their young a month earlier. As already mentioned, the face-markings of the calves are similar to those of the adults; but in newly dropped calves these markings are stated to be less distinct.

Sable antelope have the reputation of being the most high-couraged of all the antelope tribe; and a wounded bull at bay, with its tremendously powerful and wide-reaching horns, is an antagonist which should on all occasions be treated with respect and caution. Nevertheless, they do not often charge their adversaries, preferring to maintain a defensive rather than to assume an aggressive attitude.

. . .

P. 294

Some years ago the Duke of Bedford had a small herd of sable antelope at Woburn Abbey, where these antelopes habitually resorted to certain bracken-clad slopes. As they stood among the brown fern in autumn they afforded some idea of the beautiful sight a herd must present in its native haunts.

Editorial Headnote

1877 (Tring, Hertfordshire)–1923

Nathaniel Charles Rothschild (known as Charles) was a banker but is most remembered as an entomologist and conservationist.

Charles was the son of the First Baron Rothschild and worked in his banking empire. He was educated at Harrow and Cambridge. It is in the fields of entomology and land conservation, however, that Rothschild is most remembered and his contributions to both were considerable. It is believed that he personally discovered about 500 species of flea, including the one responsible for transmitting the Black Death in the fifteenth century. Evidence of this and other collections can be seen today at the Natural History Museum in Tring, Hertfordshire, where he grew up.

The conservation of nature was also a passion of Rothschild. In 1899, Rothschild bought Wicken Fen, a Cambridgeshire remnant of the East Anglian Fens, and handed it over to the National Trust two years later. Wicken Fen hence became the first British nature reserve. Rothschild then set about expanding this model of conservation, acquiring a series of locations throughout the country for what became known as 'Rothschild's List'. Other prominent reserves created from this original list include Bass Rock, an island in the Firth of Forth, and Blakeney Point on the North Norfolk coast.

In May 1912, Charles Rothschild held a meeting to discuss his radical idea about preserving natural wildlife habitats. His aim was to organize 'persons interested in the preservation of the natural fauna and flora of the United Kingdom' (Rothschild Archive 2021). Importantly for the evolution of conservation, this meant focusing on the preservation of the habitat as well as particular species of animal. The meeting established the Society for the Promotion of Nature Reserves (SPNR). In the extract, it is evident that there was recognition that Britain was behind the US and other states in this regard. By 1915, the SPNR had designated some 284 sites as 'worthy of protection'. The SPNR is now the Wildlife Trust, a prominent force for conservation in Britain today, which defines itself accordingly: 'Our purpose is to bring wildlife back, to empower people to take meaningful action for nature, and to create an inclusive society where nature matters' (Wildlife Trust 2022). Hence, today Rothschild's legacy is an organization with over 870,000 members which was a founding member of the International Union for the Conservation of Nature (IUCN), the world's foremost global institution for the preservation of nature.

Rothschild was committed to public service in a wider sense and also worked with the Red Cross. He was driven to suicide by encephalitis and so died before seeing the full realization of his ambitions with the establishment of the National Parks Commission in 1949 (Rothschild Archive 2021).

45

NATURE RESERVES: FORMATION OF A NEW SOCIETY

Charles Rothschild

Source: Charles Rothschild, *Nature Reserves: formation of a new society* (1912)

In his recent address to the Zoological Section of the British Association at Dundee, Dr. Chalmers Mitchell made a strong appeal for the organized preservation of the world's fauna. "It is only by the deliberate – and conscious interference of man," he said, "that the evil wrought by man has been arrested": and again, "Each generation is the guardian of the existing resources of the world; it has come into a great inheritance, but only as a trustee" – a trustee, that is to say, for generations that are to be. That the larger wild creatures are steadily disappearing from the face of the earth with the advance of civilization needs little demonstration. But coincidently with the wholesale extermination of mammals there is in progress a no less disastrous process of destruction among the lesser creatures – birds, fishes, reptiles, insects, and plants – also of geological, remains, and in almost every case this is the result of "the deliberate and conscious interference of man."

To arrest this destructive tendency serious consideration is being given to the subject in many countries. There exist in the United States "reserves" for the vanishing human races; in Norway, Sweden and North Russia, the Lapps are efficiently protected; in New Zealand as elsewhere in the British Dominions beyond the seas, large tracts of land have been fenced off, and laws enacted to prevent the traffic of alcohol and other goods harmful to the primitive races.

Elsewhere the duty of maintaining particular phases of human life and of preserving natural objects is recognized and performed by the community as a whole, acting through the State; but in the United Kingdom it has been left to private enterprise and private munificence to establish and finance such refuges and nature reserves as we actually possess. Something has been attempted, it is true, to check the wanton destruction of animal life, by various Acts of Parliament, the arrangement of "close" seasons, sanctuaries, &c. and in the National Trust we have a body equipped with the necessary authority to take over and safeguard such gifts of land as may be made by public enterprise or private liberality. Much has already been accomplished in this direction by certain societies

DOI: 10.4324/9781003194651-56

349

and individuals; but all students and lovers of nature generally are now invited to combine in support of the Society for the Promotion of Nature Reserves.

This Society has recently been formed with the following objects: –

1. To collect and collate information as to areas of land in the United Kingdom which retain their primitive conditions and contain rare and local species liable to extinction owing to building, drainage, and dis afforestation, or in consequence of the cupidity of collectors. All such information to be treated as strictly confidential.
2. To prepare a scheme showing which areas should be secured.
3. To obtain these areas and hand them over to the National Trust under such conditions as may be necessary
4. To 'preserve for posterity' as a national possession some part at least of our native land, its fauna, flora, and geological features.
5. To encourage the love of Nature, and to educate public opinion to a better knowledge of the value of Nature study.

The society exacts no subscription; members are formally elected by invitation of the Executive Committee (marked with * below), and all interested are invited to communicate with the secretaries. The control of the society's affairs is in the hands of a representative council consisting at present of the following: –

> President, the Right Hon. J. W. Lowther, M.P., Dr. I. Bayley Balfour, F.R.S., Sir Edward H. Busk, Sir Francis Darwin, F.R.S., Dr. F. D. Drewitt, *G. Claridge Druce, Professor J. BretJand Farmer, F.R.S., L. Fletcher, F.R.S., the Right Hon. Sir Edward Grey, Bt., K.G., M.P., the Right Hon. L. V. Harcourt, M.P., *Sir Robert Hunter, K.C.B., Lord Lucas, *E. G. B. Meade-Waldo, *the Hon. E. S. Montagu, M.P., the Earl of Plymouth, C.B., Professor E. B. Poulton, F.R.S., Sir David Prain, F.R.S., *the Hon. N. C. Rothschild, *W. H. St. Ouintin, Dr. R. F. Scharff, W. M. Webb. *Ex-officio*: Hon. Treasurer, *C. E. Fagan, I.S.O.; Hon. Secretaries, *W. R. Ogilvie-Grant, and *the Hon. F. R. Henley.

The Trustees of the British Museum have kindly given permission to the committee to use the Natural History Museum, Cromwell-road, London, S.W., as the temporary address of the society.

To carry out the objects of the society prompt action must be taken, for year by year suitable areas become fewer; and local plants and insects are found to have been extirpated when the acquisition of a few acres of land would have saved them. Such land is often unsuitable for other purposes; an isolated spot on Government property, a piece of marshland, a bird-haunted cliff, or a stretch of wood and copse where the undergrowth has been allowed to follow its own devices are admirable subjects for nature reserves. Above all, it is essential that the land selected or reserved should as far as possible retain its primitive wildness. Such lands still exist in the United Kingdom, though each year they become more rare, and once deprived of their indigenous occupants they can never be restored to a natural state. It should be borne in mind that if in the course of time, owing to the growth of a city, or for some other reason, a nature reserve has ceased to serve its purpose, the ground would still be valuable as an open space.

On the Continent, as already observed, the importance of nature reserves has been widely recognized. In Germany, particularly, a large amount of land has been reclaimed, and in a recently published book, Herr H. Conwentz, Prussian State Commissioner for the Care of Natural Monuments, gives a detailed account of the work done in the several States of the Empire. Bavaria, more than a hundred years ago, bought up the Bamberg suburban woods, afterwards forbidding indiscriminate forestry, and ordering the foresters to preserve and catalogue the chief natural features. Later, a general committee composed of delegates from the municipality and from local and artistic societies have been exceptionally successful in securing wild "parks" for rare plants. In Hessen and Oldenburg special attention has been paid to the preservation of primeval forest land; while in the first years of the new century Prussia began to recognize the necessity of protecting nature reserves, and these have since been regularly registered and mapped, Parliament, the Education Department, and the Department of Agriculture and Domains acting conjointly to assist the movement. Thus, Memmert, an uninhabited island between Juist and Borkum in the German Ocean, is now reserved as a bird sanctuary, with a watcher to look after it during the breeding season; and a tract of salt marsh near Artern perpetuates the plant association of the locality. Elsewhere spots especially favoured by wild nature have been similarly secured; for example, the Prussian Government, the local authorities and societies, and private individuals have all co-operated to secure the forest district of Chorin, near Berlin, including fenland and a small lake, also a tract of forest in the Hartz Mountains. Saxony has followed this example. In Holland, the Naardermeer, in the south of the Zuider Zee, with its rich avifauna, is now effectively isolated, while in Sweden immense stretches of country in the far north and elsewhere have been closed to the collector, not before it was necessary. It is common knowledge that before the reservation of the magnificent Lapland country round the Tornea Trdsk, and simultaneously with the opening of the Baltic-Atlantic railway the district was ruthlessly over-collected by dealers and others; in one summer a single individual is credited with the removal of 10,000 plants. In Hungary there are several reserved areas; one of them at Puszta-Peszer, in the Pest Comitat. In France good work has been done by the Forest Board in the protection of undergrowth and by some local prohibitions in the departments of Isere and Savoie on behalf of a few Alpine plants. Much the same may be said of Switzerland, where a few cantons have issued edicts against the destruction of Edelweiss and other "threatened" flowers. In Belgium, though at present little has been done officially in the way of protection, the Royal Botanical Society has completed an admirable survey of desirable natural sites ("Pour la Protection de la Nature en Belgique," Jean Massart, 1912), and this work has aroused general public interest.

In the United States, where it is obvious that the conditions are entirely different as far as the acquisition of primitive land is concerned, the system of "National Parks" has been inaugurated, but unfortunately too late to save a large part of the indigenous fauna. Canada, Australia, New Zealand, and South Africa have set the Mother Country a splendid example of what can be done in this direction. In England, where space is limited, and the population numerous, a beginning has been made by the acquisition for the nation of a part of Wicken Fen, in Cambridgeshire, the shingle and salt-marshes of Blakeney, in Norfolk (described in The Times of November 30), and the "Ruskin Reserve" near Oxford: all these retain their primitive character. Much more remains to be done, and it is hoped that the "Society for the Promotion of Nature Reserves" will meet with wide and sympathetic support.

2.3

CONSERVATION AND FEAR OF THE FUTURE

Editorial Headnote

1853 (Durham)–unknown

William Delisle Hay was a natural scientist, specializing in mycology, as well as a pioneer of science-fiction and, particularly, disaster stories. Hay lived for some time in New Zealand, as is evident in this passage where he contrasts the British urban environment unfavourably with life in the antipodes.

The Doom of the Great City depicts the recollections of a survivor of an apocalyptic fog in London some years after the event after they have emigrated to New Zealand. The work represents an early incarnation of both science and disaster fiction.

The novella was obviously inspired by the recent upsurge in London 'peasouper' fogs, and Hay does highlight the principal causal factor behind this as the overuse of coal. This is, at one level, clearly linked to the scientific and political response to urban pollution highlighted in in this volume part. However, the use of Disraeli's term 'Modern Babylon' and the painting of parallels between environmental and moral decay also bear the hallmarks of elitist conservatism. Indeed, the destruction of London is even portrayed as something of divine retribution.

Hay followed up this work with an even more apocalyptic tale the following year, Three Hundred Years Hence; Or, a Voice from Posterity. This work depicts – and appears to justify through twisted Social Darwinian and Malthusian logic – the genocide of non-whites in a future race war.

The Doom of the City represented part of a new wave of apocalyptic disaster fiction in the late Victorian age seemingly produced by the rapid social and economic changes of the time. A number of other works at this time mined a similar seam. For example, global calamity is depicted in Herbert Fyfe's 'How Will the World End?' (1900), which imagined the onset of a new ice age, and H.G. Wells's 'The Star' (1897), which portrays a disastrous collision with Earth by a meteor. The newly expanded London metropolis, however, was the focus for many such works highlighting the particular fears associated with urbanization. William Jefferies's After London welcomes the destruction of the great city as nature is allowed to reclaim the banks of the Thames (Jefferies 1885). Fred White's The Doom of London sees the capital brought to its knees – though ultimately survive – by a combination of pollution, epidemics and earthquake (White 1905). Whilst many Britons revelled in their country's powerful political and economic position in the world at the end of the nineteenth century, there were clearly also fears that this might not last and that the country could crash and burn.

pp. 32–38

46

THE DOOM OF THE GREAT CITY. BEING THE NARRATIVE OF A SURVIVOR

William Delisle Hay

Source: William Delisle Hay, *The Doom of the Great City. Being the Narrative of a Survivor* (1880)

As we came out into the high-road, we overtook a gentleman who was proceeding in the same direction as ourselves. He was a neighbour of the Forresters, and was known to them, so we fell into conversation. Like us, he had been much perturbed by the non-appearance of the postman, and he was now on his way to try and obtain tidings of him. From him we gained the first startling piece of intelligence. This gentleman had seen the "special edition" of an evening paper the previous night, and in it, he said, was an account of the accident in Bermondsey. The report said that over five hundred lives were certainly lost, but that, owing to the dense fog in the locality, and the difficulty of getting men to enter it, the exact total could not yet be known. It went on to add that although people in the adjacent district asserted the cause of the calamity to have been simply a sudden and overwhelming access of fog, this could not have been the true reason, *because it was contrary to all previous experience*; "wherefore," said this sapient journal, "we must suppose that a gush of foul sewer-gas, or some similar poisoning of the thick and heavy air, produced the fatal effect;" a piece of reasoning which almost moved Wilton to laughter. This is a fair illustration of how strangely fixed in the London mind was the notion that their fog was always to be, what it always *had been*, innocuous to the generality of people – an idea which had served to prevent any steps being taken in the direction of rendering it really so. Now, as we had seen reason to admit the possibility of the mere fog acting as a direct destroyer, we were sadly disheartened by this confirmation of the evil news. It is easy now to follow the train of conclusions which made our vague anxieties assume a more vivid shape.

Firstly, supposing it proved that the fog could kill an individual – and Wilton had proved that – what was to hinder its killing a number of individuals in a certain spot? and *that* was now proved to our minds. Again, if the fog could attain to such virulence over any special locality, there was no just reason for supposing

DOI: 10.4324/9781003194651-58

357

that its area of destructive maleficence might not be enlarged to an almost indefinite extent. So thinking and talking, we passed on down the road towards East Dulwich.

As we entered that part of Lordship Lane which formed the main street of East Dulwich, and where such shops and public-houses as the suburb boasted were to be found, we became aware of a very great commotion going on. The fog was here somewhat denser than on the higher ground we had left, though it was still only a whitish mist. But the usually quiet street, so far as we could see through the mist, presented a most unaccustomed spectacle. People were rushing wildly to and fro, groups were gathered in the roadway, on the pavement, inside and outside of the public-houses and the shops; all seemed imbued with ungovernable and frantic excitement, and on every face might be traced the same expression, panic, terror, fear! What was the matter?

Hastily we mingled with the throng, anxiously we questioned first one and then another. None seemed to know exactly what had occurred; none were possessed of details, yet the very vagueness; of the thousand rumours lent potency to their fears, while all concurred in one frenzied outburst – THE FOG! Some told us that all access to town was shut off by an impenetrable wall of fog; others said that no person or vehicle of any kind had come out of town that morning. Some told us that all access to town was shut off by an impenetrable wall of fog; others said that no person or vehicle of any kind had come out of town that morning. Some spoke of the entire cutting; off of all communication with London as a temporary nuisance and a good joke, but their blanched faces and quivering lips too plainly showed the dread that was at work within them; while others there were who told of men that had essayed to penetrate the vaporous veil, and who had returned, scared and choking, to speak of dead; men lying; in the street whose bodies they had stumbled over, to tell of the suffocating intensity of the dreadful fog. So asking and so answered, we came to Champion Hill railway station, where a large but awestricken crowd was gathered. Here we learnt the fullest details; that were yet known. All traffic into and out of London was indeed suspended, or rather, had never commenced. No trains had come out from the London termini, no response had been received to signals or telegrams; while men who had started to walk into town had either never returned, or else had shortly retraced their footsteps, panting and half-strangled. Telegrams from other suburbs and outskirts of town brought intelligence of a precisely similar state of things existing in those localities. No one had come from London, no one had succeeded in entering it. Such public conveyances as were wont to start every morning with their freight of "City men," had made efforts to do so in vain. They had been forced to relinquish the attempt, owing not only to the black obscurity, but also to the unbreathable character that the fog seemed to have assumed.

Crowds of men who lived in the suburbs and were employed in the City by day, thronged the stations, a dreadful panic having taken possession of them and altered their usual demeanour. Instead of the accustomed noise, bustle, and brisk hurry, white-faced groups consulted together in whispering tones; and many,

THE DOOM OF THE GREAT CITY. BEING THE NARRATIVE OF A SURVIVOR

utterly demoralized by excess of terror, had gone home to carry off their families to some place of greater safety. All round the "Great City" lay a wide belt of suburban districts, and these were now – so it seemed – given up to confusion, peopled with panic, and invaded with dismay. What were my feelings now?

Judge for yourselves. Do you suppose I can tell you? A man came down the station steps, as we terrified wretches cowered together below, loudly exclaiming: – "I tell you, it's damned nonsense; they CAN'T be all killed in London!" All killed! The words went to my heart like a knife. Can you fancy the very extravagance of dread? It was mine then. Can you imagine the utmost climax of terror? I knew it at that moment. How I looked, what I said or did, what I thought even, these things I know not. The awful pang had shot into my heart and brain, had benumbed my inmost soul.

Fear! It was scarcely such a sense: I had no thought of personal danger, hardly a recollection even of the too possible fate of those dear ones who were more to me than life; the agony that held me then, that has pursued me through sixty years of time to hold me now, was no common sense of fear. It was that overwhelming, all-mastering dread which men alone can know who are on a sudden taught their own immeasurable littleness; who are witnesses of some stupendous event, whose movement shows the hand sublime of Nature, the supremacy of offended God!

Yes, you know now, though I knew not then, the full extent of that hideous catastrophe: how, like the sudden overflow of Vesuvius upon the towns below; like of yore the wings of the angel of death had overshadowed the sleeping hosts of Assyria; or like that yet older tale, a world had sunk beneath the waters, so, in like manner, the fog had drawn over midnight London an envelope of murky death, within whose awful fold all that had life had died. Can you understand now the train; of reasoning; which led your grandfather to expatiate on all that was vile and wicked in the once-entitled "Modern Babylon"? Do you not see why I rather recall the evil and forget the good? Else were not my grief multiplied a thousand-fold, my anguish of pity more absorbing? And thus reflecting, may I not look up to Heaven still reverencing Just God; still dwelling in earnest faith on the love and mercy of Him Who is the Father of His creatures?

Although our knowledge of what had actually taken place was as yet extremely vague and limited, still we were sensible that the "Great City" beyond us lay stupefied, paralysed, to all seeming devoid of life, and that at an hour – it was now approaching noon – when it was usually busiest. This was alone unparalleled and horrifying, and as minute chased minute by and still no news relieved prevailing fears, and still the horrid fever of suspense made things seem darker, so the first consternation spread and deepened until a vast wave of awful, unheard-of terror rushed back from the outskirts of London. By this time every vehicle that could be put in motion was loaded with goods and with women and children, while crowds of people of all stations and sexes were hurrying along the roads which led to the country. Whither, none knew or cared; their only anxiety was to get away beyond the influence of the LONDON FOG, which their magnified panic believed was steadily advancing outward from the town. I cannot think that my own faculties had remained unshaken amid the frenzy of fear that boiled up around me; yet the deep sense of awe that fell upon me seemed to banish all merely personal fears. By-and-by, soon after noon I think, I noticed a sensible alteration; in the fog; it became lighter around us, while puffs of wind were now to be felt at short intervals. The line of mansions along the crest of Champion Hill, previously invisible from the lower ground where we were, now came out into view. I was pretty sure that the fog was becoming more tenuous – "lifting," in short. The recollection of my mother and sister came before my mind so strongly that I resolved instantly to make my way to them. I intimated my resolution to the Forresters, my companions. They did not attempt to dissuade me, but the old man wrung my hand and said, "Come back to us, my lad, if –" and he nodded and turned away. Then I passed on my road into London.

Editorial Headnote

1823 (Monmouthshire)–1913

Alfred Wallace was the epitome of the Victorian polymath, best remembered as a naturalist and explorer but also a geologist, poet, painter, political campaigner and more. Wallace's most lasting legacy is in having helped develop the idea of natural selection. He worked with Darwin in developing the theory of evolution and was, in his day, very well known for this. His personal role in this paradigm shift came to be overshadowed by the rise of Darwinism, but Darwin himself freely acknowledged the importance of his friend and colleague's contribution to evolutionary theory. Wallace's legacy regarding evolution, naturalism and ecology has, of late, come again to be better acknowledged.

Wallace was from a middle-class family that had fallen on hard times. He worked as a builder and surveyor with his brother as a young man and, in his spare time, developed a passion for entomology. In 1848, Wallace travelled to Brazil with his friend and fellow naturalist Henry Bates to collect specimens from the Amazon rainforest. They spent over four years travelling extensively across South America, and much of this adventure is chronicled in Wallace's book A Narrative of Travels on the Amazon and Rio Negro. In this work, as well as documenting the insect species he discovers, he notably shows his admiration for the peaceful lives of the Amazonian natives he encounters, comparing them favourably with Englishmen (Wallace 1853). Wallace's boat sank on his return journey to England, and many of his valuable notes and specimens were lost. He was, however, rescued and soon resumed his career as a naturalist.

After a short return to England, Wallace then travelled to Malay in 1854 and continued his extensive collecting there and wrote The Malay Archipelago, a popular account of this adventure. It was on this expedition that he started to develop his belief in natural selection and came to correspond with Darwin on this. Most notably he was struck by how Malay butterflies appeared to have physically adapted to suit their particular surroundings. In 1858, Darwin presented Wallace's findings alongside his own in a presentation on evolutionary theory to the Linnean Society. On returning to Britain in the 1860s, Wallace then befriended Darwin, as well as the other notable scientists Charles Lyell and Thomas Huxley (both profiled earlier in this volume part). Although they came to have some differences regarding evolutionary theory, Wallace remained friends with Darwin and was a pallbearer at his funeral in 1882 (Encyclopedia Britannica).

It was in the 1880s that Wallace became interested in radical politics and an admirer of the early 'utopian socialist' Robert Owen. He became the first president of the Land Nationalisation Society created in 1881 to advance the case for collectivization and limits on private land ownership. This organization was a more radical incarnation of the previous Land Tenure Reform Association, set up by John Stuart Mill in 1868, which had campaigned to end the practice of primogeniture in land ownership.

In the selected extract, an elderly Wallace gives his retrospective overview of the successes and failures of the nineteenth century. In this final, concluding chapter of his book, there is no doubt that he considers the failures to far outweigh the successes attributable to industrialization. In an angry polemic, he laments the 'reckless destruction' of the Earth in the pursuit of profit. His religious socialist convictions are apparent in criticizing the voraciousness and ungodliness of capitalism. Interestingly, this includes the oil industry, which, at the time, was very much in its infancy and not yet the environmental pariah it would later become. As can be seen, Wallace highlights resource depletion, deforestation, soil erosion and the dumping of waste as among the damning indictments of the age. On a human level, he also damns the British as culpable for the famines in India and having committed what would come to be known as genocides in Australia and Tasmania. The clear message from this critique of the times is that the prevailing economic system is not only immoral but also unsustainable.

Wallace's radical politics doubtless contributed to his marginalization from public prominence in his later life. However, his eclecticism also saw him endorse some causes, such as phrenology, spiritualism and opposing vaccinations, that damaged his scientific credentials. Wallace's conviction that evolution was not purely functional and was guided by spiritual forces was a point of departure from Darwin and was criticized by devotees of Darwinism. It is worth remembering, though, that spiritualism had many high-profile advocates at the time, including the author Arthur Conan-Doyle and the renowned scientist Robert Angus Smith, profiled in earlier in this volume part.

47

THE PLUNDER OF THE EARTH

Alfred Russel Wallace

Source: Alfred Russel Wallace, *The Plunder of the Earth* (1898)

CHAPTER XXI

The Plunder of the Earth – Conclusion

Commerce has set the mark of selfishness,
The signet of its all-enslaving power,
Upon a shining ore, and called it GOLD;
Before whose image bow the vulgar great,
The vainly rich, the miserable proud,
The mob of peasants, nobles, priests, and kings,
And with blind feelings reverence the power
That grinds them to the dust of misery.

– Shelley.

THE struggle for wealth, and its deplorable results, as sketched in the preceding chapter, have been accompanied by a reckless destruction of the stored-up products of nature, which is even more deplorable because more irretrievable. Not only have forest-growths of many hundreds of years been cleared away, often with disastrous consequences, but the whole of the mineral treasures of the earth's surface, the slow products of long-past eons of time and geological change, have been and are still being exhausted, to an extent never before approached, and probably not equalled in amount during the whole preceding period of human history.

In our own country, the value of the coal exported to foreign countries has increased from about three to more than sixteen millions sterling per annum, the quantity being now about thirty millions of tons; and this continuous exhaustion of one of the necessaries of existence is wholly in the interest of landlords and capitalists, while millions of our people have not sufficient for the ordinary needs or comforts of life, and even die in large numbers for want of the vital warmth which it would supply. Another large quantity of coal is consumed in the manufacture of iron for export, which amounts now to about two millions of tons per

DOI: 10.4324/9781003194651-59

363

annum. A rational organization of society would ensure an ample supply of coal to every family in the country before permitting any export whatever; while, if our social organization was both moral and rational, two considerations would prevent any export: the first being that we have duties toward posterity, and have no right to diminish unnecessarily those natural products which cannot be reproduced; and the second, that the operations of coalmining and iron-working being especially hard and unpleasant to the workers, and at the same time leading to injury to much fertile land and natural beauty, they should be restricted within the narrowest limits consistent with our own well-being.

In America, and some other countries, an equally wasteful and needless expenditure of petroleum oils and natural gas is going on, resulting in great accumulations of private wealth, but not sensibly ameliorating the condition of the people at large. Such an excellent light as that afforded by petroleum oil is no doubt a good thing; but it comes in the second grade, as a comfort, not a necessity; and it is really out of place till everyone can obtain ample food, clothing, warmth, house room, and pure air and water, which are the absolute necessaries of life, but which, under the conditions of our modern civilization – more correctly barbarism – millions of people, through no fault of their own, cannot obtain. In these respects we are as the Scribes and Pharisees, giving tithe of mint and cummin, but neglecting the weightier matters of the law.

Equally disastrous in many respects has been the wild struggle for gold in California, Australia, South Africa, and elsewhere. The results are hardly less disastrous, though in different ways, than those produced by the Spaniards in Mexico and Peru four centuries ago. Great wealth has been obtained, great populations have grown up and are growing up; but great cities have also grown up with their inevitable poverty, vice, overcrowding, and even starvation, as in the Old World. Everywhere, too, this rush for wealth has led to deterioration of land and of natural beauty, by covering up the surface with refuse heaps, by flooding rich lowlands with the barren mud produced by hydraulic mining; and by the great demand for animal food by the mining populations leading to the destruction of natural pastures in California, Australia, and South Africa, and their replacement often by weeds and plants neither beautiful nor good for fodder.

It is also a well-known fact that these accumulations of gold-seekers lead to enormous social evils, opening a field for criminals of every type, and producing an amount of drink-consumption, gambling, and homicide altogether unprecedented. Both the earlier gold-digging by individual miners, and the later quartz-mining by great companies, are alike forms of gambling or speculation; and while immense fortunes are made by some, others suffer great losses, so that the gambling spirit is still further encouraged and the production of real wealth by patient industry, to the same extent diminished and rendered less attractive. For it must never be forgotten that the whole enormous amount of human labor expended in the search for and the production of gold; the ships which carry out the thousands of explorers, diggers, and speculators; the tools, implements, and machinery they use; their houses, food, and clothing, as well as the countless gallons of liquor of various qualities which they consume, are all, so far as the well-being of the community is concerned, absolutely wasted. Gold is not wealth; it is neither a necessary nor a luxury of life, in the true sense of the word. It serves two purposes only: it is an instrument used for the exchange of commodities, and its use in the arts is mainly as ornament or as an indication of wealth. Nothing is more certain than that the appearance of wealth produced by large gold-production is delusive. The larger the proportion of the population of a country that devotes itself to gold-production, the smaller the numbers left to produce real wealth – food, clothing, houses, fuel, roads, machinery, and all the innumerable conveniences, comforts, and wholesome luxuries of life. Hence, whatever appearances may indicate, gold-production makes a country poor, and by furnishing new means of investment and speculation helps to keep it poor; and it has certainly helped considerably in producing that amount of wretchedness, starvation, and crime which, as we have seen, has gone on increasing to the very end of our century.

But the extraction of the mineral products stored in the earth, in order to increase individual wealth, and to the same extent to the diminution of national well-being, is only a portion of the injury done to posterity by the "plunder of the earth." In tropical countries many valuable products can be cultivated by means of cheap native labor, so as to give a large profit to the European planter. But here also the desire to get rich as quickly as possible has often defeated the planter's hopes. Nutmegs were grown for some years in Singapore and Penang; but by the exposure of the young trees to the sun, instead of growing them under the shade of great forest-trees, as in their natural state, and as they are grown in Banda, they became unhealthy and unprofitable. Then coffee was planted, and was grown very largely in Ceylon and other places; but here again the virgin forests were entirely removed, producing unnatural conditions, and the growth of the young trees was stimulated by manure. Soon there came disease and insect enemies, and coffee had to be given up in favor of tea, which is now grown over large areas both in Ceylon and India. But the clearing of the forests on steep hill slopes, to make coffee plantations, produced permanent injury to the country of a very serious kind. The rich soil, the product of thousands of years of slow decomposition of the rock, fertilized by the humus formed from decaying forest trees, being no longer protected by the covering of dense vegetation, was quickly washed away by the tropical rains, leaving great areas of bare rock or furrowed clay, absolutely sterile, and which will probably not regain its former fertility for hundreds, perhaps thousands of years. The devastation caused by the great despots of the Middle Ages and of antiquity, for purposes of conquest or punishment, has thus been reproduced in our times by the rush to obtain wealth.

Even the lust of conquest, in order to secure slaves and tribute and great estates, by means of which the ruling classes could live in boundless luxury, so characteristic of the early civilizations, is reproduced in our own time. The Great Powers of Europe are in the midst of a struggle, in order to divide up the whole continent of Africa among themselves, and thus obtain an outlet for the more energetic portions of their populations and an extension of their trade. The result, so far, has been the sale of vast quantities of rum and gunpowder; much bloodshed, owing to the objection of the natives to the seizure of their lands and their cattle; great demoralizations both of black and white; and the condemnation of the conquered tribes to a modified form of slavery. Comparing our conduct with that of the Spanish conquerors of the West Indies, Mexico, and Peru, and making some allowance for differences of race and of public opinion, there is not much to choose between them. Wealth, and territory, and native labor, were the real objects of the conquest in both cases; and if the Spaniards were more cruel by nature, and more reckless in their methods, the results were much the same. In both cases the country was conquered, and thereafter occupied and governed by the conquerors frankly for their own ends, and with little regard to the feelings or the material well-being of the conquered. If the Spaniards exterminated the natives of the West Indies, we have done the same thing in Tasmania, and almost the same in temperate Australia. And in the estimation of the historian of the future, the Spaniards will be credited with two points in which they surpassed us. Their belief that they were really serving God in converting the heathen, even at the point of the sword, was a genuine belief shared by priests and conquerors alike – not a mere sham, as is ours when we defend our conduct by the plea of introducing the "blessings of civilization." And, in wild romance, boldness of conception, reckless daring, and the successful achievement of the well-nigh impossible, we are nowhere when compared with Cortez and his five hundred Spaniards, who, with no base of supplies, no rapid steam communication, no supports, imperfect weapons and the ammunition they carried with them, conquered great, populous, and civilized empires. It is quite possible that both the conquests of Mexico and Peru by the Spaniards, and our conquests of South Africa, may have been real steps in advance, essential to human progress, and helping on the future reign of true civilization and the well-being of the human race. But if so, we have been, and are, unconscious agents, in hastening the great "far-off, divine event to which the whole creation moves."

We deserve no credit for it. Our aims have been, for the most part, sordid and selfish; and if, in the end, all should work out for good, as no doubt it will, much of our conduct in the matter will yet deserve, and will certainly receive, the severest condemnation.

Our whole dealings with subject races have been a strange mixture of good and evil, of success and failure, due, I believe, to the fact that, along with a genuine desire to do good and to govern well, our rule has always been largely influenced, and often entirely directed, by the necessity of finding well-paid places for the less wealthy members of our aristocracy, and also by the constant craving for fresh markets by the influential class of merchants and manufacturers. Hence the enormous fiscal burdens under which the natives of our Indian Empire continue to groan; hence the opium monopoly and the salt tax; hence the continued refusal to carry out the promises made or implied on the establishment of the Empire, to give the natives a continually increasing share in their own government, and to govern India solely in the interest of the Indians themselves.

It is the influence of the two classes above referred to that has urged our governments to perpetual frontier wars and continual extensions of the Empire, all adding to the burdens of the Indian people. But our greatest mistakes of all are, the collection of revenue in money, at fixed times, from the very poorest cultivators of the soil; and the strict enforcement of our laws relating to landed property, to loans, mortgages, and foreclosures, which are utterly unsuited to the people, and have led to the most cruel oppression, and the transfer of numbers of small farms from the ryots to the money-lenders. Hence, the peasants become poorer and poorer; thousands have been made tenants instead of owners of their farms; and an immense number are in the clutches of the money-lenders, and always in the most extreme poverty. It is from these various causes that the periodical famines are so dreadful a scourge, and such a disgrace to our rule. The people of India are industrious, patient, and frugal in the highest degree; and the soil and climate are such that the one thing wanted to ensure good crops and abundance of food is water-storage for irrigation, and absolute permanence of tenure for the cultivator. That we have built costly railways for the benefit of merchants and capitalists, and have spent upon these and upon frontier-wars the money which would have secured water for irrigation wherever wanted, and thus prevented the continued recurrence of famine whenever the rains are deficient, is an evil attendant on our rule which outweighs many of its benefits.

The final and absolute test of good government is the well-being and contentment of the people – not the extent of empire or the abundance of the revenue and the trade. Tried by this test, how seldom have we succeeded in ruling subject peoples! Rebellion, recurrent famines, and plagues in India; discontent, chronic want, and misery; famines more or less severe, and continuous depopulation in our sister-island at home – these must surely be reckoned the most terrible and most disastrous failures of the nineteenth century.

"Hear then, ye Senates! hear this truth sublime;
They who allow Oppression share the crime."

Editorial Headnote

1841 (London)–1929

The Twelfth Earl of Meath (known as Lord Meath) was born into an aristocratic Anglo-Irish absentee landlord family. Meath was Eton-educated and embarked on a diplomatic career after his father blocked his ambitions to enter military service (Springhall 1970). Meath worked as a diplomat in Germany, which served to foment a particular dislike of that country (Springhall 1970). He resigned to pursue social reform and philanthropy whilst serving as a Conservative politician in the House of Lords. An arch imperialist, he was responsible for getting 'Empire Day' introduced by parliament in 1916.

A combination of his imperialism, nationalism and Social Darwinism led Meath to embrace the cause of combatting urban pollution for particularly nationalistic reasons: the fear that this was causing the physical degeneration of Britain's youth and so also her military capabilities. He established the Public Gardens Association in 1882 to promote the establishment of urban parks, including Meath Park in Bethnal Green named in his honour. In 1898, with artist William Blake Richmond, he helped found – and later lead – the Coal Smoke Abatement Society (CSAB) which pressured the London County Council to prosecute firms violating anti-pollution legislation. In 1899, he also created the 'Lads Drill Association' to promote the fitness of British boys.

This speech in the House of Lords drew on a series of published articles and the book 'Prosperity or Pauperism?' (Brabazon 1888) highlighting the physical decline of the working classes resulting from urban smog. This was a phenomenon seemingly proven by British defeats in several early battles in the Boer War. As evidenced in Meath's words, it was not just pollution but urbanization itself that was also considered responsible for this physical decline since fitness levels were claimed to be higher in a rural population compared to an urban one. In particular, this is said to be because urban living is linked to cultural decline, poorer diet and alcoholism. Interestingly, in spite of his Germanophobia, Meath cites his experience of seeing fresh milk deliveries made to Berlin residents as one way of countering this national problem.

The CSAB was later central to the introduction of the 1926 Public Health (Smoke Abatement Act) and the 1956 Clean Air Act, prompted by the notorious Great London Smog of 1952. The organization still exists today as Environmental Protection UK.

48

THE NATIONAL STANDARD OF PHYSICAL HEALTH

Reginald Brabazon (Lord Meath)

Source: Reginald Brabazon (Lord Meath), *National Standard of Physical Health* (1903)

THE NATIONAL STANDARD
OF PHYSICAL HEALTH

House of Lords July 6, 1903

My Lords, I rise to draw the attention of His Majesty's Government to the Report of the Royal Commission on Physical Training in Scotland, and to the Report of the Inspector-General of Recruiting for 1902, in which he states that the one subject, which causes anxiety in the future as regards recruiting, is the gradual deterioration of the physique of the working classes from which the bulk of the recruits must always be drawn"; and to ask His Majesty's Government whether they would be prepared to issue a Royal Commission or a Committee of Inquiry with a view of ascertaining whether the poorer populations in our large towns are exposed to conditions which, if continued, must inevitably contribute to a low national standard of physical health and strength, seeing that if such be the case it would constitute a grave national peril. The Report of the Royal Commission on Physical Training in Scotland, over which my noble friend the Earl of Mansfield presided, and to whom and his colleagues we owe a deep debt of gratitude for bringing before the public in so concise and lucid a manner the present physical conditions of the people of that country, unanimously reported that – there exists in Scotland an undeniable degeneration of individuals of the classes where fond and environment are defective, which calls for attention and amelioration in obvious ways, one of which is a well regulated system of physical training. Do these words apply only to Scotland, or are they applicable to the rest of the United Kingdom? This is the question I desire His Majesty's Government to take into their most serious consideration. The subject to which I am anxious to draw the attention of the Government and of your Lordships' House is to my mind one of the most important of our social problems. It is a question of self-preservation. If my contention that a very large proportion of the population in our large cities are physically weak, be true, and that that degenerate portion is rapidly on the

DOI: 10.4324/9781003194651-60

increase, then I think there can be no question about the urgent importance of the subject and the need of Government action. That wise statesman Lord Beaconsfield once said – The public health is the foundation on which repose the happiness of the people and the power of a country. The care of the public health is the first duty of a Statesman. I am fully aware that the most important and the most interesting subject can be made unbearably dull by being over-weighted with statistics. I shall, therefore, do my best to spare your Lordships unnecessary figures; but, at the same time, I do not think it is possible for a subject of this character to be adequately and seriously discussed without occasional reference to statistics. I hope, therefore, your Lordships will bear with me, remembering the difficulty that there is in making clear such a subject without quoting figures.

In order that there may be no misapprehension in the minds of your Lordships in regard to the nature of the social problem to which I have called the attention of the Government and of this House, I should like to make it perfectly clear that I do not contend that physical deterioration is taking place among all classes in this country, nor, indeed, that any class is actually deteriorating, for the exact reverse is certainly the case in regard to some sections of society. Indeed, there can be no doubt that the physical condition of the upper and middle classes has on the whole improved. Evidence is doubtful as to whether the artisan and well-to-do labouring classes have improved or not; they probably have remained more or less stationary. Nor do I even assert that degeneration has taken place amongst the poorer classes in either town or country. What I desire to emphasise is that even should it be proved that the average individual member of a poor town population is physically the equal, or even slightly the superior, of his poor town predecessor, the overwhelming increase which has taken place in recent years in the numbers of poor men and women who live in towns has completely altered the physical condition of England, and turned a negligible national defect into one of the most serious gravity. There can be no doubt that the poor of to-day are born and live under much better conditions than the poor of a century, or even of half a century ago, and that the death-rate, both in town and country, has diminished, and it is therefore possible, and even probable, that the general average health and strength of even the poorest and most neglected in the towns are greater than those formerly enjoyed by a class similarly miserable. But although there may be degrees of misery, and because there may be a slight diminution in the physical weakness of these wretched classes, it is no reason why the national conscience should be satisfied, if it can be shown that physical weakness in these classes is still excessive, is far greater than that to be found amongst the more well-to-do, and can be avoided, especially when it can be shown that people residing in urban districts already number nearly four-fifths of the population and are rapidly increasing, whilst the country bred, which in the past recruited the weakened blood of the cities, are either stationary in number or actually decreasing.

In 1851 the urban population of England and Wales numbered only 8,990,809 out of a total population of 17,927,609, or just 50 per cent.; according to the last census the urban districts are now inhabited by more than 25,000,000 souls out of

THE NATIONAL STANDARD OF PHYSICAL HEALTH

32,527,843, or 77 per cent. of the total population. Scotland shows a very similar state of things. There 3,367,280, or 75.3 per cent of the population, live in urban districts. These figures mean that the population of Great Britain is largely town bred, and that for one man who lives in the country there are more than three who reside in the town. For purposes of comparison, and to show of how much greater importance this subject is to us than to neighbouring countries, I may state that whereas the urban inhabitants of Great Britain are 77 per cent, and those of Scotland 75.3 per cent, the town inhabitants of Germany are only 36 per cent, and those of France only 25 per cent of their entire populations. Dwellers in cities need not necessarily be of inferior physique. I have no doubt I shall be told that some of the finest athletes come from the towns. That is so, but they come from that portion of the population who are in comparatively comfortable circumstances, who are well fed, live in healthy homes, and have leisure for outdoor exercise. The great public schools of Great Britain are filled with the healthy and sturdy sons of the professional classes living largely in towns, but then, as a rule, their parents are healthy, and they come of a healthy stock. The sons of the upper and middle classes, educated at the great seminaries, far from degenerating, have increased in stature and weight above the limits attained by their predecessors. From statistics taken it can be shown that in 1901 the average Marlburian boy of thirteen years of age was 5½ lbs. heavier and 2 inches taller than his predecessor of 1874, and that the Rugby boy of thirteen in 1901 was 6 lbs. heavier and 2½ inches taller than his predecessor of 1879.

But if we consider the condition of the less favoured classes, we are confronted with an entirely different set of figures. Mr. Charles Roberts, in a Report to the Royal Commission on Secondary Education, says that – The more intelligent classes are taller and heavier at corresponding ages than the less intelligent, the more favoured classes than the less favoured; and he gives the following figures in support of his statement. He states that the public school boy, between eleven and twelve years of age, averages 55 inches in stature, and 78.7 lbs in weight; the elementary school child 52.6 inches in height, and 67.8 lbs. in weight; the factory child 51.6 inches in height, and 67.41 lbs in weight; and those at Industrial and Reformatory Schools, whom Mr. Roberts, I think inaccurately, describes as representing the slum population, 50.8 inches in height, and 64.63 lbs in weight. It must be remembered that the Industrial and Reformatory Schools, though they recruit their inmates largely from the slums of cities, do not in their statistics actually represent the physical conditions of the children of the slums, for, as the Royal Commission on Physical Training in Scotland have pointed out, these boys and girls are well fed, live in healthy dwellings, amid good sanitary surroundings, and under a healthy discipline, which rapidly improves their physique and morale, so that, on leaving the school, 80 per cent. turn out good and useful citizens. Therefore, my contention is that Mr. Roberts's figures, although they are bad enough in themselves, do not represent the real state of affairs, and that, if we could obtain accurate anthropometric measurements of the children inhabiting city slums, we should possibly find that the figures were much lower than those given by Mr. Roberts. These figures are corroborated by Dr. Hunt, medical officer of the School Board of Halifax, who examined fifty boys, between the ages of ten and eleven, attending the schools, for weight, and 450 for height. These boys came from three categories of schools – country, suburban, and central, and the figures he gives show that the upper and middle class boy averages about 3 inches more in height, and 11 pounds more in weight than the average elementary school boy; and 4 inches in height, and 14 pounds, or one stone, more in weight, than the slum or factory boy.

The Royal Commission on Physical Training in Scotland found that in Edinburgh nearly 30 per cent. of the elementary school children were badly nourished, 19.17 per cent were in poor health, 12.33 per cent were mentally dull, and 78 per cent were more or less physically weak and suffering from some kind of disease. And the gentlemen who carried out these investigations for the noble Earl and his colleagues stated that the percentage of defective children would be larger if slight affections of throat and ear were included. Out of 30,000 children in Edinburgh, Dr. Leslie Mackenzie calculated that some 50 per cent – that is, a total of 15,000 children – were suffering from the throat, and some 40 per cent, or 12,000, from slight affections of the ear, making a total of 27,000 children out of 30,000 suffering from ear and throat. In the course of his examination he found that 259 male children out of 299 and 294 females out of 298 were suffering from either affections of the ear or throat. These figures are the more alarming as one would imagine that Edinburgh, with its magnificent situation, in close proximity to its splendid Queen's Park and picturesque Arthur's Seat, would produce healthier children than, say, the enormous industrial city of Glasgow. If the children of Edinburgh are in this lamentable condition, what must be the condition of those of Glasgow and of some of the more crowded cities of England? In Liverpool we know that its medical officer has reported that out of 4,574 children there is an infantile mortality of 2,229 – or about 50 per cent. This is less than the average mortality amongst working-class children, which is 55 per cent as against 18 per cent in the upper classes. One child in every six dies in the British Isles in its first year, and, of course, many more if we consider only children of the working classes. If Edinburgh is as bad as has been stated, what must be the condition of the children of Manchester, Birmingham, Leeds, Newcastle, Bradford, Bristol – I could go through an endless list of manufacturing towns into the slums of which the sun scarcely ever penetrates, and where the air is polluted with vicious vapours and impregnated with black soot.

To combat these evils Lord Mansfield and his colleagues acknowledge that many reforms are needed. In his "Essays on Education" Herbert Spencer said – To be a good animal is the first requisite to success in life, and to be a nation of good animals is the first condition to national prosperity. To be good animals children must have strong and healthy parents, good and ample food, plenty of fresh air and exercise, be properly housed, and lead regular disciplined lives. It is only necessary to mention these requisites for health in order to see at once how impossible it is that a race of healthy and strong children can, under present

THE NATIONAL STANDARD OF PHYSICAL HEALTH

conditions, be reared in the poorer parts of our large cities. Mr. John Burns, M.P., has very truly said that – The conditions essential to manhood begin before the baby is born – a healthy home, reasonable labour, temperate living on the part of the father and mother, these are the indispensable preliminaries to healthy life in children. Again, this admirable representative of all that is best amongst the artisan class – an exemplification in his own person of mental combined with physical vigour – has said that if our future working class are to be healthy – The fathers must drink less beer and the mother's less tea. I would add that the mothers of the future must be taught knowledge necessary to the proper nurture of children. At present there are working-class mothers – I trust not many – who are under the impression that babies flourish on gin, pork, bacon, and cabbage; and if they should cry and show physical discomfort from the effects of this diet, that all can be set right by a dose of some much advertised soothing syrup.

Without proper feeding we cannot have a sturdy nation. It must be seen that pure, fresh milk be brought within the reach of the poor both in town and country, and this is of even more importance in the country than in the town, for it is a sad fact that in many parts of the rural districts it is almost impossible for the labouring classes to obtain fresh milk. The future mothers must be taught not only that milk is the proper food for babes, but that the greatest care must be taken to see that the milk is sweet, for a large proportion of infantile mortality is due to decomposing or septic milk. The death-rate among breast-fed children is only about one-thirtieth of that among those who are fed otherwise. A most laudable effort, and one which should be largely followed, has been made by the Battersea Borough Council in order to enable mothers to obtain pure, fresh milk at a reasonable charge. The Council has started a milk depôt for mothers. The milk is humanised and sterilised, and at this moment some 300 babes are being daily fed at a charge of 1s. 9d. a week for those from six to eight months, and at 2s. for older babies A baby fund has also been started to assist the poorer mothers, and arrangements have been made with the local Poor Law Guardians in the case of absolute paupers. As long ago as 1870, when I was in the diplomatic service, there existed in Berlin a model dairy which brought pure milk to the very doors of the poor by means of locked perambulating milk and cream carts, which passed at regular hours through the poorer quarters of the town and stopped at fixed points. The people could themselves fill their jugs from taps in the vehicle, over which was clearly painted the kind of milk and price. Owing to the cans being locked it was quite impossible for anyone to tamper with the supply. I cannot help thinking that something of that sort might be done nearer home.

I am quite prepared to be met with the statement that the average city child is both taller and heavier than the city child was, say, when her late Majesty Queen Victoria came to the Throne. This may very possibly be true, but such a statement, if proved, would not weaken my argument. Our knowledge of the laws of health and of sanitation has vastly improved; our factory laws have been passed since those days; we have established an universal and compulsory system of education; we have passed special laws for the protection of children, and public opinion is much more alive to their interests than it was in 1837. It would, then, be indeed sad if we could not point to some physical improvement in the case of city children of the poorer classes, even though it has been estimated, with what truth I know not, that 3,250,000 persons in the British Isles live in overcrowded dwellings, with an average of three persons in each room. I desire to point out, that whereas city children in 1837 constituted a comparatively insignificant portion of the infantile population of the country, they now form an overwhelming majority, and, as such, must in the future materially influence the national physical average, and that annually this urban and weaker element is growing more and more numerous to the serious detriment of the nation. I, for one, shall never be satisfied as long as such a material difference can be shown between the physical condition of the children of the richer and of the poorer classes. I believe that science and municipal effort, supported by a sensitive public conscience and the spread of knowledge of the laws of health and of sanitation amongst the future mothers of England, can to a very large extent neutralise the advantages which at present those classes enjoy who can live in the country and need not consider money in the bringing up and training of their children. Before I leave the subject of the children, I must draw attention to the fact that the population of this country is not increasing as it used to do. Lord Rosebery has remarked that it is useless to possess an Empire unless it is inhabited by an Imperial race. At this moment the population of Australia is practically stationary. What our colonies need is a continued steady stream of healthy agriculturists to develop their boundless resources. If the increase of population in Great Britain had proceeded since 1881 in the same ratio as it did previous to that period, there would in 1891 have been 2,434,000 more children in the country than there actually were. Since that period the birth and marriage rates show a still further decline. I now come to the youths and adults. Lord Selborne has been good enough to cause me to be supplied with a Return of the boys and youths medically examined from the 1st of January to the 31st of December, 1902, at the Royal Marine Recruiting Offices for the Royal Navy and Royal Marines, and he has remarked that – He thinks it desirable to point out that this list by no means covers the whole number of men and boys who apply for entry into either of these services, as a very large percentage of the applicants are turned away by the recruiting sergeants for some physical deficiency, such as defective teeth without being brought before the doctors at all. This Return shows that, during that period, 6,169 lads offered themselves, out of which number 1,686, or 27.3 per cent, were rejected as unfit. This proportion is a little better than that which is recorded in the case of Army recruits. The General Inspector of Recruiting for the Army, in his Report for the year 1901, states that the percentage of rejections on grounds of physical development all over the kingdom of those who offered themselves for the Army was 29.04. But from statistics I have obtained, through the kindness of the First Lord of the Admiralty, it would appear that just under 33 per cent of the lads who desired to enter Greenwich Hospital with a view to joining the Navy had to be rejected. This is the more extraordinary, as these lads must be sons of former seamen or marines, and, one would fancy, would consequently enjoy the advantage of, at all events, a healthy father.

It must not be forgotten that in this case also no account is taken of those who were rejected by the recruiter's for physical defects so apparent as to be noticed on sight. None of these figures, therefore, show the numbers of those who were rejected by the sergeants as being obviously unfit, and it must always be remembered that there is a direct pecuniary inducement to a recruiting officer to bring a recruit before the doctor, so that those rejected by the recruiters must have been physically hopelessly defective. There is nothing to show how large was the number thus rejected, but report puts it at about half those who presented themselves. This may be an exaggeration, but, if true, it would mean that over 50 per cent. of the young men and lads offering themselves for the Army and Navy have to be rejected. Let us, however, leave out of consideration those rejected by the recruiting sergeants. The figures are quite large enough in all conscience, and I have no desire to exaggerate the matter. I do not, however, believe that there would be much, if any, exaggeration in saying that some 50 per cent of those who offer themselves for the Army and Navy are rejected between recruiting officers and medical men, and subsequent dismissals for inferior physique. I have been shown a statement in writing from an Admiralty provincial recruiting officer, in which he asserts that fully 50 per cent of the candidates for the Navy are rejected for physical causes, and General Sir Frederick Maurice has lately informed the public that, out of five men who enlist, only two remain effective soldiers after two years, and that the men who slipped through the officers tests, and afterwards had to be turned out of the Army, were – Miserable, anæmic specimens of humanity, fit to do no proper man's work in any position of life. Let us leave these extra rejections out of consideration. It will then be seen that considerably more than one-fourth of those who offer themselves from both town and country for the Army and Navy are rejected for physical defects. That more than a fourth of the young men and lads who desire to serve their country in Army or Navy should be unfit to do so, is surely a very serious matter. What makes it still more serious is that it is reported for 1901 that the proportion of men rejected was highest in the class headed "labourers, servants, husbandmen, etc.," the rejections amongst labourers being 18.37 per 1,000. In 1902, owing probably to the great efforts made to obtain recruits during the war, the rejections for the Army were nearly 50 per cent in excess of the figures for the previous year. The actual figures were: 100,771 recruits offered themselves, and 47,916, or nearly 50,000, were rejected. In Germany, town life exercises a similarly harmful influence on national physique, for whereas 80 per cent of the recruits from the country are found to be physically fit for military service, only 38 per cent of those coming from Berlin can take their places in the ranks, and it must be remembered that these figures represent the average physical condition of the entire young male population of Berlin, and not only those coming from the poorer districts, as is the case in dealing with town recruits in the British Isles.

The Royal Commission on Physical Training in Scotland showed that the condition of life under which the poor lived in Edinburgh was detrimental to health and strength, but in considering the rejections for the Navy from this town we find in 1902 only 23.6 per cent were rejected, whilst 24.9 were rejected from Bristol, 30.3 from Exeter, and 35.9 from London, so that Edinburgh is not so bad as some towns in England. In Manchester, from figures supplied by Colonel Leathern, the chief recruiting officer, it appears that in 1899, during the early part of the Boer War, some 11,000 men offered their services to the Army; of these only 3,000 could be accepted, and eventually it was found that out of these 3,000 only 1,072 were fit for service in the Regular Army, 2,107 being relegated to the Militia. So that in round numbers, out of 11,000 men from Manchester, 8,000 were rejected, whilst only 1,000 were found fit to fight the battles of their country. These figures were not peculiar to the year 1899, for in 1900, out of 12,235 who offered to enlist in Manchester, 8,205 were rejected, and in 1901, out of 11,896 who came forward, 8,820 were found physically incapable of military service. It may be said that these figures relate to men brought up in the slums and who are out of employment owing to physical incapacity to do any hard work. This probably is more or less true, but it only strengthens the force of my argument for inquiring into the condition of life of the poorer populations in our large cities. But that physical weakness is not confined only to the very poor in our towns is shown by the recent statement publicly made by the colonel of the Birmingham Volunteers, who complained that he had to reject some 32 per cent of the young men who applied to him for admission into his battalion, and that on one occasion he had to reject eleven out of thirty-one recruits. Now, these men must have been men of a superior social position to the ordinary Army recruit, and should not have been subject to the influences hurtful to health entailed by extreme poverty.

Mr. Cantlie, F.R.C.S., after making some most exhaustive inquiries, has come to the conclusion that pure-bred Londoners cannot exist beyond the third generation, showing that without the infusion of country blood the populations in our large cities would, under present conditions, inevitably die out. Mr. Cantlie has also made inquiries in the country, and found that rickets is one of the commonest ailments in country districts. He ascribes this to want of food, insufficient food, or the wrong food. It is probably owing to want of milk, which in some parts of the country it is almost impossible for the poor to obtain, as milk farmers are under contract to send their entire supply to the large centres of population, and cannot, therefore, sell it locally. This is a very serious grievance, and one which should be remedied. There are other causes, however, which lead to a low physical condition amongst the people. The Royal Commission on Physical Training in Scotland has pointed out that many reforms are needed in order to ensure a physically healthy population, and that all these reforms must proceed pari passu, or more harm than good may be done; for instance, they have shown how harmful physical exercises can prove in the case of underfed and sickly children, though the same exercises are indispensable to proper development, and most beneficial when carried out under medical supervision.

Briefly stated, the principal requisites in the production of a physically capable population are: first, healthy parents; secondly, sanitary homes; thirdly, good, abundant and well-cooked food, including a cheap supply of fresh milk; fourthly, pure air and water; fifthly, facilities for exercise and healthy recreation; sixthly, a good educational system, which shall combine physical with mental and moral training, and shall instruct the young, especially the girls, in the elements of hygiene, dietetics, and the care of infants and home sanitation, and shall bring them up under good and healthy moral surroundings. It is only necessary to mention the above, which are but a few of the indispensable requisites to the production of a healthy population, in order to show how much remains to be done before we can hope to attain, not perfection, but even a moderately healthy standard of national life. If this moderate standard is to be reached, it will not be sufficient for one Department of Government to move in the right direction. The subject, when investigation has pointed out the proper course to be pursued, must be made a national one, and Government and people combined, must throw their entire energies into the matter, and insist on a general advance along the lines of national health and strength, so that future generations may be able fearlessly to face and bear the burden which fierce foreign competition and the ever increasing responsibilities of extending Empire have placed, and will place, on the shoulders of the subjects of King Edward. I am no pessimist. I firmly believe in the capabilities and energy of the Anglo-Saxon, and have confidence that, with the ancient pluck of their race, the future of the Empire will be made by its sons and daughters even more glorious than its memorable past, if only we, the fathers of the rising generation, do not neglect our duties, but give our sons and our grandsons a chance to equip themselves properly for the contest, and see that, in founding the mightiest Empire the world has ever known, we do not, by our indifference and carelessness, hinder nature in her efforts to people that Empire with an Imperial race.

Editorial Headnote

Late nineteenth-century elitist alarm at the apparent inverse correlation between British urbanization and its morality, national interest and empire was not the sole preserve of the political right. Many liberals also came to rail against the rotting fruits of free trade and industrialization, as evidenced in this multi-authored volume bringing together a number of young radical Whig politicians.

Charles Masterman (1873[Sussex]–1927) was an influential Liberal MP who served in government in the Lloyd George administration that laid the foundations of the welfare state and again during the Great War as head of the War Propaganda Bureau. He was from a wealthy rural family and was privately schooled and graduated from Cambridge. Masterman was from the non-conformist religious liberal tradition and was a passionate social reformer. Perhaps ironically for someone here criticizing the 'hooliganism' of the 'City Type' alcoholism and drug abuse contributed to his early death in his fifties (Hopkins 1999).

Philip Whitwell Wilson (1875 [Kendal]–1956) was a Liberal politician, journalist and writer. He was the son of a rector and was raised in Lakeland before studying mathematics at Cambridge University. He was elected as a Liberal MP in 1906 and served until 1910 when he switched to journalism. Wilson had a prominent journalistic career, serving as a political correspondent for the Daily News (previously founded by Charles Dickens) and working for the New York Times. He consequently became a well-known figure in US political circles and a personal friend of President Theodore Roosevelt. Wilson published on religious matters as well as a range of political and social affairs. His religious convictions are very apparent in these passages which lament the onset of urbanization and portray city living as unnatural and ungodly.

Although Masterman and Whitwell Wilson were young, radical Liberals who were committed to social reform, it is noticeable that their arguments are still nationalistic and imperialistic in extolling the virtues of the British Empire and the 'Anglo Saxon race'. Proto-ecological sentiment is also evident in asserting that 'man is vile' and an urban environment unleashes this since it creates an unnatural separation from nature. Hence, a very high value is put on the non-human world, an eco-centric line of reasoning.

49

THE HEART OF THE EMPIRE

Charles Masterman and Philip Whitwell Wilson, eds.

Source: Charles Masterman and Philip Whitwell Wilson (ed), *The Heart of the Empire* (1901)

PREFACE

THE Victorian Era has definitely closed. For many years it was manifest that the forces characteristic of that period had become expended, and that new problems were arising with a new age. But during the latter years of the nineteenth century men were content to confront the evils of national life with the old remedies. There had indeed been some modification in the general tendency of opinion, but this had by no means kept pace with the altered conditions of the world. The rapidity of social and economic change will perhaps be more easily realised now that the death of the Queen and of the century have reminded us all that nature and time spare nothing, however customary, honoured, and secure. The present can never take refuge behind the past. Foremost among the changes which have taken place has been the stupendous growth of cities. Vast herds of human beings are penned into small areas from which nature is excluded, and there live, breed, and die. The aspect of life has by that fact been altered; no longer brought into direct contact with the forces of nature, man has carved out for himself new and artificial conditions. The cities which we have to-day are different, not merely in degree but in character, from the large towns of former years; the City population is cut off from the country, in a manner previously unknown. It has developed sympathies and passions of its own, differing in essential characteristics from those of a bygone age.

Parallel with this city growth there has been an enormous increase of wealth. On every side production has advanced in a manner which would have filled our forefathers with astonishment. The fortunes which have accumulated in the hands of private persons have given them unprecedented powers over the lives of men and women. For the first time we are fully conscious how astonishing are the contrasts between the lives of the rich and of the poor, of their complete separation not only in sympathy and feeling, but in actual geographical aggregation. In old days all classes lived together in small towns and villages, the employee boarding sometimes with, always near, his master. To-day we have East and West Ends, business quarters, manufacturing quarters, residential quarters, endless vistas of villadom, acres of Lambeth and Whitechapel.

DOI: 10.4324/9781003194651-61

At the one end of the scale the lives of a large proportion of the rich are far from satisfactory. Separated from many of the realities of life, they are unable to find natural ways of expending their money, and, in con sequence, are driven to indulge in sumptuous living or in vulgar display. Thousands of pounds representing the toil of years in the cultivation of choice flowers or rare wines are dissipated for the gratification of a few guests at an evening party. Nor do the owners of this wealth really profit by their indulgence. Tyrannised over by their own conventions, slaves to their servants, frequently devoid of any real appreciation of the beautiful, their lives are spent without knowledge of the highest forms of happiness, with disastrous loss of energy and opportunity a loss that falls on all.

At the other end of the scale are the very poor-the broken classes – who suffer most from bad homes, bad education, intemperance, and want of any ideal either ethical or religious. It is here that the social reformer is apt to despair of any effective progress.

The town life is manifesting its influence not only upon these two extreme types, but also upon the great bulk of its inhabitants – the labourers, the artisans, the clerks-the "average" men of the coming century. A higher standard of comfort is counterbalanced by conditions of life more and more artificial; shortened hours of labour are compensated by a widening distance between home and place of work, and a continual increase in the time cut out of the margin of life in the transit. Improved facilities of education and the stimulating effect of the city are more than outweighed by the increasing monotony of occupation, the separation of classes, and the dulness and dreariness of the districts in which these populations are segregated. The whole result has been the upgrowth of a problem scarcely less urgent than that of the very rich and the very poor.

It must also be remembered that these new characteristics are only just beginning to show themselves. They will be far more developed, for good or for evil, after the lapse of a few generations. Thus on every side the strange and artificial growth of our cities confronts us. In every class we cannot but observe the evil effects of the enforced severance from natural conditions of life.

In presence of these problems which involve the future value of human life in England, one dark sign is the paralysis of the legislative machine and the sterility of the progressive party.

In municipal government, indeed, a party has arisen stimulated by a consistent ideal and determined to realise a definite scheme of reform. The "London Programme" is already passing from the region of idea to the region of fact: point by point its provisions are being translated into practical realities: the continuous success of its upholders terminating in their latest victory at the polls, produces an object lesson in the necessity of appealing to the people with a clear and definite policy.

But in the wider sphere of national politics the party of progress has fallen upon evil days. The champions fight as those that beat the air. Programmes are adopted at one election and abandoned at the next. "Social reform" is extolled in pompous phraseology, but when examined is often found to disappear in a maze of verbiage. Many of both parties seem endeavouring to ascertain what the country wants rather than what it needs. While the ruling party shows itself ever more blandly content to shelve real schemes of social improvement, men look in vain to the Opposition, either for appreciation of the gravity of the coming problems or for the importunate advocacy of any consistent measures of reform.

Meanwhile the problems themselves deepen in magnitude and gravity, and the opportunity for solving them in some peaceful and adequate manner becomes daily less favourable.

There are no doubt many who will regard such subjects as of only parochial interest, who will turn with a shrug of the shoulders to the wide questions of Imperial advance. They will assert that it is in the great Empire lying beyond the sea, and not within the narrow limits of the British Isles that the social problems are likely to find solution. To these we would point out the fact that four-fifths of the white subjects of the King are still living within the United Kingdom, and the great bulk of them are citizens of our towns. The policy demanded and approved by the great towns of England and Scotland will be the policy that, during this century at least, will rule the Empire. In order that this policy may be wise and just, it is essential that those who ultimately control it should be capable and intelligent citizens. "The bald-headed man who sits at the back of the 'bus" no longer governs the Empire from behind his solemn and voluminous penny paper. His political influence has devolved on to a different and less solid type of street politician, whose news and politics are supplied by the halfpenny press. It is impossible to say in what direction this change will eventually work as regards the conduct of Imperial politics. But at present the only essential differences between the modern elector and the "bald-headed man" appear to be greater ignorance and more shallow excitability.

Not only the policy but the material of Empire will come from England. The future colonisers and soldiers, not to mention the traders, who hold the Empire together, will henceforth be more and more the product of the city. It should also be remembered that increased inter the ideas of London to the Colonies, at least as effectually as they bring colonial ideas to London.

Thus an adequate knowledge of the state of our city population is essential. In spite of the researches of Mr. Charles Booth, many people are still ignorant of the fundamental divisions of the working classes; they confound the artisan, the labourer and the casual in one appellation – "the poor."

It is mainly a common apprehension of the gravity of the problems confronting this new England that has united the authors of these essays in the production of this book. They trust to be able to clear themselves from the charge of dogmatism or of arrogance; however definite their assertions they desire frankly to confess their own conclusions and remedies as but tentative and suggestive. Most of them claim, however, to possess a first-hand knowledge of the new city race. Some of the authors have lived in settlements; some in block-dwellings; others have been brought by voluntary effort or the demands of business into direct contact with the districts abandoned to the labouring classes.

They recognise the ineffectiveness of purely academic consideration and of programmes formed in the study alone. And they venture to hope that this immediate practical knowledge may give them some excuse for addressing those who have never penetrated into the desolate regions east of Liverpool Street Station or south of Waterloo.

Over and above the specific suggestions presented in the following essays, the object of the writers is to aid in removing the causes of the indifference which constitutes the most formidable obstacle to social reform. Our foreign policy has now for some years occupied the time, expended the money, and absorbed the energies of the country; and we have to ask ourselves whether the continuance of a state of things admittedly detrimental to domestic progress is either necessary or intrinsically desirable. A discussion of Imperialism in theory and practice thus forms a natural pendant to a volume that attempts to deal with the problems that face us at the Heart of the Empire.

In conclusion, they would state that in the production of a work dealing with so many subjects, entire agreement has not been attempted. Their unity is of spirit and aim. They all recognise the evils set forth in this preface, they all hope to see more active warfare against them. But individuality and freedom of treatment has been taken as the principle of the book, so that any statement made, or opinion advanced by any one of the writers, must be accredited to him alone.

. . .

pp. 6–7

Masterman 'Realities at Home'

It would be futile to deny that great changes, and in many respects great improvements, have taken place in large areas since men first awakened in the mid-century to the vital importance of the "Condition of the People" problem. Those observers who have concentrated their attention on the evils noted by former critics may indeed be pardoned if they but note the continuous triumph of light over darkness; if they hold that the forces still working are certain in the long run to produce a final victory. Utter lack of sanitation, great districts neglected by public bodies and private charity, a population hidden behind the trodden ways of men growing up in undisturbed heathendom and bestiality: these appear no longer possible. Public bodies, the London County Council and similar authorities in the great provincial cities, have been pushing their activities into the dark places of the earth; slum areas are broken up, sanitary regulations enforced, the policeman and the inspector at every corner. A series of factory acts, building acts, public health acts, have continually assailed the worst of these evils; and although an amount remains to be done which may well tax the energies of philanthropist and statesmen for many years to come, yet we may agree that the forces of progress are against these older social diseases, which eventually must disappear before the machinery which is brought against them.

But while men have slept other forces have arisen and changes taken place even as yet unappreciated by the majority of the people. Throughout the century the population of England has exhibited a continuous drift into the great cities; and now, at the opening of a new era, it is necessary to recognise that we are face to face with a phenomenon unique in the world's history. Turbulent rioting over military successes, Hooliganism, and a certain temper of fickle excitability has revealed to observers during the past few months that a new race, hitherto unreckoned and of incalculable action, is entering the sphere of practical importance – the City type" of the coming years; the "street-bred" people of the twentieth century; the "new generation knocking at our doors."

The England of the past has been an England of reserved, silent men, dispersed in small towns, villages, and country homes. The England of the future is an England packed tightly in such gigantic aggregations of population as the world has never before seen. The change has been largely concealed by the perpetual swarm of immigrants from the surrounding districts, which has permeated the whole of such a town as London with a healthy, energetic population reared amidst the fresh air and quieting influences of the life of the fields. But in the past twenty – five years a force has been operating in the raw material of which the city is composed. The texture itself has been transformed as by some subtle alchemy. The second generation of the immigrants has been reared in the courts and crowded ways of the great metropolis, with cramped physical accessories, hot, fretful life, and long hours of sedentary or unhealthy toil. The problem of the coming years is just the problem of this New Town type; upon their development and action depend the future progress of the Anglo-Saxon Race, and for the next half-century at least the policy of the British Empire in the world.

. . .

pp. 233–234

Whitwell Wilson 'The Distribution of Industry'

We are often informed that the land has gone out of cultivation, and irrevocably. It may be so, but at any rate we might grow our own vegetables (other than the human variety), and occasionally it is refreshing to taste a new-laid egg. There is no doubt that in a properly constituted village community, butter, eggs, vegetables, and a good deal of fruit would be grown locally. In many instances the workpeople themselves would take to gardening as a hobby, especially if the master had the sense to encourage such pursuits. But there would always be room for a regular market gardener, who could bring into cultivation an acre or two, and more if necessary. It is not pretended that this constitutes a settlement of the great agricultural problem of the last sixty years. But it is astonishing how much may be done by intelligent men of education towards inducing the artisan to provide food for himself.

As for education, it is hopeless in a big city. The only plan is to get the children into the fields. No doubt many of our village schools are grievously inefficient, while in London or Birmingham the exact contrary is true. But any one who travels up and down day by day on local railways, in the Metropolis must, if he has any discernment at all, become grievously dissatisfied with the finished product of the London Board School. The pedagogue has not a chance against the degrading influences that damn the finer senses. And the reason is obvious. God meant men to live in a world where natural, non-human sights and sounds, like the braying of an ass or the glory of a field of buttercups, should on the whole predominate his leisure hours. It is not that these farmyard rusticities are always grateful, either to eye or ear. But they are wholesome. A city is a place where man has a monopoly, and where man is therefore almost wholly vile. Humanity is an admirable institution when it is well diluted, but we should ever consider that Adam and Eve – alone – were too human for the garden of Eden. Sectarianism and muddle may have worked the usual havoc with our educational system, but in the main it is the adequate village school which turns out the really successful men.

A yet more dangerous symptom is that in the big towns an increasing proportion of these children who do struggle precariously to a pasty-faced puberty are obviously only born with half a brain, which half is saturated in youth with all the filth – pictorial, verbal, and dietary – that a rotten civilisation can devise. These are the "hands" that the employer has to employ, if he persists in glueing his factory to an eligible central situation on the Thames, where the devil has a monopoly of men, women, and children. And what chance has he with such human instruments of competing successfully against nations which realise the value of health and happiness to an artisan or to a factory girl? The manufacturer who is truly up to date will recognise that just as his machinery must be of the latest, so his employes must be "all there" – full of vigour, – instinct with loyalty, filled with esprit de corps and a devotion to the locality which flourishes by their toil. The apathy which we display towards these considerations, our utter failure to appreciate the financial value of a carefully trained workman, and our consequent neglect of all those measures which would secure to us intelligence in the artisan classes, are akin to our idiotic helplessness in the face of the new situation created by American and German improvements in machinery. If only our capitalists were Christians, they would be better men of business. Their religion would impel them to consider the happiness of their employes, and indirectly they would find that their profits would increase, owing to the enhanced capability of each wage-earner. Yet even as it is, a millowner, who will definitely establish a village industry, will, ipso facto, have the pick of every respectable and God-fearing working man in the trade. Ask the proprietors of Port Sunlight if this is not the case.

Editorial Headnote

1866 (Bromley)–1946

Herbert George Wells was a novelist and social critic widely hailed as the father of science fiction. He is probably best remembered for the enduring classic War of the Worlds.

Wells was from a poor background and left school at fourteen to take up an apprenticeship with a draper. After a series of similar jobs, at eighteen he won a scholarship to study biology at the Normal School of Science under the distinguished academic Thomas Huxley (discussed earlier in this volume part). Wells graduated and subsequently became a science teacher and writer. His first publication was the decidedly non-fictional Textbook of Biology in 1893. Two years later, however, he applied his scientific mind to fiction with his first novel, The Time Machine, which proved to be a huge success.

In A Modern Utopia, Wells applied Malthusian logic to his vision of human progress towards utopia. In particular, he argues that there is a need for the state to regulate the population and save people from themselves. He also advocates a world-state run by a voluntary nobility – a Samurai – which has one currency and one language. Hence, this fanciful vision actually contained many of the ideas that would come to underpin political notions of global governance, such as the functionalist theory of international cooperation later developed by David Mitrany (1975) in particular. Viewing humanity as 'the rebel child of nature', Wells appears to see us as a unique species, not only capable of using technology to tame the environment but also one that needs to better appreciate and respect its place in this tough order. Later in the novel, Wells goes on to imagine that human ingenuity and technology could be utilized in the interests of other species by ending slaughterhouses and making farming more humane.

Wells was a socialist and joined the Fabian Society in 1903. Most of his works are predicated on the belief that humanity could evolve to be something better. Later in his career he lent his support to the emergent 'science' of eugenics as a means of curbing overpopulation and improving humanity through genetic interventions (Wells 1931). Wells was also anti-religious and an open advocate of sexual freedom. World War II, late in his life, apparently crushed his spirit and much of his optimism for human progress and a future utopia (Encyclopedia Britannica).

pp. 135–174

50

A MODERN UTOPIA

H.G. Wells

Source: H.G. Wells, *A Modern Utopia* (1905)

CHAPTER THE FIFTH FAILURE
IN A MODERN UTOPIA

THE OLD UTOPIAS – save for the breeding schemes of Plato and Campan-
ella – ignored that reproductive competition among individualities which is the
substance of life, and dealt essentially with its incidentals. The endless variety of
men, their endless gradation of quality, over which the hand of selection plays,
and to which we owe the unmanageable complication of real life, is tacitly set
aside. The real world is a vast disorder of accidents and incalculable forces in
which men survive or fail. A Modern Utopia, unlike its predecessors, dare not
pretend to change the last condition; it may order and humanise the conflict, but
men must still survive or fail.

Most Utopias present themselves as going concerns, as happiness in being; they
make it an essential condition that a happy land can have no history, and all the
citizens one is permitted to see are well looking and upright and mentally and mor-
ally in tune. But we are under the dominion of a logic that obliges us to take over
the actual population of the world with only such moral and mental and physical
improvements as lie within their inherent possibilities, and it is our business to
ask what Utopia will do with its congenital invalids, its idiots and madmen, its
drunkards and men of vicious mind, its cruel and furtive souls, its stupid people,
too stupid to be of use to the community, its lumpish, unteachable and unimagina-
tive people? And what will it do with the man who is "poor" all round, the rather
spiritless, rather incompetent low-grade man who on earth sits in the den of the
sweater, tramps the streets under the banner of the unemployed, or trembles – in
another man's cast-off clothing, and with an infinity of hat-touching – on the verge
of rural employment?

These people will have to be in the descendant phase, the species must be
engaged in eliminating them; there is no escape from that, and conversely the
people of exceptional quality must be ascendant. The better sort of people, so far
as they can be distinguished, must have the fullest freedom of public service, and
the fullest opportunity of parentage. And it must be open to every man to approve
himself worthy of ascendency.

DOI: 10.4324/9781003194651-62

391

ROMANTICIZING NATURE

The way of Nature in this process is to kill the weaker and the sillier, to crush them, to starve them, to overwhelm them, using the stronger and more cunning as her weapon. But man is the unnatural animal, the rebel child of Nature, and more and more does he turn himself against the harsh and fitful hand that reared him. He sees with a growing resentment the multitude of suffering ineffectual lives over which his species tramples in its ascent. In the Modern Utopia he will have set himself to change the ancient law. No longer will it be that failures must suffer and perish lest their breed increase, but the breed of failure must not increase, lest they suffer and perish, and the race with them.

Now we need not argue here to prove that the resources of the world and the energy of mankind, were they organised sanely, are amply sufficient to supply every material need of every living human being. And if it can be so contrived that every human being shall live in a state of reasonable physical and mental comfort, without the reproduction of inferior types, there is no reason whatever why that should not be secured. But there must be a competition in life of some sort to determine who are to be pushed to the edge, and who are to prevail and multiply. Whatever we do, man will remain a competitive creature, and though moral and intellectual training may vary and enlarge his conception of success and fortify him with refinements and consolations, no Utopia will ever save him completely from the emotional drama of struggle, from exultations and humiliations, from pride and prostration and shame. He lives in success and failure just as inevitably as he lives in space and time.

But we may do much to make the margin of failure endurable. On earth, for all the extravagance of charity, the struggle for the mass of men at the bottom resolves itself into a struggle, and often a very foul and ugly struggle, for food, shelter, and clothing. Deaths outright from exposure and starvation are now perhaps uncommon, but for the multitude there are only miserable houses, uncomfortable clothes, and bad and insufficient food; fractional starvation and exposure, that is to say. A Utopia planned upon modern lines will certainly have put an end to that. It will insist upon every citizen being properly housed, well nourished, and in good health, reasonably clean and clothed healthily, and upon that insistence its labour laws will be founded. In a phrasing that will be familiar to everyone interested in social reform, it will maintain a standard of life. Any house, unless it be a public monument, that does not come up to its rising standard of healthiness and convenience, the Utopian State will incontinently pull down, and pile the material and charge the owner for the labour; any house unduly crowded or dirty, it must in some effectual manner, directly or indirectly, confiscate and clear and clean. And any citizen indecently dressed, or ragged and dirty, or publicly unhealthy, or sleeping abroad homeless, or in any way neglected or derelict, must come under its care. It will find him work if he can and will work, it will take him to it, it will register him and lend him the money wherewith to lead a comely life until work can be found or made for him, and it will give him credit and shelter him and strengthen him if he is ill. In default of private enterprises it will provide inns for him and food, and it will – by itself acting as the reserve employer – maintain a

A MODERN UTOPIA

minimum wage which will cover the cost of a decent life. The State will stand at the back of the economic struggle as the reserve employer of labour. This most excellent idea does, as a matter of fact, underlie the British institution of the workhouse, but it is jumbled up with the relief of old age and infirmity, it is administered parochially and on the supposition that all population is static and localised whereas every year it becomes more migratory; it is administered without any regard to the rising standards of comfort and self-respect in a progressive civilisation, and it is administered grudgingly. The thing that is done is done as unwilling charity by administrators who are often, in the rural districts at least, competing for low-priced labour, and who regard want of employment as a crime. But if it were possible for any citizen in need of money to resort to a place of public employment as a right, and there work for a week or month without degradation upon certain minimum terms, it seems fairly certain that no one would work, except as the victim of some quite exceptional and temporary accident, for less.

The work publicly provided would have to be toilsome, but not cruel or incapacitating. A choice of occupations would need to be afforded, occupations adapted to different types of training and capacity, with some residual employment of a purely laborious and mechanical sort for those who were incapable of doing the things that required intelligence. Necessarily this employment by the State would be a relief of economic pressure, but it would not be considered a charity done to the individual, but a public service. It need not pay, any more than the police need pay, but it could probably be done at a small margin of loss. There is a number of durable things bound finally to be useful that could be made and stored whenever the tide of more highly paid employment ebbed and labour sank to its minimum, bricks, iron from inferior ores, shaped and preserved timber, pins, nails, plain fabrics of cotton and linen, paper, sheet glass, artificial fuel, and so on; new roads could be made and public buildings reconstructed, inconveniences of all sorts removed, until under the stimulus of accumulating material, accumulating investments or other circumstances, the tide of private enterprise flowed again.

The State would provide these things for its citizen as though it was his right to require them; he would receive as a shareholder in the common enterprise and not with any insult of charity. But on the other hand it will require that the citizen who renders the minimum of service for these concessions shall not become a parent until he is established in work at a rate above the minimum, and free of any debt he may have incurred. The State will never press for its debt, nor put a limit to its accumulation so long as a man or woman remains childless; it will not even grudge them temporary spells of good fortune when they may lift their earnings above the minimum wage. It will pension the age of everyone who cares to take a pension, and it will maintain special guest homes for the very old to which they may come as paying guests, spending their pensions there. By such obvious devices it will achieve the maximum elimination of its feeble and spiritless folk in every generation with the minimum of suffering and public disorder.

But the mildly incompetent, the spiritless and dull, the poorer sort who are ill, do not exhaust our Utopian problem. There remain idiots and lunatics, there remain perverse and incompetent persons, there are people of weak character who become drunkards, drug takers, and the like. Then there are persons tainted with certain foul and transmissible diseases. All these people spoil the world for others. They may become parents, and with most of them there is manifestly nothing to be done but to seclude them from the great body of the population. You must resort to a kind of social surgery. You cannot have social freedom in your public ways, your children cannot speak to whom they will, your girls and gentle women cannot go abroad while some sorts of people go free. And there are violent people, and those who will not respect the property of others, thieves and cheats, they, too, so soon as their nature is confirmed, must pass out of the free life of our ordered world. So soon as there can be no doubt of the disease or baseness of the individual, so soon as the insanity or other disease is assured, or the crime repeated a third time, or the drunkenness or misdemeanour past its seventh occasion (let us say), so soon must he or she pass out of the common ways of men.

The dreadfulness of all such proposals as this lies in the possibility of their execution falling into the hands of hard, dull, and cruel administrators. But in the case of a Utopia one assumes the best possible government, a government as merciful and deliberate as it is powerful and decisive. You must not too hastily imagine these things being done – as they would be done on earth at present – by a number of zealous half-educated people in a state of panic at a quite imaginary "Rapid Multiplication of the Unfit."

No doubt for first offenders, and for all offenders under five-and-twenty, the Modern Utopia will attempt cautionary and remedial treatment. There will be disciplinary schools and colleges for the young, fair and happy places, but with less confidence and more restraint than the schools and colleges of the ordinary world. In remote and solitary regions these enclosures will lie, they will be fenced in and forbidden to the common run of men, and there, remote from all temptation, the defective citizen will be schooled. There will be no masking of the lesson; "which do you value most, the wide world of humanity, or this evil trend in you?" From that discipline at last the prisoners will return.

But the others; what would a saner world do with them?

Our world is still vindictive, but the all-reaching State of Utopia will have the strength that begets mercy. Quietly the outcast will go from among his fellow men. There will be no drumming of him out of the ranks, no tearing off of epaulettes, no smiting in the face. The thing must be just public enough to obviate secret tyrannies, and that is all.

There would be no killing, no lethal chambers. No doubt Utopia will kill all deformed and monstrous and evilly diseased births, but for the rest, the State will hold itself accountable for their being. There is no justice in Nature perhaps, but the idea of justice must be sacred in any good society. Lives that statesmanship has permitted, errors it has not foreseen and educated against, must not be punished by death. If the State does not keep faith, no one will keep faith. Crime and bad lives are the measure of a State's failure, all crime in the end is the crime of the community. Even for murder Utopia will not, I think, kill.

A MODERN UTOPIA

I doubt even if there will be jails. No men are quite wise enough, good enough and cheap enough to staff jails as a jail ought to be staffed. Perhaps islands will be chosen, islands lying apart from the highways of the sea, and to these the State will send its exiles, most of them thanking Heaven, no doubt, to be quit of a world of prigs. The State will, of course, secure itself against any children from these people, that is the primary object in their seclusion, and perhaps it may even be necessary to make these island prisons a system of island monasteries and island nunneries. Upon that I am not competent to speak, but if I may believe the literature of the subject – unhappily a not very well criticised literature – it is not necessary to enforce this separation.

About such islands patrol boats will go, there will be no freedoms of boat building, and it may be necessary to have armed guards at the creeks and quays. Beyond that the State will give these segregated failures just as full a liberty as they can have. If it interferes any further it will be simply to police the islands against the organisation of serious cruelty, to maintain the freedom of any of the detained who wish it to transfer themselves to other islands, and so to keep a check upon tyranny. The insane, of course, will demand care and control, but there is no reason why the islands of the hopeless drunkard, for example, should not each have a virtual autonomy, have at the most a Resident and a guard. I believe that a community of drunkards might be capable of organising even its own bad habit to the pitch of tolerable existence. I do not see why such an island should not build and order for itself and manufacture and trade. "Your ways are not our ways," the World State will say; "but here is freedom and a company of kindred souls. Elect your jolly rulers, brew if you will, and distil; here are vine cuttings and barley fields; do as it pleases you to do. We will take care of the knives, but for the rest – deal yourselves with God!"

And you see the big convict steamship standing in to the Island of Incurable Cheats. The crew are respectfully at their quarters, ready to lend a hand overboard, but wide awake, and the captain is hospitably on the bridge to bid his guests good-bye and keep an eye on the movables. The new citizens for this particular Alsatia, each no doubt with his personal belongings securely packed and at hand, crowd the deck and study the nearing coast. Bright, keen faces would be there, and we, were we by any chance to find ourselves beside the captain, might recognise the double of this great earthly magnate or that, Petticoat Lane and Park Lane cheek by jowl. The landing part of the jetty is clear of people, only a government man or so stands there to receive the boat and prevent a rush, but beyond the gates a number of engagingly smart-looking individuals loiter speculatively. One figures a remarkable building labelled Custom House, an interesting fiscal revival this population has made, and beyond, crowding up the hill, the painted walls of a number of comfortable inns clamour loudly. One or two inhabitants in reduced circumstances would act as hotel touts, there are several hotel omnibuses and a Bureau de Change, certainly a Bureau de Change. And a small house with a large board, aimed point-blank seaward, declares itself a Gratis Information Office, and next to it rises the graceful dome of a small Casino. Beyond, great hoardings

395

proclaim the advantages of many island specialities, a hustling commerce, and the opening of a Public Lottery. There is a large cheap-looking barrack, the school of Commercial Science for gentlemen of inadequate training. . . .

Altogether a very go-ahead looking little port it would be, and though this disembarkation would have none of the flow of hilarious good fellowship that would throw a halo of genial noise about the Islands of Drink, it is doubtful if the new arrivals would feel anything very tragic in the moment. Here at last was scope for adventure after their hearts.

This sounds more fantastic than it is. But what else is there to do, unless you kill? You must seclude, but why should you torment? All modern prisons are places of torture by restraint, and the habitual criminal plays the part of a damaged mouse at the mercy of the cat of our law. He has his little painful run, and back he comes again to a state more horrible even than destitution. There are no Alsatias left in the world. For my own part I can think of no crime, unless it is reckless begetting or the wilful transmission of contagious disease, for which the bleak terrors, the solitudes and ignominies of the modern prison do not seem outrageously cruel. If you want to go so far as that, then kill. Why, once you are rid of them, should you pester criminals to respect an uncongenial standard of conduct? Into such islands of exile as this a modern Utopia will have to purge itself. There is no alternative that I can contrive.

REFERENCES

Anderson, B. (1991) *Imagined Communities*. London: Verso.

Austen, J. (1796) *Letter to Cassandra, from London August 23, 1796 in Le Faye, Deirdre. A Chronology of Jane Austen*. Cambridge: CUP, 2006.

Austen, J. (1815) *Emma*. London: John Murray.

Bailey, R., Hatton, T., & Inwood, K. (2018) 'Atmospheric Pollution, Health, and Height in Late Nineteenth Century Britain', *The Journal of Economic History*, 78(4): 1210–1247.

Bate, J. (1999) 'Culture and Environment: From Austen to Hardy', *New Literary History*, 30(3): 541–560.

Bate, J. (2003) *John Clare: A Biography*. New York City: Farrar, Straus and Giroux.

Bate, J. (2020) *Radical Wordsworth: The Poet Who Changed the World*. London: William Collins.

Beenstock, Z. (2016) *Politics of Romanticism: The Social Contract and Literature*. Edinburgh: Edinburgh University Press.

Bookchin, M. (1971) *Post-Scarcity Anarchism*. Berkeley, CA: The Ramparts Press.

Brabazon (1888) *Prosperity or Pauperism*? London: Longmans.

Briggs, A. (1962) *William Morris: Selected Writings and Designs*. Harmondsworth: Penguin.

Carlyle, T. (1858) *Signs of the Times Volume Three of the Collected Works of Thomas Carlyle*, 16 volumes. London: Chapman and Hall.

Carpenter, E. (1916) *My Days and Dreams: Being Autobiographical Notes*. London: Allen and Unwin.

Carroll, A. (2019) '"Rivers Change Like Nations" Reading Eco-apocalypse in the Waters of Edera', in Mazzeno, L., & Morrison, M. (eds) *Victorian Environmental Nightmares*. London: Palgrave MacMillan: 145–166.

Clare, J. (1908) *Poems by John Clare*. London: Henry Frowde.

Clarke, R. (2005) 'Informal Adult Education Between the Wars: The Curious Case of the Selbourne Lecture Bureau', *Discussion Paper*. Birkbeck BIROn – Birkbeck Institutional Research Online https://eprints.bbk.ac.uk/id/eprint/8256/1/Clarke_2005_InformalAEBtwWars-Selsoc_A5.pdf (accessed 23.11.2021).

Cobbett, W. (1830) *Rural Rides*. London: Wm. Cobbett.

Coleridge, S.T. (1850) *Coleridge's Essays in His Own Times*. London: William Pickering.

Disraeli, B. (1845) *Sybil; Or, the Two Nations*. London: Henry Colburn.

Eliot, G. (1863) *Scenes of Clerical Life and Silas Marner*. Edinburgh & London: William Blackwood.

REFERENCES

Fyfe, H. (1900) 'How Will the World End?', *Pearson's Magazine*, 12(4).

Hansard (1903) House of Lords Debate 06 July 1903, vol. 124 cc1324–1356.

Hardy, T. (1883) 'The Dorsetshire Labourer', *Longman's Magazine*, July: 252–269.

Hardy, T. (1887) *The Woodlanders*. London: Macmillan.

Hay, W. (1880) *The Doom of the Great City. Being the Narrative of a Survivor*. London: Newman & Co.

Hill, O. (1877) *Our Common Land (and Other Short Essays)*. London: MacMillan.

Hopkins, E. (1999) *Masterman, C. (1873–1927), Politician and Journalist: The Splendid Failure*. Lewiston, NY: The Edward Mellen Press.

Jefferies, W. (1885) *After London*. London: Duckworth.

Jennings, L. (1884) 'Wellington to Crocker, 6 March 1833', in *The Correspondence and Diaries of J. W Crocker from 1809 to 1830*, volume II. London: John Murray: 205–206.

Jessop, R. (2012) 'Coinage of the Term Environment: A Word Without Authority and Carlyle's Displacement of the Mechanical Metaphor', *Literature Compass*, 9(11): 708–720.

Kaufman, E. (1998) 'Naturalizing the Nation: The Rise of Naturalization Nationalism in the United States and Canada', *Comparative Studies in and Society and History*, 40(4): 666–695.

Kerry, P., & Hill, M. (2010) *Thomas Carlyle Resartus: Reappraising Carlyle's Contribution to the Philosophy of History, Political Theory and Cultural Criticism*. Cranbury, NJ: Associated University Presses.

Kumar, K. (2000) 'Nation and Empire: English and British National Identity in Comparative Perspective', *Theory and Society*, 29(5), October: 575–608.

Lowenthal, D. (1991) 'British National Identity and the English Landscape', *Rural History*, 2(2): 205–230.

Lydekker, R. (1908) *The Game Animals of Africa*. London: Rowland Ward.

MacCarthy, F. (1994) *William Morris. A Life for Our Time*. London: Feber & Feber.

Mallett, P. (1995) 'The City and the Self', in Wheeler, M. (ed) *Ruskin and Environment: The Storm-Cloud of the Nineteenth Century*. Manchester: Manchester University Press: 38–57.

Masterman, C., & Wilson, P.W. (ed) (1901) *The Heart of the Empire*. London: Fisher Unwin.

Mitrany, D. (1975) *The Functional Theory of Politics*. London: Robertson.

Monbiot, G. (2012) 'John Clare, the Poet of the Environmental Crisis – 200 Years Ago', *The Guardian*, 9 July.

Morris, W. (1889) 'Under an Elm-Tree; or, Thoughts in the Country Side', *Commonweal*, 5(182): 6 July: 212–213.

Muir, J. (1894) *The Mountains of California*. New York: The Century Co.

Muir, J. (1916) *A Thousand Mile Walk to the Gulf*. Boston: Houghton Mifflin.

National Trust (2022) www.nationaltrust.org.uk/features/octavia-hill-her-life-and-legacy (accessed 14.04.2022).

Obituary Notices (1941) 'Herbrand Russel', *Bibliographical Memoirs of Fellows of the Royal Society*, 3(9), January: 499–502.

Ouida (1900) *The Waters of Edera*. London: T. Fisher Unwin.

Pontin, B. (2014) 'Environmental Law-Making Pubic Opinion in Victorian Britain: The Cross-Currents of Bentham's and Coleridge's Ideas', *Oxford Journal of Legal Studies*, 34(4): 759–790.

Raffles, T. (1825) 'London Zoological Society Prospectus', 1 March: 13–16.

REFERENCES

Ranlett, J. (1983) 'Checking Nature's Desecration: Late-Victorian Environmental Organization', *Victorian Studies*, 26(2): 197–222.

Rintala, M. (1968) 'Two Compromises: Victorian and Bismarckian', *Government and Opposition*, 3(2), Spring: 207–221.

Ritvo, H. (2009) *The Dawn of Green: Manchester, Thirlmere and Modern Environmentalism*. Chicago: University of Chicago Press.

Rothschild Archive (2021) https://family.rothschildarchive.org/people/104-nathaniel-charles-rothschild-1877-1923 (accessed 02.06.2022).

Rothschild, C. (1912) 'Nature Reserves: Formation of a New Society', *The Times*, 18 December.

Ruskin, J. (1843) *Modern Painters*. London: Smith, Elder and Co.

Ruskin, J. (1876) *A Protest Against the Extension of Railways in the Lake District Robert Somervell* (preface by Ruskin). London: Simpkin, Marshall & Co.

Scherren, H. (1905) *The Zoological Society of London. A Sketch of its Foundation and Development*. London: Cassell.

Sewell, A. (1898) *Black Beauty. The Autobiography of a Horse*. London: Jarrolds.

Sierra Club (2020) 'Pulling Down Our Monuments', www.sierraclub.org/michael-brune/2020/07/john-muir-early-history-sierra-club (accessed 23.28.2022).

Smith, A. (1991) *National Identity*. London: Penguin.

Springhall, J.O. (1970) 'Lord Meath, Youth and Empire', *Journal of Contemporary History*, 5(4).

Tapper, G. (1996) 'The Chairman's Notes', *The Thomas Hardy Journal*, 12(1): 17–19.

Victoriaweb (2002) 'Ouida', https://victorianweb.org/authors/ouida/biography.html (accessed 1.06.2023).

Wallace, A. (1853) *A Narrative of Travels on the Amazon and Rio Negro: With an Account of the Native Tribes, and Observations on the Climate, Geology, and Natural History of the Amazon Valley*. London: Reeve & Co.

Wallace, A. (1898) *Our Wonderful Century*. Toronto: George Morang.

Wells, H.G. (1897) 'The Star', in *The Graphic*, 25 Decemberth.

Wells, H.G. (1931) 'Introductory Remarks', *Economica*, 31, February: 1–4.

White, F. (1905) *The Doom of London Reissued (2019)*. Glasgow: Good Press.

Wildlife Trust (2022) www.wildlifetrusts.org/about-us (accessed 12.04.2022).

Woburn Abbey (2022) www.woburnabbeydeerfarm.co.uk/history/ (accessed 12.12.2021).

Woods, M. (2005) *Contesting Rurality: Politics in the British Countryside*. Aldershot: Ashgate.

Wordsworth, W. (1814) *The Excursion*. London: Longman, Hurst, Rees, Orme, and Brown.

Wordsworth, W. (1844) 'Sonnet on the Projected Kendal and Windermere Railway', *London Morning Post*, 16 October.

INDEX

Note: Page numbers in *italics* indicate a figure on the corresponding page.

acid rain 155–159
Africa 343–346
Africans 319
agriculture: biodiversity decline and 43–46; St Helena and 25, 27–34
alcoholism 381
Alkali Act 11
Amazon 361
Anglo Saxon race 371–379, 381–388
animal rights and animal welfare 271–276, 277
animals 335–340; game 341, 343–N
anthropocene 41, 43–45
anthropology 57, 59–61
anti-Semitism 305, 319; *see also* race and racism
apartheid 70
aristocracy: conservation and 207–208
Arnold, Matthew 206
Arrhenius, Svante 11
arsenic 143, 145–147
Arts and Crafts movement 205–206; *see also* Morris, William
atmosphere 173–177
Austen, Jane 299, 301–303
Australia 21, 362

bank holidays 263–270
Banks, Joseph 21
Bates, Henry 361
Bazalgette, Joseph 161
bears 45
Beatson, Alexander 7–8, 25, 27–34
beavers 8, 45
Bentham, Jeremy 12, 243
Bessemer, Henry 5

big game 208, 343–346
biodiversity decline 6–8; agriculture and 43–46
birds 15, 17–19; of prey 45
birth control 9
Black Beauty 271–276
Black Forest 204
Boer War 209, 369
Bonaparte, Napoleon 143, 257
Boors 38
Booth, Charles 385
botany 7, 21, 23–24; ecology and 73; St Helena and 25, 27–34
Botany Bay 21
Brazil 44, 361
British Humanitarian League 277
British Vegetation Committee 69
Brown, John Croumbie 127, 129–132
Burchell, William John 7, 35, 37–39
Burns, John 375

Calcutta Botanic Garden 21
Cape Town 37–39
capitalism 363–367
Cardiff 165
Carlyle, Thomas 189, 235, 319–325
Carpenter, Edward 283, 284–289
Carson, Rachel 12, 143
catastrophism 41
Cathedral Peak 295
cattle 31–33
children 371–N
cholera 11, 95, 149, 151–154, 161
Clare, John 257–261
Clean Air Act (1956) 369
Cleghorn, John 113, 115–117, 119

400

INDEX

climate change 11; droughts and 8
climate science 171, 173–177
coal 9–10, 11, 103, 105–111, 363–364;
  acid rain and 155–159; *see also* smoke
  pollution
Coal Smoke Abatement Society 201
Coal Smoke Abatement Society (CSAB) 369
Cobbett, Richard 305–311
Cobbett, William 201
cod 117, 125; *see also* fish and fishing
coffee 365
Coleridge, Samuel Taylor 201, 213–216,
  217–218
colonialism 7, 335, 362–367
Colorado beetles 143
commons 265–270; *see also* enclosures
Commons Preservation Society 201, 206
Conan-Doyle, Arthur 362
consciousness 287
conservation 7, 204; aesthetes and
  205–207; aristocracy and 207–208;
  country-side and 253–256; fear of future
  and 208–209
Conservatives 207–209, 218, 313
Cook, James 7, 21
corn 29; St Helena and 29–34
Corn Laws 313
cotton 5, 100
countryside: Surrey 301–303, 307–311;
  Yosemite National Park 293–296
Cremation Society 341
crime 365, 393, 394–395

Darwin, Charles 6, 8, 25, 47, 49–55, 119,
  207, 361; Malthusian influence on
  77–78; uniformitarianism and 41
Deep Green Ecology 70
deforestation 8, 9
degeneration 371–379
democracy 288
desertification 9
Dickens, Charles 201, 205–206, 319
diseases 89, 316
Disraeli, Benjamin 207, 313–318; *see also*
  Young England
Disused Burial Grounds Act 201, 263
dodos 63
Dog Act (1871) 277
dogs 277
Dorsetshire 329–333
droughts 8, 25, 32–34, 279
Dutch Cape Colony 35

East India Company 335
East India Corporation 25
eco-anarchism 251
ecocentrism 291
ecocide 218
ecology 5, 6, 72–73
ecosystems 69–70
Ehrlich, Paul 8–9
El Nino 25
Eliot, George 243, 245–249
elitism 214, 236
elm trees 253–256, 257
Emerson, Ralph Waldo 319
emigration 100
Emma 299, 301–303
empire 367; conservation and 207–209;
  physical health and 379, 381,
  383–388
Empire Day 369
employment 92
enclosures 9, 206, 266; *see also* Commons
  Preservation Society
environmental determinism 57, 243,
  245–249
epidemics 89, 101
epidemiology 95
epistemic communities 7
ethnology 57, 59–61
Evans, Mary Ann *see* Eliot, George
evolution 47, 49–55
Excursion, The 219–224
extinction 63, 65–67

Fabian Society 285
famines 25, 32, 34, 77, 362, 367
Faraday, Michael 161, 163–164
Farr, William 9, 95, 97–102
feminization of nature 277
fens 201, 347
feudalism 208
fish and fishing 113, 115–117, 119–126
flour 30–31; *see also* wheat
flowers 23–24; South Africa and
  38–39
fog 355, 357–360; *see also* smoke
food 371–379, 387
forest schools 133, 135–139, 207
Forestry Act (1919) 133
forestry and forest management 127,
  129–132, 365; economic aspects 133,
  135–139
fossil fuels 364; *see also* coal

INDEX

free trade 313
French Revolution 218
Fuller, Henry William 143, 144–147
Fyfe, Herbert 355

Galapagos 25
game animals 341, 343–346
gas lighting 11
geology 41, 43–45; evolution and 54
Germany 6–7, 10, 207; Technische
  Anleitung Luft and 11
Gilbert White Museum 15
gnus 341, 343–344
Godwin, William 77
gold 364
Graham, John William 189, 191–194
Grasmere 235–236
great auks 63, 65–67
Great Exhibition 251
Great Fog of 1755 11
Great Fog of 1873 12
Great Stink (1858) 161
Green Belt 263
greenhouse effect 171, 173–177

Haeckel, Ernst 6
Hallam, Arthur Henry 225
Hardin, Garret 9, 85
Hardy, Thomas 201, 327, 329–333
Hart, Ernest 179–187
Hay, William Delisle 355, 357–360
Heincke, Friedrich 113
Henry IV 129–130
herring 113, 115–117, 125; see also fish
  and fishing
Hill, Octavia 179, 182, 201, 263–270
holidays 263–270
horses 271–276
Hottentots 35, 38
humans 57, 59–61; population and 77,
  78–84, 97–102; population control and
  87–93
Hume, David 77
Hunter, Robert 206, 263
husbandry 29
Huxley, Thomas 6, 9, 47, 113, 119–126,
  171, 361

Iceland 63, 65–67
In Memoriam A.H.H.' 227–234
India 25, 362, 367; botany and 21; forests
  in 130–131

indigenous people 8
industrialization 243, 277; machines and
  323–325
insects 44
International Council for the Exploration
  of the Seas 120
International Union for the Conservation
  of Nature (IUCN) 347
Ireland 204; forests in 136
iron 5

Jansens, Jan 35
Java 335
Jevons paradox 103
Jevons, William 10, 103, 105–111
Jewish Relief Act (1858) 313
Jews 208, 305, 308, 313

Kendal-to-Windermere rail line
  217–218, 235
Kew Gardens 21, 23, 35
Kyrle Society 263

labour and labourers 98–99, 329–333
laissez-faire economics 189
Lake District 237–241
Lake District Defence Society 201,
  206, 235
Lake Hoffman 295
Lakeland 206, 217, 381
Land Nationalisation Society 361
Land Tenure Reform Association 361–362
Lankester, Edwin 119
Lankester, Ray 113
Lantern Yard 243, 245–249
laws of nature 286
Lewes, George Henry 52
Liberals 12, 189, 209, 313, 381
Light Railways Act (1896) 201, 236;
  see also railways
Lloyd, William Forster 9, 85, 87–93;
  see also Tragedy of the Commons, The
London 163–164, 299; commons and 266;
  destruction of 209; fog and 355
London Zoo 335
Lydekker, Richard 341, 343–346
Lyell, Charles 41, 43–45, 47, 361
Lyrical Ballads 213, 217

machines 322–325
malaria 316
Malay 361

402

INDEX

Malthus, Thomas 9, 77, 79–84, 85, 87–88, 207
Marsh Test 143
Materman, Charles 381–388
meat 138
Meath, Lord 369, 371–N
medievalism 251
military 376–379
milk 375
Mill, John Stuart 327, 362
Millais, John 205
milu 341
mining 364–365; coal 103, 105–111
Monbiot, George 257
morality 381
Morris, William 189, 201, 205–206, 251, 253–256, 283; *see also* Arts and Crafts movement
mountains 39, 204
Mt. Hoffman 293–296
Muir, John 201, 205, 291–296
Muntjac deer 341

Naess, Arne 70
national parks 291, 293–296; *see also* nature reserves
National Parks Commission 348
National Trust 263
nationalism 203–205, 209; naturalistic 209
natural history 15, 17–19; of humans 57, 59–61; zoology and 335–400
natural resources 363–367
natural selection 47, 49–55
nature reserves 349–352; *see also* national parks
Neo-Malthusians 9
New Poor Laws 313
Newton, Alfred 63, 64–67
novels: *Black Beauty* 271–276; *Emma* 300–303; *Silas Marner* 243, 245–249; *Sybil* 315–318

Octavia Hill Woodlands *270*
oil 364
Origin of Species 47, 49–55
ornithology 45, 63
Ouida 277–282
overfishing 10, 113, 115–117, 119–126
overpopulation 8–9, 77, 78–85, 87–93; economic value and 97; utopia and 389–396

Owen, Robert 361
oysters 126; *see also* fish and fishing

Paris Green 143
parks 45, 205, 208, 267, 291; *see also* national parks; zoos
partridges 145–147
Peel, Robert 313
pesticides 143, 144–147; arsenic and 145–147
Peterloo Massacre 305
Pharmacy and Poisons Act (1933) 143
Phillips, Eliza 207
physical health 371–379, 381–388
pine trees 294
plague 101
ploughs 28–29
poetry: 'In Memoriam A.H.H.' 227–234; 'Remembrances' 259–261; 'Sonnet on the Projected Kendal and Windermere Railway' 217–218; *Excursion, The* 219–224; Raven, The 215–216
political ecology 85
pollution 10–12; acid rain and 155–159; arsenic and 145–147; cholera and 149, 151–154; coal and 355; Rural Sanitary Authorities (RSAs) and 167–170; smoke abatement 179–187, 189, 191–194; Thames and 161–164
population and population control 77, 78–84, 85, 87–93; economic value and 97–102; utopia and 389–396
potatoes 29; St Helena and 29–34
Pre-Raphaelites 201, 205, 251; *see also* Millais, John; Morris, William; Rossetti, Dante Gabriel; Woolner, Thomas
Prevalsky's horses 341
Prichard, James Cowles 8, 57, 59–61
progress 321–325
Prussia 7
Pryce, Joseph 95
Public Garden Association 369
Public Health Acts 11, 369, 386

Quakers 57, 189, 271

race and racism 57, 59–61, 70, 291, 319, 355, 366; urbanization and 208; *see also* social Darwinism
radiation 173–177
Raffles, Thomas Stamford 335–340
ragged schools 263

403

INDEX

railways 131; Kendal-to-Windermere rail line 217–218, 235; Lake District and 237–241
Ramée, Louise de la *see* Ouida
rape 277
rationality 283
Raven, The 215–216
Rawnsley, Hardwicke 263
Remembrances' 259–261
resource curse theory 10
resource depletion 8–9
revolution 218
Ricardo, David 77
Richmond, William Blake 369
river pollution 165, 167–170
River Pollution Prevention Act 11
rivers 279–282; pollution of 161–164
Rivers Pollution Prevention Act (1876) 165
romantic poets 257; *see also* Burns, John; Clare, John; Coleridge, Samuel Taylor; Wordsworth, William
Roosevelt, Theodore 205, 291, 381
Rossetti, Dante Gabriel 205, 251
Rothschild, Nathaniel Charles 347, 349–352
Rothschild's List 347
Rousseau, Jean-Jacques 77
Roxburgh, William 21, 23–24
Rural Sanitary Authorities (RSAs) 164–165, 167–170
Ruskin, John 189, 217, 235, 237–241, *241*, 263
Russell, Herbrand 341
Russell, Ian 341

sable antelopes 341, 344–346
salmon 123–125; *see also* fish and fishing
Salmon Acts 125
schools, forestry 127, 129–132
science fiction 357–360, 389
scientific method 283, 285–289
Scotland 204; forests in 129–132
Selborne 17–19
Selborne Society 15, 201; Tennyson, Alfred, and 225
Sequoia National Park 201
serfdom 305, 327, 331
Sewell, Anna 201, 271–276
sewers 151–154
Shaw, Bernard 285
Sierra 293–296
Sierra Club 205, 291

Silas Marner 243, 245–249
Simon, Julian 95
Singer, Peter 70
slavery and slave trade 63, 319, 365–366; capitalism and 255; St Helena and 29
Smith, Adam 31
Smith, Roberts Angus 6, 10–11, 155–159, 362
smog 369
Smoke Abatement Act (1926) 369
Smoke Abatement Committee 179, 183–187
Smoke Abatement League 189
smoke pollution 179–187, 189, 191–194
Smuts, Jan 70
Snow, John 149, 151–154
social Darwinism 47, 3355
social reform 381–386
socialism 251, 285, 389
Society for the Preservation of Ancient Buildings (SPAB) 251
Society for the Promotion of Nature Reserves (SPNR) 201, 347–353
Society for the Protection of Birds (SPB) 207, 225
Somervell, William 206
Sommerville, William 133, 135–139
Sonnet on the Projected Kendal and Windermere Railway' 217–218
South Africa 37–39
South Wales 165–next
Spencer, Herbert 47, 55, 374
St Helena 21, 25, 27–34, 35
St Kilda 63
steel 5
suburban commons 266–267
sunlight 191–192
supply and demand 103
Surrey 299, 301–303, 305–311
Sweden 11
Sybil 315–318

Tansley, Arthur 69–73
Tennyson, Alfred 15, 201, 225–234
Thames 161–164
Thirlmere Defence Association (TDA) 206
timber 135–139; *see also* forestry and forest management
Tragedy of the Commons, The 85, 206; *see also* Lloyd, William Forster
Tyndall Effect 171
Tyndall, John 6, 119, 171, 173–177

INDEX

uniformitarianism 41, 43–46
United States 71–72, 99–100, 138, 349, 352
university extension lectures 283
urbanization 165, 205–209, 218, 355, 369, 381
utilitarianism 12
utopia 391–396

vaccinations 179; *see also* diseases
vegetarianism 149, 283; *see also* animal rights and animal welfare
village greens 85
vivisection 189, 283; *see also* animal rights and animal welfare
Von Humboldt, Alexander 7, 8

Wales 204
Wallace, Alfred 361, 363–367
war 89
Warming, Eugenius 69
water 279–282; cholera and 149, 151–154, *154*
wealth 383–384
Webb, Philip 251
Webb, Sidney 285
Wells, H.G. 355, 389–396
whales 61, 116; *see also* overfishing

wheat 30; arsenic and 147; *see also* flour
Whistler, James 235
White, Gilbert 6, 15, 17–next, *19*, 116
Wicken Fen 201, 347
Wilberforce, William 335
Wild Birds Protection Act (1880) 207
Williams, John 10
Williamson, Emily 207
willow-larks 17
Wilson, Philip Whitwell 381–388
Woburn Safari Park 341
wolves 45
woodlands 327
Woolner, Thomas 206
Wordsworth, William 201, 213, 217–224

X Club 6, 119, 171

Yosemite National Park 201, 291, 293–296
Young England 201, 313–314; *see also* Disraeli, Benjamin

zebras 35
Zoological Society of London 201, 335–340, 341
zoos 335–340